THE FUNDAMENTALS OF QUÉBEC BUSINESS LAW AND ETHICS

FIRST EDITION

FRANK CROOKS
B.Comm., L.L.L., L.L.B., M.A.

NICK PAPATHEODORAKOS
B.A., M.A., B.C.L

Paladin
Publications

Disclaimer

Every reasonable attempt has been made to trace the owners of copyright material used in this book. Any errors or omissions brought to the publisher's attention will be rectified in future printings.

Those involved in this publication and its content do in no way offer this work as legal opinion or professional advice and take no responsibility for inaccuracies or actions taken based on the content of this publication. Readers are cautioned to refer to the full and complete statement of the law in the official government text. A legal professional should be consulted for all legal advice.

ISBN 978-0-9869322-3-6

Inquiries or comments should be addressed to the publisher:

PALADIN PUBLICATIONS

info@paladinpublications.com

SUMMARY TABLE OF CONTENTS

TABLE OF CONTENTS

Depending on which community we examine, these rules may have developed over a long period of time as part of the habits or customs of the community, passed on by example or word-of-mouth from one generation to another. On the other hand, they may have been written down, and were therefore more widely known by everyone. An early example of this is the codification (collection in a written form) of the law, engraved on a stone column, by the legal scholars in the time of King Hammurabi of Babylon in 2100 B.C.

When our civilization was in its early stages of development, these laws and the methods creating them were very simple. The earlier communities were mostly homogeneous, small societies with similar ethnic and cultural backgrounds. Over time, these communities grew in population, increasing the potential for friction and conflict. Additionally, with the development of technologies, such as transportation and communication, these communities interacted more often with other varying communities or became themselves more diverse with people of different cultures and ethnicities migrating to their borders. As such, more complex laws were required to insure security and certainty.

1.2.2 The Role of Law in Society Today

Law ensures *security*. It has an important peace-keeping function through which it minimizes disruptions of the equilibrium in society. It does this by providing for punishment of those who seriously disturb our social order. In addition, the law enables those who suffer loss or damage because of the conduct of others, to obtain compensation.

It might work in this way. Paul bought a dog as a pet. He had been warned that the dog had a bad temper and should be kept tightly under control at all times. Sometime later he was showing his new dog to his friend, Fred. As a joke Paul unleashed the dog and told it to "go get" Fred. The dog seemed to understand the order as an instruction to attack. Fred was injured and his clothes were torn.

If the injury and damage were not serious, perhaps it would be sufficient to simply ask Paul to pay for any resulting expenses.

If Paul was being reckless and totally disregarded the possibility of injury to others (e.g., if he said, "It's up to you to take care of yourself, and if you don't, it's too bad"), the court may look much more harshly on this behaviour, and in addition to requiring payment for the injury and damages caused, the court might require the offender to spend some time in detention.

> ? *...is this the way?...*
>
> *What do you think of the way in which the "dog owner" might be treated by the law? Do you agree, or do you have some other suggestions?*

Law establishes and enforces *standards of conduct* in the community. It tells people what kind of behaviour is not acceptable, thereby reducing friction between citizens. For example, since free enterprise and competition in business are important in our country, Canadian laws include penalties which are applied to anyone unlawfully monopolizing a market or unduly reducing competition.

Law maintains the *status quo*. This means that the standards of conduct stated in the law remain in force until changed by the lawmaking authority. Our law contains the mechanism or process by which existing laws may be changed or replaced. When the legislators believe the law should be changed, they use this process to make the amendments they think the people want, and which they believe are appropriate for the society. Not everyone will agree with what the law states, but the process of amendments allows for changes to take place in an orderly way, avoiding disturbances and upheavals of the social order.

Another function of the law is to enable people to exercise their right to express themselves as individuals. The extent to which this will be considered a "freedom" is determined by the ideas and objectives of the legislators, as well as by the way they obtained their authority.

Canadian law often defines an individual's rights by stating the duties and responsibilities a person may have toward other members of the community. Thus, one may drive a car on the public highways but must exercise care not to cause injury or damage to others. We can therefore say that our law allows us to use our rights as freely as possible, as long as we do not interfere with the right of others to do the same thing. The civil law would regard such interference as an "abuse of rights."

1.2.3 Who Decides

As discussed above, sometimes a community as a whole decides what will be considered as the law through custom and usage. People become accustomed to doing things in a particular way. Over a long period of time, these customs become so widely accepted and used in the community that they become the "only way."

Or, the people in the community may recognize one person as the "wisest" and accept that person's rules as the laws by which they should all be governed.

In other countries, a group of people may declare themselves "rulers." If they control the power to enforce rules of behaviour they consider proper, they will be "in authority" to make new laws for everyone.

? *...as you read ask yourself...*

What is the best way for a community to develop laws?

Would you select any of the ideas referred to here...or do you have some other thoughts?

When one country goes to war against another, the victor will often impose its own system of law upon the loser. The citizens of the conquered country have no choice but to obey the laws of the new ruler. Under these circumstances, a country's laws are not determined by the community itself, but by the community of greater strength which can enforce its intention to rule the weaker nation by armed power.

In countries where people believe in the principles of democracy, the people themselves determine who will make the laws that govern them. They choose, by election, a group of people who will form a "government" for a limited period of time. These elected lawmakers are given the authority, during their term of office, to repeal (cancel) old laws they no longer consider valid and to pass new laws they consider necessary. As an example, in 1993 the Québec government repealed the old *Civil Code* and brought into the law a new and very different *Civil Code.*

If the citizens of the country are satisfied that these laws reflect the values that are important to them, the lawmakers or "legislators" will be re-elected to continue their work. If the people are not satisfied, then at the next election, others will be chosen to take over this authority.

This brief review indicates that the way in which the laws of a community are created is a consequence of the type of government that rules the community. The lawmaking authority can be controlled by a dictator, a religious leader, the military, or by the population itself. Most people in Canada seem to agree on the principle that each individual in the community should participate in selecting the lawmakers. This springs from the idea that in this way, the laws will be designed to allow maximum freedom for everyone, while still providing for harmony within the community.

LAW & JUSTICE
Section 1.3

While considering the nature of law, we should give some thought to the idea of justice. Are these two the same, or is there a distinction between them?

Let's look at it in terms of a recent case. A doctor who is on staff at the Lakeshore General Hospital received an emergency call at 7 a.m. A premature baby in the hospital was trembling and had an accelerated heart rate. The staff was concerned that the child might go into convulsion, with the possibility of brain damage or death.

The doctor drove toward the hospital knowing that the sooner he reached the hospital and treated the infant, the more likely tragedy would be averted. On the way, he went through a 30-km/h zone at 62 km/h. A police officer stopped him, and gave him a speeding ticket.

When the doctor appeared before the judge in Pierrefonds Municipal Court, he was found guilty of speeding and fined $132. On appeal the Court upheld the fine, saying that he could have driven to the hospital without speeding or he might have taken a faster alternate route.

The doctor argued that responding to a life-threatening situation overrides his responsibility to stop at stop signs or red lights or to obey speed limits.

The judge quoted a decision of the Supreme Court of Canada and stated:

> *"No system of positive law can recognize any principle which would entitle a person to violate the law, because in his view, the law conflicted with some higher social value. Such doctrine could well become the last resort of scoundrels and...it could very easily become simply a mask for anarchy."*
>
> *(Note: In this context, "positive" means written.)*

In this example we can identify several important elements that can help us in the discussion of law and justice. These elements, taken together or each on its own, have a direct influence on the fine balance between the nature of law and justice, on striking a sense of balance between what is allowed and what is right.

First, we must recognize that the law consists of the words written by the lawmakers. These words and sentences have no emotion or feeling; they are simply ink on paper—they are the law. However, words have meaning. They tell us what standards of behaviour the legislators require of people living in our community.

Second, the law does not apply itself. It is applied or enforced by the judges in our courts. Judges are men and women who live in our community also. They understand how citizens go about their daily lives. It is with this understanding that they apply the law.

Generally, the law allows judges discretion as to the manner in which the law is to be applied. A judge might simply apply the words of the law as they are: You were speeding and therefore pay the fine. A judge might be compassionate and say: You were speeding, but I understand it was in order to save a life, and therefore you should be excused. A judge might look very harshly at the doctor and say: You were speeding and therefore endangering the lives of pedestrians or other motorists. You must pay the fine and lose your licence for six months.

We can now distinguish between the law and justice. The words of the law are clear. They tell us what is permitted or prohibited. The judges apply the law, and we can seek justice in how the law is applied. Not every case will have the same results, because each is different, and the judge will apply the law differently.

Third, we see, in the quotation from the Supreme Court judgment, how the law is used as an instrument for enforcing standards of conduct and for building a particular type of society. In other words, the majority or those who hold power will occasionally impose their standards of behaviour on the nation. These standards will apply to everyone, including the minority who may not find justice in the law.

Now that we have a better understanding of the difference between law and justice, consider the following questions and develop opinions regarding each one:

- Must we always obey the law?
- Can we ever disregard a law with which we do not agree?
- Why should we obey the laws that we had nothing to do with creating?
- Are there any circumstances under which we might be justified in disregarding the law?

Give these questions some careful thought and develop some opinions on them. Be prepared to discuss your ideas and defend your opinions in the next class.

LAW & ETHICS
Section 1.4

Equally important to the discussion of law is an understanding of ethics and what role it plays in law. It can be argued that law and ethics are one in the same, since ethics is a set of principles or moral values of a society, distinguishing right from wrong, and that law simply reflects these values. While this may be true, it is not uncommon for a law and an ethical principle to contradict each other. For instance, a certain act by an individual or business may be legal, but at the same time be considered unethical. A Canadian business that has its products manufactured in a developing country, so as to take advantage of cheap labour, is acting within the law. However, it may be considered unethical by Canadians because they believe it is not right for the business to take advantage of these people. On the other hand, an act may be illegal and ethical at the same time. A good example of this is a soldier who refuses to fight in a war because he believes it is wrong. While he will be punished, his conscientious objection could be considered ethical.

The topic of ethics and how it relates to business and law will be further developed in the next chapter.

UNDERSTANDING THE DOMAINS OF LAW
Section 1.5

1.5.1 Private Law vs. Public Law

All laws fall into one of two domains (fields), private or public. A person can determine the domain of law by examining the objective of the law itself or by simply asking oneself "what acts does the law cover?"

The **private law** consists of the rules that regulate the legal relationship and obligations between individual citizens. C*ontract law* deals with the legal relationship in matters such as leases and employment, *commercial law* explains how to set up an enterprise and to provide goods or services, *property law* helps us to settle boundary differences with your neighbour and *civil liability law* determines the consequences of an individual's negligence, are among a few examples.

The **public law** governs the relationship between citizens and their state or nation or country. Examples of such laws are Criminal Law, Taxation Law, Highway Law, Language Laws and Bankruptcy Law. Generally, public laws attempt to regulate behaviour that affects the entire community and impose strict punishment on those breaking these laws. For instance, criminal law sets out the type of behaviour that we do not want in our society, such as murder, arson, theft, rape, assault, etc. People who engage in these activities commit an offence not only against the victim, but also against our whole society. This is why criminal offences may be punished with the most severe penalty—loss of personal freedom through imprisonment.

In criminal law matters, a person is accused of criminal behaviour, and upon being tried may be found *guilty* or *innocent* of the charge. The words innocent and guilty are reserved for use in discussing criminal proceedings. These terms are often used incorrectly, and it is important to understand how they should be used.

In contrast, private law, which is the focus of this book, uses terms that are different. A person is sued (not charged) for not having paid a debt or fulfilled an obligation. At the end of the trial, the person may be found responsible or not responsible for payment of money or for failing to carry out certain activities that were agreed upon between the parties.

1.5.2 Civil Law vs. Common Law

Generally, countries follow either a civil law or common law approach and sometimes even a combination of the two as their basis of law. Essentially, the difference between civil law and common law is who decides the law.

In a **civil law** society, the fundamental basis for law resides in legislation. The law, which is based on general principles, is largely decided upon by governing officials who then codify them into a systematic organization of statutes within their respective subjects. These codes, be they of a private or public nature, are applied by the courts. Each decision rendered by a court must be based on the letter of the law, without taking into account any previous judgments. In other words, a civil law society emphasizes legislative supremacy.

In a **common law** society, the basis for law is grounded in the principle of precedence and case law or jurisprudence. Every court decision has to take into account past judgments of similar nature so as to apply a similar judgment. If the case facts diverge or are of a new nature from past judgments, then the court's decision may formulate and declare new law. Of course most common law societies do have use of legislative powers to adopt new laws, but these laws tend to deal with very specific subjects. In other words, a common law society emphasizes judge made law.

The Canadian legal system is a combination of both civil and common law. With regards to public law, common law is largely the dominant basis of law across the state. In private law, however, two separate systems exist: the civil law system of Québec and the common law of the other provinces. This is the result of two different legal systems being historically introduced to this country, first by the French settlers who brought with them the principles of French law and then by the incorporation of common law when the British took over the colony. But whether we are in Québec or Alberta, the private law has the same function: it helps private citizens regulate their personal and business matters and provides a background of rules that everyone can understand.

SUBSTANTIVE & ADJECTIVAL LAW Section 1.6

A distinction is to be made between the part of the law that tells us what our rights are, and the part of the law that tells us how to exercise these rights.

In general, the *Civil Code* contains the rules of law that explain the **substantive law** - that part of the law where we can find the "substance" of our rights. Thus, we look to the *Civil Code* to see what rights we have if someone sells us defective merchandise, or fails to pay rent, or damages our property.

The *Civil Code* does not, however, tell us how to exercise our rights. Once we are aware of our rights, we must then turn to the *Québec Code of Civil Procedure*, to find the **adjectival law**, which contains the procedures enabling us to obtain what is rightfully ours under the substantive law. In the following section we examine some of these procedural rules.

TO SUE – THE FIVE Ws
Section 1.7

1.7.1 What and Why?

You may believe that someone owes you money and is refusing to pay or that someone is obliged to do something for you and is neglecting this obligation. In such a case you may choose to enforce your right to be paid or have the work done by bringing the matter before a court. This procedure is called "suing."

"To sue" someone, then, means to start legal proceedings, with the intention of having a judge listen to your reasons why you believe the other party has an obligation to you and asking the judge to order the other party to fulfil the obligation.

The procedure begins with an exchange of documents between the parties. In these documents, the party that is suing explains why payment is demanded and the other party explains why payment is denied. After each side has detailed its arguments in these documents, the parties then appear in court to "argue" or "plead" their case before a judge.

1.7.2 Who?

The parties involved in a civil action will vary depending on their respective rights or responsibilities. Outside of any court proceeding, the parties are referred to as **creditors** and **debtors**, the former having a claim against the latter. This claim may involve monies owed or even goods and services as agreed upon by the contracting parties in their initial dealings. The claim of a creditor against a debtor may also be the result of civil liability, damage resulting from one's fault due to his actions or inactions. Of course, there may be multiple creditors and multiple debtors affected by a similar claim.

When a creditor takes a legal action against a debtor, such as a proceeding or ultimately a court action, the parties are then referred to as plaintiff and defendant respectively. In any legal action, a case may involve multiple defendants and multiple plaintiffs. If multiple creditors, who are not associated, wish to undertake legal proceedings against a common debtor together, they must request permission from the court to institute a **class action suit**.

Creditor	A person who claims to be owed money, services or goods by someone.
Debtor	A person who owes money, services or goods to someone.
Plaintiff	A creditor who takes legal action against a debtor who owes him or her money, services or goods.
Defendant	A debtor who is sued by a plaintiff.

1.7.3 Where?

When a civil action is instituted, the plaintiff has to select where it will be taken. Several choices are available. The province of Québec is divided geographically into many judicial districts. Article 68 CCP (*Code of Civil Procedure*) states that, in general, an action may be instituted before the Court of the place where:

- the defendant lives;
- the defendant has property;
- the whole cause of action has arisen;
- the contract that gives rise to the action was made;
- the property in dispute is situated.

If the claim, however, arises out of contractual obligations, then as a general rule the case must be instituted where the contract was concluded by the parties involved.

1.7.4 When?

How long does one have to institute an action? The *Civil Code* limits many of our rights. We have a period of time within which to exercise the rights we have against other persons. If we fail to exercise them within this time period, then these rights expire.

Prescription is the legal method which the civil law establishes for a person to acquire or to lose rights by the mere lapse of time. For example, a right of ownership to real property may be acquired by prolonged continuous possession. A right to sue may be lost due to inaction for a specific period of time on the part of the creditor. In the common law jurisdictions, the prescription periods are dealt with in a *Statute of Limitations*.

It is logical to expect the law to place limits or delays within which certain rights can be exercised. This means that at some time, all rights will be terminated and lawsuits will not be instituted over matters that no one can remember and after the evidence is lost or destroyed.

The overall principle is that everything is prescribed after ten years. There are, however, shorter and longer prescription periods, the most common of which is three years. Some examples are given below.

Examples of prescriptive periods include:

1. A ten-day delay to Appear or to Plead to a Civil Action.
2. A one-year delay to disavow a child.
3. A three-year delay to claim damages resulting from personal injury or damage to property.
4. A three-year delay to acquire ownership of movable property.
5. A ten-year delay to acquire ownership of immovable property after continuous possession.

6. A ten-year delay within which a creditor in a Judgment of the court in a civil matter may still execute the Judgment against the debtor.

7. A thirty-year delay for a person to establish his/her filiation.

8. A one year delay to claim damages from defamation.

From the Civil Code

531. Any interested person, including the father or the mother, may, by any means, contest the filiation of a person whose possession of status is not consistent with his act of birth.

However, the presumed father may contest the filiation and disavow the child only within one year of the date on which the presumption of paternity takes effect, unless he is unaware of the birth, in which case the time limit begins to run on the day he becomes aware of it. The mother may contest the paternity of the presumed father within one year from the birth of the child.

2875. Prescription is a means of acquiring or of being released by the lapse of time and according to the conditions fixed by law; prescription is called acquisitive in the first case and extinctive in the second.

2892. The filing of a judicial demand before the expiry of the prescriptive period constitutes a civil interruption, provided the demand is served on the person to be prevented from prescribing not later than sixty days following the expiry of the prescription period.

2904. Prescription does not run against persons if it is impossible in fact for them to act by themselves or to be represented by others.

2905. Prescription does not run against a child yet unborn.

Nor does it run against a minor or a person of full age under curatorship or tutorship with respect to remedies he may have against his representative or against the person entrusted with his custody.

2906. Married or civil union spouses do not prescribe against each other during cohabitation.

2918. A person who has for 10 years possessed an immovable as its owner may acquire the ownership of it only upon judicial demand.

2919. The possessor in good faith of movable property acquires the ownership of it by three years running from the dispossession of the owner.

Until the expiry of that period, the owner may revendicate the movable property unless it has been acquired under judicial authority.

2924. A right resulting from a judgment is prescribed by ten years if it is not exercised.

2925. An action to enforce a personal right or movable real right is prescribed by three years, if the prescriptive period is not otherwise established.

2929. An action for defamation is prescribed by one year from the day on which the defamed person learned of the defamation.

A LEGAL SYSTEM
Section 1.8

If we examine any culture or society, we find the elements of a legal system. In comparison to Canadian standards, other legal systems may be quite primitive or much more advanced, but each one possesses the same three essential elements. The elements that make up a legal system are:

1. **Structure** of the lawmaking machinery - some method or system by which laws come into existence;
2. **Law** - the rules of behaviour imposed or accepted in the society;
3. **Administration and enforcement of the laws** - making sure the laws are followed by those who are subject to them.

Understanding the Québec legal system makes it easier for us to know and exercise our rights and freedoms within this society. In Québec, as a result of the events of history, our legal system includes elements borrowed from both France and England. Both these countries exercised a strong influence at different times on the development of government and law in this province.

Chapter 3, The Quebec Legal System, will cover each element of our legal system in greater detail.

LEGAL TERMS

In your reading, you came across the following terms. Be sure that you can explain each, to ensure your understanding of the material you have been reading. If you are uncertain as to the meaning of any term, review the material in the chapter for clarification. If necessary, consult a dictionary for further information or discuss the term(s) with your instructor.

System of law	Justice	Law
Ethics	Damage	Substantive law
Criminal law	Status quo	Codification
Injury	Custom	Democracy
Private law	Government	Public law
Civil law	Adjectival law	Common law
Prescription	Plaintiff	

REVIEW QUESTIONS

1. From your own experience, prepare an example of a case which illustrates the difference between "law" and "justice."

2. Is it necessary for a community to have "some order" to regulate its activities? Explain your answer, with examples from your own experience or taken from material you have read in other courses.

3. Mr. Rudolph called a roofing contractor to repair the roof of his house. The contractor gave him a verbal estimate of repairs in the amount of $1,200 "...for cash—no bill and no tax." If he wants a bill, he has to pay an additional sales tax to the $1,200. If he pays cash, and saves the tax, does this harm the community? Explain why or why not.

4. Can a society survive without having any "formal" laws?

5. Give two examples of civil law and criminal law.

6. In your opinion, what is the best way for a community to develop laws? Explain why you think this is best.

7. Explain, with examples, each of the following functions of law discussed in this chapter:

   a) Ensure security
   b) Establish and enforce standards of conduct
   c) Maintain the status quo.

8. Can you describe any other functions of law that are not mentioned in this chapter?

9. If the headline in tomorrow's newspaper read, "All laws have been abolished," do you think there would be any difference in how people behave? Explain what you think the differences would be, if any, and why they would come about. If you do not think there would be any difference, explain why not.

10. Does it make any difference how laws develop in a community? Won't the result always be the same? Explain your answer.

Chapter 2

ETHICS

OBJECTIVES

This chapter was prepared to enable you to achieve the following objectives:

1. To develop an understanding of the principles of ethics.
2. To distinguish between "ethics" and "law".
3. To identify important ethical issues faced by Canadian companies doing business outside of Canada.
4. To appreciate the importance of professional standards and corporate codes of conduct.
5. To understand the fundamental steps involved in the ethical problem resolution process.
6. To introduce the concept of responsible investing.
7. To become familiar with the principles of corporate governance.

INTRODUCTION TO ETHICS
Section 2.1

2.1.1 Definition

People should act in an ethical fashion. From this writer's experience, while most people would agree with this statement if asked, each person questioned would come up with different interpretations as to what the expression ethical behavior entails. In this chapter, we will introduce the reader to some of the important ethical principles that one should be conscious of and take into consideration in one's dealing with others.

While there does not exist any universal definition for the term Ethics, ethics reflects a concern for the well-being of people and of society. Ethical principles are not absolute nor are they carved in stone, as ideas and beliefs will develop and change over time as the views of society change. What is considered acceptable behavior in one country may be considered unethical or even illegal in another country. What is considered immoral behavior today in one country might be considered ethical ten years from now in the same country. Needless to say, ethical behavior is a very subjective concept which changes from one time period to another, from one country to another and from one culture to another. Ethical behavior is sometimes referred to as being a reflection of a society's moral values.

If one accepts the premise that ethical behavior should reflect the moral values of a society, then we must next attempt to identify what are the fundamental principles in determining whether an action has in fact been taken in an ethical fashion.

2.1.2 Fundamental Principles of Ethic

As ethical behavior should reflect a respect for others and for society, ethical action should promote a climate of fairness, conciliation and good faith. These principles should be reflected in both one's personal life and in business dealings. From a personal perspective when dealing with one's peers, one should take into consideration ethical principles including but not limited to the following:

- Be respectful of others;
- Act honestly and fairly;
- Comply with the law;
- Do not act maliciously;
- Inspire trust.

In one's business dealings with one's employer, employees, clients, competitors and other parties, one should take into consideration ethical principles including but not limited to the following:

- Maintain objectivity and impartiality;
- Act prudently and diligently;
- Ensure confidentiality and full disclosure;
- Avoid actual or potential conflicts of interest;
- Comply with professional standards of practice, company policies and the law.

To put it simply, ethical behavior promotes the philosophy of treating others in the same fashion as you would like to be treated yourself.

LAW VS ETHICS
Section 2.2

It is important to remember that law and ethics reflect two very separate yet interrelated and interdependent principles. To take the approach that strict compliance with the requirements of a law will ensure that one's activity will not be subject to legitimate criticism is risky from an ethical point of view. For example, the law sets out a minimum wage that employers must pay to employees. In a market where there is a surplus of unemployed labour an employer may be able to hire skilled workers at minimum wage since these workers are desperate for work. The employer has complied with the requirements of the law, but is the employer acting ethically? Is a minimum wage equal to a fair wage?

While many ethical principles may have been incorporated into legislation and therefore have acquired a legal status that all must respect, ethics is not law. Law sets out specific standards that all must respect, however the mere compliance with legal standards may not meet the ethical demands placed on business today by society. Take the example of a local Canadian company that decides to shut down operations and build a new plant in a country overseas. Does Canadian and Quebec law prevent this type of action? Generally speaking, as long as legal requirements respecting employee severance, taxation and creditor's rights, among others, are respected, a Canadian company could shut down its local plant and move its operations overseas. The fact that the company respects the law does not address the ethical issues that hundreds of local workers are now unemployed, that numerous small local suppliers have lost their major customer, that the municipality has lost a very important municipal taxpayer, that local merchants see a huge drop in retail sales as families of the laid off workers drastically cut back on personal spending and that local schools are faced with potential shut down as unemployed families move away from the community in search of jobs elsewhere. As illustrated above, these corporate actions which comply strictly with the requirements of the law may be viewed by many as being immoral and wrong.

Law alone does not always provide an adequate solution to social issues. Although law sets out rules that govern society, the legislative process by which laws are adopted is often slow to address new subjects of social concern. For this reason current issues of public concern are often not adequately addressed in law and those whose rights are affected find themselves in legal limbo. The recent recognition by both the courts and the law makers of the principle of same sex marriage is an example of how law was slow to recognize and embrace changing social attitudes and beliefs. The ongoing debate over the assisted right-to-die issue is another example of this phenomenon. The legal dispute resolution process, that of the court system, has been criticized by many as being a very time consuming and excessively expensive process that favours the party who has the most financial resources. Just because one believes that he/she has been wronged, does not necessarily mean that the aggrieved party can afford the time and financial costs that are required to institute a court action that can take years to be resolved.

INTERNATIONAL BUSINESS ETHICS
Section 2.3

2.3.1 New Frontiers

Gone are the days when businesses were viewed as being enterprises catering solely to, and being served and supplied by, local domestic interests. The emergence of the global marketplace, while opening new economic frontiers for Canadian businesses, has also opened our eyes to the disparity in business standards found in different countries. Canadian companies, at home, are faced with a set of strict legal requirements that govern all aspects of business operations from employees' rights to environmental protection. The local rules governing business operations in many developing countries are often less stringent than the Canadian standards, or in some cases are non-existent.

It is a well-recognized principle of international law that one is always subject to the laws of the country in which one is operating (host country), and as a general rule the laws of Canada do not apply outside of the sovereign borders of Canada. What is the impact of this principle on a Canadian company that decides to open a factory in a host country? Clearly the Canadian company's day-to-day operations in the host country will be governed by the laws of that country. Assuming that the host country's laws are weaker than Canadian laws with regards to the protection of workers' rights, health and safety issues, discrimination against women and the protection of the environment; does this mean that the Canadian company can simply comply in good conscience with the laws of the host country? Canadian corporate management certainly cannot deny that the absence of strict legislative protections in the host country creates a defacto economic advantage for the Canadian company. Why, in fact, did the Canadian company decide to build a factory, thousands of kilometers away from its home base, in a host country where language, climatic and cultural issues may pose operational obstacles? One answer that comes immediately to mind is that it is a lot cheaper to manufacture products in a host country that does not burden the Canadian company with pro-labour and pro-environmental protection requirements.

?...Can you identify Canadian companies operating in foreign countries?...
What do you think of the way they are doing business?
Are they acting ethically?

To pose the question differently, should a Canadian company, free from the legal constraints of its home country, operating in strict compliance with the less stringent laws of the host country, be considered a good corporate citizen? Since the Canadian company has broken no laws, either at home or in the host country, how can one argue that their behavior is in any way faulty or delinquent? From an ethical point of view, the Canadian company should in fact actively promote within its organization the philosophy that acting as a good ethical corporate citizen is not an obligation imposed by law, but rather is an act of conscience and the right thing to do. The mere fact that local host country laws do not recognize many of the basic protections that workers, the community and the environment as a whole benefit from in Canada, should not be an excuse for the Canadian company to actively ignore these rights when operating in the host country.

Should the Canadian company use its power and influence to try to force the host country government to adopt stronger protections for workers and the environment? Adopting such a confrontational approach may in fact be counterproductive and may lead to accusations of "imperialist/colonialist behavior" whereby the Canadian company is accused of trying to forcefully impose outside "western values" on to the host country. A less confrontational approach might enable the Canadian company not only to achieve its objectives of improving the conditions of its workers but also to influence the views of local business community and officials. By voluntarily adopting standards that are higher than those required in the host country, the Canadian company may be able to demonstrate that cleaner, safer and fairer working conditions can in fact improve workers' productivity, decrease absenteeism and turnover, and create a more profitable business model.

2.3.2 United Nations Global Compact (UNGC)

The United Nations Global Compact (UNGC), launched in the year 2000, is an example of an international initiative whereby over 7,000 companies from over 140 countries have voluntarily agreed to adopt a set of ethical business standards on a world-wide basis. Wherever a signatory company operates in the world it pledges to respect the following ten principles of the UNGC:

The UN Global Compact's ten principles in the areas of human rights, labour, the environment and anti-corruption enjoy universal consensus and are derived from:

- The Universal Declaration of Human Rights
- The International Labour Organization's Declaration on Fundamental Principles and Rights at Work
- The Rio Declaration on Environment and Development
- The United Nations Convention Against Corruption

The UN Global Compact asks companies to embrace, support and enact, within their sphere of influence, a set of core values in the areas of human rights, labour standards, the environment and anti-corruption.

TABLE: 2.1

Human Rights	
Principle 1:	Businesses should support and respect the protection of internationally proclaimed human rights; and
Principle 2:	Make sure that they are not complicit in human rights abuses.
Labour	
Principle 3:	Businesses should uphold the freedom of association and the effective recognition of the right to collective bargaining;
Principle 4:	The elimination of all forms of forced and compulsory labour;
Principle 5:	The effective abolition of child labour; and
Principle 6:	The elimination of discrimination in respect of employment and occupation.
Environment	
Principle 7:	Businesses should support a precautionary approach to environmental challenges;
Principle 8:	Undertake initiatives to promote greater environmental responsibility; and
Principle 9:	Encourage the development and diffusion of environmentally friendly technologies.
Anti-Corruption	
Principle 10:	Businesses should work against corruption in all its forms, including extortion and bribery.

http://www.unglobalcompact.org/AboutTheGC/TheTenPrinciples

2.3.3 Extra-Territoriality

It is important to note that in certain specific situations a Canadian company could be considered in breach of Canadian law for actions taken outside of Canada. This principle is referred to as **extra-territoriality** whereby Canadian courts can assert jurisdiction and prosecute in Canada actions taken by Canadians outside of Canada. Extra-territoriality is an exception to the general rule that a court only has jurisdiction for actions taken within its sovereign territory.

An example of the application of this principle of extra-territoriality is the recent investigations involving alleged bribery of foreign officials outside of Canada by Canadian companies under the Corruption of Foreign Public Officials Act (CFPOA). The argument that bribery was not considered an offense under the laws of the host country where said acts allegedly took place would not be a valid legal defense under the CFPOA.

> ? *...as you read ask yourself...*
>
> *Does this mean that Canadian businesses, wanting to do business in a foreign country, are not allowed to give gifts to host country officials in order to compete on a similar footing with other multinational companies doing business in that country? What if there is a well-established culture of gift-giving in the host country as an acceptable practice of doing business? If the Canadian company refuses to offer any gifts, does that put the Canadian company at a competitive disadvantage? Should all gifts be considered as bribes?*

RESOLVING ETHICAL ISSUES
Section 2.4

How does one resolve an ethical issue? Company A's manufacturing plant in Montreal is 20 years old, employs 500 workers and needs to be refurbished. If Company A invests in robotic technology it will be able to get rid of 75% of its low skilled workforce, reducing its total workforce to 100 people. As long as the requirements of the applicable laws are respected, Company A could proceed with this refurbishment and downsizing of its workforce. Even if legal, would these actions taken by Company A be ethical? The owners of Company A will argue that since they built this company from scratch, working 7 days a week and 20 hours a day for years, have they not earned the right to do what they want with their business? To each of the above questions, there is no "right" or "correct" answer.

Unlike the structured mechanism used to enforce rights created by law, that of the court system, whereby each party has his/her day in court to argue his/her side of the story, which is then resolved by a biding decision rendered by an impartial adjudicator, the judge, there is no structured system in place to render binding and enforceable ethical decisions. So how does one resolve an ethical issue?

Even though there is no absolute answer to the above question, a company should ensure that it has put in place an internal process by which questions, complaints and/or concerns can be addressed. This does not mean that a company merely installs a Suggestion Box in the employees' lunchroom but never bothers to either read or address the issues raised in the employees' letters. Failure to provide an effective internal conflict resolution process can lead to a stressful working environment and a frustrated workforce. The failure to adequately address legitimate complaints and concerns also runs the risk of promoting a corporate culture of unethical business activity. When honest workers realize that wrongdoers go unpunished or worse, are rewarded for cutting corners, the perception that unethical behavior is acceptable can develop within an organization.

In resolving ethical issues the interests of the various stakeholders need to be weighed off against each other to enable the decision maker to come up with what he/she feels is the most viable solution based on all of the circumstances. The principle stakeholders whose interests may conflict include the business owner, employees, management, customers, clients, suppliers, creditors and the community. Ethical decision making should, to the extent possible, promote a win-win situation where all stakeholders feel that their own interests have been fairly taken into consideration. While not everybody will be happy with the final decision, it is important that all affected parties feel that they have been granted an opportunity to present their side of the story before a decision is made.

While not always possible, every effort should be made to avoid placing employees in questionable ethical dilemmas. Aside from a reactive internal process addressing a new ethical issue, a proactive approach is also highly recommended in which employees are given a clear set of guidelines indicating what is considered acceptable ethical behavior. These include Professional Standards of Practice and a Corporate Code of Conduct.

PROFESSIONAL STANDARDS AND CORPORATE CODES OF CONDUCT
Section 2.5

Ethical behavior is very important in the business community and helps to instill confidence and trust in the minds of clients, employees and employers. Professional standards of practice and company codes of conduct are examples of ethical agreements that business persons voluntarily undertake to abide by and to respect.

2.5.1 Professional Standards of Practice

Professional standards of practice establish a set of ethical rules and behavior which all persons who wish to be recognized as members in good standing of a professional association agree to respect. These rules govern a professional's relationship with clients, employers, members of the profession, the community in general and the professional organization itself. Professional standards of practice promote fair and ethical business practices and strive to protect the reputation of the professional organization in the eyes of general public. Professional standards of practice deal with many issues including but not limited to the following areas of concern.

2.5.1.1 Objectivity

A professional should use his/her own judgment and make decisions based on his/her own sound analysis of the relevant business problem. A professional should not be influenced by the opinion of his/her client and/or employer. The role of a professional is not simply to give the client and/or employer whatever answer they want to hear.

2.5.1.2 Compliance with the law

Professionals must respect all regulatory and licensing requirements that govern their profession and all civil and criminal laws governing society in general.

2.5.1.3 Inappropriate conduct

A professional must not only respect the law, but must also act in a manner that does not bring disrepute to the profession as a whole. An example of inappropriate conduct would be a professional who is noticeably intoxicated on the job on a regular basis.

2.5.1.4 Confidentiality

Confidential information is information that is not readily available to the general public. In a business setting confidential information might refer to future business initiatives, financial earnings, client lists, intellectual property, R & D and other matters that competitors and/or the capital markets would be interested in learning about. Confidential information also includes all personal information regarding a company's employees.

In order to perform one's job, a professional will often be required to use confidential information belonging to a client or an employer. The professional is not permitted to use confidential information belonging to a client or to one's employer for personal profit, or for the profit of a third party, without having obtained the prior express consent of the client and/or employer.

2.5.1.5 Duty of care

A professional should act in the interests of his/her client/employer. In this respect a professional will be required to demonstrate that he/she took reasonable care and acted prudently in reaching a well-reasoned decision. There is no requirement in either ethics or law that states that a professional's decision must always in hindsight have been the "best/right" decision, as long as the professional can demonstrate that his/her decision was based on a reasonable and adequate examination of the various options available.

In determining whether a professional has respected his/her duty of care, one has to look at the particular facts of the case in question and the nature of the work to be performed. Where a client has little or no familiarity with the subject in question, and where the professional has discretionary power to make decisions on behalf of the client, the professional may be held to a higher duty of care, known as a fiduciary duty.

The **fiduciary duty** requires a professional not only to act in a reasonable manner, but to act in the best interest of the client. An example of fiduciary duty would be a stockbroker who has discretionary authority to invest a client's retirement fund. The client is a typical middle class employee earning a modest salary, having little disposable income and no knowledge of the stock market. In this case, the client relies exclusively on the broker to make investment decisions. If the broker invests this client's money in heavily leveraged speculative investments, resulting in large financial losses, the broker will probably be held in breach of his/her fiduciary duty to act in the best interest of the client. Such speculative investments are clearly not appropriate for this type of client, and the broker as a professional is required to know better. It would not be a defense for the broker to say that the client, when asked, had approved the broker's choice of investments, since the client did not have the knowledge to understand the full implications of this type of investment.

2.5.1.6 Conflict of interest

In the event that there are circumstances that could reasonably be expect to impede a professional's ability to act in an objective fashion, then the professional must disclose these circumstances in advance to the client and/or employer. Best practices would dictate that the professional decline to perform the task in the event of an actual or an apparent conflict of interest.

An example of an apparent conflict of interest would be a lawyer hired by a client to purchase several pieces of land. The lawyer immediately realizes that one of the pieces of land in question belongs to his mother-in-law. Can this lawyer go ahead and negotiate the purchase of this piece of land? What if the lawyer does not disclose the family relationship to the client but goes ahead and negotiates a reasonable sale price which is fair, based on market factors, to both the mother-in-law and to the client? What if the client, after disclosure of the relationship, tells the lawyer to go ahead and make a deal with his/her mother-in-law?

2.5.2 Corporate Codes of Conduct

A corporate code of conduct sets out the acceptable rules and guidelines that all employees in a company must respect. It is a valuable tool to educate employees as to what types of behavior, while not illegal, will not be tolerated within a corporate environment. By making the employee aware of what conduct is expected of him/her, and by setting out what the disciplinary consequences for non-respect will be, the company is able to minimize claims from aggrieved employees that they have been wrongfully punished for breaches of rules that they were unaware of.

When implementing a code of conduct for a company, it is important to ensure that employees view this corporate document as an important and serious commitment.

For this reason it is essential that top management demonstrates its own commitment to respect and to abide by the code of conduct. Leading by example is the best ethical practice to adopt when it comes to motivating employees to respect the value and importance of a corporate code of conduct.

In addition to the areas of concern discussed above for professional standards of practice, corporate codes of conduct should also address the issue of gifts and whistleblowing.

2.5.2.1 Gifts

A code of conduct should clarify what types of incidental gifts employees will be permitted to receive in the performance of their job. Acceptable gifts must not exceed a specified dollar value and must be only offered to employees as a demonstration of business etiquette and courtesy. As a general rule, gifts in cash must be avoided. Since the acceptance of a gift could be viewed as a bribe affecting the employees' objectivity and impartiality, employees are not allowed to solicit gifts.

For example, buying your client a $20 lunch to celebrate a successful business deal between your two companies should not be a problem. However, buying the same client and his/her family a $2,000 dinner in the best restaurant in town might be perceived as problematic. Buying your client and his/her family an all-inclusive week-long cruise in the Caribbean to celebrate this business deal will most likely be perceived as problematic. What should an employee do when offered a gift from a grateful client? The answer is to disclose the gift to your immediate supervisor or to the company's compliance officer if a particular person has been designated to handle these inquires, and ask them to decide if the gift is permitted. Just because you have closed a billion dollar deal on behalf of your company does not mean that the gift that you are allowed to accept from the other party can be worth a lot more money than the gift that you would be allowed to accept for closing a $10,000 deal.

2.5.2.2 Whistle blowing

Corporate codes of conduct should include whistle blowing provisions by which clearly defined reporting channels are provided for employees to report any inappropriate business activities that they may become aware of within their organization.

Whistle blowing involves the disclosure of inappropriate business practices by a member of an organization. In a typical situation, an employee will become aware of problematic behavior within an organization, be it financial impropriety, pollution, product safety or of another areas of concern to society. Normally a concerned employee's first reaction will be to report this wrongdoing or dangerous situation to his/her supervisor. The employee is acting in good faith, assumes that his/her disclosure will be welcomed by the supervisor and that the problem will be dealt with without delay. What happens when the employee's disclosure falls on to deaf ears and nothing is done to correct the problem? This is where the principles of whistle blowing come into play. Having followed the normal corporate channels of communication and not having received any results, the employee is now faced with a dilemma. Should the employee say nothing and forget about the problem, or should the employee disclose this information outside of the normal corporate channels? If the employee decides to continue his/her pursuit to resolve the problem then the next step usually involves circumventing the corporate chain of command, going around the supervisor, and reporting the problem directly to higher administration. This process is called internal whistle blowing.

Should senior administration fail to address the problem, the next step that the employee could take is referred to as external whistle blowing. External whistle blowing is the process by which the employee takes the problem public and discloses all of the facts to the government and/or media.

When an employee external whistle blows, he/she usually discloses confidential information about the company. Can the employee be fired for this disclosure? While an employee has a duty to respect the confidential information of the employer, the employee also has a duty to protect society and the public in general. Which of these duties should prevail? Do co-workers respect an employee who blows the whistle, or do they see the whistle blower as a "rat"?

RESPONSIBLE INVESTING
Section 2.6

Responsible investing, often referred to as socially responsible investing, represents a new ethical approach to evaluating a business enterprise. The traditional business model for corporations focuses on generating financial growth and profitable returns for the shareholders. Investors, in deciding whether to invest in a business enterprise, would examine financial statements to ascertain whether a company had the potential of generating profitable short-term returns for them, either in the form of dividends or through material increases in the value of publicly traded shares.

Contrary to the short-term profit driven evaluation approach, responsible investing adopts an ethical long-term approach to evaluating investments. An enterprise's social impact, including its labour practices, its respect for human rights and its position on environmental protection play an important role in creating long-term value, and are factors important in the assessment made by the responsible investor.

One important strategy employed in responsible investing is the principle of refusing to invest in certain types of industries or in companies with poor ethical track records. Industries that are viewed as harmful to society are often excluded from the responsible investment portfolio even though these companies may generate substantial profits. Examples of these "harmful" industries would include toxic chemicals, alcohol, tobacco, gambling, munitions and industries generating harmful emissions.

Institutional investors such as public or private pension funds wield enormous power and influence in the capital markets (stock markets, private placements, debt financing). As more and more pension funds have adopted a responsible investing philosophy over the last decade, a strong message has been sent to businesses world-wide that corporate management must not focus strictly on pleasing its shareholders with maximum profits, but must actively take into consideration the effects that companies' business activities have on a wide range of stakeholders (including those stakeholders referred to in Section 2.4 hereof).

A recent case that highlights the principles of responsible investing is that of an American candy manufacturer who for years has been buying raw materials from West African suppliers located in a geographical region known to actively use slave child labour. A pension fund shareholder of this candy company asked management for assurances that the company was not dealing with plantations that enslaved children. Corporate management was not prepared to disclose the information requested, so the pension fund instituted a court action to force the company to provide details concerning the identity of its suppliers. The pension fund argued that since the candy company knew that its raw materials were coming from an ethically suspect part of the world, the company had a duty to demonstrate to its stakeholders that it was not tacitly promoting child slavery by supporting unethical businesses in that region.

? *...as you read ask yourself...*
Could the candy company argue that it has done no wrong since it has no direct control over the African raw material suppliers? In your opinion, will this be a valid defense?

CORPORATE GOVERNANCE
Section 2.7

The last decade has been plagued with shocking examples of the failure of corporations and financial markets, from Enron and WorldCom to the subprime mortgage fiasco. Who suffered from these failures? Was it merely the rich banks and industrialists who lost a portion of their enormous fortunes? No, it was ordinary citizens, salaried workers, small investors and residential homeowners who suffered. Why did these dramatic financial failures occur and why did no one within the management of the corporations in question see these failures coming?

The principle of corporate governance looks at how companies are managed. Corporate governance involves setting up ethical procedures and controls to monitor and regulate the often conflicting interests of, and the interaction among, the shareholders, the Directors and the Officers (business managers) of a corporation. In the traditional corporate model the shareholders (owners of the company) do not participate in managing the company, however they elect the Directors who are empowered to manage the company. The Board of Directors has the authority to appoint the Officers who run the company on a day-to-day basis. While shareholders have no power to manage the company, their power to elect and consequently dismiss a Director creates a situation where the majority shareholder could conceivably "pressure or influence" the Directors' decisions. Since the Directors appoint the Officers of the company, the Directors can also assert influence over the nature and scope of decisions that the Officers take. As company law generally does not prohibit a shareholder, who is a human being and not a corporation, from also being a Director and Officer of the company, the separation among the roles of these three stakeholders is even more blurred. In Canada, a vast majority of companies are small to medium sized businesses owned and operated by shareholders who also concurrently perform the role of director and officer.

Corporate governance recognizes the need to create an ethical decision making process within a corporation by promoting the election of autonomous external (independent) Directors to help balance the decision making power of the insider Directors. Insider Directors are those persons who are either shareholders themselves or who have personal relationships with the shareholders of the company. Another important governance principle is to ensure that the person who exercises the role of Chairman of the Board of Directors is not the same person who holds the position of Chief Executive Officer (CEO) of the company. A CEO, who is not subject to the undue influence of insider Directors, is perceived as a more unbiased leader, more open to listen to the opinions and advice of independent Directors and of other interested parties.

As Directors have a duty to act in the best interest of the company, corporate governance also addresses the issue of what competencies and qualifications are necessary to be a Director. Simply because a person or his/her family owns shares in a company does not guarantee that this person has the business savvy necessary to run a corporation. Inexperience in leadership ability can not only result in erroneous actions and serious oversights, but can also send the dangerous message down the corporate chain of command that impropriety and incompetence will not be punished. Corporate governance promotes the election of competent independent Directors who can bring relevant industry experience and dynamic leadership skills to the boardroom.

Principles of ethical governance also require a corporation to act with transparency. Transparency refers to the process of operating in an open and above-board fashion, allowing interested stakeholders to verify that proper channels and procedures have been respected with regards to the calling and holding of meetings, the voting process, the appointment of Officers and senior management, the negotiation of material contract and the adoption of other business decisions. Transparency also requires that the details of all business decisions are properly documented in written corporate records (minutes). Transparency plays an important role in building investor confidence in a company by clearly disclosing all forms of remuneration that Directors and Officers will be receiving for their services. Best ethical business practices call for tying Directors' and Officers' remuneration, stock options, bonuses and other perks not simply to short-term financial profit but to a long term sustainable agenda, therefore sending a strong ethical message to the Directors and Officers.

LEGAL TERMS

In your reading, you came across the following terms. Be sure that you can explain each, to ensure your understanding of the material you have been reading. If you are uncertain as to the meaning of any term, review the material in the chapter for clarification. If necessary, consult a dictionary for further information or discuss the term(s) with your instructor.

Ethics	Morals	Extra-territoriality
Duty of care	Objectivity	Conflict of interest
Confidentiality	Code of conduct	Professional standards
Bribery	UNGC	Transparency
Disclosure	Fiduciary duty	Corporate governance
Stakeholders	Whistle blowing	Responsible investing

REVIEW QUESTIONS

1. Explain the difference between internal and external whistle blowing.

2. Does Canadian law apply outside of the borders of Canada? Explain your answer.

3. Under what circumstances would a company employee be permitted to accept a gift from a corporate supplier?

4. What are the differences, if any, between a duty of care and a fiduciary duty?

5. Does the best interest of the company equal the best interest of the majority shareholder? To whom do the Directors owe a duty?

6. Explain what is meant by the term "UNGC" and describe what areas of ethical concern are addressed by this initiative.

7. A Canadian based municipal pension fund is interested in investing in South American agricultural and mining interests. Based on your understanding of responsible investing, what are some of the important factors that the pension fund managers should look into when choosing their investments?

Chapter 3

THE QUEBEC LEGAL SYSTEM

OBJECTIVES

This chapter was prepared to enable you to achieve the following objectives:

1. To identify the three components of the Québec legal system.
2. To explain why "sovereignty" is the first step in establishing how laws come into existence.
3. To see how statutes, which are the statement of the law, are the logical outcome of a constitution.
4. To identify and understand the sources of law in our legal system.
5. To understand the legal profession.
6. To identify the role of the courts in the explanation, interpretation, and application of statute law.
7. To understand the function of the Governor General and Lieutenant Governors.

STRUCTURE
The First Element of the Québec Legal System
Section 3.1

"The Rule of Law as a principle of legality—the notion that governments can do nothing except that which they are authorized to do by law, and individuals can do everything except that which they are expressly prohibited from doing by law."

Prof. Frank R. Scott, former Dean of McGill Law Faculty

> *...What do you think Prof. Scott meant by this comment? Where would you look to find the "authority" to which he refers?*

We have considered the nature and function of law and the historical events that have resulted in the legal system found in this province today. We can now consider the following questions:

- Where does the authority come from to make laws for the citizens of Québec?
- Who has this authority?
- How far does this authority extend?
- What power, if any, exists to back up this authority?
- How are laws made?

3.1.1 Sovereignty

To answer these and similar questions we begin by looking at the concept of **sovereignty** and the power conferred by nationhood.

Every independent nation is sovereign. This means that the people who inhabit the country have, within their control, the supreme and absolute power to govern themselves in whatever way they choose. They can make laws, enforce these laws, impose and collect taxes, make war or peace, and enter into treaties, to name only some of their powers.

Every nation must decide how it will deal with its sovereignty. If the citizens choose to keep the sovereign power within their own hands, they will each have a voice, and they will meet regularly to make decisions as to how the nation will be governed. An example of this is small city states, such as Athens during the 500 B.C. period.

If this structure becomes too large, making it unwieldy or even impossible for such meetings to take place, it may be decided to have representatives chosen by groups of people. These representatives would meet, each bringing to the meeting the views of the people they represent. This group of representatives would then make the laws that would apply to everyone in the society.

If those who are chosen to represent the nation's citizens fail in their duties or manipulate their authority for personal gain, the inhabitants may replace them through accepted means, such as an election. Revolution and violence might also be used by the inhabitants to gain back their sovereign authority when the representatives govern by the use of force.

If, on the other hand, the chosen representatives act wisely, in the opinion of their fellow citizens, they will govern for the benefit of everyone. This may lead to prosperous national growth and citizens who may be content enough to allow the chosen group to continue to lead them for an extended period of time.

Obviously this is a highly oversimplified view of how sovereignty works, but it may assist you to grasp the basic idea.

There are, of course, limits to the use of sovereign rights. Generally, these are physical limits, i.e., the borders of the nation. A country can exercise its sovereignty within its own borders but not beyond. Thus, Canada cannot make laws telling the citizens of Switzerland how to behave, for this would interfere with the Swiss sovereignty.

3.1.2 Authority to Enact Law

Since 1982, with the adoption of the *Constitution Act*, Canada has been a fully sovereign nation, with the right to decide its government and make its own laws.

At that time, we decided to adopt the former *British North America (BNA) Act* as the basis for our Constitution, and to build on it.

The Constitution sets up the structure of our government (federal and provincial), and gives to each of the two levels the right to pass laws—but only in the specified fields assigned to them.

The federal parliament, situated in Ottawa, has the right to pass laws for the "Peace, Order and Good Government of Canada." These laws apply to all Canadian citizens, everywhere in the country. They also apply to residents and visitors who may not be citizens.

Although this appears to be a very wide grant of legislative authority, the Constitution restricts it by stating that the federal government cannot make laws relating to those matters that are given to the provinces.

The provincial legislatures are given the right to pass laws on those subjects that the Constitution says are reserved exclusively for them. There are ten provincial lawmaking bodies, each having its headquarters in the capital city of each province, e.g., Québec City, Winnipeg, Victoria, etc.

3.1.3 The Canadian Legislative Process

Now that we understand the principle of sovereignty with regards to law making authority within a state, we can examine the mechanism by which representatives make law and bring it into force.

We have seen how the Constitution of Canada sets up both a federal government and provincial governments. Both of these levels of government are given the right, by our Constitution, to pass laws on subjects that are within their sphere of authority. It is therefore appropriate to ask the question: if one of these governments wants to pass a particular law, how does it do so?

Federal laws are made by Parliament. This refers to the mechanism created to make laws at the federal level in Canada. There are three elements to the federal Parliament:

1. House of Commons (elected members)
2. Senate (appointed members)
3. Queen

When the federal government wants to pass a law on a particular subject, it begins by having the proposed law introduced by a Minister of the government, and it is given "first reading." If the members do not reject it, it is then printed in the form of a booklet and distributed to the members of the House of Commons. It is referred to as a "Bill" and given a number (e.g., Bill 96) for easy reference.

A few weeks later, it is brought up for discussion in the House, and the Minister explains why the government wants it to become a law of Canada. The opposition members will give their response as they debate the Bill in this "second reading."

The Bill then is given to a Committee to be examined in detail. The Committee will report back to the House with its recommendations for any changes it considers useful. The Bill is then ready for "third reading." At this time the Members have a last chance to make changes to the Bill and vote on it.

If the Bill passes the third reading, it is then sent to the Senate, where it goes through the same procedure and another three readings.

Once the Bill has passed both the House of Commons and the Senate, it is ready for "Royal Assent." This means it is signed into law by the Queen or her personal representative. For practical reasons, laws are rarely, if ever, signed by the Queen herself. It has become the custom for her personal representative to carry out this task.

After this, it is no longer a "Bill"; it has become a "law" and is now called by its proper name (e.g., the *Bank Act*; the *Income Tax Act*; the *Criminal Code*, etc.)

Normally, it is the government in power which successfully introduces new legislation. On occasion, however, Private Members' Bills proposed by Members of Parliament from any party can also become law.

3.1.4 The Québec Legislative Process

In each province, the laws are made by the legislature. This is the technical term for the provincial lawmaking mechanism. In Québec, it consists of two elements:

1. National Assembly
2. Queen

When the provincial government wants to pass a law, the process is quite similar to that which applies at the Federal level. A "Bill" is introduced into the National Assembly and must be read three times.

After the three readings, it is ready to be signed into law by the Queen or her personal representative in the province. It then becomes law.

?...and in the province...
How does one become a member of the National Assembly?

3.1.5 Representatives of the Crown & their Role in Lawmaking

The **Governor General** is the representative of the Crown in Canada. The Queen, upon the recommendation of the Canadian government, appoints the person who holds this position.

The Queen is the Canadian Head of State, but the Governor General is authorized *"to exercise, on the advice of the Canadian ministers, all Her Majesty's powers, and authorities in respect of Canada."*

One of the most important responsibilities of the Governor General is to ensure that the country always has a Prime Minister. If this office should become vacant because of death or resignation, it is the Governor General's responsibility to see that the post is filled. The same applies if the government resigns following a defeat in the House of Commons or in an election.

As one of the three elements of the Canadian Parliament, the Governor General summons Parliament (calls members to opening session), prorogues Parliament (adjourns current session) and dissolves the existing Parliament (terminates pending new election). Equally important, the Governor General also gives assent to those bills passed by both houses of the parliament, which then become Acts of Parliament and have the force of law.

The Governor General is Canada's host to visiting heads of state and other distinguished visitors from foreign countries, and also represents this country abroad in an official capacity.

The **Lieutenant Governor** is the Queen's representative in each province of Canada, and exercises the powers of the Queen granted under the Constitution, with respect to the province.

? *...In the next class, you will be asked...*
Who is Canada's Governor General?
Who is Québec's Lieutenant Governor?

3.1.6 Branches of Law

Parliament and the provincial legislatures use the lawmaking machinery we have just described to adopt various laws covering virtually every type of personal and business activity that Canadian citizens engage in. Some examples are:

Labour	Environment	Custom Duties
Marriage & Divorce	Communication	Contracts
Packaging	Copyright	Education
Railway	Highways	Companies
Bankruptcy	Patents	Income Tax
Aviation	Food & Drugs	Competition

Our interest, in this book, is in the law of Québec which regulates those activities most of us will encounter or work with. Therefore, we shall be dealing generally with the civil law, and in particular the law of contracts, so that we can identify the essential elements of a contract, and understand the nature of such contracts as sale, lease, mandate, etc.

Other areas of the civil law to be considered are property, ownership, prescription, civil responsibility, and some of the elements of civil procedure which outlines the rules to be followed in exercising the rights we have under the *Civil Code*.

LAW
The Second Element of the Québec Legal System
Section 3.2

The law element of the Québec legal system, which we defined in the previous chapter as the rules of behaviour imposed or accepted in the society, has six sources. Each of these sources contributes towards the development or restriction of new laws.

3.2.1 The Canadian Constitution: Cornerstone of Confederation and Canadian Society

The *Constitution Act, 1982*, tells us in section 52 that "*the Constitution of Canada is the supreme law of Canada, and any law that is inconsistent with the provisions of the Constitution is, to the extent of inconsistency, of no force or effect.*" For information on who in Canada can pass laws, on a particular subject, we can examine sections 91 and 92 of the *Constitution Act, 1867*.

What would a document written in 1867 have to say about who has authority over aviation, labour laws, outer space satellites, radio and television broadcasting, and employment insurance in Canada? Most of these subjects did not exist in 1867.

These and many other subjects have arisen since the Canadian Constitution was first drafted. All have been settled, some by agreement between the federal and provincial governments, and some by decisions of the courts.

To summarize, the only source of authority to make laws in Canada is the Constitution. The citizens of Canada have adopted this Constitution as the framework by which they wish to be governed. This document tells us which of the governments has the right to enact legislation on specific matters and limits all governments from imposing any arbitrary laws contradicting the rights granted by the Constitution. Where there is an area of ambiguity or uncertainty, we seek the answer through the courts that will make a declaratory judgment by interpretation based on the Constitution as a whole.

?...Go online and look at sections 91 and 92. Which government can pass laws for:

a) protecting an invention?
b) tavern licences?
c) incorporating?
d) divorce?
e) money?
f) banks?

3.2.2 Federal and Provincial Statute Law

The first source of law in our legal structure is our Constitution. The second is contained in the laws made by the federal and provincial governments.

Once we know which government has the right to pass laws on a certain subject, we can turn to the laws themselves to learn what they say about the subject.

Every year, each government passes many acts or statutes (laws) and at the end of the year these are all printed in one volume called "Statutes of Canada, 20XX," or "Statutes of Québec, 20XX."

From time to time, laws are revised, changed or even repealed (cancelled). When that happens, those who work in the legal profession must read the original law and update their copies of it to include these changes.

After a few years, with many changes having been made, it becomes somewhat complicated to know exactly how the law reads. In order to make the latest version of the laws more accessible to citizens, the governments consolidate the statutes every fifteen years or so, that is, they reprint them with all of the changes in a set of books called *The Revised Statutes of Canada* or *The Revised Statutes of Québec* with the year of revision. These sets of books contain all the laws currently in force modified to include all the changes made during the years since the previous revision. If we wish to know what law applies today, we must read the most recent Revised Statutes and then look for any changes to that law made since the revision.

A "Code," such as the *Civil Code of Québec* is also a "statute," for it is enacted (passed) in the same way. The distinction between the two lies in their content and interpretation. Strictly speaking, a **statute** deals with only one subject, e.g., taxation, insurance, bankruptcy. Our Canadian Constitution is a special and unique statute. A **code** deals with many subjects in a broad area. For example, the *Civil Code* has provisions (rules) concerning marriage, domicile, contracts, minors, prescription, birth certificates, etc., but all of these are within the field we consider to be part of the "civil" or "private" law. The federal *Criminal Code* deals with murder, treason, impaired driving, arson, and other subjects within the field we call the criminal law.

A statute is usually interpreted more strictly than a code, and the full intent of the lawmakers must be found "within the four corners of the Act." That is, the meaning of any unclear portion must be found by looking at the rest of the statute to see if the same or similar words are used in other paragraphs which are clearer. On the other hand, the interpretation of a code can be made with the aid of outside sources such as previous laws or decisions, as well as in the writings of respected jurists.

An important example of a Québec statute is the *Québec Charter of Human Rights and Freedoms*, which has significant implications for all who live in Québec. Discussion of the *Québec Charter* will be undertaken in the next chapter concerning personal rights and freedoms.

3.2.3 Case Law - Jurisprudence

The third source of law is found in the judgments of the courts rendered in past cases. These, collectively, form an ever-growing body of case law - **jurisprudence.**

In a stable legal system, it is essential that the law always be applied in the same way. When a difference of opinion between two people cannot be decided by the parties themselves, they may bring it before a court. The judge makes a decision, and the parties accept and comply with it. If a similar situation arises a year or two later between two other people, the same solution should apply. The judgment in the previous case would be referred to as an example of how the law is applied.

In order to obtain uniformity in the application of the law, the courts will generally consider previous decisions quite carefully and follow them whenever it is reasonable to do so. If, however, the legislators have passed a statute that conflicts with the "case law," then the statute has overriding authority. It must be remembered that the courts in Québec are not supposed to make law; their function is to apply and interpret the laws made by the Legislature.

A distinction should be noted between the authority of decided cases in the civil law environment of the province of Québec and the common law system in force in the other provinces of Canada. In the common law system, once a Court has made a decision, this decision is considered to have the force of law unless and until it is changed by a new statute. This is the doctrine of **stare decisis**, meaning "let the decision stand," and the courts are bound to follow previous decisions, wherever they apply. However, Québec courts are not bound to follow past judgments, although the judges carefully consider them in the interest of maintaining uniformity in the application of the law.

3.2.4 Doctrine

The fourth source of the law is the **doctrine** or written commentary on the law. Many highly respected lawyers and judges, having made their own careful study and analysis of various subjects of the Québec law, have then written articles or books explaining what they have found in their work. These writings may often help us better understand the nature and underlying principles of the law.

This written material forms what is referred to as the doctrine. It is not unusual for a lawyer to refer to one or more of these articles or books when pleading a case in court, in an attempt to convince the court to accept the explanation of the author. Obviously, the more often the courts accept these writings as being the proper explanation of the law, the more highly respected will be the person who has written the material.

3.2.5 Custom or Tradition

A fifth source to consider are the **customs** or usage commonly accepted in a particular community or industry. Providing there is no statute law that conflicts with such custom, the fact that something has been done in a particular way for a long period of time may help a court to declare that such a custom has virtually hardened into a law. This can, of course, be replaced at any time by a new law which provides for a different rule to be followed.

An example is found in a 1976 case heard in Alberta. A contract was entered into for the sale of a bull to be used as a breeder. The buyer later found that the bull was unable to perform this service, and sued the seller for damages. There was no law specifically covering this matter, but the Court found that there was a custom in the agricultural community that if a bull could not perform, the purchase price should be refunded. The judge followed this custom and ordered the money to be returned.

?...a good time for a pause...

Pause here to ask yourself, do you know of any customs?
What statutes do you believe came from customs?

3.2.6 Administrative Regulations

The sixth and final source of law is a rapidly growing one, the body of **regulations** brought into force under the authority of various statutes.

In many laws, the government sets up a special committee, board, or commission to take charge of the application of that particular law. These administrative boards are given the authority to pass regulations which are the detailed rules setting out precisely how the law is to be respected, enforced, or applied. One such body is the "Office de la langue française," set up under Bill 101. There are more than four hundred such administrative organizations in Canada, established under federal or provincial laws. A few examples are:

Federal	Provincial
Canadian Radio-Television Commission	Régie du logement
Canadian Wheat Board	Commission des droits de la personne
Immigration Appeal Board	Régie des alcools des courses et des jeux
Canada Labour Relations Board	Régie des rentes du Québec
Human Rights Commission	Commission de la santé et de la sécurité du travail (CSST)

? *...as you read ask yourself...*
Which source of law is most prevalent in our legal system?
Has it always been this way or has it changed and why?

ADMINISTRATION & ENFORCEMENT
The Third Element of the Québec Legal System
Section 3.3

We have looked at the make-up of the legislative bodies in Canada to whom the function of lawmaking is given, as well as the process by which laws come into effect.

Once the laws have been passed, it is up to the courts to interpret and apply them. We have confidence in our judges, that with the experience and understanding these men and women have gained, they are capable of explaining how the laws should be used in going about our daily activities.

While judges use their best talents to fulfil a difficult and lonely task, they are human. Recognizing this, and the fact that people may have different opinions about anything, including the meaning of a law, we have a system of courts made up of several levels.

To better understand the administration and enforcement element, we will first examine the court system and then the legal profession.

3.3.1 The Court System

People, as individuals or business managers, may have a difference of opinions as to how a law should be applied or interpreted. Quite often, people may even have a difference of opinions on how an agreement, entered into by the parties, should be applied. In such situations, our legal system entitles them to present their differences to a court and have a judge render a decision to settle the matter.

Depending on the nature of a case or perhaps on the amount of money involved, the procedural rules may entitle people to seek a decision or the reversal of a court decision at various **forums** (levels). In this section, we shall look at the structure of the court system and discuss the differences between the various courts in Québec.

The *Constitution Act, 1867*, states in Sec. 92(14) that the provinces have exclusive rights with respect to:

> *"the administration of justice in the Province, including the constitution, maintenance and organization of Provincial Courts, both of civil and criminal jurisdiction..."*

In the *Courts of Justice Act*, we find the names and details of the various courts that have authority in Québec. The Courts of Québec, in civil, criminal and mixed matters, are:

The Court of Appeal
The Superior Court
The Court of Québec
The Municipal Courts

Each of these courts has a specified **jurisdiction** over the administration and enforcement of laws. In other words, different courts have different levels of competencies, which may refer to either:

a) the nature, or type of cases brought before that court - e.g., civil, criminal, bankruptcy, divorce, etc., or the maximum amount of money the court has the authority to decide upon i.e., the financial jurisdiction;

or

b) the geographic area of the province where the court may hold its sittings, and from which it may hear cases.

In this book, the first meaning will be the one most frequently used.

COURT STRUCTURE

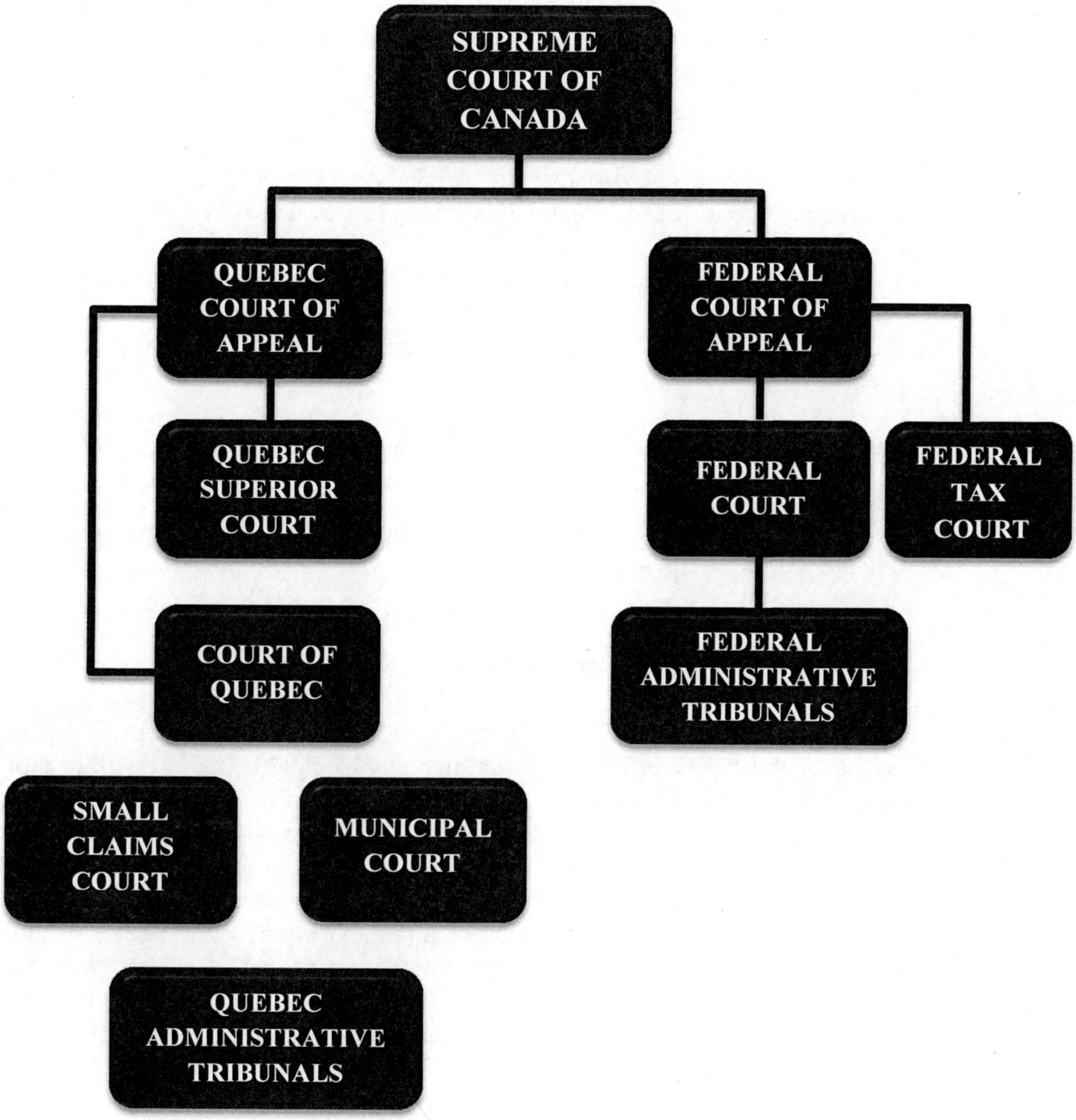

3.3.1.1 The Municipal Court

Each city (municipality) in the province is given the right to set up a Municipal Court. There are over eighty such courts in Québec. Except for Montreal, Laval, and Québec cities, the municipal court is usually a "part-time" court, sitting one or two evenings and/or afternoons each week. This is simply because there are generally not enough cases to occupy a court on a full-time basis. The judges of these courts are often lawyers who live in the community, and are appointed by the Minister of Justice of Québec to exercise the role of a municipal judge.

In Montreal, Laval and Québec City, the Municipal Courts maintain a full-time daily schedule, often with several courtrooms in session at the same time. In these cities, the judges are appointed to permanent positions.

The Municipal Court has jurisdiction to hear matters related to violations of municipal by-laws (e.g., traffic, health, zoning, noise, municipal taxes) and minor criminal matters under Part XXVII of the *Criminal Code of Canada* for which offences are punishable by summary conviction (e.g. mischief, shoplifting, gambling). Appeals for criminal offences are heard by the Superior Court. The Municipal Court does not hear civil cases in which a person is suing someone else for money owed.

3.3.1.2 The Court of Québec

Cases that fall within the jurisdiction of the Court of Québec are brought to this Court and heard by one judge. Since cases come to this Court the first time they are heard, it is called a Court of First Instance.

This Court has three divisions. They are the Civil Division (which includes the Small Claims Court), the Youth Division and the Criminal and Penal Division. With respect to the civil jurisdiction of this Court, it may, in general, hear cases of the following types:

a) where the value claimed, or the contract in dispute, is more than $7000 and less than $70,000 (except for matters of alimentary pension or alimony)

b) to cancel a lease when the amount claimed for rent and damages is less than $70,000

c) to recover unpaid municipal or school taxes

d) to cancel a real estate valuation roll on which taxes would be assessed.

A judgment of the Court of Québec can be appealed to the Court of Appeal only if the value of the object in dispute is greater than $50,000. Cases dealing with amounts below $50,000 cannot be appealed and the decision of the Court of Québec is the final judgment. However, an appeal may be allowed if it can be demonstrated the case involves a question of law, a question of principle or a new issue that contradicts judicial precedence and is in the public's interest that it be addressed by the court.

In Youth matters, the Court has exclusive jurisdiction respecting adoption, and exercises the powers and functions of the Youth Court under the *Young Offenders Act* (federal) and the *Youth Protection Act* (Québec).

It has exclusive jurisdiction to hear appeals from the Québec Administrative Tribunal and any other administrative tribunal that allows appeals.

The judges of the Court of Québec are appointed by the provincial government for life.

3.3.1.3 The Small Claims Court (division of the Court of Québec)

In order to relieve the backlog of cases and pressure on the higher courts, the Province organized a Small Claims Court in 1972. An important objective at the time was to enable people to obtain faster and less expensive settlement of minor court cases.

This Court uses the **inquisitive method**. One judge hears the parties, asks them about the relevant facts, and renders a decision.

In order to meet the objectives set out for the Court, some essential conditions apply:

a) The claim must be no more than $7,000.

b) The claim must arise out of a contract, or from an accident which resulted in damage.

c) The debtor (person sued) does not have to reside in Québec.

d) The debt must be owed personally or directly to the creditor (the person suing).

e) An association, partnership or corporation suing must not have had more than five employees working for it during the previous twelve months.

f) Lawyers are not permitted to represent people in this court, except if given permission due to the complexity of the case.

A person suing or being sued in this Court should come to the Court in person. If it is impossible to do so, a **mandate** (authority to act for another person) may be given in writing to someone else that may then represent the person, but this must be done without charge.

If a business (corporation) sues or is sued, it must be represented by a director or officer or by a person who is a full-time employee of the business, and in this case, the employee may be a lawyer.

A creditor may voluntarily decide to reduce the amount he or she is owed to less than $7,000 in order to bring the claim to the Small Claims Court. For example, a person owed $7,250 might claim a reduced amount of $7,000. In doing so, however, the creditor loses forever the right to claim the additional amount, even if he or she wins the case.

The judge will attempt to bring the parties to reconciliation, but if this is not successful, a judgment will be made.

There is no appeal from the judgments of the Small Claims Court. Once a judgment is rendered, the money owed must be paid within ten days. If it is not, the creditor has the right to return to the Court and request that the debtor's salary or property (movables only) be seized to satisfy the judgment.

To file a motion with the Small Claims Court, the petitioner must deposit a sum for costs. The following costs were in effect as of June 1, 2013. The law provides for these to be indexed every year on April 1. Anyone considering making use of the Small Claims Court should verify the charges in effect at the time.

The creditor must deposit the following sum, based on the amount involved in the case and on whether they are acting as a person (Natural Person) or a corporation (Legal Person):

Claim Amount	Natural Person	Legal Person
Up to $999.99	$73.75	$124
Between $1000 to $2999.99	$105	$156
Between $3000 to $4999.99	$136	$185
Between $5000 to $7000	$167	$218

A debtor, who intends to contest an action, must deposit the following amount of costs:

Claim Amount	Natural Person	Legal Person
Up to $999.99	$62	$110
Between $1000 to $2999.99	$93.75	$143
Between $3000 to $4999.99	$124	$174
Between $5000 to $7000	$156	$204

The judgment debtor, aside from being ordered to pay bailiff fees, must also pay the costs of execution in the amount of:

Claim Amount	Natural Person	Legal Person
Up to $999.99	$62	$93.75
Between $1000 to $2999.99	$87.25	$118
Between $3000 to $4999.99	$110	$143
Between $5000 to $7000	$136	$156

3.3.1.4 The Superior Court

This is the Court of original general jurisdiction and like the Court of Quebec cases are heard by one judge alone. This means that it hears every case that is brought to court for the first time, unless a paragraph of law directs that such a case must be brought before another court - e.g., if the amount is below $70,000, or if it is an adoption matter or a labour dispute.

The Superior Court also has superintending and reforming power over all other courts in the province, except for the Court of Appeal, as well as over corporations. This means that if another court should exceed its jurisdiction (rendering a decision beyond its level of authority), a request may be made to the Superior Court to remedy the situation.

In its capacity to deal with the decisions of corporations, the Court will generally only consider whether the firm has the right to make the decision that is contested, and it will not question the soundness of the decision unless the court feels management breached its duty of care. If the firm did not have the right to make the decision, the Court can cancel or modify such decisions.

Most of the decisions of the Superior Court may be appealed automatically or with leave (permission) from the Court of Appeal.

3.3.1.5 The Court of Appeal

This is the general Appeal Court for the province. It is the Court to which appeals are brought from the Superior Court, and in special cases, from the Court of Québec. It has “appellate jurisdiction” (the right to hear appeals) over all cases where an appeal is allowed by law, except those where the law specifically says the appeal must be heard by a different body.

In the Court of Appeal, each case is heard by more than one judge—there may be three, five, or seven judges who listen and decide a case. Decisions are made by a majority of the judges present; it is not necessary for the decision to be unanimous. Any judge who disagrees with the other judges may write a “dissenting opinion,” in which the reasons for the difference of opinions are set out.

The whole case is not argued again in this Court. The evidence and transcripts from the lower court are carefully reviewed by the judges before the hearing, and the lawyers will argue only the grounds (reasons) for the appeal. Note that the grounds for appeal may be based only on error of law and or error of fact.

The Court can rule in one of three ways. It can allow the lower court decision to stand, it can overrule the lower court decision and substitute it with its own judgment or it can order that the case be heard once again from the start by the lower court.

3.3.1.6 The Supreme Court of Canada

This is the highest Court in Canada, and is the final court to which one may bring appeals in all matters, civil or criminal. There is only one Supreme Court of Canada, and it hears appeals from all of the courts in all provinces of the country.

There are nine judges in this court, appointed by the federal government. The judges are chosen from across Canada, with three of them always being appointed from Québec.

Cases are heard by an odd number of judges and decisions are by majority. Like the Court of Appeal, it can rule to maintain a lower court decision, substitute the previous decision with its own or order a new trail. Although some matters may be appealed "of right," generally anyone wishing to bring a case to this Court must first ask permission from the Court. A panel of judges will examine the request, and decide if "leave to appeal" will be granted.

3.3.1.7 The Federal Court of Canada

This special Court deals with matters that concern the federal government. It has both a first instance section as well as an appeal section.

It deals with a wide variety of administrative matters, disagreements between citizens and the federal government and hears, in appeal, cases decided by other federal courts such as the Tax Court, and citizenship matters.

3.3.1.8 Administrative Tribunals (Boards)

Both the federal and provincial laws often bring into existence bodies that are given the power to enact administrative regulations. These regulations, once approved, have the force of law, and impose rules as to how a particular law is to be enforced. These regulations often intervene in the rights of citizens to enter into contracts or to arrange their business or financial matters to their advantage.

Citizens who disagree with the decisions of these boards can often appeal such decisions through a review board built into the law itself or through the Québec Administrative Tribunal, which oversees all other administrative bodies. But, it must be noted that not all decisions made by one of these government agencies or departments may be challenged before the Tribunal. Quite often a decision by an administrative board is final and there is generally no further recourse. Examples of such boards are the Canada Employment Insurance Commission and the Commission de la santé et de la sécurité du travail (CSST), which awards workers' compensation benefits.

3.3.2 THE LEGAL PROFESSION

3.3.2.1 Judges

Judges of the Québec Superior Court, Court of Appeal, Supreme Court of Canada and all federal courts are appointed and their salaries are paid by the federal government. Judges in the lower courts are paid and appointed by the provincial government.

In order to be appointed as a judge, a person must be a lawyer with a minimum of ten years' experience. Upon being appointed, the person must give up private practice and terminate any business relationships. The retirement age is seventy for judges of the Court of Quebec.

When positions are open, the Québec government advertises them in the publications distributed to the legal profession. Those interested may apply, and a special panel is set up to review the applications and make hiring recommendations to the government.

It is an essential part of a judge's position to make decisions on matters that are brought before him or her. The law says:

> *A Judge cannot refuse to adjudicate under the pretext of the silence, obscurity or insufficiency of the law. (Interpretation Act, Sec. 41.2)*

In performance of this responsibility, a judge may ask questions to clarify responses or assist in the application of the law, but in a very limited form. Unlike the **inquisitive** approach found in the courts of France, where the judge asks questions and carries out cross-examinations, our system is based on the **adversarial** approach. The parties, usually represented by their lawyers, are opponents or adversaries. They each present fact and legal arguments, and the judge decides which of the two adversaries has developed a stronger case, based on the preponderance (weight) of the evidence. The inquisitive method, however, is used in the Small Claims Court (a division of the Court of Québec), where no lawyers are permitted.

The adversarial system is used in the courts of England as well as in the United States, which has followed the British system quite closely.

3.3.2.2 Lawyers & Notaries

The **lawyer** (avocat) gives legal advice, assists in setting up new businesses, prepares contracts, and has the exclusive right to represent clients and plead cases before the courts. Only a lawyer may make a claim for payment on behalf of another person with the threat of legal proceedings as a consequence of non-payment.

The **notary** (notaire) also gives legal advice on personal and business matters, but has the exclusive right to prepare certain contracts such as real estate transactions involving a hypothec (mortgage), marriage contracts, notarial wills, and authentic documents. The notary, however, cannot appear in court to argue a case on behalf of a client.

These two legal professions in Québec have evolved from a blend of elements taken from both England and France.

In England and other common law countries, the legal profession is divided into **solicitors** and **barristers**. The solicitor deals with the public, providing legal advice on all matters. Arguing cases in court is handled by a barrister, who specializes in court procedure and litigation. A person cannot be both a solicitor and a barrister, nor can such individuals practise in partnership together.

In France, the legal profession is more specialized. There are four kinds of lawyers, each having somewhat different responsibilities. The **avocat**, like the English barrister, is the lawyer who pleads cases before the courts, both civil and criminal. The **avoué** is an officer of the court who may deal directly with clients and who prepares all the written documents and pleadings. Avoués are more similar to the English solicitors. The **agréés** are lawyers who practise before the commercial courts, in a manner similar to the avoué. The **notaire** is a specialist and is the only member of the French legal profession who can handle real estate transactions, prepare marriage contracts and liquidate successions. A person cannot be both an avocat and a notaire. Although they share the right to handle some matters, other areas of legal activity are reserved specifically for one or the other.

In the common law provinces of Canada, there is no division in the legal profession. The only professional is the lawyer or attorney. All lawyers are trained to carry out any legal function, to handle matters related to all types of contracts, and to plead both civil and criminal cases.

Both lawyers and notaries in Québec receive essentially the same legal training before entering their chosen profession. After two years at CEGEP, they usually proceed to a three-year undergraduate university degree such as Bachelor of Arts (B.A.), Bachelor of Commerce (B.Com.), or Bachelor of Science (B.Sc.). The next step is the three-year law school program leading to the Bachelor of Civil Law (B.C.L.). One additional year of study is required for a student wanting to obtain the Common law degree as well, the Bachelor of Laws (LL.B.).

To complete his or her training, the future lawyer takes the course given by the Bar of Québec (Barreau du Québec), spends a period of time "articling" or working as a "*stagaire*" with a lawyer, and writes the Bar examinations. The future notary takes the course given by the Board of Notaries (Chambre des notaires), "articles" with a practising notary, and writes the Board exams. Finally, some nine years after leaving high school, the legal professional is in a position to begin providing legal services to the public.

Only one profession can be carried on. A person must select either the profession of lawyer or that of notary. One cannot be both in Québec.

3.3.2.3 The Notarial System

The profession of notary is unique to the Province of Québec. The "notaire" or notary was the first legal profession practised in Canada or New France. Jean Gloria was appointed the first Royal Notary in the French colony on September 20, 1663. The notary has played and continues to play a significant role in Québec and in the French Civil Law system. It has its roots in the French legal profession as practised in France, and has since developed with certain differences arising from the Québec experience.

The right of the separate existence of the notarial profession was assured when, on April 30, 1785, Lieutenant Governor Hamilton declared the professions of lawyer and notary to be incompatible. Since that time, the two professions have existed on their own.

The notarial system has great importance in the Québec legal structure. The notary is an expert in the drafting of legal documents, and has the authority to prepare **Authentic Acts** (*actes authentiques*). These are documents drawn up by the notary and signed by the parties in the presence of the notary. The original copy, with the signatures of the parties, remains in the notary's possession. The parties receive authentic copies of the document, with their names typed and the copy is signed by the notary as being a true copy of the original.

The value of the authentic act is that it "makes proof of its own contents" i.e., it does not have to be proven in court, as would any other document. The mere fact of the notary's signature is sufficient evidence for any Québec judge to accept the document as being valid.

The authentic act is prepared on special paper designated by the Board of Notaries as having the proper linen content and weight, so that it will last many years without seriously deteriorating. The signatures must be in good quality ink. Marginal notes must be initialled by all the parties and lastly by the notary.

A notarial document is prepared either **en minute** or **en brevet**. Deeds (documents) en minute are kept separate and are numbered consecutively in the notary's records, and the notary issues copies or extracts from them. The notary is obliged by law to preserve the original documents which are kept in fire-proof vaults or cabinets. Deeds en brevet are executed with one or more originals which are delivered to the parties.

Notaries are legal practitioners and public officers whose chief duty is to prepare and execute deeds and contracts. The notary may also use the title "legal advisor," "title attorney," or "notary public" for affidavits to be used outside the province of Québec.

The profession is regulated by the Board of Notaries, the professional corporation given this responsibility. The inspectors of the Board periodically examine the documents, trust books, and records of the notary to ensure that all of the required rules are being followed. The Board has the power to fine, suspend or disbar a notary who is found to have violated the rules of the profession.

Certain documents must be passed (signed) before a notary. These include gifts inter-vivos (between living persons); hypothecary loans (mortgages); inventory of the property of a person who has become incapable (physically and/or mentally) of looking after his or her own affairs; sale of property belonging to minors or incapable persons; wills in authentic form; trust deeds and marriage contracts.

The notary is also an expert in the examination of title to real estate. This is done to ensure that there are no irregularities in past transactions which may interfere with a person being the true owner of property that he or she buys.

In the preparation of authentic documents, the notary has the obligation to observe certain facts:

1. to establish the identity of the parties,
2. to ensure that the parties understand the nature of the document they are about to sign,
3. to verify that the parties clearly consent to the obligations they are about to undertake,
4. to ensure that the date and place of the signing of the document are clearly indicated.

3.3.3 Commissioner of Oaths

It is sometimes necessary for a person to sign a document and solemnly declare under oath that the information it contains is true. Such a "solemn declaration" or affidavit may be received by a lawyer or notary. Because it is not always convenient to go to the office of a legal professional, the Québec government authorizes certain persons to be Commissioners of Oaths (*Commissaire à l'assermentation*). The Commissioner may receive solemn declarations when the person takes the oath and signs the document in the presence of the Commissioner. Such documents have the same validity as if made in open court under oath.

Commissioners do not have, nor do they require any legal training. They are people of good character who apply to be appointed as Commissioners. The Commissioner is not responsible to verify the truth of the information in an affidavit, only to ensure that the person who signs the document has solemnly declared that the information it contains is true.

An example of an affidavit is shown below. The person making it signs it after taking the oath, and the Commissioner of Oaths then signs it in the JURAT, which is the section at the bottom left hand corner, to certify that the person declared it to be true.

AFFIDAVIT

I, the undersigned John Henderson, automobile mechanic, residing and domiciled at 8399 Montplaisir Avenue in the City and District of Montreal, having been duly sworn, do hereby declare the following:

1. THAT I have known the late George Caplan for the last fifteen years;

2. THAT I am not related to the late George Caplan either directly or by marriage;

3. THAT I have frequently been in his company, and on many occasions I have seen his handwriting and his signature;

4. THAT I have taken cognizance of the document alleged to be the Last Will and Testament of the late George Caplan in Holograph form;

5. THAT I can identify the handwriting on the said document as being that of the late George Caplan, including the signature at the end of the document.

AND I HAVE SIGNED:

John Henderson

JOHN HENDERSON

SOLEMNLY DECLARED BEFORE ME
IN THE CITY OF MONTREAL ON THIS
11th day of August, 2013

Gilles Menard
Commissioner of Oaths
in and for the
District of Montreal

Commissioners of Oaths cannot charge more than $5 dollars for their services and cannot sign affidavits for members of their own family, such as parents, brothers or sisters, consort or children.

In addition to Commissioners of Oaths, the law also authorizes mayors, councillors, priests, ministers, and justices of the peace to receive sworn statements.

3.3.4 Legal Aid

The purpose of the Legal Aid Act is to provide the services of a lawyer or notary, free of charge, to anyone who cannot afford to pay for such services. Free legal aid is available to any person who can prove that his revenue and assets, or those of the family, do not exceed the established levels set by government.

The law sets out the maximum weekly income a person can earn and those whose earnings are below these levels will qualify for legal aid assistance, provided the type of service they seek is not excluded. The schedule of earnings changes from time to time, so that any interested person should verify what the levels are at the time.

A person who qualifies for assistance calls the Legal Aid office (blue pages of the telephone directory) and arranges to fill out an application. Once this is reviewed and accepted, a certificate of eligibility for legal aid will be issued.

The person may then choose to have the case handled by one of the lawyers who work permanently for the Legal Aid office, or any other lawyer or notary in private practice who is willing to look after the case.

Once the case is concluded, the lawyer or notary sends the bill to the Legal Aid office, and there is no charge to the client.

Legal aid is available in the following cases:

a) criminal defence matters in first instance
b) certain family matters
c) alimentary obligation
d) cases under the Youth Protection Act

Certain legal proceedings are excluded from legal aid. They are:

a) taking action for defamation or libel (but available to defendant);
b) to contest the results of an election;
c) taking action for breach of promise of marriage;
d) defending a parking violation.

For legal aid phone numbers and eligibility rules contact

The Commission des services juridiques

www.csj.qc.ca

LEGAL TERMS

In your reading, you came across the following terms. Be sure that you can explain each, to ensure your understanding of the material you have been reading. If you are uncertain as to the meaning of any term, review the material in the chapter for clarification. If necessary, consult a dictionary for further information or discuss the term(s) with your instructor.

sovereignty	constitution	statute
repealed	consolidate	assent
code	interpretation	bill
jurisprudence	case law	custom
stare decisis	doctrine	prorogue
regulations	administrative boards	

REVIEW QUESTIONS

1. Sunita, who works for a large investment firm, is preparing a full report on the law related to banks.

   Explain in detail what steps Sunita will take in order to be sure that she has located all the information necessary to prepare this report.

2. The fishing boats of a foreign country have been taking fish from an area 25 km outside the limits of Canadian territorial waters (The limit is 200 nautical miles or 370 km from shore). The Canadian government instructed its enforcement officers to board the foreign ships and arrest the captain and crew in order to stop this over fishing.

   Explain the legal basis for this action to show whether or not Canada has the right to take this action.

3. Explain whether Québec courts are bound by previous judgments.

4. Gérard, the owner of Lo-price Furniture Store Inc., is planning an important sale. He ordered 100,000 advertising pamphlets from his printer, intending to distribute them to all the homes in his area of the city.

   The printer delivered 91,267 pamphlets. Gérard called the printer to complain, and insisted on receiving the balance. The printer explained that he had run short of paper, and that there was a custom in the printing industry that a client had to accept up to 10 percent more or less than the quantity ordered. He said that he could not supply the balance at the same price.

   Gérard is very angry, as it means that he will miss sending the pamphlets to many homeowners. What defence might the printer use if Gérard sues him to produce the balance at the same price, and how could the printer support this defence?

5. The Governor General and the Lieutenant Governors are the Queen's representatives in Canada and the provinces. Do you think these positions are needed or should they be abolished? If you think they should be eliminated, how could this be done, and what would be the effect on our lawmaking process?

6. Some islands in the Atlantic Ocean just off the coast of Argentina belong to and have been ruled by England for many years. The government of Argentina has decided that, since the islands are much closer to Argentina than to England, it would be better for Argentina to govern them.

   The government of Argentina has passed a law stating that all people living on these islands must pay income tax to Argentina. Comment on this situation and support your remarks by referring to the material you have read in this chapter.

7. Although laws in Canada are passed by Parliament or the Legislatures, we speak of "case law" in this chapter. What is the difference between the laws passed by the government and "case law"?

8. The Canadian Radio-Television Commission (CRTC) makes decisions about who can be licensed to operate radio or television stations and who can sell various telecommunication services. Recently the CRTC agreed that one firm should have the exclusive right (i.e., a monopoly) to sell Direct-to-Home satellite TV services. The Canadian government reacted to this decision by ordering the CRTC to allow other firms to apply for the right to sell the same service.

   Does the Canadian government have the right to intervene in this matter? Why or why not?

   Why do you think the Canadian government would want to intervene in this matter?

9. In this chapter there is a brief list of various branches of law. Can you add five more subjects to this list?

Chapter 4

PERSONAL RIGHTS

OBJECTIVES

This chapter was prepared to enable you to achieve the following objectives:

1. To understand what rights and freedoms existed prior to the *Constitution Act, 1982.*
2. To appreciate the importance of the *Canadian Charter of Rights and Freedoms.*
3. To understand the guarantees provided by "entrenchment" versus a simple statute.
4. To appreciate the importance of the *Québec Charter of Human Rights and Freedoms*.
5. To introduce the principles of application for both Charters.
6. To understand how limitations may be imposed on Charter rights and freedoms.
7. To appreciate the rights and freedoms offered by the *Québec Civil Code*.

INTRODUCTION
Section 4.1

In a free and democratic society, rarely will we find complete agreement on issues. Public opinion, on any given issue, is made up of those who form the majority and those of the minority. As a result, much of what we practice as a democratic society has centered on trying to balance the interrelated, but often conflicting principles of majority rule, societal objectives and individual rights. Thomas Jefferson's quote identifies best the importance of this balance:

> ***"All, too, will bear in mind this sacred principle, that though the will of the majority is in all cases to prevail, that will, to be rightful, must be reasonable; that the minority possess their equal rights, which equal laws must protect, and to violate would be oppression."***
>
> ***Thomas Jefferson***

This chapter will attempt to draw on this principle of balance by highlighting three important documents, whose purpose is the protection of individual and minority rights. These documents are the *Canadian Charter of Rights and Freedoms*, the *Québec Charter of Human Rights and Freedoms* and the *Book on Persons* of the *Civil Code of Québec.*

THE CANDIAN CHARTER OF RIGHTS AND FREEDOMS
Section 4.2

4.2.1 Entrenched Rights

Prior to the adoption of the *Canadian Charter of Rights and Freedoms*, in 1982, Canadians had very little guaranteed protections against government encroachment on their freedoms. Canada was founded on the principle of parliamentary supremacy, which was reinforced by not including in the *BNA Act* a Charter or a Bill protecting individual rights. It was believed that an elected government, composed of the common citizen, would be more legitimate and better suited in making laws that would protect its citizens, than unelected judges – who could use a constitutional Charter to make laws as they saw fit through judicial activism.

In general, politicians and scholars argued a Charter was not necessary since people could rely on various statutes, such as the *Criminal Code of Canada*, provincial and federal labour codes, the *Civil Code* for those residing in Québec or the *Canadian Bill of Rights* that was adopted in 1960, as a means of protecting their rights. Additionally, there existed a belief in an implied (assumed) Bill of Rights, found in the preamble of the *BNA Act, 1867*, which reads:

> *"Whereas the Provinces of Canada, Nova Scotia and New Brunswick have expressed their Desire to be federally united into One Dominion under the Crown of the United Kingdom of Great Britain and Ireland, with a Constitution similar in Principle to that of the United Kingdom..."*

The words *"similar in Principle"* underscore the Founding Fathers' intent to create a country based on the fundamental principles of a parliamentary system. Such a system requires the participation of its citizens and could not function if laws were invoked to curtail free speech, freedom of association and assembly rights. Therefore, any such law would be in violation of the *BNA Act*, 1867, and struck down by the courts.

Canadian history, though, demonstrates these statutes and theoretical beliefs were not enough to protect citizens from having their rights arbitrarily violated or systematically diminished by local, provincial and federal government agencies. Statutes could easily be changed or ignored. Even the *Canadian Bill of Rights* had limited enforcement since it was simply a statute placed on equal footing with other statutes or worse, was over-ridden by a new statute hindering rights found in the *Bill.*

This changed with the adoption of the *Constitution Act, 1982*, containing as its central part the *Canadian Charter of Rights and Freedoms*. This document entrenches and protects the basic rights which are guaranteed to every Canadian. When we say that these rights are **"entrenched"** in the Constitution, this means that they can be changed (amended) only in the same way that the *Act* can be amended, and that is by agreement between the federal and provincial governments – neither level of government can change it alone. Seven provinces containing at least 50% percent of the population of Canada need to approve an amendment for it to pass (the *seven-fifty formula*).

As a result, this required procedure provides a much stronger guarantee for these rights and freedoms than if they were contained in a law passed only by the federal Parliament or only by the Québec legislature.

4.2.2 Application

Unlike any previous provincial human rights statute or the federal *Bill of Rights*, which bound only the governments that adopted these protections, the *Canadian Charter of Rights and Freedoms* required upon its inception an adherence to it by both the federal and provincial legislatures. This is enshrined in section 32(1). It reads:

> ***32.** (1) This Charter applies*
>
> *(a) to the Parliament and government of Canada in respect of all matters within the authority of Parliament including all matters relating to the Yukon Territory and Northwestern Territories; and*
>
> *(b) to the legislature and government of each province in respect of all matters within the authority of the legislature of each province.*

But, section 32(1) adherence is not limited to just these two levels of government. The words *"all matters within the authority"* extend this obligation to include all levels of government regardless of geographic location, level of importance or jurisdictional authority. For instance, municipal governments, police, schools, hospitals and for that matter any institution or person identifiable as an agent of the government is required to not violate the *Charter* through their actions. On a more micro level, one may be able to argue a lifeguard working at a community pool, who denies access to an individual based on ethnicity, would be violating the *Charter* – making himself and the municipal authority liable for his actions.

A key point of section 32(1) is its limited application to the actions of government and its agents. An employee of a private business, who is warned about wearing a religious ornament while at work and subsequently fired for refusing to remove it, will not be able to invoke the *Charter* to sue for discrimination. The *Canadian Charter* applies only to matters as they relate to government. In other words, an individual can use the *Canadian Charter* only if they have been wronged by government. Violations between private individuals are not protected by the *Charter*.

4.2.3 Protected Rights

The rights and freedoms protected by the *Charter* include the following:

1. Fundamental Freedoms (s. 2)

The basic freedoms guaranteed by this section include freedom of religion, thought and expression, freedom of the press and other media, and the right to assemble and associate. These rights are considered to be the basic minimum needs for every citizen of a democratic society to develop and flourish. Some examples of activities protected under this section include publishing information critical of the government, associating and protesting decisions made by the government, joining unions and striking as a means of empowering the individual worker, and deciding how and when to practice your religion.

2. **Democratic Rights (s. 3 - 5)**

These rights include the right to vote for elected members of the House of Commons or the National Assembly, and also the right to be qualified to stand for election. The Supreme Court has given these sections a wider definition and scope by finding that every citizen must be allowed to "play a meaningful role" during an election process. As a result, various groups left out of voting in the past, such as judges, now have a right to vote. Additionally, electoral districts that are too large in comparison to other districts can be challenged as diminishing effective representation.

3. **Mobility Rights (s. 6)**

The right to move to, or live in any part of Canada, or look for work anywhere in the country, and even to leave Canada, is assured under the *Canadian Charter*. The Supreme Court has in a series of cases enlarged the scope of section 6 by interpreting it to include the right of a person or corporation to do business anywhere in the country.

4. **Legal Rights (s. 7 - 14)**

Every person has the right to life, liberty, and security, but does not have the right to euthanasia or assisted suicide.

They also include protections against unreasonable search or detention and cruel and unusual punishment, which are extended to non-citizens in Canada.

A person who is arrested has the right to consult a lawyer, to be informed promptly of the reasons for the arrest, and to be presumed innocent until proven guilty.

5. **Equality Rights (s. 15)**

Every Canadian is entitled to equal treatment in law and to protection against discrimination. The Supreme Court of Canada, in *Law v. Canada,* [1999], found discrimination under section 15 exists when a law or act of a government meets the following three conditions:

i. It causes a differential treatment based on a personal characteristic or doesn't take into consideration the characteristic.
ii. It is described or associated to what is listed in section 15.
iii. It imposes an unnecessary burden on the person or perpetuates a stereotype.

6. **Official Languages of Canada (s. 16 - 22)**

The *Charter* states that English and French are the official languages of Canada. This applies only in those areas where the federal government has authority under the *Constitution*, such as the post office, employment offices and the military.

Therefore, all Canadians have the right to communicate with the federal government or its departments in either of these languages.

7. Minority Language Education Rights (s. 23)

Three main criteria determine the right of children to be educated in either English or French in any province. These are based on the mother tongue of the parents, the language in which the parents were educated in Canada, or the language in which other children in the family are receiving their education in Canada.

The full text of the Canadian Charter of Rights and Freedoms is found in Appendix "4-A" at the end of this chapter.

4.2.4 Limitations

No federal or provincial government can "opt out" from the *Charter*. Section 33 and section 1 of the *Charter*, however, allow governments to adopt laws that may limit individual rights and freedoms. The inclusion of these two sections in the *Charter* was to curtail judicial activism and maintain legislative authority within the hands of elected officials, rather than appointed judges.

4.2.4.1 The Notwithstanding Clause – Section 33

Section 33 empowers the federal or provincial governments to pass laws "notwithstanding" some of the provisions of the *Charter*. In other words, a government can adopt a statute that will be protected from a court striking it down, even though it may violate a *Charter* right. For instance, if the government wanted to pass a law limiting certain religious practices in public and make sure it isn't declared unconstitutional, they could include within the statute the notwithstanding clause.

The use of section 33, however, is restricted in two forms. First, it can only be used to limit rights set out in sections 2 and 7–15 of the *Charter*. All the other rights in the *Charter* are protected from the notwithstanding clause. Second, once section 33 is used, it will operate for not more than five years. This is called the **sunset clause**. Once the five years have expired, so does the limitation. The government is then forced to reintroduce the statute through the legislative process and face public scrutiny again.

4.2.4.2 The Oakes Test – Section 1

Section 1 of the *Charter,* like section 33, can also be used to limit rights and freedoms, but two important differences exist. The first reinforces *Charter* protections. Unlike section 33, which can be applied without judicial challenge, section 1 imposes upon the government the obligation to demonstrate why a statute infringing a *Charter* protection should be maintained. Once a legal challenge against such a law has been instituted, it falls on the government to show why individual rights should be diminished in favour of societal objectives. The second difference weakens Charter protections. Unlike section 33, which is limited to section 2 and 7 – 15, section 1 has a much broader reach. The government can attempt to make laws limiting any of the rights and freedoms found in the *Charter*.

In *R. v. Oakes* [1986], the Supreme Court of Canada developed a test determining how section 1 would be applied and what the government would need to prove so that a right may be limited. Oakes had been caught with 10 vials of hashish oil and $619.45 dollars. Oakes claimed the drugs were for his own use and the money was from his workers' compensation cheque. Nevertheless he was charged with possession intended for trafficking under the *Narcotic Control Act*. Section 8 of the *Act* imposed upon the defendant the responsibility to demonstrate he did not intend on trafficking the drugs, a **reverse onus**, which rendered him guilty until he proved his innocence. Oakes argued this reverse onus violated section 11 (d) of the *Charter*. The Supreme Court of Canada agreed with Oakes by applying a two part test. The first part of the test verifies that the limitation has "an objective related to concerns which are pressing and substantial in a free and democratic society." In other words, it must be an important problem. The second part of the test verifies that the means chosen to limit the right is "reasonable and demonstrably justified." The government must demonstrate the right is being limited as little as possible and there is no other way of achieving its goals with milder restrictions.

THE QUEBEC CHARTER OF HUMAN RIGHTS AND FREEDOMS
Section 4.3

4.3.1 Québec Charter vs. Canadian Charter

In June 1975, long before the *Canadian Charter of Rights and Freedoms* was entrenched in our Constitution, the Québec government passed into our provincial law the *Québec Charter of Human Rights and Freedoms*. Although it may seem at first glance that the two documents are simple duplications of each other, raising the question why the need for two charters, the difference in their application is significant enough to render both equally beneficial to individuals seeking to correct damages done to them.

First, the Canadian Charter applies only to government infringement of citizens' rights and freedoms. The *Québec Charter*, on the other hand, applies to both government matters and the actions of private individuals towards their fellow citizens. If an individual in Québec faces discrimination, they have an option to invoke either of the two documents depending on the author of the act.

A second important distinction is the difference in the "guarantee" which these two charters offer. The *Canadian Charter* is "entrenched"—it cannot be changed without a complex process of approval by both federal and provincial governments. The *Québec Charter*, however, is like any other law of the province, and can be changed at any time by the provincial government of the day without notice. To reinforce the *Québec Charter*, section 52 was incorporated into the text. This section expressly forbids any derogation from certain fundamental rights (sections 1 – 38) by any other law adopted before or after the *Charter*. This special status accorded to the

Charter places it above all other laws, unless said law expressly allows for derogation from a right.

4.3.2 Protected Rights

The rights and freedoms protected by the *Québec Charter* include the following:

1. Fundamental Freedoms and Rights (s. 1 - 9)

The freedoms and rights protected in these sections include the right to one's own physical protection and integrity over one's own body, to make their own choices free of others or government influence, even when their life is in peril. Euthanasia or assisted suicide, however, is prohibited. Should a person's life be in peril and they desire help, then the *Québec Charter* imposes an obligation on society to come to their assistance.

Closely associated with these rights is the freedom to believe in any religion or hold any opinion and to express them within any lawful means through public expression, association and assembly.

Included in these rights is the protection of reputation and privacy. For instance, private information given under confidence to a government agency or a person bound to secrecy by law, such as a priest or a lawyer, cannot be disclosed without authorization from the person giving the information.

By extension of these personal rights, the property of a person is also protected. A person is allowed to peacefully enjoy his property within the law and it is protected against encroachment by others. In other words, nobody can take or enter your property unless the law allows it and the property can be used in any means as long as it does not interfere with others' rights and respects the law, such as playing loud music all night.

2. Right to Equal Recognition and Exercise of Rights and Freedoms (s. 10 - 20.1)

These sections focus on discrimination. Section 10 defines discrimination as an act based on "distinction, exclusion or preference" that causes a right to be nullified or diminished. But, it must be noted that only the acts listed in section 10 are considered discriminatory. For instance, refusing to rent an apartment to a family because they have kids is covered under s.10. A landlord, however, can include a clause in a lease prohibiting pets.

Along the lines of section 10, no one may harass or incite discrimination against a person. Nor may they prohibit a person from entering into a juridical act (e.g. a contract) or have a discriminatory clause included in a juridical act. One exception is insurance or pension contracts, which under section 20.1 allows providers to set premiums or even deny coverage based on personal information causing a distinction.

A person must also not be restricted from accessing public transportation or a public place. Jurisprudence has found that not only must clubs, restaurants, airlines, city transport and any other place frequented by the general public refrain from restricting access, but must also accommodate people with physical or mental conditions unable to access the facilities. A business or government may argue undue hardship, such as severe financial constraints, as a means of avoiding accommodation responsibility.

Additionally, all employment related activities, such as application forms, interviews, hiring, training, compensation and dismissals, must not violate the section 10 list. However, an employer is free to hire and offer different wage levels based on the person's aptitudes or qualifications in comparison to others.

3. **Political Rights (s. 21 - 22)**

These sections affirm the right of every person to be heard by their legislators in matters of concern. Each person, within legal limits, also possesses the right to vote and present themselves for election to public office.

4. **Judicial Rights (s. 23 - 38)**

Similar to the Legal Rights of the *Canadian Charter*, every person accused of an illegal activity has the right to a fair and impartial hearing by a tribunal. Nobody may be detained except as provided by law and they must be treated with humanity. All people are protected from unreasonable search and seizure of property.

5. **Economic and Social Rights (s. 39 - 48)**

Unlike the *Canadian Charter*, the *Québec Charter* provides economic and social protections for various members of the community. For children, it provides protection, security and free public education. For employees, it offers reasonable and safe work conditions. For spouses, it confirms their equal authority and obligations to each other. Lastly, for aged persons, it offers security and protection from exploitation.

Some selected sections of the Québec Charter are reproduced in Appendix "4-B".

4.3.3 Enforcement of Rights and Freedoms

Should any of these rights and freedoms be infringed, section 49 of the *Québec Charter* gives the victim several legal recourses. One such legal recourse involves asking the court to issue an **injunction** ordering the offending party to stop an ongoing violation. Another allows the victim to receive compensation for possible moral (e.g. psychological distress) or material (e.g. loss of income) damages. Additionally, if the infringement was intentional, then the victim may also request **punitive damages**. Punitive damages are granted by a court as a means of punishing the defendant to teach them a lesson, so that they do not violate somebody else's rights and freedoms in the future. It also has a preventative objective to discourage others from acting in such a manner.

Two simple examples highlight intentional interference. In one case, a town decides that all its police officers must be of a certain height for safety reasons. As a result, a few applicants are refused and some officers are fired because they do not meet the height criteria. These applicants and officers can sue for discrimination and seek moral and material damages, but not punitive damages. The criteria's purpose was safety, but its negative consequence was discrimination. In another case, a women applies to rent an apartment, but is refused because she is pregnant. She can sue for material, moral and punitive damages. The refusal is a direct discrimination based on personal characteristics listed in section 10, thus intentional.

It should be noted that if the defendant pleads or is found guilty of a criminal charge, the plaintiff may have no right to punitive damages in a civil trial. Since a criminal finding is considered to be a tool to teach the defendant a lesson and prevent future reoccurrence, then awarding punitive damages would result in a double punishment for the same offence.

4.3.4 Limitations

The *Québec Charter*, like the *Canadian Charter*, also has in place a mechanism by which the government may limit certain rights and freedoms for the purpose of protecting larger societal objectives and limiting judicial activism. Section 9.1 of the *Québec Charter*, allows the legislature to limit any of the Fundamental Freedoms and Rights found between section 1 and section 9, but under a legal challenge it would have to justify any such limit using the principles of the Oakes Test.

THE CIVIL CODE OF QUEBEC
Section 4.4

The *Book on Persons* of the *Civil Code* compliments the larger principles of rights and freedoms set out by the *Québec Charter*. Selected topics closely related to the theme of this chapter will be discussed. These include the following:

1. **Enjoyment and Exercise of Civil Rights (art. 1 - 9)**

   All persons born alive and viable, meaning able to survive on their own after birth, have a juridical personality and can exercise all civil rights. Included in these rights is a **patrimony**, which is the sum of a person's property value minus any obligations, and personal rights that include life, integrity, reputation and privacy. None of these rights, however, may be exercised in **bad faith** or for the purpose of causing others harm. In other words, even though the law may allow a person certain legal recourses, using these recourses solely as a means of causing another person difficulty would constitute an abuse of rights and therefore bad faith. These rights can then be denied.

2. **Integrity of the Person (art. 10)**

   Every person is protected from any interference, except if the law allows it or the person has given a free and enlightened consent. Consent is valid only if it was given free of physical or physiological pressure and the person fully understood, with an explanation if necessary, what the interference would entail.

3. **Care (art. 11 - 25)**

   An adult has the right to refuse any and all medical care, even if the refusal may mean the person's life would be placed at risk. Medical care can only be forced upon a person if they are incapable of giving consent, because they are unconscious or mentally incompetent of communicating their wishes, and their life is in danger.

Care for a minor is authorized by a tutor (parent), but a minor aged fourteen years old or more may consent on their own. A minor fourteen years or older may also refuse care as long as it isn't life threatening. If they refuse, parents would need to obtain court authorization for care.

An adult is free to donate a body part or submit themselves to medical experiments as long as it does not risk their lives and the benefits are significantly higher than the disadvantages. Donating a body part must be done for free and a person submitting themselves to experiments can receive only a small compensation for inconvenience.

4. Respect of Children's Rights (art. 32 - 34)

All children have a right to protection, security and attention from their parents or appointed guardians and every decision concerning them must be made in their best interest. In situations involving a court proceeding, a child may be heard by the judge if possible.

5. Respect of Reputation and Privacy (art. 35 - 41)

No person may invade the privacy or harm the reputation of another. A list of what is considered an invasion of privacy is found in article 36. It reads:

> **36.** The following acts, in particular, may be considered as invasions of the privacy of a person:
>
> (1) entering or taking anything in his dwelling;
> (2) intentionally intercepting or using his private communications;
> (3) appropriating or using his image or voice while he is in private premises;
> (4) keeping his private life under observation by any means;
> (5) using his name, image, likeness or voice for a purpose other than the legitimate information of the public;
> (6) using his correspondence, manuscripts or other personal documents.

Protection of privacy also includes strict rules on who can keep a file or collect information on a person. The person keeping a file on another must have a legitimate reason, they must give the person free access to their file and must not share this information with a third party without the subject's consent.

6. Change of Name (art. 57 - 70)

Every person, including minors aged fourteen years and older, can request a change of their family name for serious reasons. They may also request a change because their existing family name conflicts with their birth certificate, is foreign, difficult to pronounce or write, can be easily made fun of or has taken on a negative association due to another person with the same name.

7. Change of Designation of Sex (art. 71 - 73)

A person, who has undergone a surgical operation altering their gender and has been residing in Québec for at least one year, may request a change in their birth certificate designation and given name.

Some selected articles of the Civil Code of Québec are reproduced in Appendix "4-C".

APPENDIX "4-A"
Constitution Act, 1982

PART I
CANADIAN CHARTER OF RIGHTS AND FREEDOMS

Whereas Canada is founded upon principles that recognize the supremacy of God and the rule of law:

Guarantee of Rights and Freedoms

1. **The Canadian Charter of Rights and Freedoms** guarantees the rights and freedoms set out in it subject only to such reasonable limits prescribed by law as can be demonstrably justified in a free and democratic society.

Fundamental Freedoms

2. Everyone has the following fundamental freedoms:

(a) freedom of conscience and religion;

(b) freedom of thought, belief, opinion and expression, including freedom of the press and other media of communication;

(c) freedom of peaceful assembly

(d) freedom of association.

Democratic Rights

3. Every citizen of Canada has the right to vote in an election of members of the House of Commons or of a legislative assembly and to be qualified for membership therein.

4. (1) No House of Commons and no legislative assembly shall continue for longer than five years from the date fixed for the return of the writs at a general election of its members.

(2) In time of real or apprehended war, invasion or insurrection, a House of Commons may be continued by Parliament and a legislative assembly may be continued by the legislature beyond five years if such continuation is not opposed by the votes of more than one-third of the members of the House of Commons or the legislative assembly, as the case may be.

5. There shall be a sitting of Parliament and of each legislature at least once every twelve months.

Mobility Rights

6. (1) Every citizen of Canada has the right to enter, remain in and leave Canada.

(2) Every citizen of Canada and every person who has the status of a permanent resident of Canada has the right

(a) to move to and take residence in any province; and

(b) to pursue the gaining of a livelihood in any province.

(3) The rights specified in subsection (2) are subject to

(a) any laws or practices of general application in force in a province other than those that discriminate among persons primarily on the basis of province of present or previous residence; and

(b) any laws providing for reasonable residency requirements as a qualification for the receipt of publicly provided social services.

(4) Subsections (2) and (3) do not preclude any law, program or activity that has as its object the amelioration in a province of conditions of individuals in that province who are socially or economically disadvantaged if the rate of employment in that province is below the rate of employment in Canada.

Legal Rights

7. Everyone has the right to life, liberty and security of the person and the right not to be deprived thereof except in accordance with the principles of fundamental justice. Everyone has the right to be secure against unreasonable search or seizure.

8. Everyone has the right to be secure against unreasonable search or seizure.

9. Everyone has the right not to be arbitrarily detained or imprisoned.

10. Everyone has the right on arrest or detention

(a) to be informed promptly of the reason therefor;

(b) to retain and instruct counsel without delay and to be informed of that right; and

(c) to have the validity of the detention determined by way of habeas corpus and to be released if the detention is not lawful.

11. Any person charged with an offence has the right

(a) to be informed without unreasonable delay of the specific offence;

(b) to be tried within a reasonable time;

(c) not to be compelled to be a witness in proceedings against that person in respect of the offence;

(d) to be presumed innocent until proven guilty according to law in a fair and public hearing by an independent and impartial tribunal;

(e) not to be denied reasonable bail without just cause;

(f) except in the case of an offence under military law tried before a military tribunal, to the benefit of trial by jury where the maximum punishment for the offence is imprisonment for five years or a more severe punishment;

(g) not to be found guilty on account of any act or omission unless, at the time of the act or omission, it constituted an offence under Canadian or international law or was criminal according to the general principles of law recognized by the community of nations;

(h) if finally acquitted of the offence, not to be tried for it again and, if finally found guilty and punished for the offence, not to be tried or punished for it again; and

(i) if found guilty of the offence and if the punishment for the offence has been varied between the time of commission and the time of sentencing, to the benefit of the lesser punishment.

12. Everyone has the right not to be subjected to any cruel and unusual treatment or punishment.

13. A witness who testifies in any proceedings has the right not to have any incriminating evidence so given used to incriminate that witness in any other proceedings, except in a prosecution for perjury or for the giving of contradictory evidence.

14. A party or witness in any proceedings who does not understand or speak the language in which the proceedings are conducted or who is deaf has the right to the assistance of an interpreter.

Equality Rights

15. (1) Every individual is equal before and under the law and has the right to the equal protection and equal benefit of the law without discrimination and, in particular, without discrimination based on race, national or ethnic origin, colour, religion, sex, age or mental or physical disability.

(2) Subsection (1) does not preclude any law, program or activity that has as its object the amelioration of conditions of disadvantaged individuals or groups including those that are disadvantaged because of race, national or ethnic origin colour, religion, sex, age or mental or physical disability.

Official Languages of Canada

16. (1) English and French are the official languages of Canada and have equality of status and equal rights and privileges as to their use in all institutions of the Parliament and government of Canada.

(2) English and French are the official languages of New Brunswick and have equality of status and equal rights and privileges as to their use in all institutions of the legislature and government of New Brunswick.

(3) Nothing in this chapter limits the authority of Parliament or a legislature to advance the equality of status or use of English and French.

17. (1) Everyone has the right to use English or French in any debates and other proceedings of Parliament.

(2) Everyone has the right to use English or French in any debates and other proceedings of the legislature of New Brunswick.

18. (1) The statutes, records and journals of Parliament shall be printed and published in English and French and both language versions are equally authoritative.

(2) The statutes, records and journals of the legislature of New Brunswick shall be printed and published in English and French and both language versions are equally authoritative.

19. (1) Either English or French may be used by any person in, or in any pleading in or process issuing from, any court established by Parliament.

(2) Either English or French may be used by any person in, or any pleading in or process issuing from, any court of New Brunswick.

20. (1) Any member of the public in Canada has the right to communicate with, and to receive available services from, any head or central office of an institution of the Parliament or government of Canada in English or French, and has the same right with respect to any other office of any such institution where

(a) there is a significant demand for communications with and services from that office in such language; or

(b) due to the nature of the office, it is reasonable that communications with and services from that office be available in both English and French.

(2) Any member of the public in New Brunswick has the right to communicate with, and to receive available services from, any office of an institution of the legislature or government of New Brunswick in English or French.

21. Nothing in sections 16 to 20 abrogates or derogates from any right, privilege or obligation with respect to the English and French languages, or either of them, that exists or is continued by virtue of any other provision of the Constitution of Canada.

22. Nothing in sections 16 to 20 abrogates or derogates from any legal or customary right or privilege acquired or enjoyed either before or after the coming into force of this Charter with respect to any language that is not English or French.

Minority Language Educational Rights

23. (1) Citizens of Canada

(a) whose first language learned and still understood is that of the English or French linguistic minority population of the province in which they reside, or

(b) who have received their primary school instruction in Canada in English or French and reside in a province where the language in which they received that instruction is the language of the English or French linguistic minority population of the province,

have the right to have their children receive primary and secondary school instruction in that language in that province.

(2) Citizens of Canada of whom any child has received or is receiving primary or secondary school instruction in English or French in Canada, have the right to have all

their children receive primary and secondary school instruction in the same language.

(3) The right of citizens of Canada under subsections (1) and (2) to have their children receive primary and secondary school instruction in the language of the English or French linguistic minority population of a province

(a) applies wherever in the province number of children of citizens who have such a right is sufficient to warrant the provision to them out of public funds of minority language instruction; and

(b) includes, where the number of those children so warrants, the right to have them receive that instruction in minority language educational facilities provided out of public funds.

Enforcement

24. (1) Anyone whose rights or freedoms, as guaranteed by this Charter, have been infringed or denied may apply to a court of competent jurisdiction to obtain such remedy as the court considers appropriate and just in the circumstances.

(2) Where, in proceedings under subsection (1), a court concludes that evidence was obtained in a manner that infringed or denied any rights or freedoms guaranteed by this Charter, the evidence shall be excluded if it is established that, having regard to all the circumstances, the admission of it in the proceedings would bring the administration of justice into disrepute.

General

25. The guarantee in this Charter of certain rights and freedoms shall not be construed so as to abrogate or derogate from any aboriginal, treaty or other rights or freedoms that pertain to the aboriginal peoples of Canada including

(a) any rights or freedoms that have been recognized by the Royal Proclamation of October 7, 1763; and

(b) any rights or freedoms that may be acquired by the aboriginal peoples of Canada by way of land claims settlement.

26. The guarantee in this Charter of certain rights or freedoms shall not be construed as denying the existence of any other rights or freedoms that exist in Canada.

27. This Charter shall be interpreted in a manner consistent with the preservation and enhancement of the multicultural heritage of Canadians.

28. Notwithstanding anything in this Charter, the rights and freedoms referred to in it are guaranteed equally to male and female persons.

29. Nothing in this Charter abrogates or derogates from any rights or privileges guaranteed by or under the Constitution of Canada in respect of denominational, separate or dissentient schools.

30. A reference in this Charter to a province or to the legislative assembly or legislature of a province shall be deemed to include a reference to the Yukon Territory and the Northwest Territories, or to the appropriate legislative authority thereof, as the case may be.

31. Nothing in this Charter extends the legislative powers of any body or authority.

Application of Charter

32. (1) This Charter applies

(a) to the Parliament and government of Canada in respect of all matters within the authority of Parliament including all matters relating to the Yukon Territory and Northwestern Territories; an

(b) to the legislature and government of each province in respect of all matters within the authority of the legislature of each province.

(2) Notwithstanding subsection (1),

section 15 shall not have effect until three years after this section comes into force.

33. (1) Parliament or the legislature of a province may expressly declare in an Act of Parliament or of the legislature, as the case may be, that the Act or a provision thereof shall operate notwithstanding a provision included in section 2 or sections 7 to 15 of this Charter.

(2) An Act or a provision of an Act in respect of which a declaration made under this section is in effect shall have such operation as it would have but for the provision of this Charter referred to in the declaration.

(3) A declaration made under subsection (1) shall cease to have effect five years after it comes into force or on such earlier date as may be specified in the declaration.

(4) Parliament or a legislature of a province may re-enact a declaration made under subsection (1).

(5) Subsection (3) applies in respect of a re-enactment made under subsection (4).

Citation

34. This Part may be cited as the Canadian Charter of Rights and Freedoms.

PART II
RIGHTS OF THE ABORIGINAL PEOPLES OF CANADA

35. (1) The existing aboriginal and treaty rights of the aboriginal peoples of Canada are hereby recognized and affirmed.

(2) In this Act, "aboriginal peoples of Canada" includes the Indian, Inuit and Métis peoples of Canada.

PART V
PROCEDURE FOR AMENDING CONSTITUTION OF CANADA

38. (1) An amendment to the Constitution of Canada may be made by proclamation issued by the Governor General under the Great Seal of Canada where so authorized by

(a) resolutions of the Senate and House of Commons; and

(b) resolutions of the legislative assemblies of at least two-thirds of the provinces that have, in the aggregate, according to the then latest general census, at least fifty percent of the population of all the provinces.

(2) An amendment made under subsection (1) that derogates from the legislative powers, the proprietary rights or any other rights or privileges of the legislature or government of a province shall require a resolution supported by a majority of the members of each of the Senate, the House of Commons and the legislative assemblies required under subsection (1).

(3) An amendment referred to in subsection (2) shall not have effect in a province the legislative assembly of which has expressed its dissent thereto by resolution supported by a majority of its members prior to the issue of the proclamation to which the amendment relates unless that legislative assembly, subsequently, by resolution supported by a majority of its members, revokes its dissent and authorizes the amendment.

(4) A resolution of dissent made for the purposes of subsection (3) may be revoked at any time before or after the issue of the proclamation to which it relates.

39. (1) A proclamation shall not be issued under subsection 38(1) before the expiration of one year from the adoption of the resolution initiating the amendment procedure thereunder, unless the legislative assembly of each province has previously adopted a resolution of assent or dissent.

(2) A proclamation shall not be issued under subsection 38(1) after the expiration of three years from the adoption of the resolution initiating

the amendment procedure thereunder.

40. Where an amendment is made under subsection 38(1) that transfers provincial legislative powers relating to education or other cultural matters from provincial legislatures to Parliament, Canada shall provide reasonable compensation to any province to which the amendment does not apply.

An amendment to the Constitution of Canada in relation to the following matters may be made by proclamation issued by the Governor General under the Great Seal of Canada only where authorized by resolutions of the Senate and House of Commons and of the legislative assembly of each province:

(a) the office of the Queen, the Governor General and the Lieutenant Governor of a province;

(b) the right of a province to a number of members in the House of Commons not less than the number of Senators by which the province is entitled to be represented at the time this Part comes into force;

(c) subject to section 43, the use of the English or the French language;

(d) the composition of the Supreme Court of Canada; and

(e) an amendment to this Part.

42. (1) An amendment to the Constitution of Canada in relation to the following matters may be made only in accordance with subsection 38(1):

(a) the principle of proportionate representation of the provinces in the House of Commons prescribed by the Constitution of Canada;

(b) the powers of the Senate and the method of selecting Senators;

(c) the number of members by which a province is entitled to be represented in the Senate and the residence qualifications of Senators;

(d) subject to paragraph 41(d), the Supreme Court of Canada;

(e) the extension of existing provinces into the territories; and

(f) notwithstanding any other law or practice, the establishment of new provinces.

(2) Subsections 38(2) to (4) do not apply in respect of amendments in relation to matters referred to in subsection (1).

43. An amendment to the Constitution of Canada in relation to any provision that applies to one or more, but not all, provinces including:

(a) any alteration to boundaries between provinces, and

(b) any amendment to any provision that relates to the use of the English or the French language within a province,

may be made by proclamation issued by the Governor General under the Great Seal of Canada only where so authorized by resolution of the Senate and House of Commons and the legislative assembly of each province to which the amendment applies.

44. Subject to sections 41 and 42, Parliament may exclusively make laws amending the Constitution of Canada in relation to the executive government of Canada or the Senate and House of Commons.

45. Subject to section 41, the legislature of each province may exclusively make laws amending the constitution of the province.

46. (1) The procedures for amendment under sections 38, 41, 42 and 43 may be initiated either by the Senate or the House of Commons or by the legislative assembly of a province.

(2) A resolution of assent made for the purposes of this Part may be revoked at any time before the issue of a proclamation authorized by it.

47. (1) An amendment to the Constitution of

Canada made by proclamation under sections 38, 41, 42 or 43 may be made without a resolution of the Senate authorizing the issue of the proclamation if, within one hundred and eighty days after the adoption by the House of Commons of a resolution authorizing its issue, the Senate has not adopted such a resolution and if, at any time after the expiration of that period, the House of Commons again adopts the resolution.

(2) Any period when Parliament is prorogued or dissolved shall not be counted in computing the one hundred and eighty day period referred to in subsection (1).

48. The Queen's Privy Council for Canada shall advise the Governor General to issue a proclamation under this Part forthwith on the adoption of the resolutions required for an amendment made by proclamation under this Part.

49. A constitutional conference composed of the Prime minister of Canada and the first ministers of the provinces shall be convened by the Prime Minister of Canada within fifteen years after this Part comes into force to review the provisions of this Part.

PART VII
GENERAL

52. (1) The Constitution of Canada is the supreme law of Canada, and any law that is inconsistent with the provisions of the Constitution is, to the extent of the inconsistency, of no force or effect.

(2) The Constitution of Canada includes

(a) the **Canada Act**, including this Act;

(b) the Acts and orders referred to in Schedule I; and

(c) any amendment to any Act or order referred to in paragraph (a) or (b).

(3) Amendments to the Constitution of Canada shall be made only in accordance with the authority contained in the Constitution of Canada.

53. (1) The enactments referred to in Column I of Schedule I are hereby repealed or amended to the extent indicated in Column II thereof, and, unless repealed, shall continue as law in Canada under the names set out in Column III thereof.

(2) Every enactment, except the *Canada Act*, that refers to an enactment referred to in Schedule I by the name in Column I thereof is hereby amended by substituting for that name the corresponding name in Column II thereof, and any *British North America Act* not referred to in Schedule I may be cited as the *Constitution Act* followed by the year and number, if any, of its enactment.

55. A French version of the portions of the Constitution of Canada referred to in Schedule I shall be prepared by the Minister of Justice of Canada as expeditiously as possible and, when any portion thereof sufficient to warrant action being taken has been so prepared, it shall be put forward for enactment by proclamation issued by the Governor General under the Great Seal of Canada pursuant to the procedure then applicable to an amendment of the same provisions of the Constitution of Canada.

56. Where any portion of the Constitution of Canada has been or is enacted in English and French or where a French version of any portion of the Constitution is enacted pursuant to section 55, the English and French versions of that portion of the Constitution are equally authoritative.

57. The English and French versions of this Act are equally authoritative.

58. Subject to section 59, this Act shall come into force on a day to be fixed by proclamation issued by the Governor General under the Great Seal of Canada.

60. This Act may be cited as the Constitution Act, 1982, and the Constitution Acts 1867 and 1975 (No. 2) and this Act may be cited together as the *Constitution Acts, 1867 to 1982*.

APPENDIX "4-B"
SELECTED SECTIONS FROM

The Québec Charter of Human Rights and Freedoms (1975)

Whereas every human being possesses intrinsic rights and freedoms designed to ensure his protection and development;

Whereas all human beings are equal in worth and dignity, and are entitled to equal protection of the law;

Whereas respect for the dignity of the human being and recognition of his rights and freedoms constitute the foundation of justice and peace;

Whereas the rights and freedoms of the human person are inseparable from the rights and freedoms of others and from the common well-being;

Whereas it is expedient to solemnly declare the fundamental human rights and freedoms in a Charter, so that they may be guaranteed by the collective will and better protected against any violation;

Therefore, Her Majesty, with the advice and consent of the National Assembly of Québec, enacts as follows:

PART I
HUMAN RIGHTS AND FREEDOMS

Chapter I
Fundamental Freedoms and Rights

1. Every human being has a right to life, and to personal security, inviolability and freedom.

He also possesses juridical personality.

2. Every human being whose life is in peril has a right to assistance.

Every person must come to the aid of anyone whose life is in peril, either personally or calling for aid, by giving him the necessary and immediate physical assistance, unless it involves danger to himself or a third person, or he has another valid reason.

3. Every person is the possessor of the fundamental freedoms, including freedom of conscience, freedom of religion, freedom of opinion, freedom of expression, freedom of peaceful assembly and freedom of association.

4. Every person has a right to the safeguard of his dignity, honour and reputation.

5. Every person has a right to respect for his private life.

6. Every person has a right to the peaceful enjoyment and free disposition of his property, except to the extent provided by law.

7. A person's home is inviolable.

8. No one may enter upon the property of another or take anything therefrom without his express or implied consent.

9. Every person has a right to non-disclosure of confidential information.

No person bound to professional secrecy by law and no priest or other minister of religion may, even in judicial proceedings, disclose confidential information revealed to him by reason of his position or profession, unless he is authorized to do so by the person who confided such information to him or by an express provision of law.

The tribunal must, *ex officio*, ensure that professional secrecy is respected.

9.1 In exercising his fundamental freedoms and rights, a person shall maintain a proper regard for democratic values, public order and the general well-being of the citizens of Québec.

In this respect, the scope of the freedoms and rights, and limits to their exercise, may be fixed by law.

Chapter I.1
Right to Equal Recognition and Exercise of Rights and Freedoms

10. Every person has a right to full and equal recognition and exercise of his human rights and freedoms, without distinction, exclusion or preference based on race, colour, sex, pregnancy, sexual orientation, civil status, age except as provided by law, religion, political convictions, language, ethnic or national origin, social condition, a handicap or the use of any means to palliate a handicap.

Discrimination exists where such a distinction, exclusion or preference has the effect of nullifying or impairing such right.

10.1. No one may harass a person on the basis of any ground mentioned in section 10.

11. No one may distribute, publish or publicly exhibit a notice, symbol or sign involving discrimination, or authorize anyone to do so.

12. No one may, through discrimination, refuse to make a juridical act concerning goods or services ordinarily offered to the public.

13. No one may in a juridical act stipulate a clause involving discrimination.

Such a clause is deemed without effect.

14. The prohibitions contemplated in sections 12 and 13 do not apply to the person who leases a room situated in a dwelling if the lessor or his family resides in such dwelling, leases only one room and does not advertise the room for lease by a notice or any other public means of solicitation.

15. No one may, through discrimination, inhibit the access of another to public transportation or a public place, such as a commercial establishment, hotel, restaurant, theatre, cinema, park, camping ground or trailer park, or his obtaining the goods and services available there.

16. No one may practise discrimination in respect of the hiring, apprenticeship, duration of the probationary period, vocational training, promotion, transfer, displacement, laying-off, suspension, dismissal or conditions of employment of a person or in the establishment of categories or classes of employment.

17. No one may practise discrimination in respect of the admission, enjoyment of benefits, suspension or expulsion of a person to, of or from an association of employers or employees or any professional orders or association of persons carrying on the same occupation.

18. No employment bureau may practise discrimination in respect of the reception, classification or processing of a job application or in any document intended for submitting an application to a prospective employer.

18.1. No one may, in an employment application form or employment interview, require a person to give information regarding any ground mentioned in section 10 unless the information is useful for the application of section 20 or the implementation of an affirmative action program in existence at the time of the application.

18.2. No one may dismiss, refuse to hire or otherwise penalize a person in his employment owing to the mere fact that he was convicted of a penal or criminal offence, if the offence was in no way connected with the employment or if the person has obtained a pardon for the offence.

19. Every employer must, without discrimination, grant equal salary or wages to the members of his personnel who perform equivalent work at the same place.

A difference in salary or wages based on experience, seniority, years of service, merit, productivity or overtime is not considered discriminatory if such criteria are common to all members of the personnel.

20. A distinction, exclusion or preference based on the aptitudes or qualifications required for an employment, or justified by the charitable, philanthropic, religious, political or educational nature of a non-profit institution or of an institution devoted exclusively to the well-being of an ethnic group, is deemed non-discriminatory.

20.1 In an insurance or pension contract, a social benefits plan, a retirement, pension or insurance plan, or a public pension or public insurance plan, a distinction, exclusion or preference based on age, sex or civil status is deemed non-discriminatory where the use thereof is warranted and the basis thereof is a risk determination factor based on actuarial data.

In such contracts or plans, the use of health as a risk determination factor does not constitute discrimination within the meaning of section 10.

Chapter II
Political Rights

21. Every person has a right of petition to the National Assembly for the redress of grievances.

22. Every person legally capable and qualified has the right to be a candidate and to vote at an election.

Chapter III
Judicial Rights

23. Every person has a right to a full and equal, public and fair hearing by an independent and impartial tribunal, for the determination of his rights and obligations or of the merits of any charge brought against him.

The tribunal may decide to sit *in camera*, however, in the interests of morality or public order.

24. No one may be deprived of his liberty or of his rights except on grounds provided by law and in accordance with prescribed procedure.

24.1 No one may be subjected to unreasonable search or seizure.

25. Every person arrested or detained must be treated with humanity and with the respect due to the human person.

26. Every person confined to a house of detention has the right to separate treatment appropriate to his sex, his age and his physical or mental condition.

27. Every person confined to a correctional facility while awaiting the outcome of his trial has the right to be kept apart, until final judgment, from prisoners serving sentence.

28. Every person arrested or detained has a right to be promptly informed, in a language he understands, of the grounds of his arrest or detention.

28.1. Every accused person has a right to be promptly informed of the specific offence with which he is charged.

29. Every person arrested or detained has a right to immediately advise his next of kin thereof and to have recourse to the assistance of an advocate. He has a right to be informed promptly of those rights.

30. Every person arrested or detained must be brought promptly before the competent tribunal or released.

31. No person arrested or detained may be deprived without just cause of the right to be released on undertaking, with or without deposit or surety, to appear before the tribunal at the appointed time.

32. Every person deprived of his liberty has a right of recourse to *habeas corpus*.

32.1. Every accused person has a right to be tried within a reasonable time.

33. Every accused person is presumed innocent until proven guilty according to law.

33.1. No accused person may be compelled to testify against himself at his trial.

34. Every person has a right to be represented by an advocate or to be assisted by one before any tribunal.

35. Every accused person has a right to a full and complete defense and has the right to examine and cross-examine witnesses.

36. Every accused person has a right to be assisted free of charge by an interpreter if he does not understand the language used at the hearing or if he is deaf.

37. No accused person may be held guilty on account of any act or omission which, at the time when it was committed, did not constitute a violation of the law.

37.1. No person may be tried again for an offence of which he has been acquitted or of which he has been found guilty by a judgment that has acquired status as *res judicata.*

37.2. Where the punishment for an offence has been varied between the time of commission and the time of sentencing, the accused person has a right to the lesser punishment.

38. No testimony before a tribunal may be used to incriminate the person who gives it, except in a prosecution for perjury or for the giving of contradictory evidence.

Chapter IV
Economic and Social Rights

39. Every child has a right to the protection, security and attention that his parents or the persons acting in their stead are capable of providing.

40. Every person has a right, to the extent and according to the standards provided for by law, to free public education.

41. Parents or the persons acting in their stead have a right to give their children a religious and moral education in keeping with their convictions and with proper regard for their children's rights and interests.

42. Parents or the persons acting in their stead have a right to choose private educational establishments for their children, provided such establishments comply with the standards prescribed or approved by virtue of the law.

43. Persons belonging to ethnic minorities have a right to maintain and develop their own cultural interests with the other members of their group.

44. Every person has a right to information to the extent provided by law.

45. Every person in need has a right, for himself and his family, to measures of financial assistance and to social measures provided for by law, susceptible of ensuring such person an acceptable standard of living.

46. Every person who works has a right, in accordance with the law, to fair and reasonable conditions of employment which have proper regard for his health, safety and physical well-being.

47. Married or civil union spouses have, in the marriage or civil union, the same rights, obligations and responsibilities.

Together they provide the moral guidance and material support of the family and the education of their common offspring.

48. Every aged person and every handicapped person has a right to protection against any form of exploitation.

Such a person also has a right to the protection and security that must be provided to him by his family or the persons acting in their stead.

Chapter V
Special and Interpretative Provisions

49. Any unlawful interference with any right or freedom recognized by this Charter entitles the victim to obtain the cessation of such interference and compensation for the moral or material prejudice resulting therefrom.

In case of unlawful and intentional interference, the tribunal may, in addition, condemn the person guilty of it to punitive damages.

49.1 Any complaint, dispute or remedy the subject-matter of which is covered by the Pay Equity Act (chapter E-12.001) shall be dealt with exclusively in accordance with the provisions of that Act.

Moreover, any question concerning pay equity between a predominantly female job class and a predominantly male job class in an enterprise employing fewer than 10 employees shall be settled by the Commission de l'équité salariale in accordance with section 19 of this Charter.

50. The Charter shall not be so interpreted as to suppress or limit the enjoyment or exercise of any human right or freedom not enumerated herein.

50.1 The rights and freedoms set forth in this Charter are guaranteed equally to women and men.

51. The Charter shall not be so interpreted as to extend, limit or amend the scope of a provision of law except to the extent provided in section 52.

52. No provision of any Act, even subsequent to the Charter, may derogate from sections 1 to 38, except so far as provided by those sections, unless such Act expressly states that it applies despite the Charter.

53. If any doubt arises in the interpretation of a provision of the Act, it shall be resolved in keeping with the intent of the Charter.

54. The Charter binds the State.

55. The Charter affects those matters that come under the legislative authority of Québec.

PART III
AFFIRMATIVE ACTION PROGRAMS

86. The object of an affirmative action program is to remedy the situation of persons belonging to groups discriminated against in employment, or in the sector of education or of health services and other services generally available to the public.

An affirmative action program is deemed non-discriminatory if it is established in conformity with the Charter.

An equal access employment program is deemed not to discriminate on the basis of race, colour, gender or ethnic origin if it is established in accordance with the Act respecting equal access to employment in public bodies.

An equal access to employment program established for a handicapped person within the meaning of the Act to secure handicapped persons in the exercise of their rights with a view to achieving social, school and workplace integration is deemed to be non-discriminatory if it is established in conformity with the Act respecting equal access to employment in public bodies

APPENDIX "4-C"
SELECTED ARTICLES FROM
The Civil Code of Québec

TITLE ONE
ENJOYMENT AND EXERCISE OF CIVIL RIGHTS

1. Every human being possesses juridical personality and has the full enjoyment of civil rights.

2. Every person has a patrimony.

The patrimony may be divided or appropriated to a purpose, but only to the extent provided by law.

3. Every person is the holder of personality rights, such as the right to life, the right to the inviolability and integrity of his person, and the right to the respect of his name, reputation and privacy.

These rights are inalienable.

4. Every person is fully able to exercise his civil rights.

In certain cases, the law provides for representation or assistance.

5. Every person exercises his civil rights under the name assigned to him and stated in his act of birth.

6. Every person is bound to exercise his civil rights in good faith.

7. No right may be exercised with the intent of injuring another or in an excessive and unreasonable manner which is contrary to the requirements of good faith.

8. No person may renounce the exercise of his civil rights, except to the extent consistent with public order.

9. In the exercise of civil rights, derogations may be made from those rules of this Code which supplement intention, but not from those of public order.

TITLE TWO
CERTAIN PERSONALITY RIGHTS

Chapter I
Integrity of the Person

10. Every person is inviolable and is entitled to the integrity of his person. Except in cases provided for by law, no one may interfere with his person without his free and enlightened consent.

Division I
Care

11. No person may be made to undergo care of any nature, whether for examination, specimen taking, removal of tissue, treatment or any other act, except with his consent.

If the person concerned is incapable of giving or refusing his consent to care, a person authorized by law or by mandate given in anticipation of his incapacity may do so in his place.

12. A person who gives his consent to or refuses care for another person is bound to act in the sole interest of that person, taking into account, as far as possible, any wishes the latter may have expressed.

If he gives his consent, he shall ensure that the care is beneficial notwithstanding the gravity and permanence of certain of its effects, that it is advisable in the circumstances and that the risks incurred are not disproportionate to the anticipated benefit.

13. Consent to medical care is not required in case of emergency if the life of the person is in danger or his integrity is threatened and his consent cannot be obtained in due time.

It is required, however, where the care is unusual or has become useless or where its consequences could be intolerable for the person.

14. Consent to care required by the state of health of a minor is given by the person having parental authority or by his tutor.

A minor 14 years of age or over, however, may give his consent alone to such care. If his state requires that he remain in a health or social services establishment for over 12 hours, the person having parental authority or tutor shall be informed of that fact.

15. Where it is ascertained that a person of full age is incapable of giving consent to care required by his or her state of health, consent is given by his or her mandatary, tutor or curator. If the person of full age is not so represented, consent is given by his or her married, civil union or *de facto* spouse or, if the person has no spouse or his or her spouse is prevented from giving consent, it is given by a close relative or a person who shows a special interest in the person of full age.

16. The authorization of the court is necessary where the person who may give consent to care required by the state of health of a minor or a person of full age who is incapable of giving his consent is prevented from doing so or, without justification, refuses to do so; it is also required where a person of full age who is incapable of giving his consent categorically refuses to receive care, except in the case of hygienic care or emergency.

The authorization of the court is necessary, furthermore, to cause a minor 14 years of age or over to undergo care he refuses, except in the case of emergency if his life is in danger or his integrity threatened, in which case the consent of the person having parental authority or the tutor is sufficient.

17. A minor 14 years of age or over may give his consent alone to care not required by the state of his health; however, the consent of the person having parental authority or of the tutor is required if the care entails a serious risk for the health of the minor and may cause him grave and permanent effects.

18. Where the person is under 14 years of age or is incapable of giving his consent, consent to care not required by his state of health is given by the person having parental authority or the mandatary, tutor or curator; the authorization of the court is also necessary if the care entails a serious risk for health or if it might cause grave and permanent effects.

19. A person of full age who is capable of giving his consent may alienate a part of his body *inter vivos*, provided the risk incurred is not disproportionate to the benefit that may reasonably be anticipated.

A minor or a person of full age who is incapable of giving his consent may, with the consent of the person having parental authority, mandatary, tutor or curator and with the authorization of the court, alienate a part of his body only if that part is capable of regeneration and provided that no serious risk to his health results.

20. A person of full age who is capable of giving his consent may submit to an experiment provided that the risk incurred is not disproportionate to the benefit that can reasonably be anticipated.

21. A minor or a person of full age who is incapable of giving consent may not be submitted to an experiment if the experiment involves serious risk to his health or, where he understands the nature and consequences of the experiment, if he objects.

Moreover, a minor or a person of full age who is incapable of giving consent may be submitted to an experiment only if, where the person is the only subject of the experiment, it has the potential to produce benefit to the person's health or only if, in the case of an experiment on a group, it has the potential to produce results capable of conferring benefit to other persons in the same age category or having the same disease or handicap. Such an experiment must be part of a research project approved and monitored by an ethics committee. The competent ethics committees are formed by the Minister of Health and Social Services or designated by that Minister among existing research ethics committees; the composition and operating conditions of the committees are determined by the Minister and published in the *Gazette officielle du Québec*.

Consent to experimentation may be given, in the case of a minor, by the person having parental authority or the tutor and, in the case of a person of full age incapable of giving consent, by the mandatary, tutor or curator. Where a person of full age suddenly becomes incapable of consent and the experiment, insofar as it must be undertaken promptly after the appearance of the condition giving rise to it, does not permit, for lack of time, the designation of a legal representative, consent may be given by the person authorized to consent to any care the person requires; it is incumbent upon the competent ethics committee to determine, when examining the research project, whether the experiment meets that condition.

Care considered by the ethics committee to be innovative care required by the state of health of the person concerned does not constitute an experiment.

22. A part of the body, whether an organ, tissue or other substance, removed from a person as part of the care he receives may, with his consent or that of the person qualified to give consent for him, be used for purposes of research.

25. The alienation by a person of a part or product of his body shall be gratuitous; it may not be repeated if it involves a risk to his health.

An experiment may not give rise to any financial reward other than the payment of an indemnity as compensation for loss and inconvenience.

Chapter II
Respect of Children's Rights

32. Every child has a right to the protection, security and attention that his parents or the persons acting in their stead are able to give to him.

33. Every decision concerning a child shall be taken in light of the child's interests and the respect of his rights.

Consideration is given, in addition to the moral, intellectual, emotional and physical needs of the child, to the child's age, health, personality and family environment, and to the other aspects of his situation.

34. The court shall, in every application brought before it affecting the interest of a child, give the child an opportunity to be heard if his age and power of discernment permit it.

Chapter III
Respect of Reputation and Privacy

35. Every person has a right to the respect of his reputation and privacy.

No one may invade the privacy of a person without the consent of the person unless authorized by law.

36. The following acts, in particular, may be considered as invasions of the privacy of a person:

(1) entering or taking anything in his dwelling;

(2) intentionally intercepting or using his private communications;

(3) appropriating or using his image or voice while he is in private premises;

(4) keeping his private life under observation by any means;

(5) using his name, image, likeness or voice for a purpose other than the legitimate information of the public;

(6) using his correspondence, manuscripts or other personal documents.

37. Every person who establishes a file on another person shall have a serious and legitimate reason for doing so. He may gather only information which is relevant to the stated objective of the file, and may not, without the consent of the person concerned or authorization by law, communicate such information to third persons or use it for purposes that are inconsistent with the purposes for which the file was established. In addition, he may not, when establishing or using the file, otherwise invade the privacy or damage the reputation of the person concerned.

38. Except as otherwise provided by law, any person may, free of charge, examine and cause the rectification of a file kept on him by another person with a view to making a decision in his regard or to informing a third person; he may also cause a copy of it to be made at reasonable cost. The information contained in the file shall be made accessible in an intelligible transcript.

39. A person keeping a file on a person may

not deny him access to the information contained therein unless he has a serious and legitimate reason for doing so or unless the information is of a nature that may seriously prejudice a third person.

40. Every person may cause information which is contained in a file concerning him and which is inaccurate, incomplete or equivocal to be rectified; he may also cause obsolete information or information not justified by the purpose of the file to be deleted, or deposit his written comments in the file.

Notice of the rectification is given without delay to every person having received the information in the preceding six months and, where applicable, to the person who provided that information. The same rule applies to an application for rectification, if it is contested.

41. Where the law does not provide the conditions and modalities of exercise of the right of examination or rectification of a file, the court, upon application, determines them.

Similarly, if it becomes difficult to exercise those rights, the court, upon application, settles the difficulty.

Division III
Change of Name

57. No change may be made to a person's name, whether of his surname or given name, without the authorization of the registrar of civil status or the court, in accordance with the provisions of this section.

58. The registrar of civil status has competence to authorize a change of name for a serious reason in every case that does not come under the jurisdiction of the court, and in particular where the name generally used does not correspond to that appearing in the act of birth, where the name is of foreign origin or too difficult to pronounce or write in its original form or where the name invites ridicule or has become infamous.

The registrar also has competence where a person applies for the addition to the surname of a part taken from the surname of the father or mother, as declared in the act of birth.

59. A person of full age who is a Canadian citizen and who has been domiciled in Québec for at least one year may apply for a change of name. If the application concerns the surname, it is also valid as an application in respect of the person's minor children who bear the same surname or part of that surname.

A person may also apply for the change of the given names of the minor children or the addition of a part to their surname taken from the person's own surname.

60. The tutor to a minor may apply for the change of the name of his pupil, if the latter is a Canadian citizen and has been domiciled in Québec for at least one year.

62. Except for a compelling reason, no change of name of a minor child may be granted if the tutor or the minor, if 14 years of age or over, has not been notified of the application or objects to it.

However, in the case of an application for the addition to the surname of the minor of a part taken from the surname of the father or mother, only the minor has the right to object.

63. Before authorizing a change of name, the registrar of civil status shall ascertain that the notices of the application have been published, unless a special exemption from publication has been granted by the Minister of Justice for reasons of general interest; he shall give to third persons who so request the opportunity to state their views.

The registrar may also require the applicant to furnish any additional explanation and information he may need.

66. A minor 14 years of age or over acting alone may present an application for a change of name, but he shall in such a case give notice of the application to the person having parental authority and to the tutor.

The minor acting alone may also object to an application.

67. A change of name produces its effects from the time the judgment authorizing it acquires the authority of a final judgment (*res judicata*) or from the time that the decision of the registrar of civil status is no longer open to review.

Notice of the change is published in the *Gazette officielle du Québec* unless a special exemption from publication is granted by the Minister of Justice for reasons of general interest.

68. A change of name nowise alters the rights and obligations of a person.

69. All documents made under the former name of a person are deemed to be made under his new name.

Division IV
Change of Designation of Sex

71. Every person who has successfully undergone medical treatments and surgical operations involving a structural modification of the sexual organs intended to change his secondary sexual characteristics may have the designation of sex which appears on his act of birth and, if necessary, his given names changed.

Only a person of full age who has been domiciled in Québec for at least one year and is a Canadian citizen may make an application under this article.

72. The application is made to the registrar of civil status; it is accompanied with, in addition to the other relevant documents, a certificate of the attending physician and an attestation by another physician practising in Québec to the effect that the treatments and operations were successful.

73. The application is subject to the same procedure as an application for a change of name and to the same publication requirements and the same duties. The rules relating to the effects of a change of name, adapted as required, apply to a change of designation of sex.

CASE 4.1

COURT OF APPEAL (QUEBEC)

DATE: March 4, 2004

COMMISSION SCOLAIRE MARGUERITE-BOURGEOYS
Appellant—respondent
v.
BALVIR SINGH MULTANI
BALVIR SINGH MULTANI, in his capacity as tutor for his son **GURBAJ SINGH MULTANI**
Respondents—petitioners

No: 500-09-012386-025

JUDGMENT OF LEMELIN J.A. (AD HOC)

[6] Appellants are appealing the Superior Court decision granting the respondents' motion for declaratory judgment and allowing Gurbaj Singh to wear his kirpan to school so long as he respected certain conditions.

[7] The respondent, twelve years old at the time, was a Sikh student attending a Secondary I welcoming class at École Sainte-Catherine-Labouré, an institution part of the appellant Commission scolaire Marguerite-Bourgeoys (CSMB).

[8] On November 19, 2001, in the schoolyard, the respondent dropped the kirpan he was wearing beneath his clothes. The school administration prohibited him from bringing this object to school again.

[9] On December 21, 2001, the CSMB granted the Multani family's request to allow their son to wear his kirpan to school, requiring that the kirpan be placed in a scabbard with a flap sown securely shut to ensure that it could not be either voluntarily or accidentally removed from the scabbard and be used as an offensive or defensive weapon. School authorities could make checks at any time to ensure that these conditions were being respected.

[10] The governing board, which, in accordance with the Education Act , counts among its members certain parents, staff members and community representatives, among others, refused to approve this proposal.

[12] The appellant's council of commissioners upheld the decision of the governing board. On March 11, 2002, taking note of the unanimous recommendation of the review committee that reviewed the issue at the respondents' request, the council of commissioners adopted the following resolution:

- That the decision of the administration of École Sainte-Catherine-Labouré to prohibit G.S.M. from wearing the kirpan at school in accordance with the school's Code of Conduct be upheld;

- That the proposal for accommodation formulated by Mtre Grey on behalf of Mr. Multani, father of G.S.M., regarding the wearing of the kirpan in school not be upheld;
- That the Commission scolaire accept the wearing of the symbolic kirpan as a pendant or in any other form and of a material that would make it harmless.

[17] The Superior Court judge declared the decision of the appellant's council rendered March 19, 2002, void and of no effect. She allowed respondent Gurbaj Singh to wear the kirpan to École Sainte-Catherine-Labouré, subject to the following conditions:

- that the kirpan be worn under his clothes;
- that the kirpan be carried in a scabbard made of wood and not metal, to prevent it from causing injury;
- that the kirpan be placed in its scabbard and wrapped and sewn in a sturdy fabric pouch, and that this pouch be sewn to the guthra;
- that school personnel be authorized to verify, in a reasonable fashion, that these conditions were being followed;
- that the petitioner be required to keep the kirpan in his possession at all times, and that its disappearance be reported to school authorities immediately;
- that if the present judgment were not respected, the petitioner would definitively lose the right to wear his kirpan at school.

[18] Because this judgment was immediately enforceable notwithstanding appeal, the appellants presented a motion on July 31, 2002, to suspend execution. The respondents' lawyer then declared that the Multani son would attend a private school for the 2002-2003 school year. The appeal continues even though the present context has rendered the subject matter of the litigation less urgent.

THE EVIDENCE

[51] I have already outlined the decision-making framework and the chronology of events. However, the analysis cannot take place in a factual vacuum. I will summarize the evidence that the Court has been asked to consider in its evaluation of the decision.

[52] The respondents have filed their own affidavits, as well as one by the Chaplain Manjit Singh. Other than these affidavits, there is no other historical evidence or evidence attesting to the importance of Sikh tenets or the essential characteristics of a kirpan. In Superior Court, all parties referred without objection to extracts of documents and expert reports submitted in other Canadian and American judicial proceedings. The complete documents cannot be verified. Although interesting, this information does not carry the weight of evidence.

[53] The respondents have established that baptized Orthodox Sikhs like Gorbaj Singh must follow a dress code that requires the wearing of religious symbols known as "the five Ks": the kesh (uncut hair), the kara (steel bracelet worn on the

wrist), the kirpan (dagger, with metal blade), the kachh (specific type of underclothing) and the kangha (a wooden comb).

[54] The kirpan, a metal "dagger" with a curved blade, may be several centimetres long. It is carried in a scabbard attached to a bandolier called a guthra. The object that the Multani son dropped was a kirpan about twenty centimetres in length that had been inserted in a scabbard. According to Denis Boulanger, president of the appellant's review committee, the tip of the kirpan was sharp and pointed, piercing the cloth pouch in which it was carried, even when inserted in the scabbard. Altogether, it was a relatively heavy object and could be perceived to be a dangerous weapon; this explains the importance the trial judge placed on the material of the scabbard.

[55] Chaplain Manjit Singh teaches an introductory course on Sikhism at the Faculty of Religious Studies at McGill University. He confirms the existence of the five sacred symbols already mentioned by the respondents and points out that the kirpan must be worn at all times, even in bed.

[56] The Chaplain adds, "The kirpan is not intended as a weapon to hurt anyone." He says that the respondents' refusal to accept wearing a symbolic plastic kirpan "is a perfectly reasonably religiously-motivated interpretation; it is not novel or unusual." The Sikh religion teaches pacifism, respect and tolerance for others. This witness knows of no incidents of violence at school involving a kirpan.

[57] None of the evidence brought forward by the respondents was disputed.

[58] The appellant CSMB has never claimed that the Multani boy had behavioural or disciplinary problems, nor that it had ever been informed of any violent incident involving the wearing of a kirpan at school.

[59] Seventeen affidavits of school administrators and interveners from the field emphasize the serious safety problems in Montreal area schools, relating violent incidents that have occurred over the last few years. This climate has required supervision and safety measures to be tightened up in order to reduce the level of risk.

[60] Denis Leclerc is a psychoeducator who has collaborated on a study involving fourteen secondary schools in the CSMB. The study was carried out in order to draw a general portrait of the socio-educational environment and to act as an assessment tool to help schools prevent various social problems, particularly violence, that affect success in school.

[61] He testified that 9% of students claim to have been attacked or threatened with a weapon by another student, that the majority of students and teachers in the participating schools have a negative perception of their safety, and that it is essential to remedy the situation. The presence of kirpans at school increases the feeling of insecurity, even if no incidents have occurred yet. In his affidavit, he goes on to explain that allowing this object in schools may also have other consequences on the behaviour and attitude of the students. I will refer to this later.

[62] The respondents have produced no evidence to dispute the facts regarding the environment and the context in which the decision was made.

[63] The resolution of the council of commissioners prohibiting Gurbaj Singh from wearing his kirpan to school is based on a rule of conduct that is imposed on all students with the objective of ensuring an environment conducive to their development and safety. However, even if the decision has a valid objective and there is no intent to infringe on a fundamental freedom, as in the case at bar, the effects of the decision must be considered. Infringement, even unintentional or indirect, is sufficient.

[64] The appellant, by uniformly applying the rule prohibiting the carrying of a weapon or dangerous object to school and by refusing to make an exception for Gurbaj Singh, has prevented him from following a tenet of his religion. The respondents conclude that this infringes on their freedom of religion. In addition, the respondents also contend that the appellant has infringed on their equality rights, pleading the discriminatory effects of the decision.

[65] Freedom of conscience and religion is a fundamental freedom protected under s. 2(a) of the Canadian Charter and s. 3 of the Quebec Charter. The legislators have also entrenched in these charters the equal right of all individuals to enjoy their fundamental freedoms (s. 15 (1) Canadian Charter and s. 10, Quebec Charter).

[67] Freedom of conscience and religion protects not only beliefs but also the practices that these beliefs dictate, as the two are very frequently inseparable. The Charter exists not merely to encourage tolerance; it is also a generator of rights. A logical consequence of recognizing a right is the obligation to respect and take measures to protect the exercise of that right.

[68] The respondents have proved the existence of the tenet of the "five Ks" for baptized orthodox Sikhs. The fact that some Sikh parents accept that their children do not wear the kirpan at school is not conclusive. We must recognize that people who profess the same religion may adhere to the dogma and practices of that religion to varying degrees of rigour.

[69] The conscience of each individual justifies his or her choice, and this freedom of conscience is also protected by the Charters. What is important is the sincerity of the individual invoking the existence of a tenet.

[70] Even if there are different interpretations from that of the respondents regarding the necessity of wearing the same type of kirpan, they have nevertheless met the burden of establishing that their religious belief is sincere and neither unique nor capricious.

[71] Therefore, the decision of the council of commissioners infringes on the full exercise of the respondents' freedom of religion and conscience as it "has the effect of impeding conduct integral to the practice of [the respondent's] religion."

[72] However, without placing the rights of some over those of others, it remains

that the exercise of freedoms, even fundamental ones, does not enjoy absolute protection. The Charter must be interpreted as a whole. As Iacobucci and Major JJ. pointed out in B.(R.) v. Children's Aid Society of Metropolitan Toronto, "although the freedom of belief may be broad, the freedom to act upon those beliefs is considerably narrower, and it is the latter freedom at issue in this case." A public organization cannot accept requests or actions that go against public order or the security and well-being of the community. There is a greater likelihood that the enjoyment of a freedom that contains within it an actual threat to the security of others will rightly be restrained because it may represent an impingement on the fundamental liberties of others.

[73] In the Children's Aid case, La Forest J. pointed out that the Supreme Court has consistently refrained from imposing internal limits on the scope of the freedom of religion, suggesting that s. 1 of the Canadian Charter is a more flexible tool with which to balance competing rights and that it is up to the legislator to explain its position. The legislator, or the decision-maker, must justify the position taken.

[74] It appears to me that the grounds limiting the respondents' freedom of religion are the same as those authorizing State intervention. Section 1 of the Canadian Charter and s. 9.1 of the Quebec Charter define the scope of such intervention:

> 1. The Canadian Charter of Rights and Freedoms guarantees the rights and freedoms set out in it subject only to such reasonable limits prescribed by law as can be demonstrably justified in a free and democratic society.
>
> 9.1. In exercising his fundamental freedoms and rights, a person shall maintain a proper regard for democratic values, public order and the general well-being of the citizens of Québec.
>
> In this respect, the scope of the freedoms and rights, and limits to their exercise, may be fixed by law.

[75] I am unable to conceive of a justification sufficient to satisfy these two provisions if there exists reasonable accommodation. The application of these articles allows us to circumscribe the limits of the appellant's a priori duty to accommodate. It is not necessary to show that the council of commissioners' decision was contrary to s. 15(1) of the Canadian Charter or s. 10 of the Quebec Charter. Merely the infringement of the freedom of religion opens the door to a claim for the right to accommodation.

[76] In short, in order to avoid an accommodation being imposed, the appellant must meet the test articulated by the Supreme Court in Oakes.

[77] The decision of the CSMB was motivated by an urgent and real objective, namely, to ensure an environment conducive to the development and learning of the students. This requires them to ensure the safety of the students and the staff. This duty is at the core of the mandate entrusted to educational institutions.

[78] Moreover, the obvious importance of this objective has been acknowledged by all parties. The task now is to determine whether the appellants have

established that the measures taken to achieve this objective were justifiable in a free and democratic society. The essence of this analysis is laid out by McIntyre J. in Simpsons-Sears:

> This general concept of freedom of religion has been well-established in our society and was a recognized and protected right long before the human rights codes of recent appearance were enacted. Difficulty arises when the question is posed of how far the person in entitled to go in the exercise of his religious freedom. At what point in the profession of his faith and the observance of its rules does he go beyond the mere exercise of his rights and seek to enforce upon others conformance with his beliefs? To what extent, if any, in the exercise of his religion is a person entitled to impose a liability upon another to do some act or accept some obligation he would not otherwise have done or accepted? [...] How far, it may be asked, may the same requirement be made of fellow employees and, for that matter, of the general public?

[81] This is the reasoning followed by the Canadian Human Rights Tribunal in Nijar, reconciling the rights at issue with the context in which they were invoked. The Tribunal concluded that the restriction of the wearing of the kirpan in airplanes is legitimate as a way to protect the clientele.

[82] Similarly, in the Hothi case, Dewar J. of the Manitoba Queen's Bench held that a safe environment is essential to the good administration of justice and prohibited an accused from wearing his kirpan in the courtroom.

[86] There is most certainly a direct and rational connection between prohibiting the wearing of the kirpan or the carrying of a weapon or dangerous object in educational institutions and the objective of maintaining an orderly and safe environment for both the students and staff.

[87] This regulation from the Code of Conduct cannot go so far as to prohibit the possession of any object which can cause injury; indeed, even a pencil can be used to inflict injury. Nevertheless, a reasonable line must be drawn, and an inherently dangerous object falls beyond that line.

[91] It remains to be seen whether there is a reasonable accommodation that would allow Gurbaj Singh to wear his kirpan to school while respecting the appellant's duty to the community it serves. A school board that administers schools attended by students from different countries—eighty different countries, according to the appellant's lawyer —has a duty of tolerance. The appellant has the obligation to develop an educational plan that respects the freedom of conscience and religion of the students, the parents, and the school staff, in accordance with its enabling Act. However, it also has the obligation to ensure their safety.

[99] Allowing the kirpan to be worn, even under conditions similar to those upheld by the Superior Court judge, would oblige the appellant to depart from important policy objectives by reducing security standards with respect to the individual respondent and the protection of its clientele as a whole. Such a compromise was determined to be "undue hardship" in British Columbia (Superintendent of Motor Vehicles) v. British Columbia (Council of Human Rights).

[101]Thus, the appellant has adopted rules of conduct within the limits of its jurisdiction by concluding that it could not, without undue hardship, accede to the request of the Multani family. The various branches of the appellant's organization were called on to evaluate the measures required to fulfill its mandate. The council of commissioners' resolution on March 19, 2002, was not unreasonable and does not warrant judicial intervention.

[102]Given this conclusion, it is not necessary to proceed with a separate analysis of the infringement of equality rights under s. 15 of the Canadian Charter and s. 10 of the Quebec Charter. If, hypothetically, there were a violation of equality rights according to the criteria set out in Law, the appellants submit essentially the same justification arguments under s. 1 of the Canadian Charter and s. 9.1 of the Quebec Charter. As to reasonable accommodation, it must be considered not only in terms of the infringement of the freedom of religion but also the right to equality.

[103]For these reasons, I would allow the appeals with costs and dismiss the application for declaratory judgment, with costs.

CASE 4.2

SUPREME COURT OF CANADA

CITATION: Multani *v.* Commission scolaire Marguerite-Bourgeoys, [2006] 1 S.C.R. 256, 2006 SCC 6

DATE: 20060302
DOCKET: 30322

BETWEEN:

Balvir Singh Multani and Balvir Singh Multani, in his capacity as tutor to his minor son Gurbaj Singh Multani
Appellants
v.
Commission scolaire Marguerite-Bourgeoys and Attorney General of Quebec
Respondents

Present: McLachlin C.J. and Major, Bastarache, Binnie, LeBel, Deschamps, Fish, Abella and Charron JJ.

ON APPEAL FROM THE COURT OF APPEAL FOR QUEBEC

G and his father B are orthodox Sikhs. G believes that his religion requires him to wear a kirpan at all times; a kirpan is a religious object that resembles a dagger and must be made of metal. In 2001, G accidentally dropped the kirpan he was wearing under his clothes in the yard of the school he was attending. The school board sent G's parents a letter in which, as a reasonable accommodation, it authorized their son to wear his kirpan to school provided that he complied with certain conditions to ensure that it was sealed inside his clothing. G and his parents agreed to this arrangement. The governing board of the school refused to ratify the agreement on the basis that wearing a kirpan at the school violated art. 5 of the school's *Code de vie* (code of conduct), which prohibited the carrying of weapons. The school board's council of commissioners upheld that decision and notified G and his parents that a symbolic kirpan in the form of a pendant or one in another form made of a material rendering it harmless would be acceptable in the place of a real kirpan. B then filed in the Superior Court a motion for a declaratory judgment to the effect that the council of commissioners' decision was of no force or effect. The Superior Court granted the motion, declared the decision to be null, and authorized G to wear his kirpan under certain conditions. The Court of Appeal set aside the Superior Court's judgment. After deciding that the applicable standard of review was reasonableness *simpliciter*, the Court of Appeal restored the council of commissioners' decision. It concluded that the decision in question infringed G's freedom of religion under s. 2(*a*) of the *Canadian Charter of Rights and Freedoms* ("*Canadian Charter*") and s. 3 of Quebec's *Charter of human rights and freedoms* ("*Quebec Charter*"), but that the infringement was justified for the purposes of s. 1 of the *Canadian Charter* and s. 9.1 of the *Quebec Charter*.

Held: The appeal should be allowed. The decision of the Court of Appeal should be set aside and the decision of the council of commissioners should be declared to be null.

Per McLachlin C.J. and Bastarache, Binnie, Fish and Charron JJ.: In the case at bar, it is the compliance of the commissioners' decision with the requirements of the *Canadian Charter* that is central to the dispute, not the decision's validity from the point of view of administrative law. There is no suggestion that the council of commissioners did not have jurisdiction, from an administrative law standpoint, to approve the *Code de vie*. Nor is the administrative and constitutional validity of the rule against carrying weapons in issue. Since the complaint is based entirely on freedom of religion, the Court of Appeal erred in applying the reasonableness standard to its constitutional analysis. The administrative law standard of review was not relevant. [18-20]

The *Canadian Charter* applies to the decision of the council of commissioners, despite the decision's individual nature. Any infringement of a guaranteed right that results from the actions of a decision maker acting pursuant to its enabling statute is also a limit "prescribed by law" within the meaning of s. 1. Where the legislation pursuant to which an administrative body has made a contested decision confers a discretion and does not confer, either expressly or by implication, the power to limit the rights and freedoms guaranteed by the *Canadian Charter*, the decision should, if there is an infringement, be subjected to the test set out in s. 1 to ascertain whether it constitutes a reasonable limit. [22-23]

In the instant case, the Court does not at the outset have to reconcile two constitutional rights, as only freedom of religion is in issue here. However, that freedom is not absolute and can conflict with other constitutional rights. Since the test governing limits on rights was developed in *Oakes*, the Court has never called into question the principle that rights are reconciled through the constitutional justification required by s. 1 of the *Canadian Charter*. Since the decision genuinely affects both parties and was made by an administrative body exercising statutory powers, a contextual analysis under s. 1 will make it possible to balance the relevant competing values in a more comprehensive manner. [29-30]

The council of commissioners' decision prohibiting G from wearing his kirpan to school infringes his freedom of religion. G genuinely believes that he would not be complying with the requirements of his religion were he to wear a plastic or wooden kirpan, and none of the parties have contested the sincerity of his belief. The interference with G's freedom of religion is neither trivial nor insignificant, as it has deprived him of his right to attend a public school. The infringement of G's freedom of religion cannot be justified under s. 1 of the *Canadian Charter*. Although the council's decision to prohibit the wearing of a kirpan was motivated by a pressing and substantial objective, namely to ensure a reasonable level of safety at the school, and although the decision had a rational connection with the objective, it has not been shown that such a prohibition minimally impairs G's rights. [2] [38-41] [44] [48] [77]

The analogy with the duty of reasonable accommodation is helpful to explain the burden resulting from the minimal impairment test with respect to an individual. In the circumstances of the instant case, the decision to establish an absolute prohibition against wearing a kirpan does not fall within a range of reasonable alternatives. The arguments in support of such a prohibition must fail. The risk of G using his kirpan for violent purposes or of another student taking it away from him is very low, especially if the kirpan is worn under conditions such as were imposed by the Superior Court. It should be added that G has never claimed a right to wear his kirpan to school without restrictions. Furthermore, there are many objects in schools that could be used to commit violent acts and that are much more easily obtained by students, such as scissors, pencils and baseball bats. The evidence also reveals that not a single violent incident related to the presence of kirpans in schools has been reported. Although it is not necessary to wait for harm to be done before acting, the existence of concerns relating to safety must be unequivocally established for the infringement of a constitutional right to be justified. Nor does the evidence support the argument that allowing G to wear his kirpan to school could have a ripple effect. Lastly, the argument that the wearing of kirpans should be prohibited because the kirpan is a symbol of violence and because it sends the message that using force is necessary to assert rights and resolve conflict is not only contradicted by the evidence regarding the symbolic nature of the kirpan, but is also disrespectful to believers in the Sikh religion and does not take into account Canadian values based on multiculturalism. Religious tolerance is a very important value of Canadian society. If some students consider it unfair that G may wear his kirpan to school while they are not allowed to have knives in their possession, it is incumbent on the schools to discharge their obligation to instil in their students this value that is at the very foundation of our democracy. A total prohibition against wearing a kirpan to school undermines the value of this religious symbol and sends students the message that some religious practices do not merit the same protection as others. Accommodating G and allowing him to wear his kirpan under certain conditions demonstrates the importance that our society attaches to protecting freedom of religion and to showing respect for its minorities. The deleterious effects of a total prohibition thus outweigh its salutary effects. [51-54] [57-59] [67-71] [76] [79]

Given that G no longer attends his school, the appropriate and just remedy is to declare the decision prohibiting him from wearing his kirpan to be null. [82]

Per Deschamps and Abella JJ.: Recourse to a constitutional law justification is not appropriate where, as in this case, what must be assessed is the propriety of an administrative body's decision relating to human rights. Whereas a constitutional justification analysis must be carried out when reviewing the validity or enforceability of a norm such as a law, regulation or other similar rule of general application, the administrative law approach must be retained for reviewing decisions and orders made by administrative bodies. Basing the analysis on the principles of administrative law not only averts the problems that result from blurring the distinction between the principles of constitutional justification and the principles of administrative law, but also prevents the impairment of the analytical tools developed specifically for each of these fields. In addition, this approach allows parties and administrative bodies to know in advance which rules govern disputes involving human rights issues. [85] [103] [125]

Simply alleging that a s. 1 analysis is required does not make administrative law inapplicable. If an administrative body makes a decision or order that is said to conflict with fundamental values, the mechanisms of administrative law — including the standard of review — are readily available. It is difficult to conceive of an administrative decision being permitted to stand if it violates the *Canadian Charter*. [86] [93] [128]

A decision or order made by an administrative body cannot be equated with a "law" within the meaning of s. 1 of the *Canadian Charter*. The expression "law" used in s. 1 naturally refers to a norm or rule of general application. The *Oakes* test, which was developed to assess legislative policies, is based on the duty of the executive and legislative branches of government to account to the courts for any rules they establish that infringe protected rights. That test, which is based on an analysis of societal interests, is better suited, conceptually and literally, to the concept of "prescribed by law". The duty to account imposed — conceptually and in practice — on the legislative and executive branches is not easily applied to administrative tribunals. [112-113] [119-121]

Lastly, even if the concepts of reasonable accommodation and minimal impairment have a number of similarities, they belong to two different analytical categories. On the one hand, the process required by the duty of reasonable accommodation takes into account the specific details of the circumstances of the parties. The justification of minimal impairment, on the other hand, is based on societal interests. An administrative law analysis is microcosmic, whereas a constitutional law analysis is generally macrocosmic. These separate streams — public versus individual — should be kept distinct. [129-134]

In the instant case, it is the standard of reasonableness that applies to the decision of the school board's council of commissioners. The council did not sufficiently consider either the right to freedom of religion or the proposed accommodation measure. It merely applied literally the *Code de vie* in effect at the school. By disregarding the right to freedom of religion without considering the possibility of a solution that posed little or no risk to the safety of the school community, the council made an unreasonable decision. [99]

Per LeBel J.: It is not always necessary to resort to the *Canadian Charter* or, in the case of Quebec, the *Quebec Charter* when a decision can be reached by applying general administrative law principles or the specific rules governing the exercise of a delegated power. However, the dispute as presented makes a constitutional analysis unavoidable. Where a decision is contested on the basis that the administrative body's exercise of the delegated power is vitiated by the violation of a fundamental right, the only way to determine whether the infringement of the constitutional standard is justified is to consider the fundamental rights in issue and how they have been applied. Where the exercise of such a power has an impact on the relationship between competing constitutional rights, those rights can be reconciled in two ways. The first approach involves defining the rights and how they relate to each other, and the second consists of justification under s. 1 of the *Canadian Charter*. In the case at bar, the first approach can be dispensed with, as the evidence does not show a *prima facie* infringement of the right to security of the person. It is therefore necessary to turn to justification under s. 1. In the case of an individualized decision made pursuant to statutory authority, it may be possible to dispense with certain steps of the analysis. The existence of a statutory authority that is not itself challenged makes it pointless to review the objectives of the act. The issue becomes one of proportionality or, more specifically, minimal limitation of the guaranteed right, having regard to the context in which the right has been infringed. Reasonable accommodation that would meet the requirements of the constitutional standard must be considered at this stage and in this context. In the case at bar, the school board has not shown that its prohibition was justified and met the constitutional standard. [141-144] [153-155]

CASE 4.3

SUPREME COURT OF CANADA

British Columbia (Public Service Employee Relations Commission) *v.* BCGSEU, [1999] 3 S.C.R. 3

The British Columbia Government and Service Employees' Union
Appellant

v.

The Government of the Province of British Columbia as represented by the Public Service Employee Relations Commission
Respondent

Indexed as: British Columbia (Public Service Employee Relations Commission) *v.* BCGSEU

File No.: 26274.

1999: February 22; 1999: September 9.

Present: Lamer C.J. and L'Heureux-Dubé, Gonthier, Cory, McLachlin, Iacobucci, Major, Bastarache and Binnie JJ.

ON APPEAL FROM THE COURT OF APPEAL FOR BRITISH COLUMBIA

Judgment of McLachlin, J.

Introduction

[1] Seven years ago Tawney Meiorin was hired as a forest firefighter by the Province of British Columbia (the "Government"). Although she did her work well, she lost her job three years later when the Government adopted a new series of fitness tests for forest firefighters. She passed three of the tests but failed a fourth one, a 2.5 kilometre run designed to assess whether she met the Government's aerobic standard, by taking 49.4 seconds longer than required.

[2] The narrow issue in this case is whether the Government improperly dismissed Ms. Meiorin from her job as a forest firefighter. The broader legal issue is whether the aerobic standard that led to Ms. Meiorin's dismissal unfairly excludes women from forest firefighting jobs. Employers seeking to maintain safety may err on the side of caution and set standards higher than are necessary for the safe performance of the work. However, if men and women do not have an equal ability to meet the excessive standard, the effect may be to exclude qualified female candidates from employment for no reason but their gender. Like human

rights legislation throughout Canada, the British Columbia *Human Rights Code*, R.S.B.C. 1996, c. 210, seeks to counter this by requiring employers to justify their standards where *prima facie* discrimination is established. The question in this case is whether the Government has done so.

Facts

[4] Ms. Meiorin was employed for three years by the British Columbia Ministry of Forests as a member of a three-person Initial Attack Forest Firefighting Crew in the Golden Forest District. The crew's job was to attack and suppress forest fires while they were small and could be contained. Ms. Meiorin's supervisors found her work to be satisfactory.

[5] Ms. Meiorin was not asked to take a physical fitness test until 1994, when she was required to pass the Government's "Bona Fide Occupational Fitness Tests and Standards for B.C. Forest Service Wildland Firefighters" (the"Tests"). The Tests required that the forest firefighters weigh less than 200 lbs. (with their equipment) and complete a shuttle run, an upright rowing exercise, and a pump carrying/hose dragging exercise within stipulated times. The running test was designed to test the forest firefighters' aerobic fitness and was based on the view that forest firefighters must have a minimum "VO_2max" of 50 $ml \cdot kg^{-1} \cdot min^{-1}$ (the "aerobic standard"). "VO_2 max" measures "maximal oxygen uptake", or the rate at which the body can take in oxygen, transport it to the muscles, and use it to produce energy.

[6] The Tests were developed in response to a 1991 Coroner's Inquest Report that recommended that only physically fit employees be assigned as front-line forest firefighters for safety reasons. The Government commissioned a team of researchers from the University of Victoria to undertake a review of its existing fitness standards with a view to protecting the safety of firefighters while meeting human rights norms. The researchers developed the Tests by identifying the essential components of forest firefighting, measuring the physiological demands of those components, selecting fitness tests to measure those demands and, finally, assessing the validity of those tests.

[10] After four attempts, Ms. Meiorin failed to meet the aerobic standard, running the distance in 11 minutes and 49.4 seconds instead of the required 11 minutes. As a result, she was laid off. Her union subsequently brought a grievance on her behalf. The arbitrator designated to hear the grievance was required to determine whether she had been improperly dismissed.

[11] Evidence accepted by the arbitrator demonstrated that, owing to physiological differences, most women have lower aerobic capacity than most men. Even with training, most women cannot increase their aerobic capacity to the level required by the aerobic standard, although training can allow most men to meet it. The arbitrator also heard evidence that 65 percent to 70 percent of male applicants pass the Tests on their initial attempts, while only 35 percent of female applicants have similar success. Of the 800 to 900 Initial Attack Crew members employed by the Government in 1995, only 100 to 150 were female.

[12] There was no credible evidence showing that the prescribed aerobic capacity was necessary for either men or women to perform the work of a forest firefighter satisfactorily. On the contrary, Ms. Meiorin had in the past performed her work well, without apparent risk to herself, her colleagues or the public.

The Rulings

[13] The arbitrator found that Ms. Meiorin had established a *prima facie*case of adverse effect discrimination by showing that the aerobic standard has a disproportionately negative effect on women as a group. He further found that the Government had presented no credible evidence that Ms. Meiorin's inability to meet the aerobic standard meant that she constituted a safety risk to herself, her colleagues, or the public, and hence had not discharged its burden of showing that it had accommodated Ms. Meiorin to the point of undue hardship. He ordered that she be reinstated to her former position and compensated for her lost wages and benefits: (1996), 58 L.A.C. (4th) 159.

[14] The Court of Appeal (1997 CanLII 3694 (BC CA), (1997), 37 B.C.L.R. (3d) 317) did not distinguish between direct and adverse effect discrimination. It held that so long as the standard is necessary to the safe and efficient performance of the work and is applied through individualized testing, there is no discrimination. The Court of Appeal (mistakenly) read the arbitrator's reasons as finding that the aerobic standard was necessary to the safe and efficient performance of the work. Since Ms. Meiorin had been individually tested against this standard, it allowed the appeal and dismissed her claim. The Court of Appeal commented that to permit Ms. Meiorin to succeed would create "reverse discrimination", i.e., to set a lower standard for women than for men would discriminate against those men who failed to meet the men's standard but were nevertheless capable of meeting the women's standard.

Analysis

[18] The arbitrator held that the standard was one of the appropriate measurements available to the Government and that there is generally a reasonable relationship between aerobic fitness and the ability to perform the job of an Initial Attack Crew member. This falls short, however, of an affirmative finding that the ability to meet the aerobic standard chosen by the Government is necessary to the safe and efficient performance of the job. To the contrary, that inference is belied by the arbitrator's conclusion that, despite her failure to meet the aerobic standard, Ms. Meiorin did not pose a serious safety risk to herself, her colleagues, or the general public. I therefore proceed on the view that the arbitrator did not find that an applicant's ability to meet the aerobic standard is necessary to his or her ability to perform the tasks of an Initial Attack Crew member safely and efficiently. This leaves us to face squarely the issue of whether the aerobic standard is unjustifiably discriminatory within the meaning of the Code.

The Test

[20] In the case of direct discrimination, the employer may establish that the

standard is a BFOR by showing: (1) that the standard was imposed honestly and in good faith and was not designed to undermine the objectives of the human rights legislation (the subjective element); and (2) that the standard is reasonably necessary to the safe and efficient performance of the work and does not place an unreasonable burden on those to whom it applies (the objective element). It is difficult for an employer to justify a standard as a BFOR where individual testing of the capabilities of the employee or applicant is a reasonable alternative.

[21] If these criteria are established, the standard is justified as a BFOR. If they are not, the standard itself is struck down.

[22] A different analysis applies to adverse effect discrimination. The BFOR defence does not apply. *Prima facie* discrimination established, the employer need only show: (1) that there is a rational connection between the job and the particular standard, and (2) that it cannot further accommodate the claimant without incurring undue hardship: *O'Malley*, *supra*, at pp. 555-59, *per* McIntyre J.; *Central Alberta Dairy Pool*, *supra*, at pp. 505-6 and 519-20, *per* Wilson J. If the employer cannot discharge this burden, then it has failed to establish a defence to the charge of discrimination. In such a case, the claimant succeeds, but the standard itself always remains intact.

[27] The distinction between a standard that is discriminatory on its face and a neutral standard that is discriminatory in its effect is difficult to justify, simply because there are few cases that can be so neatly characterized. For example, a rule requiring all workers to appear at work on Fridays or face dismissal may plausibly be characterized as either directly discriminatory (because it means that no workers whose religious beliefs preclude working on Fridays may be employed there) or as a neutral rule that merely has an adverse effect on a few individuals (those same workers whose religious beliefs prevent them from working on Fridays). On the same reasoning, it could plausibly be argued that forcing employees to take a mandatory pregnancy test before commencing employment is a neutral rule because it is facially applied to all members of a workforce and its special effects on women are only incidental.

[42] This case, where Ms. Meiorin seeks to keep her position in a male-dominated occupation, is a good example of how the conventional analysis shields systemic discrimination from scrutiny. This analysis prevents the Court from rigorously assessing a standard which, in the course of regulating entry to a male-dominated occupation, adversely affects women as a group. Although the Government may have a duty to accommodate an individual claimant, the practical result of the conventional analysis is that the complex web of seemingly neutral, systemic barriers to traditionally male-dominated occupations remains beyond the direct reach of the law. The right to be free from discrimination is reduced to a question of whether the "mainstream" can afford to confer proper treatment on those adversely affected, within the confines of its existing formal standard. If it cannot, the edifice of systemic discrimination receives the law's approval. This cannot be right.

[54] Having considered the various alternatives, I propose the following three-step

test for determining whether a *prima facie* discriminatory standard is a BFOR. An employer may justify the impugned standard by establishing on the balance of probabilities:

(1) that the employer adopted the standard for a purpose rationally connected to the performance of the job;

(2) that the employer adopted the particular standard in an honest and good faith belief that it was necessary to the fulfilment of that legitimate work-related purpose; and

(3) that the standard is reasonably necessary to the accomplishment of that legitimate work-related purpose. To show that the standard is reasonably necessary, it must be demonstrated that it is impossible to accommodate individual employees sharing the characteristics of the claimant without imposing undue hardship upon the employer.

[55] This approach is premised on the need to develop standards that accommodate the potential contributions of all employees in so far as this can be done without undue hardship to the employer. Standards may adversely affect members of a particular group, to be sure. But as Wilson J. noted in *Central Alberta Dairy Pool*, *supra*, at p. 518, "[i]f a reasonable alternative exists to burdening members of a group with a given rule, that rule will not be [a BFOR]". It follows that a rule or standard must accommodate individual differences to the point of undue hardship if it is to be found reasonably necessary. Unless no further accommodation is possible without imposing undue hardship, the standard is not a BFOR in its existing form and the *prima facie* case of discrimination stands.

[56] Having set out the test, I offer certain elaborations on its application.

<u>Step One</u>

[57] The first step in assessing whether the employer has successfully established a BFOR defence is to identify the general purpose of the impugned standard and determine whether it is rationally connected to the performance of the job. The initial task is to determine what the impugned standard is generally designed to achieve. The ability to work safely and efficiently is the purpose most often mentioned in the cases but there may well be other reasons for imposing particular standards in the workplace.

[58] The employer must demonstrate that there is a rational connection between the general purpose for which the impugned standard was introduced and the objective requirements of the job.

[59] If there is no rational relationship between the general purpose of the standard and the tasks properly required of the employee, then there is of course no need to continue to assess the legitimacy of the particular standard itself. Without a legitimate general purpose underlying it, the standard cannot be a BFOR. In my view, it is helpful to keep the two levels of inquiry distinct.

Step Two

[60] Once the legitimacy of the employer's more general purpose is established, the employer must take the second step of demonstrating that it adopted the particular standard with an honest and good faith belief that it was necessary to the accomplishment of its purpose, with no intention of discriminating against the claimant.

Step Three

[62] The employer's third and final hurdle is to demonstrate that the impugned standard is reasonably necessary for the employer to accomplish its purpose, which by this point has been demonstrated to be rationally connected to the performance of the job. The employer must establish that it cannot accommodate the claimant and others adversely affected by the standard without experiencing undue hardship. When referring to the concept of "undue hardship", it is important to recall the words of Sopinka J. who observed in *Central Okanagan School District No. 23 v. Renaud*, 1992 CanLII 81 (SCC), [1992] 2 S.C.R. 970, at p. 984, that "[t]he use of the term 'undue' infers that some hardship is acceptable; it is only 'undue' hardship that satisfies this test". It may be ideal from the employer's perspective to choose a standard that is uncompromisingly stringent. Yet the standard, if it is to be justified under the human rights legislation, must accommodate factors relating to the unique capabilities and inherent worth and dignity of every individual, up to the point of undue hardship.

[65] Some of the important questions that may be asked in the course of the analysis include:

(a) Has the employer investigated alternative approaches that do not have a discriminatory effect, such as individual testing against a more individually sensitive standard?

(b) If alternative standards were investigated and found to be capable of fulfilling the employer's purpose, why were they not implemented?

(c) Is it necessary to have all employees meet the single standard for the employer to accomplish its legitimate purpose or could standards reflective of group or individual differences and capabilities be established?

(d) Is there a way to do the job that is less discriminatory while still accomplishing the employer's legitimate purpose?

(e) Is the standard properly designed to ensure that the desired qualification is met without placing an undue burden on those to whom the standard applies?

(f) Have other parties who are obliged to assist in the search for possible accommodation fulfilled their roles? As Sopinka J. noted in *Renaud*, *supra*, at pp. 992-96, the task of determining how to accommodate individual differences may also place burdens on the employee and, if there is a collective agreement, a union.

[69] Ms. Meiorin has discharged the burden of establishing that, *prima facie*, the aerobic standard discriminates against her as a woman. The arbitrator held that,

because of their generally lower aerobic capacity, most women are adversely affected by the high aerobic standard. While the Government's expert witness testified that most women can achieve the aerobic standard with training, the arbitrator rejected this evidence as "anecdotal"and "not supported by scientific data". This Court has not been presented with any reason to revisit this characterization. Ms. Meiorin has therefore demonstrated that the aerobic standard is *prima facie* discriminatory, and has brought herself within s. 13(1) of the Code.

[70] Ms. Meiorin having established a *prima facie* case of discrimination, the burden shifts to the Government to demonstrate that the aerobic standard is a BFOR. For the reasons below, I conclude that the Government has failed to discharge this burden and therefore cannot rely on the defence provided by s. 13(4) of the Code.

<u>Steps One and Two</u>

[71] The first two elements of the proposed BFOR analysis, that is (1) that the employer adopted the standard for a purpose rationally connected to the performance of the job; and (2) that the employer adopted the particular standard in an honest and good faith belief that it was necessary to the fulfilment of that legitimate work-related purpose, have been fulfilled. The Government's general purpose in imposing the aerobic standard is not disputed. It is to enable the Government to identify those employees or applicants who are able to perform the job of a forest firefighter safely and efficiently. It is also clear that there is a rational connection between this general characteristic and the performance of the particularly strenuous tasks expected of a forest firefighter. All indications are that the Government acted honestly and in a good faith belief that adopting the particular standard was necessary to the identification of those persons able to perform the job safely and efficiently. It did not intend to discriminate against Ms. Meiorin. To the contrary, one of the reasons the Government retained the researchers from the University of Victoria was that it sought to identify non-discriminatory standards.

<u>Step Three</u>

[72] Under the third element of the unified approach, the employer must establish that the standard is reasonably necessary to the accomplishment of that legitimate work-related purpose. To show that the standard is reasonably necessary, it must be demonstrated that it is impossible to accommodate individual employees sharing the characteristics of the claimant without imposing undue hardship upon the employer. In the case on appeal, the contentious issue is whether the Government has demonstrated that this particular aerobic standard is reasonably necessary in order to identify those persons who are able to perform the tasks of a forest firefighter safely and efficiently. As noted, the burden is on the government to demonstrate that, in the course of accomplishing this purpose, it cannot accommodate individual or group differences without experiencing undue hardship.

[73] The Government adopted the laudable course of retaining experts to devise a non-discriminatory test. However, because of significant problems with the way

the researchers proceeded, passing the resulting aerobic standard has not been shown to be reasonably necessary to the safe and efficient performance of the work of a forest firefighter. The Government has not established that it would experience undue hardship if a different standard were used.

[74] The procedures adopted by the researchers are problematic on two levels. First, their approach seems to have been primarily a descriptive one: test subjects were observed completing the tasks, the aerobic capacity of the test subjects was ascertained, and that capacity was established as the minimum standard required of every forest firefighter. However, merely describing the characteristics of a test subject does not necessarily allow one to identify the standard minimally necessary for the safe and efficient performance of the task. Second, these primarily descriptive studies failed to distinguish the female test subjects from the male test subjects, who constituted the vast majority of the sample groups. The record before this Court therefore does not permit us to say whether men and women require the same minimum level of aerobic capacity to perform safely and efficiently the tasks expected of a forest firefighter.

[75] While the researchers' goal was admirable, their aerobic standard was developed through a process that failed to address the possibility that it may discriminate unnecessarily on one or more prohibited grounds, particularly sex. This phenomenon is not unique to the procedures taken towards identifying occupational qualifications in this case: see generally K. Messing and J. Stevenson, "Women in Procrustean Beds: Strength Testing and the Workplace"(1996), 3 *Gender, Work and Organization* 156; K. Messing, *One-Eyed Science: Occupational Health and Women Workers* (1998). Employers and researchers should be highly mindful of this serious problem.

[76] The expert who testified before the arbitrator on behalf of the Government defended the original researchers' decision not to analyse separately the aerobic performance of the male and female, experienced and inexperienced, test subjects as an attempt to reflect the actual conditions of firefighting. This misses the point. The polymorphous group's average aerobic performance is irrelevant to the question of whether the aerobic standard constitutes a minimum threshold that cannot be altered without causing undue hardship to the employer. Rather, the goal should have been to measure whether members of all groups require the same minimum aerobic capacity to perform the job safely and efficiently and, if not, to reflect that disparity in the employment qualifications. There is no evidence before us that any action was taken to further this goal before the aerobic standard was adopted.

[77] Neither is there any evidence that the Government embarked upon a study of the discriminatory effects of the aerobic standard when the issue was raised by Ms. Meiorin. In fact, the expert reports filed by the Government in these proceedings content themselves with asserting that the aerobic standard set in 1992 and 1994 is a minimum standard that women can meet with appropriate training. No studies were conducted to substantiate the latter assertion and the arbitrator rejected it as unsupported by the evidence.

[79] Referring to the Government's arguments on this point, the arbitrator noted

that, "other than anecdotal or 'impressionistic' evidence concerning the magnitude of risk involved in accommodating the adverse-effect discrimination suffered by the grievor, the employer has presented no cogent evidence . . . to support its position that it cannot accommodate Ms. Meiorin because of safety risks". The arbitrator held that the evidence fell short of establishing that Ms. Meiorin posed a serious safety risk to herself, her colleagues, or the general public. Accordingly, he held that the Government had failed to accommodate her to the point of undue hardship. This Court has not been presented with any reason to interfere with his conclusion on this point, and I decline to do so. The Government did not discharge its burden of showing that the purpose for which it introduced the aerobic standard would be compromised to the point of undue hardship if a different standard were used.

[80] This leaves the evidence of the Assistant Director of Protection Programs for the British Columbia Ministry of Forests, who testified that accommodating Ms. Meiorin would undermine the morale of the Initial Attack Crews. Again, this proposition is not supported by evidence. But even if it were, the attitudes of those who seek to maintain a discriminatory practice cannot be reconciled with the Code. These attitudes cannot therefore be determinative of whether the employer has accommodated the claimant to the point of undue hardship.

Conclusion

[83] I conclude that Ms. Meiorin has established that the aerobic standard is*prima facie* discriminatory, and the Government has not shown that it is reasonably necessary to the accomplishment of the Government's general purpose, which is to identify those forest firefighters who are able to work safely and efficiently. Because it has therefore not been established that the aerobic standard is a BFOR, the Government cannot avail itself of the defence in s. 13(4) of the Code and is bound by the prohibition of such a discriminatory standard in s. 13(1)(b).

[84] I would allow the appeal and restore the order of the arbitrator reinstating Ms. Meiorin to her former position and compensating her for lost wages and benefits. Ms. Meiorin's union, the appellant on this appeal, shall have its costs in this Court and in the court below.

Appeal allowed with costs.

CASE 4.4

SUPREME COURT OF CANADA

Therrien (Re), [2001] 2 S.C.R. 3, 2001 SCC 35

Judge Richard Therrien,
Q.C.J. *Appellant*

v.

The Minister of
Justice *Respondent*

and

The Attorney General of
Quebec *Respondent*

and

The Attorney General for Ontario,
the Attorney General for New Brunswick,
Office des droits des détenus and
Association des services de réhabilitation
sociale du
Québec *Interveners*

Indexed as: Therrien (Re)

Neutral citation: 2001 SCC 35.

File No.: 27004.

2000: October 2; 2001: June 7.

Present: McLachlin C.J. and L'Heureux-Dubé, Gonthier, Iacobucci, Bastarache, Binnie and Arbour JJ.

(Excerpts of Judgment Summary)

ON APPEAL FROM THE COURT OF APPEAL FOR QUEBEC

Civil rights -- Equality rights -- Information relating to employment -- Criminal record -- Candidate for judicial office -- Whether selection committee may question candidate regarding criminal record -- Whether question infringes Charter of Human Rights and Freedoms -- Charter of Human Rights and Freedoms, R.S.Q., c. C-12, ss. 10, 18.1, 18.2, 20.

In 1970, the appellant was sentenced to imprisonment for one year for unlawfully giving assistance to four members of the Front de libération du Québec. After serving his sentence, he continued his legal studies. From 1976 to 1996, the appellant practised law, and in 1987, on his application, the Governor in Council granted him a pardon under s. 5(*b*) of the *Criminal Records Act*. Between 1989 and 1996, the appellant submitted his candidacy in five selection procedures for judicial appointments. In 1991 and 1993, he revealed his previous convictions and stated that he had been pardoned and his candidacy was rejected because of his criminal record. In the last selection procedures, he did not disclose his criminal record, or even that he had been pardoned. In September 1996, as a result of the favourable recommendation of the selection committee, the Minister of Justice recommended that he be appointed as a Judge of the Court of Québec. In late October, the Associate Chief Judge of the Court of Québec and chairman of the selection committee which had recommended the appellant's candidacy learned that he had been in trouble with the law. She advised the Minister of Justice of the situation and stated that the appellant had failed to disclose this information to the committee. The Minister lodged a complaint with the Quebec Conseil de la magistrature. A committee of inquiry of the Conseil found that the complaint was justified and recommended that removal procedures be initiated. The Conseil then recommended that the Minister of Justice initiate the process to remove the appellant by making a request to the Court of Appeal in accordance with s. 95 of the *Courts of Justice Act* ("*C.J.A.*").

Held: The appeal should be dismissed.

Substantive Issues

The pardon granted to the appellant under the *Criminal Records Act* did not mean that he could deny his criminal record and answer "no" to the question regarding his "trouble with the law", which the selection committee asks people qualified for appointment as judges. An objective analysis of the Act does not support the argument that the pardon retroactively wipes out his conviction. While a pardon does not make the past go away, it expunges consequences for the future. The integrity of the pardoned person is restored and he or she need not suffer the effects associated with the conviction in an arbitrary or discriminatory manner. Even if the opinion subjectively formed by the appellant had to be considered, the Court of Appeal held that the appellant's record contained sufficient evidence tending to establish that he was aware of the meaning and effect of the Act and that he deliberately subjectively ignored them.

The decision by the Minister of Justice to lodge an ethics complaint against the appellant was based primarily, perhaps exclusively, on the appellant's failure to disclose to the members of the selection committee that he had been in trouble with the law. Even though that decision was based in part on the existence of a criminal record, it did not infringe the appellant's equality rights under s. 15(1) of the *Canadian Charter*. Although there was differential treatment between the appellant and others who did not have a criminal history, and assuming, but without deciding the issue, that a criminal record is an analogous ground of discrimination for the purposes of s. 15(1), the Minister's decision cannot be regarded as discriminatory when we consider the relevant contextual factors. The Minister took into account the appellant's situation as a whole, as well as the situation of people who come before the court and are entitled to the highest degree of integrity, impartiality and independence on the part of the members of the judiciary in whom they place their confidence.

The appellant could have been asked the question about being in trouble with the law by the members of the selection committee without infringing the provisions of the *Quebec Charter*. Section 18.1 provides that no one may, in an employment interview, require a person to give information regarding any ground mentioned in s. 10 unless the information is useful for the application of s. 20. It is uncertain whether judicial office is included in the expression "employment" in s. 18.1 and a criminal record, even one for which a pardon has been granted, is not included in the grounds listed in s. 10. Even if the information related to one of the grounds listed in s. 10, the question would still be permitted in the selection process for persons qualified for appointment as judges since the distinction is based on the aptitudes or qualifications required for judicial office, which is deemed non-discriminatory by s. 20 of the *Quebec Charter*. The existence of a police file containing information relating to the appellant's criminal record is a supplementary source of information, but it cannot replace the selection committee and did not justify the appellant in not answering the question asked by the committee.

Section 18.2 of the *Quebec Charter*, which provides that no one may dismiss, refuse to hire or otherwise penalize a person in his employment owing to the mere fact that he was convicted of a penal or criminal offence, if the offence was in no way connected with the employment or if the person has obtained a pardon for the offence, cannot prevent the appellant from being removed. A careful examination of the conditions that must be met if that section is to apply clearly indicates that this provision does not apply to members of the judiciary. Judicial office is not an employment within the meaning of s. 18.2, by reason of the history of the judiciary and the nature, characteristics and requirements of the office. As well, the recommendations made by the Conseil de la magistrature and the Court of Appeal were not made owing to the mere fact that the appellant had been convicted of a criminal offence; rather, they were made solely because he had failed to disclose his criminal record to the selection committee. Lastly, the legislature, which was concerned about preserving the independence, impartiality and integrity of the judiciary, cannot have intended to deprive the government of its discretion to refuse to vest judicial authority in candidates whose past would be likely to undermine public confidence in its justice system.

Revocation of the appellant's commission is the appropriate sanction. The public's confidence in its justice system, which every judge must strive to preserve, is at the very heart of this case. The Court of Appeal made a thorough study and a balanced assessment of the appellant's situation and focused its decision on upholding the integrity of the judicial office. In the circumstances, and since it is the judicial forum appointed by the legislature to make determinations concerning the conduct of a judge, and a recommendation for removal in this case would not amount to arbitrary interference by the Executive in the exercise of the judicial function, the sanction that the Court of Appeal chose to impose should not be reviewed. The appellant's failure to be candid and to disclose relevant information when he was a candidate for the office of judge sufficiently undermined public confidence that he was incapable of performing the duties of his office.

CASE 4.5

SUPREME COURT OF CANADA

Syndicat Northcrest *v.* Amselem, [2004] 2 S.C.R. 551, 2004 SCC 47

Moïse Amselem, Gladys Bouhadana, Antal Klein and Gabriel Fonfeder *Appellants*

v.

Syndicat Northcrest *Respondent*

Present: McLachlin C.J. and Iacobucci, Major, Bastarache, Binnie, Arbour, LeBel, Deschamps and Fish JJ.

ON APPEAL FROM THE COURT OF APPEAL FOR QUEBEC

Summary:

The appellants A, B, K, and F, all Orthodox Jews, are divided co-owners of units in luxury buildings in Montréal. Under the terms of the by-laws in the declaration of co-ownership, the balconies of individual units, although constituting common portions of the immovable, are nonetheless reserved for the exclusive use of the co-owners of the units to which they are attached. The appellants set up "succahs" on their balconies for the purposes of fulfilling the biblically mandated obligation of dwelling in such small enclosed temporary huts during the annual nine-day Jewish religious festival of Succot. The respondent requested their removal, claiming that the succahs violated the by-laws, which, *inter alia*, prohibited decorations, alterations and constructions on the balconies. None of the appellants had read the declaration of co-ownership prior to purchasing or occupying their individual units. The respondent proposed to allow the appellants to set up a communal succah in the gardens. The appellants expressed their dissatisfaction with the proposed accommodation, explaining that a communal succah would not only cause extreme hardship with their religious observance, but would also be contrary to their personal religious beliefs, which, they claimed, called for the setting up of their own succahs on their own balconies. The respondent refused their request and filed an application for a permanent injunction prohibiting the appellants from setting up succahs and, if necessary, permitting their demolition. The application was granted by the Superior Court and this decision was affirmed by the Court of Appeal.

Held (Bastarache, Binnie, LeBel and Deschamps JJ. dissenting): The appeal should be allowed.

Per McLachlin C.J. and Iacobucci, Major, Arbour and Fish JJ.: Defined broadly, religion typically involves a particular and comprehensive system of faith and worship. In essence, religion is about freely and deeply held personal convictions or beliefs connected to an individual's spiritual faith and integrally linked to his or her self-definition and spiritual fulfilment, the practices of which allow individuals to foster a connection with the divine or with the subject or object of that spiritual faith.

Freedom of religion under the Quebec *Charter of Human Rights and Freedoms* (and the *Canadian Charter of Rights and Freedoms*) consists of the freedom to undertake practices and harbour beliefs, having a nexus with religion, in which an individual demonstrates he or she sincerely believes or is sincerely undertaking in order to connect with the divine or as a function of his or her spiritual faith, irrespective of whether a particular practice or belief is required by official religious dogma or is in conformity with the position of religious officials. This understanding is consistent with a personal or subjective understanding of freedom of religion. As such, a claimant need not show some sort of objective religious obligation, requirement or precept to invoke freedom of religion. It is the religious or spiritual essence of an action, not any mandatory or perceived-as-mandatory nature of its observance, that attracts protection. The State is in no position to be, nor should it become, the arbiter of religious dogma. Although a court is not qualified to judicially interpret and determine the content of a subjective understanding of a religious requirement, it is qualified to inquire into the sincerity of a claimant's belief, where sincerity is in fact at issue. Sincerity of belief simply implies an honesty of belief and the court's role is to ensure that a presently asserted belief is in good faith, neither fictitious nor capricious, and that it is not an artifice. Assessment of sincerity is a question of fact that can be based on criteria including the credibility of a claimant's testimony, as well as an analysis of whether the alleged belief is consistent with his or her other current religious practices. Since the focus of the inquiry is not on what others view the claimant's religious obligations as being, but what the claimant views these personal religious "obligations" to be, it is inappropriate to require expert opinions. It is also inappropriate for courts rigorously to study and focus on the past practices of claimants in order to determine whether their current beliefs are sincerely held. Because of the vacillating nature of religious belief, a court's inquiry into sincerity, if anything, should focus not on past practice or past belief but on a person's belief at the time of the alleged interference with his or her religious freedom.

Freedom of religion is triggered when a claimant demonstrates that he or she sincerely believes in a practice or belief that has a nexus with religion. Once religious freedom is triggered, a court must then ascertain whether there has been non-trivial or non-insubstantial interference with the exercise of the implicated right so as to constitute an infringement of freedom of religion under the Quebec (or the Canadian) *Charter*. However, even if the claimant successfully demonstrates non-trivial interference, religious conduct which would potentially cause harm to or interference with the rights of others would not automatically be protected. The ultimate protection of any particular *Charter* right must be measured in relation to other rights and with a view to the underlying context in which the apparent conflict arises.

Here, the impugned stipulations in the declaration of co-ownership infringe upon the appellants' freedom of religion under s. 3 of the Quebec *Charter*. The trial judge's approach to freedom of religion was incorrect. First, he chose between two competing rabbinical authorities on a question of Jewish law. Second, he seems to have based his findings with respect to freedom of religion solely on what he perceived to be the objective obligatory requirements of Judaism, thus failing to recognize that freedom of religion under the Quebec (and the Canadian) *Charter* does not require a person to prove that his or her religious practices are supported by any mandatory doctrine of faith. Furthermore, any incorporation of distinctions between "obligation" and "custom" or, as made by the respondent and the courts below, between "objective obligation" and "subjective obligation or belief" within the framework of a religious freedom analysis is dubious, unwarranted and unduly restrictive. On the issue of sincerity, the trial judge correctly concluded that the appellant A sincerely believed that he was obliged to set up a succah on his own property. The appellants K and F submitted expert evidence of their sincere individual belief as to the inherently personal nature of fulfilling the commandment of dwelling in a succah. Such expert testimony, although not required, suffices in positively assessing the sincerity and honesty of their belief. Lastly, the interference with their right to freedom of religion is more than trivial and thus, leads to an infringement of that right. It is evident that in respect of A the impugned clauses of the declaration of co-ownership interfere with his right in a substantial way, as a prohibition against setting up his own succah obliterates the substance of his right. In the case of K and F, they have proven that the alternatives of either imposing on friends and family or celebrating in a communal succah as proposed by the respondent will subjectively lead to extreme distress and thus impermissibly detract from the joyous celebration of the holiday. In any event, there is no doubt that all the appellants sincerely believe they must fulfill the biblically mandated obligation, perhaps not of setting up one's own succah, but of "dwelling in" a succah for the entire nine-day festival of Succot. Although the declaration of co-ownership does not overtly forbid the appellants to dwell in a succah -- in that they are free to celebrate the holiday with relatives or in a proposed communal succah --, the burdens placed upon them as a result of the operation of the impugned clauses are evidently substantial. Preventing them from building their own succah therefore constitutes a non-trivial interference with and thus an infringement of their protected rights to dwell in a succah during the festival of Succot.

The alleged intrusions or deleterious effects on the co-owners' rights to peaceful enjoyment of their property and to personal security guaranteed by ss. 6 and 1 respectively of the Quebec *Charter* are, under the circumstances, at best minimal and thus cannot be reasonably considered as imposing valid limits on the exercise of the appellants' religious freedom. The respondent has not adduced enough evidence to conclude that allowing the appellants to set up such temporary succahs would cause the value of the units, or of the property, to decrease. Similarly, protecting the co-owners' enjoyment of the property by preserving the aesthetic appearance of the balconies and thus enhancing the harmonious external appearance of the building cannot be reconciled with a total ban imposed on the appellants' exercise of their religious freedom. The potential annoyance caused by a few succahs being set up for a period of nine days each year would undoubtedly be quite trivial. Finally, the appellants' offer to set up their succahs in such a way that they would not block any doors, would not obstruct fire lanes and would pose no threat to safety or security obviated any security concerns under the circumstances. In order to respect the co-owners' property interests, however, the appellants should set up their succahs in a manner that conforms, as much as possible, with the general aesthetics of the property.

Whether one can waive a constitutional right like freedom of religion is a question that is not free from doubt. However, even assuming that an individual can theoretically waive his or her right to freedom of religion, a waiver argument, or an argument analogous to waiver, cannot be maintained on the facts of this case. First, the prohibitions can properly be construed as falling under s. 9.3 of the declaration of co-ownership, which does not absolutely prohibit, but rather, simply requires soliciting the consent of the co-owners to enclose one's balcony. Second, the appellants did not voluntarily, clearly and expressly waive their rights to freedom of religion. They had no choice but to sign the declaration of co-ownership if they wanted to reside at that complex. It would be both insensitive and morally repugnant to intimate that the appellants simply move elsewhere if they take issue with a clause restricting their right to freedom of religion. Further, there is no evidence that the appellants were aware that signing the declaration amounted to a waiver of their rights to freedom of religion. Not only would a general prohibition on constructions, such as the one in the declaration of co-ownership, be insufficient to ground a finding of waiver, but arguably so would any document lacking an explicit reference to the affected *Charter* right.

Per Bastarache, LeBel and Deschamps JJ. (dissenting): Since a religion is a system of beliefs and practices based on certain religious precepts, a nexus between the believer's personal beliefs and the precepts of his or her religion must be established. To rely on his or her conscientious objection a claimant must demonstrate (1) the existence of a religious precept, (2) a sincere belief that the practice dependent on the precept is mandatory, and (3) the existence of a conflict between the practice and the rule.

The claimant must first show that the precept in question is genuinely religious and not secular. The test is reasonable belief in the existence of a religious precept. To this end, expert testimony will be useful, as it can serve to establish the fundamental practices and precepts of a religion the individual claims to practise. In the second step, the claimant must establish that he or she has a sincere belief and that this belief is objectively connected to a religious precept that follows from a text or another article of faith. It is not necessary to prove that the precept objectively creates an obligation, but it must be established that the claimant sincerely believes he or she is under an obligation that follows from the precept. The inquiry into the sincerity of beliefs must be as limited as possible, since it will expose an individual's most personal and private beliefs to public airing and testing in a judicial or quasi-judicial setting. The sincerity of a belief is examined on a case-by-case basis and must be supported by sufficient evidence, which comes mainly from the claimant. Although consistency in religious practice may be indicative of the sincerity of a claimant's beliefs, it is the claimant's overall personal credibility and evidence of his or her current religious practices that matter. The essential test must be the claimant's intention and serious desire to obey the fundamental precepts of his or her religion. Finally, unless the impugned provisions or standards infringe the claimant's rights in a manner that is more than trivial or insubstantial, the freedom of religion guaranteed by the *Charters* is not applicable.

Even if all religious conduct, practices or expression that could infringe or affect the rights of others in a private law context are protected *a priori* by the purpose of freedom of religion, they are not necessarily protected under the right to freedom of religion. According to the first paragraph of s. 9.1 of the Quebec *Charter*, the rights and freedoms subject to s. 9.1, including the right to freedom of religion, must be exercised in relation to one another while maintaining proper regard for democratic values, public order and the general well-being of citizens. The *Civil Code of Québec* is the most important instrument for defining the principles governing public order and the general well-being of the citizens of Quebec. The first paragraph of s. 9.1 requires not merely a balancing of the respective rights of the parties; it is necessary to reconcile all the rights and values at issue and find a balance and a compromise consistent with the public interest in the specific context of the case. The court must ask itself two questions: (1) Has the purpose of the fundamental right been infringed? (2) If so, is this infringement legitimate, taking into account democratic values, public order, and the general well-being? A negative answer to the second question would indicate that a fundamental right has been violated. In the first step of the analysis, the person alleging the infringement must prove that it has occurred. [page558] In the second step, the onus is on the defendant to show that the infringement is consistent with the principles underlying s. 9.1. The reconciliation of rights is clearly different from the duty to accommodate in the context of an infringement of the right to equality guaranteed by s. 10 of the *Charter*.

In the case at bar, the prohibition against erecting their own succahs does not infringe the appellants' right to freedom of religion. Based on the evidence that was adduced and accepted, the appellants sincerely believe that, whenever possible, it would be preferable for them to erect their own succahs; however, it would not be a divergence from their religious precept to accept another solution, so long as the fundamental obligation of eating their meals in a succah was discharged. It cannot therefore be accepted that the appellants sincerely believe, based on the precepts of their religion that they are relying on, that they are under an obligation to erect their own succahs on their balconies. It is, rather, the practice of eating or celebrating Succot in a succah that is protected by the guarantee of freedom of religion set out in s. 3 of the Quebec *Charter*. The declaration of co-ownership does not hinder this practice, as it does not bar the appellants from celebrating in a succah, in that they can celebrate Succot at the homes of friends or family or even in a communal succah, as proposed by the respondent.

Assuming that the belief of the appellant A that he must erect a succah on his own balcony is sincere and that it is based on a precept of his religion, the infringement of his right to freedom of religion is legitimate, since the right to erect succahs on balconies cannot be exercised in harmony with the rights and freedoms of others and the general well-being of citizens. The rights of each of the other co-owners to the peaceful enjoyment and free disposition of their property and to life and personal security under ss. 6 and 1, respectively, of the Quebec *Charter* are in conflict with the appellant's freedom of religion. In the case at bar, the right to the peaceful enjoyment and free disposition of one's property is included in the purpose of the restrictions provided for in the declaration of co-ownership. The restrictions are aimed first and foremost at preserving the market value of the dwelling units held in co-ownership. They also protect the co-owners' right to enjoy the common portions reserved for exclusive use while preserving the building's style and its aesthetic appearance of a luxury building and permitting the balconies to be used to evacuate the building in a dangerous situation. The restrictions are justified, in conformity with art. 1056 C.C.Q., by the immovable's destination, characteristics and location. Also, preventing the obstruction of routes between balconies so that they can be used as emergency exits protects the co-owners' right to life and personal security. The argument that succahs can be erected without blocking access routes too much if certain conditions are complied with cannot be accepted at this point in the analysis, as it is based on the concept of reasonable accommodation, which is inapplicable in the context of s. 9.1.

The obligation imposed on the appellants to exercise their rights of ownership in harmony with the rights of the other co-owners is not unfair. The declaration of co-ownership was drafted in an effort to preserve the rights of all the co-owners, without distinction. It must also be borne in mind that the erection, as proposed by the respondent, of a communal succah would have had the desired result of upholding not only the parties' contractual rights, but also of the rights guaranteed by ss. 6, 1 and 3 of the Quebec *Charter*. Such a solution would be consistent with the principle that freedom of religion must be exercised within reasonable limits and with respect for the rights of others, subject to such limitations as are necessary to protect public safety, order and health and the fundamental rights and freedoms of others.

Per Binnie J. (dissenting): While freedom or religion as guaranteed by s. 3 of the Quebec *Charter* should be broadly interpreted, the Quebec *Charter* is also concerned in s. 9.1 with a citizen's responsibilities to other citizens in the exercise of their rights and freedoms. Here, the threshold test of bringing the s. 3 claim within the protected zone of religious freedom has been met but, in the circumstances of this case, the appellants cannot reasonably insist on a personal succah.

The succah ritual exists as an article of the Jewish faith and at least one of the appellants sincerely believes that dwelling in his own succah is part of his faith, subject to a measure of flexibility when a personal succah is not available. The construction of a succah on the commonly owned balconies of the building, however, is clearly prohibited by the declaration of co-ownership. Weight must fairly be given to the private contract voluntarily made among the parties to govern their mutual rights and obligations, including the contractual rules contained in the declaration of co-ownership, as well as on the co-owners' offer of accommodation. Buried at the heart of this fact-specific case is the issue of the appellants' acceptance, embodied in the contract with their co-owners, that they would not insist on construction of a personal succah on the communally owned balconies of the building. A person's right to the peaceful enjoyment of his property is one of the rights guaranteed by s. 6 of the Quebec *Charter* and the primary right asserted by the co-owners. Although s. 9.1 does not specifically impose a duty on [page560] third parties to accommodate a claimant, as a practical matter, the reasonableness of the claimant's conduct will be measured, at least to some extent, in light of the reasonableness of the conduct of the co-owners. The text of s. 9.1 puts the focus on the claimant, who must have regard to the facts of communal living, which includes the rights of third parties. Lastly, the reasonableness of a claimant's objection must be viewed from the perspective of a reasonable person in the position of the claimant with full knowledge of the relevant facts. When all the relevant facts of this case are considered, especially the pre-existing rules of the immovable accepted by the appellants as part of the purchase of their units, the appellants have not demonstrated that their insistence on a personal succah and their rejection of the co-owner's accommodation of a group succah show proper regard for the rights of others within the protection of s. 9.1. The appellants themselves were in the best position to determine their religious requirements and must be taken to have done so when entering into the co-ownership agreement in the first place. They cannot afterwards reasonably insist on their preferred solution at the expense of the countervailing legal rights of their co-owners. As found by the trial judge, the accommodation offered by the co-owners was not inconsistent with the appellants' sense of religious obligation in circumstances where a personal succah is simply not available.

CASE 4.6

SUPREME COURT OF THE UNITED STATES

GRUTTER *v.* BOLLINGER et al.

CERTIORARI TO THE UNITED STATES COURT OF APPEALS FOR THE SIXTH CIRCUIT

No. 02—241. Argued April 1, 2003–Decided June 23, 2003

The University of Michigan Law School (Law School), one of the Nation's top law schools, follows an official admissions policy that seeks to achieve student body diversity through compliance with *Regents of Univ. of Cal.* v. *Bakke,* 438 U.S. 265. Focusing on students' academic ability coupled with a flexible assessment of their talents, experiences, and potential, the policy requires admissions officials to evaluate each applicant based on all the information available in the file, including a personal statement, letters of recommendation, an essay describing how the applicant will contribute to Law School life and diversity, and the applicant's undergraduate grade point average (GPA) and Law School Admissions Test (LSAT) score. Additionally, officials must look beyond grades and scores to so-called "soft variables," such as recommenders' enthusiasm, the quality of the undergraduate institution and the applicant's essay, and the areas and difficulty of undergraduate course selection. The policy does not define diversity solely in terms of racial and ethnic status and does not restrict the types of diversity contributions eligible for "substantial weight," but it does reaffirm the Law School's commitment to diversity with special reference to the inclusion of African-American, Hispanic, and Native-American students, who otherwise might not be represented in the student body in meaningful numbers. By enrolling a "critical mass" of underrepresented minority students, the policy seeks to ensure their ability to contribute to the Law School's character and to the legal profession.

When the Law School denied admission to petitioner Grutter, a white Michigan resident with a 3.8 GPA and 161 LSAT score, she filed this suit, alleging that respondents had discriminated against her on the basis of race in violation of the Fourteenth Amendment, Title VI of the Civil Rights Act of 1964, and 42 U.S.C. § 1981; that she was rejected because the Law School uses race as a "predominant" factor, giving applicants belonging to certain minority groups a significantly greater chance of admission than students with similar credentials from disfavored racial groups; and that respondents had no compelling interest to justify that use of race. The District Court found the Law School's use of race as an admissions factor unlawful. The Sixth Circuit reversed, holding that Justice Powell's opinion in *Bakke* was binding precedent establishing diversity as a compelling state interest, and that the Law School's use of race was narrowly tailored because race was merely a "potential 'plus' factor" and because the Law School's program was virtually identical to the Harvard admissions program described approvingly by Justice Powell and appended to his *Bakke* opinion.

Held: The Law School's narrowly tailored use of race in admissions decisions to further a compelling interest in obtaining the educational benefits that flow from a diverse student body is not prohibited by the Equal Protection Clause, Title VI, or §1981. Pp. 9—32.

(a) In the landmark *Bakke* case, this Court reviewed a medical school's racial set-aside program that reserved 16 out of 100 seats for members of certain minority groups. The decision produced six separate opinions, none of which commanded a majority. Four Justices would have upheld the program on the ground that the government can use race to remedy disadvantages cast on minorities by past racial prejudice. 438 U.S., at 325. Four other Justices would have struck the program down on statutory grounds. *Id.*, at 408. Justice Powell, announcing the Court's judgment, provided a fifth vote not only for invalidating the program, but also for reversing the state court's injunction against any use of race whatsoever. In a part of his opinion that was joined by no other Justice, Justice Powell expressed his view that attaining a diverse student body was the only interest asserted by the university that survived scrutiny. *Id.*, at 311. Grounding his analysis in the academic freedom that "long has been viewed as a special concern of the First Amendment," *id.*, at 312, 314, Justice Powell emphasized that the " 'nation's future depends upon leaders trained through wide exposure' to the ideas and mores of students as diverse as this Nation." *Id.*, at 313. However, he also emphasized that "[i]t is not an interest in simple ethnic diversity, in which a specified percentage of the student body is in effect guaranteed to be members of selected ethnic groups," that can justify using race. *Id.*, at 315. Rather, "[t]he diversity that furthers a compelling state interest encompasses a far broader array of qualifications and characteristics of which racial or ethnic origin is but a single though important element." *Ibid.* Since *Bakke*, Justice Powell's opinion has been the touchstone for constitutional analysis of race-conscious admissions policies. Public and private universities across the Nation have modeled their own admissions programs on Justice Powell's views. Courts, however, have struggled to discern whether Justice Powell's diversity rationale is binding precedent. The Court finds it unnecessary to decide this issue because the Court endorses Justice Powell's view that student body diversity is a compelling state interest in the context of university admissions. Pp. 9—13.

(b) All government racial classifications must be analyzed by a reviewing court under strict scrutiny. *Adarand Constructors, Inc.* v. *Peña,* 515 U.S. 200, 227. But not all such uses are invalidated by strict scrutiny. Race-based action necessary to further a compelling governmental interest does not violate the Equal Protection Clause so long as it is narrowly tailored to further that interest. *E.g., Shaw* v. *Hunt,* 517 U.S. 899, 908. Context matters when reviewing such action. See *Gomillion* v. *Lightfoot*, 364 U.S. 339, 343—344. Not every decision influenced by race is equally objectionable, and strict scrutiny is designed to provide a framework for carefully examining the importance and the sincerity of the government's reasons for using race in a particular context. 13—15.

(c) The Court endorses Justice Powell's view that student body diversity is a compelling state interest that can justify using race in university admissions. The Court defers to the Law School's educational judgment that diversity is essential to its educational mission. The Court's scrutiny of that interest is no less strict for taking into account complex educational judgments in an area that lies primarily within the university's expertise. See, *e.g., Bakke,* 438 U.S., at 319, n. 53 (opinion of Powell, J.). Attaining a diverse student body is at the heart of the Law School's proper institutional mission, and its "good faith" is "presumed" absent "a showing to the contrary." *Id.,* at 318—319. Enrolling a "critical mass" of minority students simply to assure some specified percentage of a particular group merely because of its race or ethnic origin would be patently unconstitutional. *E.g., id.,* at 307. But the Law School defines its critical mass concept by reference to the substantial, important, and laudable educational benefits that diversity is designed to produce, including cross-racial understanding and the breaking down of racial stereotypes. The Law School's claim is further bolstered by numerous expert studies and reports showing that such diversity promotes learning outcomes and better prepares students for an increasingly diverse workforce, for society, and for the legal profession. Major American businesses have made clear that the skills needed in today's increasingly global marketplace can only be developed through exposure to widely diverse people, cultures, ideas, and viewpoints. High-ranking retired officers and civilian military leaders assert that a highly qualified, racially diverse officer corps is essential to national security. Moreover, because universities, and in particular, law schools, represent the training ground for a large number of the Nation's leaders, *Sweatt* v. *Painter*, 339 U.S. 629, 634, the path to leadership must be visibly open to talented and qualified individuals of every race and ethnicity. Thus, the Law School has a compelling interest in attaining a diverse student body. 15—21.

(d) The Law School's admissions program bears the hallmarks of a narrowly tailored plan. To be narrowly tailored, a race-conscious admissions program cannot "insulat[e] each category of applicants with certain desired qualifications from competition with all other applicants." *Bakke, supra,* at 315 (opinion of Powell, J.). Instead, it may consider race or ethnicity only as a " 'plus' in a particular applicant's file"; *i.e.,* it must be "flexible enough to consider all pertinent elements of diversity in light of the particular qualifications of each applicant, and to place them on the same footing for consideration, although not necessarily according them the same weight," *id.,* at 317. It follows that universities cannot establish quotas for members of certain racial or ethnic groups or put them on separate admissions tracks. See *id.*, at 315—316. The Law School's admissions program, like the Harvard plan approved by Justice Powell, satisfies these requirements. Moreover, the program is flexible enough to ensure that each applicant is evaluated as an individual and not in a way that makes race or ethnicity the defining feature of the application. See *Bakke, supra,* at 317 (opinion of Powell, J.). The Law School engages in a highly individualized, holistic review of each applicant's file, giving serious consideration to all the ways an applicant might contribute to a diverse educational environment. There is no policy, either *de jure* or *de facto*, of automatic acceptance or rejection based on any single "soft" variable. *Gratz* v. *Bollinger*, *ante*, p. ___, distinguished. Also, the program adequately ensures that all factors that may contribute to diversity are meaningfully considered alongside race. Moreover, the Law School frequently accepts nonminority applicants with grades and test scores lower than underrepresented minority applicants (and other nonminority applicants) who are rejected. The Court rejects the argument that the Law School should have used other race-neutral means to obtain the educational benefits of student body diversity, *e.g.,* a lottery system or decreasing the emphasis on GPA and LSAT scores. Narrow tailoring does not require exhaustion of every conceivable race-neutral alternative or mandate that a university choose between maintaining a reputation for excellence or fulfilling a commitment to provide educational opportunities to members of all racial groups. See, *e.g., Wygant* v. *Jackson Bd. of Ed.,* 476 U.S. 267, 280, n. 6. The Court is satisfied that the Law School adequately considered the available alternatives. The Court is also satisfied that, in the context of individualized consideration of the possible diversity contributions of each applicant, the Law School's race-conscious admissions program does not unduly harm nonminority applicants. Finally, race-conscious admissions policies must be limited in time. The Court takes the Law School at its word that it would like nothing better than to find a race-neutral admissions formula and will terminate its use of racial preferences as soon as practicable. The Court expects that 25 years from now, the use of racial preferences will no longer be necessary to further the interest approved today. Pp. 21—31.

(e) Because the Law School's use of race in admissions decisions is not prohibited by Equal Protection Clause, petitioner's statutory claims based on Title VI and §1981 also fail. See *Bakke, supra,* at 287 (opinion of Powell, J.); *General Building Contractors Assn., Inc.* v. *Pennsylvania,* 458 U.S. 375, 389—391. Pp. 31—32.
288 F.3d 732, affirmed.

O'Connor, J., delivered the opinion of the Court, in which Stevens, Souter, Ginsburg, and Breyer, JJ., joined, and in which Scalia and Thomas, JJ., joined in part insofar as it is consistent with the views expressed in Part VII of the opinion of Thomas, J. Ginsburg, J., filed a concurring opinion, in which Breyer, J., joined. Scalia, J., filed an opinion concurring in part and dissenting in part, in which Thomas, J., joined. Thomas, J., filed an opinion concurring in part and dissenting in part, in which Scalia, J., joined as to Parts I—VII. Rehnquist, C. J., filed a dissenting opinion, in which Scalia, Kennedy, and Thomas, JJ., joined. Kennedy, J., filed a dissenting opinion.

LEGAL TERMS

In your reading, you came across the following terms. Be sure that you can explain each, to ensure your understanding of the material you have been reading. If you are uncertain as to the meaning of any term, review the material in the chapter for clarification. If necessary, consult a dictionary for further information or discuss the term(s) with your instructor.

entrenched	judicial activism	adherence
representation	discrimination	*Canadian Bill of Rights*
notwithstanding clause	euthanasia	distinction
punitive damages	Oakes Test	sunset clause
undue hardship	interference	security
application	liable	invoke

REVIEW QUESTIONS

1. A photographer from a newspaper takes a picture of you while you are laying on the front lawn of your school relaxing. The following day, the picture appears in the newspaper along with an article about students taking it easy enjoying the spring weather. Have your rights been violated? Explain.

2. While Jane Smith was filling out an application form to rent an apartment, she noticed a clause stating smoking was prohibited anywhere in the building. Jane, a smoker, believes this is discrimination and therefore not legal so she completes the application and moves in shortly afterwards. Can Jane smoke in her apartment? Is the clause discriminatory? Explain.

3. During a visit to his niece, who was pregnant, the uncle showed her a lottery ticket and explained how he would give it to the baby for good luck. A few weeks after the baby is born, complications cause its death. Two weeks later, the uncle checks the lottery numbers and discovers it is the jackpot ticket worth millions. Who does the ticket belong to and why?

4. How does the principle of undue hardship relate to discrimination?

5. The Québec government adopted a law requiring drivers suspected of driving while under the influence of drugs to submit to a roadside medical exam. The exam works like the glucose readers sold in pharmacies. What test would determine its legality? Apply the test to determine its legality.

6. You work for a large company. On Friday you were told not to come back for work next week because you chose to continue wearing a head piece, required by your religion, even though the manager warned you to take it off because it did not fit with the company's image. Can you use the *Canadian Charter of Rights and Freedoms* to contest this action? Explain.

7. Last week, the Supreme Court of Canada struck down an important *Criminal Code* statute. What option(s) does the federal government have to protect this statute? Explain how the option(s) work.

8. What conditions must be met to sue somebody for punitive damages?

Chapter 5

MANDATE

OBJECTIVES

This chapter was prepared to enable you to achieve the following objectives:

1. To introduce the legal concept of mandate.

2. To develop an understanding as to how a contract of mandate is formed.

3. To understand the scope of a mandate.

4. To be able to describe the distinctions among the terms "mandator", "mandatary" and "third person".

5. To become familiar with the rights and the responsibilities of the various parties involved in a contract of mandate.

6. To appreciate the difference between express and tacit acceptance.

7. To understand what is meant by an apparent mandate.

INTRODUCTION
Section 5.1

Mandate is a contract between two persons, the mandator and the mandatary, by which the mandator empowers the mandatary to represent him in dealings with an outside party (third person). Under a contact of mandate, the mandatary is given the power not merely to assist the mandator in performing a task, but to act on behalf of the mandator and to bind the mandator to the agreement reached between the mandatary and a third person. The mandator is bound by the agreement as if he had signed it himself. From a practical point of view, mandate deals with two separate contractual undertakings. Firstly, there is the contract between the mandator and the mandatary, setting out the terms of the mandate; secondly, there is the contact that will be entered into between the mandatary and the third person.

For example, I am leaving the country tomorrow permanently and have already sold all my furniture, but I have not yet disposed of my television set. I ask my friend Bob to sell it for me, for at least $200, in return for which I will pay him 10% of the sale price. Bob agrees. We now have a valid contract of mandate. I leave the country; Bob puts an advertisement in the school newspaper which is seen by Linda. Linda calls Bob, meets him and buys the TV. When Bob agrees to sell Linda the television, Bob is acting on my behalf and I am legally bound by this sales agreement even though I am 10,000 KM away and have never met or spoken to Linda. This is the nature of mandate. The mandator will find himself legally bound by a contract negotiated and signed on his behalf by another person, the mandatary. Remember, the mandatary does not simply negotiate terms and conditions and then submit them to the mandator for final approval.

While the proper legal terminology used in the Province of Quebec is mandator and mandatary, one often hears the parties referred to by their Common Law names whereby the mandator is referred to as "the principle" and the mandatary is referred to as "the agent". The term mandate in Common Law is referred to as "agency".

Selected articles from the Civil Code of Québec are reproduced in Appendix "5-A" at the end of this chapter.

CHARACTERISTICS
Section 5.2

5.2.1 Formation

When is a contract of mandate validly formed? Like other contracts, the contract of mandate requires the consent of both the mandator and the mandatary. Consent, or acceptance of the contract, can be demonstrated either expressly or tacitly. Since a contract of mandate need not, as a general rule, be evidenced by a written document, a verbal agreement is sufficient to create a valid contract. The term "express acceptance" can mean one of two different things. Where a written contract of mandate exists, express acceptance is shown by demonstrating that the party signed the contractual document. Where the contract of mandate is verbal, express acceptance refers to proving that a party verbally agreed to be bound by the contract of mandate. Naturally, as the reader has probably already surmised, the specific terms and conditions of a verbal agreement could be a lot more difficult to prove than the terms and conditions of a written document bearing the signatures of both parties. Best practice dictates that one always enters into a written agreement so that there will be less risk of misinterpretation.

> ***Where a contact of mandate is in written form, it is referred to as a "power of attorney"***

A party's consent to a contract of mandate can also be demonstrated tacitly, from the actions of the party. For example, when I asked Bob to sell my television we did not sign a contract; Bob never said "yes, I agree", but Bob picked up my television set and walked out of my apartment. Is Bob's action a demonstration of his tacit acceptance of the mandate or could this act be interpreted differently?

5.2.2 Remuneration

Where the mandatary expects no payment in return for his services, the mandate is referred to as "by gratuitous title"; where payment will be received, the mandate is referred to as "by onerous title". Without proof to the contrary, a mandate entered into between two natural persons (human beings) is presumed to be by gratuitous title unless it is a professional mandate (i.e. lawyer, accountant, etc.) where the presumption will be by onerous title involving some form of payment. Best practices dictate that the remuneration to be paid to the mandatary, if any, should be clearly set out in a written contract of mandate.

5.2.3 Scope

Mandates may be special, for the performance of a specific task (i.e. sell my television), or they may be general, covering all of the business activities of the mandator (i.e. I am leaving the country for six months, take care of my affairs while I am gone). The powers of the mandatary are deemed to cover all tasks which are incidental to the performance of the mandate even if those tasks are not expressly set out in the contract of mandate. An example would be a mandate to sell a car. Even if the contract was silent, the mandatary would have the right to use the car for the purposes of taking potential buyers for test drives. This incidental right to use the vehicle infrequently would not include the right to drive the car daily for personal and recreational purposes.

OBLIGATIONS OF THE MANDATARY TOWARDS THE MANDATOR
Section 5.3

5.3.1 Prudence and Diligence

The mandatary has a duty to act with prudence and diligence in the performance of the mandate. This duty equates to an obligation on the part of the mandatary to act in a reasonable manner. This duty also requires that the mandatary perform his obligations to the best of his abilities. Determining whether the mandatary met both of these standards will be interpreted in light of the particular facts of the case.

5.3.2 Honesty and Faithfulness

In performing his duties, a mandatary must always have the mandatory's best interest in mind. The mandatary should be honest in the information he is providing and faithful in his actions, such as not releasing important data, contact lists or favouring a third person that could cause the mandator harm.

Furthermore, the mandatary must place the best interest of the mandator ahead of his own personal interest. In this regard, the mandatary must avoid any situation where his personal interests are in conflict with the interests of the mandator. The mandatary must disclose, in a timely fashion, to the mandator any actual or apparent conflict of interest.

5.3.3 Substitute Mandatary

Should the mandatary wish to have another person perform the mandate on his behalf, he may do so with the permission of the mandator. If the mandatary appoints a substitute mandatary without obtaining the mandator's consent, the mandatary will remain liable to the mandator for all actions taken by the substitute mandatary. However, in cases of urgency when the mandatary is incapable of fulfilling his obligations and he is unable to inform the mandator in due time, a third person may be appointed. The mandatary is also liable to the mandator for the actions of any person who the mandatary engages to assist him in the performance of the mandate.

5.3.4 Double Mandate

A double mandate refers to the situation where a mandatary is acting as the representative of two parties to a transaction whose interests could conflict. Take the following example: I engage Bob to be my mandatary to sell my car. Linda also engages Bob to be her mandatary to buy a good used car for her. Bob decides to sell my car to Linda. Both Linda and I pay Bob separate commissions. This is an example of a double mandate situation. A person is permitted to perform a double mandate on the express condition that he discloses the double mandate to both mandators and acts impartially towards each.

...as you read ask yourself...
In this situation, how would you interpret the expression "impartially"?

Where a mandator was unaware of the double mandate and where he suffered injury (damage), he can ask the court to nullify the transaction in question. By "nullifying" a contract, the agreement between the parties is deemed to never have existed. The nullity concept will be further developed in the Principles of Contract Law chapter.

5.3.5 Confidential Information and Property

The mandatary may not use for his own benefit any property or information that he receives in carrying out his mandate, without having obtained the authorization of the mandator. This prohibition deals with physical property as well as non-public information relating to the business of the mandator such as client lists, trade secrets, intellectual property, financial statements, business projects and other information that competitors and/or the public would find of value. A mandatary who breaches this prohibition will be liable for all damages suffered by the mandator. In addition to damages, the mandatary will also be required to pay to the mandator all profits that the mandatary made from using the information or in the case of property a rental charge for the unauthorized use of said property. The mandatary will also be liable for interest on all money belonging to the mandator that has been improperly used.

5.3.6 Mandatary as Contracting Party

The mandatary may not, directly or indirectly, become a party to the transaction that he has agreed to perform for the mandator, unless the mandator approves or is aware that the mandatary is so acting. Example: I engage Bob as my mandatary to sell my old car that I have not used for years. I tell him that I want at least $5,000 for the car. When Bob sees the car in my garage, he realizes that it is a 50-year-old highly collectable European sports car. Bob feels that the car is worth at least $20,000, but he says nothing and immediately calls his friend Linda. Linda agrees to pretend to be a buyer so that she and Bob can flip the car on eBay and make a fast profit. Linda buys the car for $5,000 and has it towed to her house. When she and Bob examine it later that day, they discover that the car has no engine and is in fact worth about $5,000 as a project car or for parts. Clearly Bob had not intended to buy this car to keep; he wanted to flip it quickly for a substantial profit. Obviously Bob breached his duty to the mandator. Bob no longer wants the car. Would this breach allow Bob to get out of the sale? The answer is no as a breach of this obligation by the mandatary only allows the mandator to annul the transaction. Should the mandatary also have the right to annul the transaction?

OBLIGATIONS OF THE MANDATOR TOWARDS THE MANDATARY
Section 5.4

5.4.1 Expenses and Remuneration

The mandator has an obligation to cooperate with the mandatary to facilitate the performance of the mandate, to reimburse reasonable expenses and to pay the remuneration that the mandatary is entitled to receive.

5.4.2 Ratification

The mandator is liable for acts performed by the mandatary within the limits of the mandate. He is therefore not liable for acts performed by the mandatary that exceed the limits of the mandate. It is possible, though, for these acts to be ratified under three circumstances. Ratification refers to the act of retroactively approving an action that has already occurred. First if the mandator chooses to ratify said actions. Second, where the mandatary was unaware the mandate had ended. Third, when the action has been performed more advantageously for the mandator, the mandator is presumed to ratify this action.

OBLIGATIONS OF THE MANDATARY TOWARDS THIRD PERSONS
Section 5.5

5.5.1 Personal Liability

A mandatary who can show that he both acted within the limits of his mandate and disclosed the existence of his mandate to the third person, is not personally liable to the third person with whom he contracted. If the mandatary did not disclose his capacity as mandatary, the third person can sue the mandatary personally for the performance of the contract. The third person can also sue the mandator once the mandator's identity becomes known to the third person.

5.5.2 Exceeding the Mandate

Where the mandatary exceeds his powers (acts outside the limits of the mandate), he is personally liable to the third person for this excess unless:

- The third person was sufficiently aware of the mandate, or
- The mandator ratifies the actions in question.

? *...as you read ask yourself...*

What would be an example of a mandatary acting outside the limits of his mandate?

5.5.3 Concealing the Name of the Mandator

Situations may arise where a mandatary agrees with his mandator not to disclose the name of the mandator in dealings with third persons. An example of where this might occur would be when a well-known company is trying to quietly purchase large tracts of land. If landowners were aware of the name of the actual buyer, they might try to demand a higher price for their land. For this reason, mandataries are often hired to undertake real estate transactions where the name of the mandator is not disclosed. A mandatary who does not disclose the name of his mandator is personally liable to the third person, so care must be taken when accepting this type of mandate. The mandatary should consult his own lawyer for appropriate guidance.

OBLIGATIONS OF THE MANDATOR TOWARDS THIRD PERSONS
Section 5.6

5.6.1 Liability for the Acts of the Mandatary

The mandator is liable for acts performed by the mandatary within the limits of the mandate. Remember, the mandatary was engaged to represent the mandator in contractual dealings with a third person, so it is reasonable to assume that a mandatary who performs his mandate properly will not be personally liable to the third person. As mentioned previously, the mandator can also be liable for acts of the mandatary that exceed the mandate if ratified by the mandator, the mandatary was unaware the mandate had ended or the act was more advantageous for the mandator.

5.6.2 Apparent Mandate

An apparent mandate may occur where the following conditions are met:

1. When you allow it to be believed that another person is acting as your mandatary, and

2. This person is not in actual fact your mandatary, and

3. Where this apparent mandatary enters into an agreement with a third person who is acting in good faith.

We are dealing with a situation where the third person has erroneously, but in good faith, thought that he was contracting with an authorized mandatary.

> ? *...as you read ask yourself...*
> *Can you think of an example of an apparent mandate?*

5.6.3 Vicarious Liability

Although as a general rule a mandator is liable for injury (damage) caused by his mandatary in the performance of the mandate, a defence is available and the mandator will not be liable if he can show that he was unable to prevent this injury. It is important to note that when we study employment law, we will see that an employer has no similar defence and is always liable for injury caused by his employee (also referred to as servants) in the performance of their duties. In practice it is very common to experience situations where a mandatary is also an employee, and the mandator is also an employer. An example would be a sale clerk in a retail store. This person is a paid employee of the store owner but he is also a mandatary of the store owner, since this sales clerk is the person who transacts sales with the customers (third persons). When determining the rights and responsibilities of the various parties, it is important to examine the nature and the scope of the legal relationship between them. In the above mentioned sale clerk example, which rules would apply, mandate or employment law?

TERMINATION OF MANDATE
Section 5.7

As a general rule, mandate may be terminated at any time by either party. The party terminating the mandate could however be liable for damages suffered by the other party if the termination is given without serious reason and at an inopportune moment. Mandate also terminates upon the death or bankruptcy of either party or upon the completion of the transaction in question. Upon termination of the mandate, the mandatary is required to render an account of his activities and to return to the mandator everything that he has received in the performance of his duties, even if what he received was not due to the mandator.

The mandatary is entitled to deduct from the money he remits to the mandator, the sums that are owed to him by the mandator, and the mandatary may also withhold property of the mandator until the sums owed to him are paid.

APPENDIX "5-A"
SELECTED ARTICLES FROM
The Civil Code of Québec

CHAPTER IX
MANDATE

DIVISION I
NATURE AND SCOPE OF MANDATE

2130. Mandate is a contract by which a person, the mandator, empowers another person, the mandatary, to represent him in the performance of a juridical act with a third person, and the mandatary, by his acceptance, binds himself to exercise the power.

The power and, where applicable, the writing evidencing it are called the power of attorney.

2131. The object of the mandate may also be the performance of acts intended to ensure the personal protection of the mandator, the administration, in whole or in part, of his patrimony as well as his moral and material well-being, should he become incapable of taking care of himself or administering his property.

2132. Acceptance of a mandate may be express or tacit. Tacit acceptance may be inferred from the acts and even from the silence of the mandatary.

2133. Mandate is either by gratuitous title or by onerous title. A mandate entered into between two natural persons is presumed to be by gratuitous title but a professional mandate is presumed to be given by onerous title.

2134. Remuneration, if any, is determined by the contract, usage or law or on the basis of the value of the services rendered.

2135. A mandate may be special, namely for a particular business, or general, namely for all the business of the mandator.

A mandate expressed in general terms confers the power to perform acts of simple administration only. The power to perform other acts is conferred only by express mandate, except where, in the case of a mandate given in anticipation of the mandator's incapacity, that mandate confers full administration.

2136. The powers of a mandatary extend not only to what is expressed in the mandate, but also to anything that may be inferred therefrom. The mandatary may carry out all acts which are incidental to such powers and which are necessary for the performance of the mandate.

2137. Powers granted to persons to perform an act which is an ordinary part of their profession or calling or which may be inferred from the nature of such profession or calling, need not be mentioned expressly.

DIVISION II
OBLIGATIONS BETWEEN PARTIES

Obligations of the mandatary towards the mandator

2138. A mandatary is bound to fulfill the mandate he has accepted, and he shall act with prudence and diligence in performing it.

He shall also act honestly and faithfully in the best interests of the mandator, and avoid placing himself in a position that puts his own interest in conflict with that of his mandator.

2139. During the mandate, the mandatary is bound to inform the mandator, at his request or where circumstances warrant it, of the stage reached in the performance of the mandate.

The mandatary shall inform the mandator without delay that he has fulfilled his mandate.

2140. The mandatary is bound to fulfill the mandate in person unless he is authorized by the mandator to appoint another person to perform all or part of it in his place.

If the interests of the mandator so require, however, the mandatary shall appoint a third person to replace him where unforeseen circumstances prevent him from fulfilling the mandate and he is unable to inform the mandator thereof in due time.

2141. The mandatary is accountable for the acts of the person he has appointed without authorization as his substitute as if he had performed them in person; where he was authorized to make such an appointment, he is accountable only for the care with which he selected his substitute and gave him instructions.

In any case, the mandator has a direct action against the person appointed by the mandatary as his substitute.

2142. In the performance of the mandate, the mandatary, unless prohibited by the mandator or usage, may require the assistance of another person and delegate powers to him for that purpose.

The mandatary remains liable towards the mandator for the acts of the person assisting him.

2143. A mandatary who agrees to represent, in the same act, persons whose interests conflict or could conflict shall so inform each of the mandators, unless he is exempted by usage or the fact that each of the mandators is aware of the double mandate; he shall act impartially towards each of them.

Where a mandator was not in a position to know of the double mandate, he may have the act of the mandatary declared null if he suffers injury as a result.

2144. Where several mandataries are appointed in respect of the same business, the mandate has effect only if it is accepted by all of them.

The mandataries shall act jointly for all acts contemplated in the mandate, unless otherwise stipulated or implied by the mandate. They are solidarily liable for the performance of their obligations.

2145. A mandatary who exercises alone powers that his mandate requires him to exercise with another person exceeds his powers, unless he exercises them more advantageously for the mandator than agreed.

2146. The mandatary may not use for his benefit any information he obtains or any property he is charged with receiving or administering in carrying out his mandate, unless the mandator consents to such use or such use arises from the law or the mandate.

If the mandatary uses the property or information without authorization, he shall, in addition to the compensation for which he may be liable for injury suffered, compensate the mandator by paying, in the case of information, an amount equal to the enrichment he obtains or, in the case of property, an appropriate rent or the interest on the sums used.

2147. The mandatary may not, even through an intermediary, become a party to an act which he has agreed to perform for his mandator, unless the mandator authorizes it or is aware of his quality as a contracting party.

Only the mandator may avail himself of the nullity resulting from the violation of this rule.

2148. Where the mandate is by gratuitous title, the court may, after assessing the extent of the mandatary's liability, reduce the amount of damages for which he is liable.

Obligations of the mandator towards the mandatary

2149. The mandator is bound to cooperate with the mandatary to facilitate the fulfilment of the mandate.

2150. Where required, the mandator advances to the mandatary the necessary sums for the performance of the mandate. He reimburses the mandatary for any reasonable expenses he has incurred and pays him the remuneration to which he is entitled.

2151. The mandator owes interest on expenses incurred by the mandatary in the performance of his mandate from the day they are disbursed.

2152. The mandator is bound to discharge the mandatary from the obligations he has contracted towards third persons within the limits of the mandate.

The mandator is not liable to the mandatary for any act which exceeds the limits of the mandate. He is fully liable, however, if he ratifies such act or if the mandatary, at the time he acted, was unaware that the mandate had terminated.

2153. The mandator is presumed to have ratified an act which exceeds the limits of the mandate where the act has been performed more advantageously for him than he had indicated.

2154. Where the mandatary is not at fault, the mandator is bound to compensate him for any injury he has suffered by reason of the performance of the mandate.

2155. If no fault is imputable to the mandatary, the sums owed to him are payable even though the business has not been successfully concluded.

2156. If a mandate is given by several persons, their obligations towards the mandatary are solidary.

DIVISION III
OBLIGATIONS OF PARTIES TOWARDS THIRD PERSONS

Obligations of the mandatary towards third persons

2157. Where a mandatary binds himself, within the limits of his mandate, in the name and on behalf of the mandator, he is not personally liable to the third person with whom he contracts.

The mandatary is liable to the third person if he acts in his own name, subject to any rights the third person may have against the mandator.

2158. Where a mandatary exceeds his powers, he is personally liable to the third person with whom he contracts, unless the third person was sufficiently aware of the mandate, or unless the mandator has ratified the acts performed by the mandatary.

2159. Where the mandatary agrees with a third person to disclose the identity of his mandator within a fixed period and fails to do so, he is personally liable.

The mandatary is also personally liable if he is bound to conceal the name of the mandator or if he knows that the person whose identity he discloses is insolvent, is a minor or is under protective supervision and he fails to mention this fact.

Obligations of the mandator towards third persons

2160. A mandator is liable to third persons for the acts performed by the mandatary in the performance and within the limits of his mandate unless, under the agreement or by virtue of usage, the mandatary alone is liable.

The mandator is also liable for any acts which exceed the limits of the mandate, if he has ratified them.

2161. The mandator may repudiate the acts of the person appointed by the mandatary as his substitute if he suffers any injury thereby, where the appointment was made without his authorization or where his interest or the circumstances did not warrant the appointment.

2162. The mandator or, upon his death, his heirs are liable to third persons for acts done by the mandatary in the performance and within the limits of the mandate after the termination of the mandate, where the acts were the necessary consequence of those already performed or could not be deferred without risk of loss, or where the third person was unaware of the termination of the mandate.

2163. A person who has allowed it to be

believed that a person was his mandatary is liable, as if he were his mandatary, to the third person who has contracted in good faith with the latter, unless, in circumstances in which the error was foreseeable, he has taken appropriate measures to prevent it.

2164. A mandator is liable for any injury caused by the fault of the mandatary in the performance of his mandate unless he proves, where the mandatary was not his servant, that he could not have prevented the injury.

2165. A mandator, after disclosing to a third person the mandate he had given, may take action directly against the third person for the performance of the obligations he contracted towards the mandatary, who was acting in his own name. However, the third person may plead the inconsistency of the mandate with the stipulations or nature of his contract and the defenses which can be set up against the mandator and the mandatary, respectively.

If proceedings have already been instituted against the third person by the mandatary, the mandator may exercise his right only by intervening in the proceedings.

DIVISION V
TERMINATION OF MANDATE

2184. Upon termination of the mandate, the mandatary is bound to render an account and return to the mandator everything he has received in the performance of his duties, even if what he has received was not due to the mandator.

The mandatary owes interest, computed from the time he is in default, on any balance in the account consisting of sums he has received.

2185. A mandatary is entitled to deduct what the mandator owes him by reason of the mandate from the sums he is required to remit.

The mandatary may also retain what was entrusted to him by the mandator for the performance of the mandate until payment of the sums due to him.

CASE 5.1

Piec Estate v. Caisse d'économie polonaise du Québec

[1999] Q.J. No. 79, **Quebec Superior Court (Civil Division)**

(Excerpts of Judgment)

TEXT OF JUDGMENT

JOHN H. GOMERY J.:— By judgment dated September 15, 1993 rendered in virtue of the last paragraph of Article 924 of the former Civil Code of Quebec ("C.C.B.C."), Plaintiff Margaret Wojcicka was appointed executrix of the intestate estate of her late aunt, Stefania Janina Wojcicka, widow of the late Bronislaw Piec. Mrs. Piec, who in her lifetime was domiciled in the City of Montreal, died on July 3, 1992 while on a visit to her native Poland.

At the time of her death Mrs. Piec was a member of the Defendant credit union of which she owned one share worth $5.00. She had on deposit in savings account No. 2470 the sum of $50.00 and was the registered owner of two term deposit certificates issued by the Defendant in the amounts of $1,000.00 and $26,000.00 respectively. The smaller term deposit certificate had interest accrued of $92.50 when Mrs. Piec died. In her capacity as executrix of Mrs. Piec's estate Plaintiff claims these amounts, totalling $27,147.52, from Defendant.

Defendant contests the action on the ground that on August 18, 1992, about six weeks after Mrs. Piec's death, all amounts that it owed to her were paid over to her nephew Tadeusz Wojcicki ("Tadeusz") at the latter's request, in accordance with a power of attorney that Mrs. Piec had signed on May 15, 1992, shortly before her departure for Poland. At the time these payments were made the Defendant's employees did not know that Mrs. Piec had died. Defendant also invokes a letter dated July 1, 1992, apparently signed by Mrs. Piec, which was delivered to Defendant by Tadeusz; the letter instructs the Caisse to pay Tadeusz $26,000.00 out of the amounts presently claimed. It has since been established that the letter is a forgery, but it is relied upon by Defendant to show that it acted in good faith. The parties have identified three questions of combined fact and law that require to be answered to dispose of the present case: was the Defendant authorized and entitled to deliver the sums deposited with it to Tadeusz on the basis of the power of attorney dated May 15, 1992? What if any effect should be given to the forged letter of instructions dated July 1, 1992? And did Defendant act with reasonable care in the circumstances, and if so, is that a valid defence to the claim?

Before considering these questions, it will be useful to review the factual background in greater detail.

Mrs. Piec, an elderly woman with a limited ability to speak English or French, became a member of the Defendant in 1983. She was well known to its manager and personnel. Following the death of her husband in 1987 the Plaintiff assisted her for a time with the settlement of his estate and often accompanied her to the

Defendant's premises. Plaintiff subsequently moved to Illinois to live, and her contacts with her aunt became less frequent.

Mrs. Piec lived for many years at 3615 Aylwin Street, Montreal. The property belonged to her until 1991 when she sold it to her good friend Mrs. Muguette Paquet, who had at one time occupied the premises as a tenant. Following the sale Mrs. Piec became Mrs. Paquet's tenant, and the latter assumed some of the functions formerly performed by Plaintiff, taking her to do her banking and assisting her in getting about.

In 1990 Tadeusz arrived in Canada from Poland as a visitor, and started to live with Mrs. Piec at 3615 Aylwin Street. When his visa expired he remained here illegally. Following the sale of the Aylwin Street property in 1991, as a result of which Mrs. Piec realized a substantial sum of money, Tadeusz seemed to wish to avoid any encounter with Mrs. Paquet, with whom he had previously had a cordial relationship.

On May 15, 1992 Mrs. Piec and Tadeusz went to the Defendant's place of business where Mrs. Piec made it known that she was planning to visit relatives in Poland, and would be away for some time. So that her affairs could be administered by Tadeusz during her absence, she signed a printed endorsement on her account card reading as follows:

> "Power of Attorney to Sign and Endorse Cheques
> I, the undersigned, authorize and by these presents give full power to Wojcicki, Tadeusz (whose signature is hereon annexed) for me and in my name, to withdraw from La Caisse D'Économie all sums or parts of sums deposited or which may hereafter be deposited to the credit of my account No. 2470 and also for me in my name to endorse all cheques, payable to my order, drawn on said Credit Union and receive payment of the same hereby confirming all payments to the said attorney on his or her receipt. And by these presents, I ratify, confirm and recognize as good and valid all payments made up to this day by the said Credit Union of all the sums or part sums deposited to my credit. These presents shall continue in full force and effect until notice in writing of the revocation hereof has been given to the said Credit Union by the depositor. In testimony of which I have signed in the presence of the undersigned witness.
>
> (s) Stefania Piec, Depositor
> (s) Tadeusz Wojcicki, Attorney
> (s) Illegible, Witness 15.05.92"

On the same occasion Mrs. Piec purchased the term deposit certificate for $26,000.00. The document which the Defendant issued to evidence the transaction specifies that it could not be redeemed before its maturity on October 26, 1992. Defendant's manager explains that in order to redeem such a deposit before maturity in spite of this condition, its internal rules require that the agreement of five members of the Caisse be obtained. In such cases no interest is paid to the depositor. The smaller term deposit certificate of $1000.00 had been issued on February 14, 1984 and renewed annually ever since; it was not subject to these conditions and could be redeemed at any time.

As already noted, Mrs. Piec died in Poland on July 3, 1992 but her death was not known to the Defendant, Mrs. Paquet or the Plaintiff until the end of August. In the meantime, Tadeusz emptied and closed the bank account, redeemed both term deposit certificates, took the proceeds in cash and disappeared. The manner in which this was accomplished leaves one with no alternative but to believe that he knew of his aunt's death before anyone else and adopted the following strategem so as to misappropriate her property.

On or about August 11, 1992 Tadeusz delivered to the Defendant a letter purportedly signed by his aunt, written in Polish, a translation of which reads as follows:

> "Kamien, le 01.07.1992
> Stefania Piec
> 36-143 Kamien
> Drzywa Wics 50
> woj. Rzeszow
>
> Au Directeur de la Caisse Polonaise 65 Sherbrooke East
> J'autorise mon neveu Tadeusz Wojcicki, né le 07.04.54 de fermer immédiatement mon compte bancaire no 2470 et transmettre la somme de 26 000,00 $ à mon neveu, comme établi (autorisation) en date du 15.05.1992.
> Je m'excuse du changement de décision qui fut prise à cause de mon état de santé ainsi que ma situation familiale.
> Je vous prie de déduire les frais administratifs du montant mentionné plus haut.
> Sincèrement,
> Stefania Piec"

Upon receiving this document, not realizing it was a forgery, Defendant's manager instructed his staff to obtain the necessary consent from five members of the credit union; this was done during the course of the following six days. On August 18, 1992 Tadeusz reappeared, redeemed both certificates, and deposited the proceeds in account no. 2470. He then drew a cheque on the account for $26,000.00 payable to "cash".

The bank notes involved must have made an impressive wad. Indeed the Defendant had had to make arrangements in advance to have this much cash on hand. None of the Defendant's employees who were heard as witnesses remembers asking Tadeusz any questions about the transaction such as why he chose to take out the money in cash, rather than in another form, or why Mrs. Piec was, in effect, liquidating her savings so abruptly, nor do they remember asking about the health problem to which she refers in the letter.

On August 25, 1992 Tadeusz returned to the Defendant's premises one last time and withdrew all of the sums remaining in Mrs. Piec's account. Her savings account was then closed.

On August 30, 1992 Mrs. Paquet received a telephone call from her daughter who told her that the Aylwin Street property, where Mrs. Piec still had her furniture and personal effects, was being systematically emptied by unknown persons. The police were called and learned that Mrs. Piec had died about two months earlier. Mrs. Paquet informed Plaintiff and Defendant of the sad news. She testifies that she is still surprised that the Defendant would have paid out all of Mrs. Piec's money to Tadeusz without so much as a phone call to her; the Defendant's employees knew of her friendship with Mrs. Piec, and knew how to get in touch with her.

Let us now deal with the three questions.

1. Was the Defendant authorized and entitled to pay Tadeusz on the basis of the power of attorney?

The power of attorney of May 15, 1992 authorizes Tadeusz to draw cheques on Mrs. Piec's bank account, to make withdrawals and generally to administer the account, but it does not give him the authority to redeem or deal with the term deposit certificates in any way. In the absence of specific language to this effect Defendant cannot rely upon the power of attorney to justify its acceptance of Tadeusz's instructions that the term deposits be redeemed. Article 1704 C.C.B.C. reads:

> "The mandatary can do nothing beyond the authority given or implied by the mandate. He may do all acts which are incidental to such authority and necessary for the execution of the mandate."

The general rule is stated in the first sentence of Article 1704, and the authority to perform acts incidental to the general authority given to the mandatary recognized in the second sentence is exceptional. As a general principle, a narrow construction should be put upon a power of attorney, particularly where it constitutes a contract of adhesion as defined by Article 1379 C.C.Q. In this case the power of attorney consisted of a preprinted form prepared by the Defendant, whose terms were not negotiated or negotiable.

The general authority conferred by the power of attorney is limited to the drawing of cheques on Mrs. Piec's account and the withdrawal of sums from it. The redemption of the term deposits was not incidental to this mandate; it was an extraordinary act and, in the case of the term deposit of $26,000.00, involved the renunciation of an important amount of accrued interest. It could be said that the redemption of the latter certificate constituted a direct contradiction of the stipulation that it should not be redeemed before October 10, 1992. Tadeusz himself appears to have recognized this contradiction; otherwise he would not have put himself to the trouble and considerable risk of using a forged document to persuade the Defendant to permit the redemption of the certificate before maturity.

It is accordingly the Court's opinion that the power of attorney did not empower

Tadeusz to redeem either of the term deposit certificates, and that the Defendant erred in acceding to his request to convert them to cash.

The same can be said of Mrs. Piec's membership in Defendant, worth $5.00. Nothing in the power of attorney can be construed as conferring the authority to terminate the banking relationship that she had had with Defendant since 1983. Tadeusz's instructions to the Defendant to close the account should at the very least have aroused the suspicions of its employees that something was amiss. Defendant pleads that the payment of the proceeds of the redemption of the term deposit certificates was made to Tadeusz in accordance with the power of attorney dated May 15, 1992, at a time when Defendant did not know of the extinction of his mandate by the death of Mrs. Piec. This argument is based upon Articles 1728 and 1729 C.C.B.C. which read:

"1728. The mandator or his legal representative is bound toward third persons for all acts of the mandatary, done in execution and within the powers of the mandate after it has been extinguished, if its extinction be not known to such third persons.

1729. The mandator or his legal representative is bound for acts of the mandatary done in execution and within the powers of the mandate after its extinction, when such acts are a necessary consequence of a business already begun.

He is bound for acts of the mandatary done after the extinction of the mandate by death or cessation of authority in the mandator, for the completion of a business, where loss or injury might have been caused by delay."

However as already noted, the redemption of the term deposit certificates was not a power which was given to Tadeusz, or incidental to such a power. Therefore his withdrawal of the proceeds of the redemptions was not "done in execution and within the powers of the mandate."

Accordingly Defendant may not rely upon the power of attorney as a defence to the claim, with the possible exception of the $50.00 on deposit in account no. 2470. We shall return to the subject of this deposit when dealing with the third question.

2. What if any effect should be given to the forged letter of instructions?

The Court is of the view that the Defendant may not rely in any way upon the forged letter of instructions, as a ground of defence. Whether the forged instrument is in the form of a bill of exchange, a cheque, or a letter of instructions, the banking institution concerned is required to recognize its customer's signature, and to detect any forgery, no matter how difficult that may be. The governing principle, supported by many judicial decisions, is enunciated by Professor L'Heureux op. cit. at page 242, as follows:

"Une jurisprudence ancienne fait obligation à la banque de reconnaître la

> signature de son client et considère qu'il y a négligence si elle fait défaut de ne pas découvrir la contrefaçon de cette signature."

The good faith of the banking institution is immaterial. In Grivna v. Banque Canadienne Nationale (1954) C.S. 169 Mr. Justice Smith concludes his judgment with the following paragraphs:

> "All things considered, therefore the Court is forced to conclude that the proof establishes that the said cheques were not signed by the plaintiff. Such being the case, the plaintiff's action must succeed since the bank was obliged to know the signature of its customer and is bound to reimburse monies paid out of his account without his authority and on a forged signature and since there is no proof that the plaintiff has ratified or is precluded from setting up the said forgery.
>
> Counsel for defendant emphasized the fact that there was a total absence of fault and negligence on the part of the defendant who cashed the said cheques in good faith and only after comparing the signatures thereon with the plaintiff's authentic signature. All of this is doubtless true; unfortunately for the defendant, however, it does not affect its responsibility towards the plaintiff in regard to the monies paid out of the plaintiff's account on a forged signature."

Defendant argues that the requirement that a banking institution recognize a forgery of its client's signature applies only to bills of exchange, and that the forged letter of instructions purportedly signed by Mrs. Piec does not constitute a bill of exchange. The Court respectfully disagrees on both counts. The doctrine and jurisprudence cited above does not limit the circumstances under which a bank is held responsible for any loss caused by a forgery of its client's signature, nor should it. In any event the letter of instructions dated July 1, 1992 conforms to all of the characteristics of a bill of exchange as they are defined in section 16(1) of the Bills of Exchange Act R.S.C., 1985, c. B-4.

The evidence of the handwriting experts called by the parties to testify has convinced the Court that the forgery of Mrs. Piec's signature was far from easy to detect, although both of them have no doubt whatsoever that it was indeed a forgery. This does not, however, exonerate Defendant from its responsibility. The law chooses to impose responsibility for a loss caused by a forgery upon the party who accepted to act on the basis of the falsified signature, even when that party is the innocent victim of a criminal act perpetrated by the person who uses the forgery. The alternative victim would be the bank depositor, with the consequence that anyone would become exposed to the danger that his or her bank account could be misappropriated by thieves presenting forged letters of instructions to the banking institution concerned, provided that the latter was honestly deceived. Such a possibility would tend to undermine the confidence to which bank customers are entitled concerning their deposits.

3. Did the Defendant act with reasonable care?

As a result of the conclusions already reached, this question is relevant only to the $50.00 on deposit in account no. 2470.

Plaintiff argues that the Defendant's suspicions should have been sufficiently aroused when Tadeusz acted as he did in August, 1992, and that it should have made some sort of enquiry before accepting his instructions. A simple phone call to Mrs. Paquet would almost certainly have resulted in the discovery that Mrs. Piec had died, or that Tadeusz was acting without her authorization.

The Court is of the opinion that a number of factors should have alerted the Defendant to the possibility that Tadeusz was exceeding the mandate that Mrs. Piec had given him, when he requested the liquidation of her holdings. These include the substantial sum of money involved, far in excess of what was required to pay her current accounts, the apparent foreign destination of the funds, and the request that the money to be transmitted to Mrs. Piec be converted into cash, most of it in small denominations. According to an expertise filed in the record by Professor L'Heureux, it is not a normal request that the transfer of funds from Canada to a foreign destination be made in cash; usually such transfers are effected by way of banker's draft, or by a wire transfer from one banking institution to another.

The Defendant should have been alerted by all of these circumstances that Tadeusz was or might be exceeding his authority. In the absence of any efforts to verify his assertion that he was entitled to wind up Mrs. Piec's affairs as he did, the Defendant should be held responsible for the misappropriation of her bank account.

FOR THESE REASONS, Plaintiff's action is maintained and the Court condemns Defendant to pay Plaintiff ès qualité the sum of $27,142.52 with interest from the date of service and the indemnity provided for by Article 1078.1 C.C.B.C., the whole with costs, including the fees and costs of Plaintiff's experts.

CASE 5.2

Dowell v. Hay-Ellis

[1998] Q.J. No. 1580, **Quebec Superior Court (Civil Division)**

(Excerpts of Judgment)

TEXT OF JUDGMENT

J. MARTIN J.:— Plaintiff Dr. Anthony Dowell has instituted the present proceedings against the defendant notary claiming reimbursement of the sum of $69,649.79. According to the plaintiff, the said sum was improperly disbursed as a consequence of the defendant's professional negligence in the administration of monies held in his trust account. It is the plaintiff's contention that the sums in question were part of a larger amount being held by the defendant for the purpose of meeting expenses in relation to an immovable property on Sauvé and Meilleur streets in the City of Montreal (hereinafter referred to as the Sauvé property) of which the plaintiff had become owner in the course of the month of October 1993. This litigation raises no difficult questions of law. Rather the issues stand to be resolved upon the nature and extent of the notary's duties and obligations in the particular circumstances of the case at bar.

The facts surrounding this transaction are a good deal more complicated than the particular issue which requires to be resolved. In view of several contradictions existing between the versions of several of the witnesses there are some aspects of the matter which remain unclear. These do not, however, bear upon the core issue of the defendant's responsibility.

Some time prior to October 13, 1993 an individual by the name of Ronald Joseph set out to orchestrate the acquisition of the Sauvé property. Whether he intended to do so on his own behalf, in concert with or on behalf of one Mortimer Davis is unclear. The property was mortgaged virtually to the hilt and the situation was further complicated by the fact that Joseph at the time was under bankruptcy protection and was therefore disqualified from engaging in such transactions. By all appearances Joseph was purely and simply attempting to short circuit the law and to enrich himself to the detriment of his creditors. Not only was Joseph ineligible to act on his own account but there were other difficulties which required to be overcome. Both the mortgage creditor and the vendors obviously had to be in agreement with regard to any proposed purchaser. Joseph therefore required a "front man" who would be acceptable to both the vendors and to the mortgage creditor, and found him in the person of Dowell. The plaintiff was in fact no stranger to Joseph having been involved with him in previous transactions. That may explain why he approached this one with a certain degree of caution.

It is happily not necessary for the purposes of this litigation to determine the length and breadth of the scheme which Joseph was attempting to put in place. It will suffice to say that Dowell was never intended to have any personal interest in the Sauvé St. property beyond that which the law imposed as a result of the purchase of same being made in his name. Furthermore he was fully aware that all transactions relative to the property were being orchestrated by Joseph and that it was anticipated that the property would in the near future again be sold or "flipped" although he had no details as to when or how this may be accomplished. Dowell was also aware that the consideration for the lending of his name for these operations was the payment of a sum of $15,000.00 which he was to receive and indeed did subsequently receive from Joseph.

The stage was set and on October 13, 1993 Joseph together with the defendant and another attended upon Dowell at his clinic in order to have him execute a series of documents in relation to the sale which the defendant had prepared at Joseph's behest. In addition to the proposed deed of purchase, it was anticipated that Dowell would execute a power of attorney in favour of Joseph mandating him to carry out all acts attendant to the eventual administration of the Sauvé property. As to whether these documents had been previously faxed or otherwise sent to Dowell for his perusal is a question upon which the evidence is somewhat contradictory. It will suffice to say however that on the 30th of October Dowell became sufficiently concerned about the possible consequences of his participation in the scheme that he sought the counsel of his attorney Me Bruce Taub prior to executing any of the documents in question. As a result of Dowell's request Taub accordingly also attended at Dowell's clinic where he received and reviewed the documents in question.

Taub was concerned for his client for it soon emerged that Dowell would at least officially become the sole purchaser of the property and his attorney set about to ensure, through the modification of both the drafts of the deed of sale and the power of attorney that some control was retained in the hands of Dowell himself. There are contradictions in the evidence as to just what Taub modified. According to him he made extensive changes to both the power of attorney and to the projected deed of sale. These two documents he states were the only ones discussed in front of him. His testimony in this regard was confirmed by Dowell. The defendant, on the other hand contends that Taub modified only the power of attorney.

Whatever the truth of it the defendant, for his part welcomed the presence of Taub in the picture. He stated that in a professional context, he felt "awkward" to employ his word in attempting to be counsel to both Joseph and Dowell and was happy when Taub came into the picture. His testimony in this regard is in my view important. On one hand it confirms that he was, as indeed he ought to have been, conscious of the risk to which Dowell was exposed for as long as he remained the owner of the property. On the other it permits me to infer that he appreciated the nature of his duty toward Dowell in relation to the trust monies of which he subsequently took control following the sale.

At the time of the sale namely October 13, 1993 the vendors deposited with the defendant the sum of $237,209.27. The accuracy of this sum is not contested and out of it the defendant proceeded to make certain payments in relation to arrears in mortgage payments and the real estate agent's commission thereby reducing the balance held in trust to $128,750.00.

On October 28, 1998 the defendant issued a cheque in the amount of $128,526.50 to Dowell who immediately endorsed same back to the defendant with the result that its proceeds were replaced in the defendant's trust account to Dowell's credit and earmarked for the management of the Sauvé property. That transaction was accompanied by a receipt for the said amount which receipt had inscribed on its face the following notation: "To be used for the management of 400 Sauvé, Montreal". It is signed by the defendant. The sum in question was in turn duly recorded on a ledger sheet in the plaintiff's name as an integral part of the records maintained by the defendant of monies held in trust for others.

An adjustment was subsequently made in the amount of $224.00 bringing the balance to $128,750.50 a figure which concords almost exactly with the balance remaining following the payment of the real estate agent's commission and the balance outstanding in relation to the mortgage payments.

The plaintiff alleges that between November 1st, 1993 and January 19, 1994 the defendant, at the sole behest of Joseph paid out of the monies held in trust for the Sauvé property sums destined for other purposes.

The defendant, for his part makes no attempt to deny the said payments. Indeed he would be hard put to do so. As a first line of defence he maintains that he had no duty or obligation toward the plaintiff inasmuch as the latter was no more than a "prête-nom" for Joseph and as such had no pecuniary interest in the sums in question. With respect that argument cannot be sustained. First of all whatever may have been the defendant's understanding of the relationship between Dowell and Joseph, Dowell in his capacity as owner of the property incurred, from the date of his acquisition of the property, obligations toward innumerable third parties such as the mortgage creditor, municipal and school authorities not to mention his obligations toward the tenants themselves. The defendant accepted sums of money which he undertook to hold in trust which money was to be used for the management of the property. This created an obligation on his part. Transactions relating to the sums in question were recorded in a ledger sheet bearing the plaintiff's name. Regardless of the nature of the relationship between Dowell and Joseph I fail to see how the defendant can pretend that Dowell's interest in the property is insufficient to trigger the defendant's duty of care toward him. This is especially true given his intimate knowledge of the nature of the transaction.

Dowell on the contrary had a clear interest in the property and in agreeing to hold monies destined for the management of same the defendant became a mandatary with the duties and obligations which arise from that capacity. These duties in turn are complemented and shaded by the special character bestowed by the defendant's profession. In that context the question which will eventually have to be answered is whether the defendant in his professional capacity met the standards imposed upon him by his profession.

In the course of the meeting at Dowell's office on October 13, 1993 the latter was required to sign three documents which he and his attorney inspected closely. These were:

1) A Power of Attorney;

2) A transfer of his rights to a numbered company namely 3096-6345 Quebec Inc.;

3) The draft of the deed of sale.

As a result of the position counselled by Taub and adopted by Dowell very substantial changes were made to the power of attorney. As the defendant put it, the power of attorney was effectively "emasculated". In fact, when Taub had finished the document could hardly be said to subsist as a mandate to manage at all. Effectively all it empowered Joseph to do was to purchase, sell or otherwise alienate the property upon such terms as he may think proper. Since the property was in any event heavily mortgaged that authority was meaningless indeed.

All of this is admittedly difficult to reconcile with testimony to the effect that Dowell wanted no personal involvement in the day-to-day administration of the property and his understanding that it was Joseph who would be looking after this aspect of the matter. This may be why Dowell, on November 1st, 1993, granted authorisation to Joseph and to one Colin O'Neill to sign leases and to arrange to have maintenance and repairs done to the Sauvé property. In the course of his examination Dowell acknowledged that the document, while in Joseph's handwriting was indeed signed by him.

The circumstances surrounding the administration of the property effectively confirm this arrangement. In point of fact it was Joseph and not Dowell who saw to the day-to-day administration of the property. It was Joseph who effectively dealt with the defendant as far as the property was concerned. According to Joseph he had full control of the Sauvé property at least during the initial period and indeed the circumstances confirm him.

It is against the foregoing factual background that the conduct of the defendant stands to be measured. Before doing so it will nevertheless be helpful to dwell for a short time on the payments which gave rise to the present proceedings.
In paragraphs 12 and 13 of his statement of claim, the plaintiff makes the following allegations:

"12. All monies left in trust with the defendant were for the express purposes of paying the maintenance charges on the Sauvé property, the whole as appears from the original receipt given by the defendant to the plaintiff and already deposited herein as Exhibit P-7;

13. Contrary to the explicit mandate accepted by the defendant from the plaintiff to use the money he had in trust for the express purposes of the maintenance of the Sauvé property, the defendant issued cheques totalling $69,649.79 for purposes other than the management of the Sauvé property, the whole as appears from copies of the said cheques, as well as the notary's ledger produced en liasse as Exhibit P-8;"

In paragraph 14 of his statement of claim, the plaintiff lists twenty-two payments made by way of cheques drawn on the defendant's trust account which, it is the plaintiff's contention, constitute payments for purposes other than the maintenance of the Sauvé property. At trial the series of twenty-seven cheques were filed under the rubric of Exhibit P-8. Of these, only 20 form part of the plaintiff's claim. The defendant's ledger duly lists two other cheques, numbers 78 and 88 as having been issued although the cheques are missing. I have in view of the testimony considered those as forming part of the plaintiff's claim. Thus, whether an item of claim is supported by cheque or by a ledger entry, I have found it to be accurate.

While cheques #60, #61, #65 and #68 do not form part of the claim as such #61 in the amount of $40,500.00 is of some interest. Dowell's fee of $15,000.00 for the use of his name was included in that amount while the balance, according to Dowell, was deposited to Joseph's credit. In short his fee of $15,000.00 was paid directly from the monies held in trust for his account.

This certainly lends some credence to the contention of the defence that Joseph was the directing mind behind the entire transaction. While that may be so it does not however lend much support to the proposition advanced by the defendant to the effect that Dowell had no interest in the monies held in trust. This is not, after all a dispute between Joseph and Dowell. Rather it is a claim against the defendant for having failed to fulfil his professional obligations according to the standards imposed by the law. The plaintiff, as I have been at pains to point out, remained liable to third parties as a result of his ownership of the property. Indeed, as the mortgage creditor's letter of February 24, 1994 makes abundantly clear his exposure, as at that date, amounted to $93,890.46. It can hardly be said that he had no interest.

From cheque #73 onwards it is however Dowell's contention that with the exception of cheques #110, #114 and #116 the payments all related to matters having nothing to do with the Sauvé property. That in essence is the basis of his claim.

The defendant made no attempt to contradict Dowell with regard to the foregoing assertion. Incredibly he took the position that Joseph was in sole and complete control of the administration of the property and therefore of the disbursement of the monies held by the defendant in trust. He therefore followed Joseph's instructions to the letter without question and did not apparently even request or verify any of the invoices in relation to the payments he was asked to make. His mandate, he maintained was a "truncated" one which had passed from Dowell to Joseph.

There is certainly nothing to support such a conclusion in the power of attorney which Taub modified and which I have discussed previously. If indeed the defendant had any basis for such a belief, and in my view he had none, it could only exist in virtue of Exhibit P-9. Even there whatever powers Dowell granted to Joseph are granted only in relation to the administration of the property.
How the defendant can support the contention that this absolved him from verifying the basis for the payments which he made is beyond my comprehension. Furthermore in his letter to Taub dated March 24, 1994 he expresses himself in part as follows:

> "With reference to the subject mentioned above, I enclose a photocopy of the trust account entries concerning our mutual client.

> ...
> All transactions were carried out at the behest of Mr. Ronald Joseph who was managing the property."
>
> (underlining mine)

Joseph was questioned closely with regard to each of the cheques in question. After a somewhat unenthusiastic attempt to justify cheque #73 which covered the cost of insurance premiums on his Ste-Marthe farm on the ground that Dowell was a guarantor of the mortgage, Joseph effectively confirmed that the payments were indeed incurred, save for two, in relation to a number of matters which had nothing whatever to do with the Sauvé property.

As far as the missing cheques #78 and #88 are concerned they are, first of all, duly recorded in the defendant's ledger as payments having been made on November 1st, 1993 and November 8, 1993 respectively. The first involves a payment to one Donald Fishman, a veterinarian in the amount of $14,000.00. This payment is in no way related to the Sauvé property. The same may be said of the second in the amount of $16,477.64 which was made payable to the Laurentian Bank.

Of all the sums forming part of the claim the only ones which Joseph was able to relate to the Sauvé property were #84 and #112. #84 was made payable to the order of Jean-Pierre Olynyk and according to Joseph was incurred for renovations to the Sauvé property. No satisfactory explanation was however furnished as to the nature and extent of these renovations let alone that they relate to the Sauvé property. Cheque #112 in the amount of $1,100.00 was made payable to one Michel Plouffe. In the course of argument it was conceded that this amount was indeed incurred in relation to the Sauvé property for the repairing or refinishing of certain floors. It will accordingly be deducted from the sum claimed in paragraph 14 reducing that amount from $64,649.79 to $63,549.79.

To that amount must be added the sum of $5,000.00 paid by way of cheque #68 again to the order of Jean-Pierre Olynyk. First of all that payment is not recorded in the defendant's ledger sheet with regard to Dowell nor has the payment been satisfactorily explained as relating to the Sauvé property.

The sums improperly paid out as alleged in paragraphs 14 and 15 total therefore $68,549.79.

It will not be necessary to embark on a long dissertation over the responsibility of the defendant in the circumstances.

Art. 1458 C.C.Q. enacts the general principle of civil liability applicable in the circumstances.

> Art. 1458 Every person has a duty to honour his contractual undertakings. Where he fails in this duty, he is liable for any bodily, moral or material injury he causes to the other contracting party and is liable to reparation for the injury; neither he nor the other party may in such a case avoid the rules governing contractual liability by option for rules that would be more favourable to them.

In addition Articles 2130 and following bear upon the contract of mandate. In particular Article 2138 provides as follows:

> Art. 2138 A mandatary is bound to fulfill the mandate he has accepted, and he shall act with prudence and diligence in performing it.
>
> He shall also act honestly and faithfully in the best interests of the mandator, and avoid placing himself in a position that puts his own interest in conflict with that of his mandator.

In the case of a notary these obligations are shaded and strengthened by the Code de déontologie des notaires (L.Q., ch. N-2, r. 3). The notary in a nutshell must act, in the exercise of his profession, with prudence and diligence.

In permitting himself to issue cheques without making even the slightest attempt to verify in what manner these requested payments related to the Sauvé property the notary fell far short of the standard of conduct which the law imposes upon him. He never even required invoices. Had he done so even the most cursory inspection of such invoices, if indeed they existed, would have demonstrated that these accounts bore no relationship to the Sauvé property. The defendant neither realised nor recognised the need for caution. On the contrary, he chose, putting it at its very best, to act blindly, putting his faith in Joseph. As a consequence the plaintiff sustained the loss of funds which he was entitled to expect would be employed solely in relation to the maintenance and upkeep of the Sauvé property. This engages the responsibility of the defendant.

FOR THESE REASONS, THE COURT:

MAINTAINS the plaintiff's action;

CONDEMNS the defendant to pay to the plaintiff the sum of $68,549.79 with interest from the date of putting in default to wit April 21st, 1994 together with the additional indemnity provided for in Article 1619 of the Civil Code.

The whole with costs.

LEGAL TERMS

In your reading, you came across the following terms. Be sure that you can explain each, to ensure your understanding of the material you have been reading. If you are uncertain as to the meaning of any term, review the material in the chapter for clarification. If necessary, consult a dictionary for further information or discuss the term(s) with your instructor.

Mandator	Mandatary	Third person
Express acceptance	Tacit acceptance	Ratification
Onerous title	Gratuitous title	Specific mandate
General mandate	Power of attorney	Double mandate
Apparent mandate	Nullity	Exceeding the mandate

REVIEW QUESTIONS

1. In the contract of mandate, to what degree does the mandator retain the power to approve the decisions taken by the mandatary in the performance of the mandate?

2. When a mandatary expressly accepts a mandate, must this acceptance be evidenced in a written document? Explain your answer.

3. In what specific situations could a mandatary be held personally liable to the third person who is not satisfied with the item that he purchased from the mandatary?

4. You meet a person in the parking lot of a large department store. He is wearing a store name-tag and tells you that he is selling store inventory at a special low price from the trunk of his car. You buy a brand new camera from him for $35. The next morning you change your mind and return to the store for an exchange. The store refuses. Can you argue apparent mandate? Explain your answer.

5. How could performing a double mandate, even with the consent of both mandators, be potentially dangerous for the mandatary? Explain your answer.

6. If you are required to conceal the name of your mandator from the third person with whom you are dealing, how can you protect yourself from being sued personally by said third person?

Chapter 6

FORMS OF BUSINESS OWNERSHIP

OBJECTIVES

This chapter was prepared to enable you to achieve the following objectives:

1. To understand that there are various legal forms that can be used for the ownership of a business.
2. To become familiar with the two principal personal forms of business ownership, the sole proprietorship and the partnership.
3. To distinguish between the general commercial partnership and the limited partnership.
4. To describe why the development of an objective form of business ownership was necessary and to explain its early development.
5. To understand the concept of corporate legal personality and the characteristics of the corporation.
6. To develop an understanding of the legal procedure used to start a business using any of the forms of ownership discussed.

INTRODUCTION
Section 6.1

In Article 1525 of the *Civil Code*, we find the following explanation:

> *The carrying on by one or more persons of an organized economic activity, whether or not it is commercial in nature, consisting of producing, administering or alienating property, or providing a service, constitutes the carrying on of an enterprise.*

The operation of a business involves the transacting of a series of acts of commerce by a merchant, generally with the object of earning a profit. By contrast, an individual who enters into a single isolated (or occasional) transaction which is not part of a continuing series would not be a merchant, and the transaction would merely be a private undertaking, for it would not be part of "an organized economic activity."

Before entering into an analysis of specific business transactions (e.g., sale, lease, etc.), we shall explore the general nature of doing business. An enterprise or business operation may be organized under one of several different ownership structures or forms.

People considering opening a business have to decide which of the various forms best suits their objectives. In selecting a particular form of business ownership, the factors that must be evaluated include the nature of the transactions to be carried out, the funds required (and available) to begin the business, the type of work to be done, and the number of people to be involved. The forms of business ownership most frequently used in Canada include:

a) Sole proprietorship

b) Partnership

c) Corporation

The authority to govern, regulate and make laws on business and commercial transactions is found in our Constitution. Section 92 (13) of the *Constitution Act, 1867* gives provinces the right to make laws about "Property and Civil Rights in the Province." From this flows the right of the provincial government to regulate sole proprietorships and partnerships, which are both "personal" forms of business ownership.

The word "personal" is used here because the law considers that the business is owned and operated by a person who undertakes the risks and keeps the profits "personally"—either alone or with others.

There have been, from time to time, areas of conflict between the federal and provincial governments with respect to which of them has the authority to regulate certain types of commercial activity. Examples are the operation of airports, cable radio and television, labour legislation, and off-shore oil reserve exploitation.

Generally, such conflicts are submitted to the *Supreme Court of Canada*. In its deliberations, the Court interprets the principles of the *Constitution Act*, carefully seeking the intention of the founders of our country, and making every effort to be faithful to these intentions.

Sometimes, it is not necessary to take the matter to the Court, as the federal and provincial governments are able to resolve the conflict by agreement.

THE SOLE PROPRIETORSHIP
Section 6.2

6.2.1 Description

A sole proprietorship is the most common form for business start-ups. By definition it encompasses any and all enterprise undertaken by one single individual, who remains the sole owner and retains full authority to manage the administration of the enterprise. Entrepreneurs, select this form of business ownership when they have very limited capital or choose to maintain only a part-time participation in the enterprise, and do not wish to take on partners or invest capital for incorporation.

Sole proprietorship is the most common form of business ownership for the simple reason that it is the least complex form. A person can begin the operation of an enterprise using his or her own personal name (not a business name), in Québec without any formalities whatever. There may, however, be requirements for a business to obtain a licence from the municipal authorities.

A married person has the same right as anyone else to open a business as a sole proprietor. However, the legal right of each consort (spouse) to dispose of property he or she owns personally may be restricted by the provisions governing their marriage regime.

A minor engaged in any type of trade or business is considered to be of full age as regards any transaction related to that business. Also, minors cannot use the defence of lesion (claiming they were unfairly taken advantage of because of their age) to escape their responsibilities under contracts entered for the purpose of their business.

6.2.2 Characteristics

6.2.2.1 Start-Up (Registration)

Any person who carries on business is required to register this fact with the Québec government authorities. A special form provided for this purpose is filed along with the required fees. An annual update is also required and a fee paid each year.

An example of a Sole Proprietor registration form is found in Appendix "6-D" at the end of this chapter.

The only exception to this requirement is the person who is using only his or her own personal name as the name of the business. In this case, the person is not required to register but may do so voluntarily.

A business owner who wishes to use some other name to operate the business is therefore required by law to register a declaration with the *Registraire des entreprise*, stating the owner's own name and address and the name and type of business he or she plans to open. The requirement for this declaration and the information it must contain is set out in detail in the *Act Respecting the Legal Publicity of Enterprises,* found in *Appendix "6-A"* at the end of this chapter. This registration of the business's name gives the owner permanent rights to its use and prevents anyone else from using the same name.

Once registered, Declarations of Sole Proprietorship are kept in a specific office, which is open to the public, and also made available online. Any person, government agency or other business can use these declarations to find out who is behind any enterprise name. This is especially useful for creditors who may make a more informed decision about extending credit to a business they have not previously dealt with.

> ?... *Did you know...*
> *All pertinent information for starting-up a business and online registration to declare a business is available at:*
>
> - *Provincial: Registraire des entreprise www.registreentreprises.gouv.qc.ca*
> - *Federal : Industry Canada www.corporationscanada.ic.gc.ca*

6.2.2.2 Ownership

(i) The Owner

A sole proprietor is one individual who maintains complete, one hundred per cent, financial control and interest over the enterprise. If an agreement should be made with another person to share the ownership, the legal form changes to partnership and exposes both to different rules and regulations.

(ii) Transfer of Ownership

Transfer of ownership is not possible. Because the enterprise and the sole proprietor are considered to be one in the eyes of the law, ownership of the enterprise can not be passed on to another person. For instance, if a sole proprietor, who is running a business, dies and an heir wishes to continue the activity, they must either inherit the assets or buy them from the estate and then register a new business ownership in their name.

6.2.2.3 Liability for Debts

The sole proprietorship is a "personal" form of business ownership. This means that the sole proprietor has unlimited and personal liability for the debts of the business. Any debts related to the operation of the business are considered to be the personal debts of the business owner. Therefore, all the property owned by the sole proprietor may be seized and sold, if need arises, in order to pay the debts of the business.

Accordingly, if the business becomes bankrupt, so does an owner whose personal assets are not sufficient to pay off the business debts. The business and the owner are, in law, one and the same.

The debt incurred for the business, by the owner, remains even upon his or her death. All debts must be paid out of the owner's estate before a division of assets can take place amongst surviving heirs.

6.2.2.4 Management

The sole proprietor is the one and only person who manages the business. He or she makes all the decisions about every aspect of the business operation and does not have to consult anyone or obtain permission or agreement for any of the business activities.

6.2.2.5 Profits

Since the sole proprietor takes all the risks and is responsible for all the debts, it is reasonable that he or she is the owner of any profits earned. These profits, considered as personal income of the business owner, are taxed along with any other income the person may have.

6.2.2.6 Termination

A sole proprietorship is terminated when the business owner dies or wishes to cease doing business. The person remains responsible for any debts undertaken while carrying on the business. A declaration should be registered stating that the person is no longer using the business name, in order to avoid responsibility for any debts that may be incurred by anyone using the name of the business after it has been closed.

6.2.3 Advantages and Disadvantages

Many aspects of sole proprietorship can be summed up into advantages and disadvantages.

6.2.3.1 Advantages

- Simple registration—easily done by owner.
- Inexpensive to start—costs under $50 to register.
- All profits belong to the owner.
- All decisions made by the owner.
- Flexibility.
- Simple to dissolve.
- Enjoyment and challenge of personal involvement.
- Operations and results can be kept secret.

6.2.3.2 Disadvantages

- Owner is personally liable for all debts—unlimited liability.
- Difficult to obtain outside financing (e.g., capital for growth).
- Depends only on skills of owner—may be too specialized.

- Lack of continuity.
- No legal distinction between owner and business.
- Restrictions on hiring members of owner's family including spouse and children under 19, under income tax regulations.
- May be difficult to sell "good will" if reputation depends very heavily on the personality of the owner.
- All profits are considered to be earned by the sole proprietor personally and are taxed at full personal income tax rates.

> ***"Good will"*** *- refers to the value of the reputation, credibility and reliability that a business has built up over a period of time. It is an intangible factor, and thus it is often very difficult to assign a financial value to it.*

THE PARTNERSHIP
Section 6.3

6.3.1 Description

When two or more people agree to operate a business together, this agreement forms a contract between them known as the **Contract of Partnership**. Contracts of partnerships must respect certain requirements set out in the *Civil Code of Québec*, found in *Appendix "6-B"* at the end of this chapter.

Under the terms of this contract, each of the partners agrees to contribute something to their common venture, and in return they share the profits (and also the losses, if there are any) resulting from their efforts. Essentially, a partnership is similar to several sole proprietors running one business together. They each have the advantages and responsibilities of a sole proprietor.

It is normal, although not required by law, for the partners to prepare a **Partnership Agreement** in which they write down the details of their business relationship. In essence, a Partnership Agreement will function as a written contract, thereby reducing any potential future disagreements as to what the partners had decided.

An example of such an agreement is found in Appendix "6-C" at the end of this chapter.

6.3.2 Characteristics (The General Partnership)

6.3.2.1 Start-Up (Registration)

All partnerships are required to register a Partnership Declaration. This document will identify the partners, the location and type of business they intend to operate. This declaration becomes a public document and can be consulted by anyone interested in knowing who the owners are of a particular partnership business.

An example of a Partnership registration form is found in Appendix "6-E" at the end of this chapter.

The requirement for this declaration and the information it must contain is set out in detail in the *Act Respecting the Legal Publicity of Enterprises,* found in *Appendix "6-A"* at the end of this chapter.

6.3.2.2 Ownership

(i) The Owners

Ownership of the assets is determined by the partners themselves and may be included in the Partnership Agreement. The division of ownership does not, though, have to be equal amongst all existing partners. It is common for some partners to have a larger share of ownership over the other partners, for whatever reason agreed upon. For instance, three partners may agree that one of them will hold fifty per cent ownership in the assets and the other two will have twenty-five per cent each.

(ii) Transfer of Ownership

Unlike in a sole proprietorship, transfer of ownership in a partnership is possible, but within limits. The partners may agree on how to deal with each partner's share of assets depending on the circumstances, such as the death of one of the partners or if a partner wishes to cease his or her involvement in the enterprise.

6.3.2.3 Liability for Debts

The partnership is also a "personal" form of business ownership. The partners are the business and they each have unlimited, personal liability for the debts of their enterprise. In a general partnership, if the business is unable to pay its debts from the assets used for the business, the partners will be called upon to pay these from their own personal assets.

Partners are **solidarily** liable for the partnership debts. This means that any one or more of the partners may be required to pay all or part of any debt owed by the business.

The partners are permitted to agree between themselves, that one or more of the partners will not have to contribute to the debts of the partnership debts; however, this agreement cannot be used against creditors of the business. Thus, a partner may be called upon to pay the business debts and then, after payment, seek out his or her partners to collect from them the portion of the debts they had agreed to pay.

6.3.2.4 Management

The partners will agree between themselves as to how the business is to be managed. Every aspect of management may be included in the Partnership Agreement, including clauses dealing with the failure of any partner to fulfill designated responsibilities. The agreement may also include a mechanism for settling any disputes between the partners by designating an independent third party to resolve questions.

The agreement should include such matters as:

- How much time each partner will devote to the business.
- What responsibilities each partner will have, e.g., sales, production, financial management, etc.
- What happens if one of the partners becomes too ill to work in the business.

6.3.2.5 Profits

The partners may agree between themselves as to whether they will be equal partners (each receiving the same share of the profits) or unequal partners with some other arrangement regarding the sharing of profits.

There is only one arrangement not permitted by the *Civil Code* and that is one which excludes a person from any share of the profits. Such an arrangement is null. Thus, by definition, a partner *must* have some share in the profits, no matter how small.

The partner's share of the profits is considered as personal earnings and is taxed as such. It makes no difference that the money may not have been actually taken out of the business, but was re-invested in it. The mere fact that the partner is entitled to it makes it taxable income in the year it is earned.

6.3.2.6 Termination

The partnership is a relatively "fragile" form of business ownership. It does not take much to bring it to an end. It can be terminated by the agreement of the partners, by the bankruptcy of the business, or upon the accomplishment of its objective. Some partnerships may be ended by the death or bankruptcy of one of the partners.

6.3.3 Characteristics (The Limited Partnership)

A special form of Partnership is permitted for situations where some partners want to invest in the business, but they are prepared to leave the management to the other partners.

The **limited partnership** differs from general partnerships in the liability for debts and in the right to participate in the management of the business.

In a limited partnership, the **general** partners are solidarily liable for the debts to an unlimited, personal extent (just as in a general partnership). However, the **special partners** are liable for the debts only to the extent of a stipulated amount they have contributed to the partnership, and is stated in the partnership declaration. If the amount is not stated, they are solidarily liable for all debts, along with the general partners.

The special partners are not permitted to take part in the day-to-day operation and running of the business. They can meet periodically with their partners to discuss the business, but they must not take an active role in the regular management activities. This role must be left to the general partners.

See selected articles from the Civil Code (Appendix 6-B) and from the Act Respecting the Legal Publicity of Enterprises (Appendix 6-A) for the rules that apply to the partnership form of business ownership.

6.3.4 Advantages and Disadvantages

Many aspects of a partnership can be summed up into advantages and disadvantages.

6.3.4.1 Advantages

- Simple registration—easily done by the partners themselves.
- Inexpensive to start—costs under $50 to register.
- Profits shared only between the partners.
- Partners able to assist each other.
- Partners pool their talents—one has skills the other(s) lack.
- Quite flexible.
- Simple to dissolve.
- More scope for specialization among the partners.
- Enjoyment of personal involvement.
- Limited Partnership allows for some limitation of liability.

6.3.4.2 Disadvantages

- Partners are personally liable for all debts and the liability is solidary (one partner may be required to pay all debts if the other partner(s) cannot or will not).
- Potential for conflict between the partners.
- Lack of continuity.
- Difficult to transfer ownership.
- May be difficult to recover one's investment.
- Requires a written agreement if partners do not share equally or if some partners are to be excluded from carrying out some of the functions of the business.
- Partner's share of the profits taxed at full personal income tax rates.
- Restriction on hiring members of partners' families.

THE CORPORATION
Section 6.4

6.4.1 Background

We have examined the rules that apply to the personal forms of business ownership. In the sole proprietorship and partnership, there is no legal distinction between the owners and the business - they are one and the same.

The important consequence flowing from this is the unlimited personal liability that the owners have for the debts of the business. In spite of this, we find many businesses using one of these two forms of business ownership today.

In most cases, these enterprises are relatively small. The owners do not object to the personal liability because, as long as the business is small, their exposure to debt may not be great enough to "wipe them out." If the business owes $10,000 or $20,000, then even if conditions force them to close the business, they will likely be able to find the resources to pay off the debts without having to totally surrender their personal assets. However, if the debts of the business should reach $500,000 or $10 million, not many people would be prepared to take the same risk. Thus, before allowing a business to grow too large, the owners will look for some way to limit their liability for debts.

We have seen the way in which the limited partnership can be used to enable the special partners to limit their liability. But there is still the full liability on the general partners.

Business people have long faced this problem. During the development of the laws on business in the 1600s, some merchants in England petitioned the King, requesting that they be formed into a company in order to undertake exploration of the new land "Canada." The idea they had was that the business community would share the risks of exploration with them. The "Company" would outfit ships and hire crews. Other businesses would supply them with clothing, food, and equipment, and extend credit for part of the costs.

If the venture was successful and the vessel returned loaded with furs or other valuable commodities, the profits would go toward paying the creditors. If, however, the vessel sank or returned empty, everyone would lose-the owners and the creditors.

The idea seemed to find a lot of support. An early example is the Charter issued in 1670 by Charles II to a group of people who set up a company called "The Governor and Company of Adventurers Trading into Hudson's Bay." This business was very successful and has continued from that time to the present where it is known as "The Hudson's Bay Company." This is the very same firm that was incorporated in 1670. The head office was moved from England to Canada, and the fur trade on which the business had been built was recently discontinued. But the company has had an unbroken history since those early days.

6.4.2 Description

The main difference between the corporation and the other forms of business that we examined is the fact that corporations are created by the government as separate **legal persons**. Obviously a corporation does not have a tangible existence in the same sense as a human being. However, apart from those activities that are clearly impossible (e.g., marriage, adoption, etc.), a corporation may engage in any activities or undertakings that are not prohibited by the law or by the Articles of Incorporation. Therefore, a corporation may own assets, have debts, enter contracts, hire people, issue cheques, sell property, share its profits with its owners, become insolvent or bankrupt, sue in the courts, and be sued. Furthermore, a corporation may be an incorporator. With the rights bestowed on it, a corporation may even form or simply buy another corporation in whole or in part with other corporations.

Everyone recognizes that this "legal person" does not really exist—it is a product of our imagination—a fiction of the law. But it is such a useful idea that most of the countries of the world have adopted the concept into their law.

This principle, that the personality of a corporation is separate and distinct from the personality of the individual members or shareholders, has been recognized in many cases, the leading one being the English case of Salomon v. Salomon & Co. (1897, AC 22). In this case, the majority shareholder, who held first mortgage bonds from the company, was permitted to rank as the first secured creditor of the company upon its bankruptcy. The Privy Council (the highest Court in England), in its judgment, reasoned that the individual and the company must be regarded as separate legal persons and therefore owners of a corporation can even sue the company, if necessary, to protect their rights.

The important point to note about a corporation's separate legal personality is that the owners, the people who set up the corporation, are not in any way liable for the corporation's debts. If the corporation does not have the funds to pay its debts, no creditor can come to the owners and ask them pay the bills. The creditors simply have to take the loss.

It is obvious, therefore, that creditors must take great care before they extend credit to corporations. They should assure themselves that the corporation is "credit-worthy"—i.e., that it has a good reputation for paying its bills and that it appears to have sufficient assets to be able to discharge its debts. Even so, this is no guarantee, and every year we see thousands of businesses, large and small, go into bankruptcy, leaving their creditors unable to collect the money owed to them.

An all-encompassing definition of a corporation is that proposed by the American Chief Justice John Marshall in the case *Dartmouth College* v. *Woodward* (1819, 4 Wheaton (U.S.) 518) in these words:

> *"A Corporation is an artificial being, invisible, intangible, and existing only in contemplation of law. Being the mere creature of law, it possesses only those properties which the charter of its creation confers upon it, either expressly, or as incidental to its very existence. These are such as are supposed best calculated to effect the object for which it was created. Among the most important are immortality, and, if the expression may be allowed, individuality..."*

6.4.3 Characteristics

6.4.3.1 Start-Up (Application)

The start-up of a corporate form of business is the most complex and expensive of those examined thus far. A corporation does not simply come into existence because of its incorporators' wishes. In order for its legal personality to become reality, an application must prepared and be approved by the government authorities. Generally, to ensure the incorporation is efficiently completed, the services of a lawyer or notary are retained. It is this approval that actually creates the corporation, and brings it to life under the terms of the law. Several decisions and steps must be taken to obtain this authorization, some of which are discussed below.

(i) Federal or Provincial Incorporation?

One of the first decisions an entrepreneur must make is whether to incorporate under federal or provincial law. In Canada, there are eleven laws under which the corporation may be formed. The federal law is the *Canada Business Corporations Act* (CBCA). The law in this province is the *Québec Business Corporations Act* (QBCA) (*Loi sur les sociétés par actions*). A similar law provides for the incorporation of businesses in each of the other provinces.

The power of the provinces to incorporate companies arises from the provision in the *Constitution Act, 1867,* which states the province may incorporate companies "...with provincial objects." This has generally been interpreted to refer to the geographic scope of the company's activities. It should be noted, however, that merely because a federally incorporated firm operates solely within one province, this does not invalidate the terms under which that business was incorporated.

In general, the decision to incorporate under one jurisdiction rather than another is guided by the "objects" of the business. These objects concern the geographical scope of the proposed business. Briefly, if it is intended that the business will carry on its activities in two or more provinces of Canada, the objects would be considered as being federal and the owners should consider using the CBCA. If the business activities will be confined to the province of Québec and will likely remain local, then the provincial law would be preferred.

A provincially incorporated company may carry on business in other provinces; however if it wishes to open a branch in another province, it will be required to obtain and pay for a licence from each province in which it wishes to operate, subject to the exception noted below. There is a reciprocal agreement in force between Québec and Ontario under which businesses incorporated in one of these two provinces are not required to obtain a licence to operate in the other

Under the *Québec Act Respecting the Legal Publicity of Enterprises*, it is required that any business incorporated outside of Québec must, if it wants to do business in this province, register and pay a separate fee to operate in Québec.

A company created under the CBCA, on the other hand, has the capacity to carry on business in all parts of Canada. Provincial governments cannot restrict the powers of federally incorporated businesses unless such restrictions apply to all companies equally. Federal companies, however, are required to comply with all provincial laws that generally apply to all firms. For instance, they must register, obtain the necessary licences, pay all applicable taxes, file annual reports, etc. They must also collect and remit the provincial sales taxes, if any.

> *An example of a form for Federal Incorporation is found in Appendix "6-F" and Provincial Incorporation in Appendix "6-G" at the end of this chapter.*

A request for a **Federal Incorporation** requires the completion and filing of a document called the *Articles of Incorporation*. This document identifies the details of the structure of the proposed corporation as well as the persons who are the original incorporators (the ones asking for the business to be incorporated).

Articles of Incorporation may be filed by any person or persons who are:

- over 18 years of age;
- of sound mind;
- not a bankrupt.

In addition, a notice is filed stating where in Canada the registered (head) office will be located, and another stating who will be the first directors of the corporation.

These documents are submitted, with the current filing fee, to *The Director, Canada Business Corporations Act* in Ottawa. If the documents are properly filed and contain all the necessary information, the government will issue the *Certificate of Incorporation*. This certificate states the file number of the corporation in the government records and the official date on which the corporation came into existence. The application may be filed online at: www.corporationscanada.ic.gc.ca.

For a **Québec Incorporation**, the procedure does not differ much from the federal procedure. In actuality, with the coming into force of the *Québec Business Corporations Act* (QBCA) in February 2011, the Québec government substantially reformed the old *Québec Companies Act* (QCA) and brought the legislation more into line with its federal and provincial counterparts. As a result, Québec's two older systems, Letters-Patent and Part IA of the QCA, gave way to one procedure for all applications. Even companies incorporated under the old procedures are now covered by the new law and have five years to submit changes to their Articles of Incorporation so as to bring themselves into conformity with the QBCA.

The procedure under the QBCA allows any one or more persons over the age of 18 and not under protective supervision or bankrupt, to file Articles of Incorporation which set out the identification of the incorporator(s), the name and share structure of the corporation, and any limitations to be imposed on its activities. The Articles are filed, with the required fees, to the government, which issues a *Certificate of Constitution*. This certificate establishes the date on which the corporation comes into existence. The application may be filed online at: www.registreentreprises.gouv.qc.ca.

An example of a Federal Certificate of Incorporation is found in *Appendix "6-H"* at the end of this chapter.

(ii) Determine By-laws

Every corporation is required to prepare a set of internal rules, called by-laws. These rules state how the company may borrow money, issue bonds or debentures, elect directors and officers, and hold meetings of shareholders. The by-laws are proposed by the Board of Directors and approved by the shareholders. They then form the basis on which the company will carry on its business activities. Any future changes to the by-laws require shareholder approval.

(iii) Identify Principal Place of Business

A corporation must maintain, under the CBCA, a registered office within Canada. Under the QBCA, the corporation must maintain a head office within Québec. The purpose of the registered or head office is to provide a place where the important documents of the corporation are to be kept. These include:

- the Articles of Incorporation and by-laws;

- the Certificate of Incorporation;
- any unanimous shareholder agreement;
- minutes of shareholder and directors' meetings;
- the register of the corporation's securities (shares);
- the official company seal if any.

(iv) Select Name of the Corporation

Selecting the name of the corporation is another important step. The name of a corporation must respect certain rules in order to be acceptable. These include the following:

- the name must not be deceptive or misleading;
- the name must not be the same or sufficiently similar (in its written form or in its sound) to that of any other business to permit confusion to occur;
- must not invoke a relation to a government body, educational institution, professional association (e.g. Quebec Bar Association) and non-profit organizations;
- the last word of the corporate name must be any one of the following: Corporation or Corp., Incorporated or Inc., Limited or Ltd./Ltée., or Société par actions de régime fédéral (SARF);
- under the CBCA, the name may be either French, English or a combination of both, which then must use Inc.;
- under the QBCA the name must be in French, and may be accompanied by versions in any other language(s); it should be noted that for a company incorporated in any other jurisdiction, it must have a name in French in order to register in Québec.

The government maintains a computerized listing of all companies incorporated in Canada called NUANS. When a new application is received, this listing is searched to ensure the proposed name does not conflict with any existing corporate name. A verification with the Québec Enterprise Registrar may also be necessary since the two systems are separate entities and do not share information.

A company may also be incorporated using a number as its name. It is not unusual to find a company name such as 7392468 Canada Inc.

The word (Canada), in brackets, may be included in the corporate name only if the business is a subsidiary of a firm with the same name incorporated under the laws of a foreign country. However, there is no restriction on the use of "Canada" (without the brackets), "of Canada," or "Canadian," as long as there is no implication that the federal government is involved in the business.

Selected sections from the QBCA are reproduced in Appendix "6-I" and selected sections from the CBCA are reproduced in Appendix "6-J" at the end of this chapter.

6.4.3.2 Ownership

(i) The Owners – Common vs. Preferred Shares

Ownership in a corporation results from the purchase, by the investors, of **shares**, the term used for the small units into which the ownership is divided. These shares, also referred to as *securities*, form the basis of the financial or capital structure of the company. They are sold by the company to investors in order to raise funds for working capital and special projects, such as expansion, acquisitions and replacement of equipment.

The law requires that there must be at least one "class", or group, of common shares. If the incorporators wish, there may also be one or more "classes" of preferred shares.

The ownership of a corporation rests in the hands of the **common shareholders**. All matters presented for the approval of shareholders are voted on by the holders of the common shares on the basis of one share - one vote. Most issues require only a simple majority of votes to be approved. Certain matters, however, such as amalgamation, amendment of the articles of incorporation or dissolution of the corporation require, by law, the approval of at least two-thirds (2/3) of the common shareholders.

The common shareholders of the company share in the profits of the business when a dividend is declared by the Board of Directors. These dividends may be expressed in terms of a monetary unit (dollars and cents) per common share, or may take the form of a stock dividend by which each shareholder receives additional common shares (or fractions) for each share held.

There is no obligation for dividends to be declared. The Board of Directors has the responsibility to decide how much, if any, of the firm's profits will be paid out as dividends and how much will remain in the company as retained earnings. Retention of profits may result in a greater profit in following years or an increase in the shareholders' equity in the corporation over time. If the Board of Directors should not declare a dividend for one or even many years, despite substantial profits, the common shareholders have no basis for legal action against the Board. Their only recourse, at the next annual general meeting, is to replace the current board members with others who may have a more liberal dividend policy.

The common shareholders further participate when the company is liquidated, sharing rateably (i.e. in proportion to the number of shares they own), in the assets remaining after all debts and preferred shares have been paid.

Common shares are referred to as "no-par value." Use of the term par value has grown through tradition but bears no relation to the real value of shares. The real value (book value) of a company's shares is arrived at by establishing the equity of the shareholders in the firm and dividing this by the number of outstanding common shares. No-par value indicates that no price has been set by the company as the value of the share. The federal law requires all companies to have only no-par value shares.

The price of a company's shares trading on the stock exchange may be different from the book value of the shares, as stock exchange prices reflect the supply and demand for the shares in the market place.

It is important to note that corporate dividends are taxed twice. The company pays income tax as it makes profits each year. When the Board of Directors pays out some or all of these profits to the shareholders in the form of dividends, this money becomes "income" to the shareholders who are required to pay tax on it again. A compensating feature, however, is that shareholders may deduct from their *tax payable* a percentage of all dividends received in the year.

Preferred shares offer ownership in the corporation, but in a limited form. When a corporation needs new capital funds, a two-sided problem may occur. Firstly, the common shareholders may not wish to reduce their voting control in the firm that would result from issuing more common shares. Secondly, those who are prepared to invest their money in the company may want to have a greater security for their investment than is provided by common shares. A solution to this problem that is frequently used is for the corporation to issue what are known as preferred shares.

The term "preferred" indicates that these shares provide for special rights and priorities as well as restrictions that do not apply to the common shares. For example, preferred shareholders will be guaranteed a certain dividend on their investment (e.g., 10 percent), which will be paid from the company's profits (when profits are made) before *any* dividends are paid to the common shareholders. Preferred shares always carry a stated or par value. In addition, preferred share dividends may be cumulative, in that if the company has an unprofitable year resulting in no dividends being paid, the dividend accumulates and is paid along with the next year's dividend, before the common shares receive their dividends. Preferred shares may also be "participating," i.e., have the right to share in the remaining profits of the company to some predetermined level, after the guaranteed dividend has been paid to them and a dividend has been declared to the common shareholders.

Another "preference" attached to these shares is the right for preferred shareholders to have their investment in the company repaid (at the par value of the shares) before any payment to common shareholders at the time of the liquidation of the corporation.

Preferred shares may also be "redeemable." This enables the company to repay the shareholders the money they have invested (at the par value of the shares) and retire the shares and the equity they represent in the firm. The result of this is to improve the equity position of the common shareholders, who then do not have to share their ownership of the firm with as many people.

In order to provide additional incentives for investors to purchase preferred shares, the company may state that at some future date, the preferred shares may be "converted" into common shares. Thus, if the price of the common shares rises, the preferred shareholders may find it to their advantage to avail themselves of this "convertibility." The advantage to the company is that it no longer is bound to pay the guaranteed dividend each year to the preferred shareholders.

The main restriction found in preferred shares is that they do not carry the right to vote at meetings of shareholders. It is the common shareholders who can make decisions regarding the operations of the company and they are the ones who elect the members of the Board of Directors. As long as the company has paid the guaranteed preferred share dividends, the preferred shareholders have received the return they are entitled to, and therefore have no right to take part in the decision-making process. Most preferred shares, however, provide that if the company does not earn sufficient profit to pay the guaranteed dividend for two successive years the preferred shareholders then obtain the right to vote. As soon as their dividend is paid they once again become non-voting shares, until there is another default.

~~~~~~~~~~~~

NOTE: Re Use of the Terms "Common"
and "Preferred" for Shares.

Under section 24 of the *Canada Business Corporations Act* and section 44 of the *Québec Business Corporations Act,* incorporated companies no longer use the
~~~~~~~~~~~~

terms Common Shares or Preferred Shares. In place of these, all shares are designated as Class "A" shares, Class "B" shares, etc. All federal and Québec corporations are required to have one class of shares entitling their holders to vote at all meetings of shareholders.

(ii) Transfer of Ownership

Transfer of ownership in a corporation is a simpler matter than under any other business form. The ownership of a sole proprietorship or partnership is a personal matter. Thus, if a sole proprietor or a partner decides to cease his or her activity, the existence of the enterprise comes to an end.

In a corporation, however, the situation is quite different. The ownership is not a personal matter, rather it is objective. The shareholder does not own machinery or buildings or trucks. The shareholder owns only units or shares, and these can be quite easily transferred to one or more other persons. The *evidence of ownership* in a corporation is the **share certificate**. Today, when shares in a company are sold by the owner, the broker simply transfers the certificates to the purchaser for the agreed upon payment. This transfer of all (or part) of a person's shares, which has become even easier and faster through internet trading, does not in any way affect the legal existence of the company, since it exists in law as a separate entity. Thus, although many shares of a company may change hands every day, the company continues to operate and carry on its business in the usual way. An example of a share certificate is found in *Appendix "6-K"* at the end of this chapter.

> ? *...Before you continue...*
> *Consider the legal effects that each of the following methods of raising capital will have on the shareholders of a corporation.*

This ease of transferring ownership also makes it possible to **raise capital** easier than the other forms of business. Corporations are created with an unlimited number of common, or Class A shares. Therefore, any time the Board of Directors wish to do so, they may raise additional capital by selling shares from the corporation's treasury. This, of course, may dilute the holdings of the existing shareholders and thus the decision to bring in more funds in this way must be made carefully, after serious consideration of the available alternatives.

The company may also raise new funds through the issue of preferred shares. The drawback to this method for the common shareholders is that they will have to wait to receive dividends until after the preferred shareholders have been paid the dividends that were guaranteed to them.

Any company proposing to sell securities (shares or bonds) to the public must file a **prospectus** with the appropriate securities regulatory commission in the province concerned and in federally (SEDAR). This prospectus sets out in detail the nature of the business activities; the financial results in recent years; the names of the major shareholders, directors and officers; special agreements or contracts in which the company is involved; lawsuits by or against the firm that have not yet been settled; and other material information. This prospectus is intended to provide a full disclosure of the business so that prospective investors may make fully informed decisions.

If the shareholders do not wish the company to raise capital through the sale of common or preferred shares, the firm may, like any other person, obtain funds by borrowing from financial institutions or private lenders, or by the sale of bonds or debentures.

When a corporation wishes to borrow large sums of money to be repaid at a set rate of interest over a long period of time, the lenders will generally insist upon having better security than ordinary creditors. This security will give the lenders a better chance of getting their money back and/or taking over the management of the company, in the event of the company's inability to meet its obligations. In order to provide such security, the firm may issue bonds or debentures. A **debenture** is a guarantee to repay, giving the creditor a preferred right to collect his or her debt. Note that the preferred right is based only on the general credit of the corporation. A **bond** provides greater security to the creditor because it usually provides for specific security such as a pledge or mortgage on all or part of the company's assets. The rights of the creditors can be found in the document called a *Trust Indenture* or *Trust Deed* for which the detailed requirements are set out in the law.

6.4.3.3 Liability for Debts

Perhaps the most important feature of incorporation is the limitation it provides for the shareholders' liability for company debts. A person who invests money in the shares of a corporation is protected against the loss of any further funds by this feature. In the event that the company should incur debts that it cannot pay, or even become bankrupt, no shareholder can be called upon to bear any portion of these debts. There exists a shielding or **corporate veil** between the investor and the corporation. This limitation of liability encourages individuals to invest their money in business corporations, secure in the knowledge that their maximum possible loss is the amount they have already paid as their investment in the purchase of shares.

It should be carefully noted that the limitation of liability applies to the shareholders, not to the corporation. The corporation remains fully liable for all its debts, without limit.

Under certain circumstances, though, this protection afforded to the shareholders may be mitigated due to their actions, which then allows creditors to pursue the shareholders personally. Four possible actions are worth noting.

First, quite often shareholders make promises to contribute capital or other assets to the corporation in the future. The reasons for such a promise will vary, but usually it is upon start-up or when seeking financing and the shareholders want to demonstrate a commitment to the corporation. Should a shareholder fail to fulfil this promise, the corporation or creditors on behalf of the corporation may hold the shareholder personally liable and pursue them for their promised contribution.

Second, the shareholder may also be held personally liable if they have participated in fraud against the corporation. Any interested party, such as a creditor or another shareholder, may ask a court to hold a shareholder, who through deception has illegally profited from the corporation, personally liable for the amount claimed along with possible damages suffered. A common example of this is when shareholders, who are running a small business, use company funds for their own personal benefit or misappropriate property belonging to the corporation.

Third, shareholders may start-up or use a corporation to avoid responsibility and commit fraud towards a third person, such as a creditor, or to break the law. For example, the owner of a corporation who undertakes telemarketing fraud against senior citizens or the owner of a company that is heading into bankruptcy and decides to maximize credit with suppliers with the intention of never paying them back. In both cases, the managing shareholder cannot hide behind the corporate veil arguing it was the corporation and not he who committed the crime or fraud. In both cases, creditors can ask a court for the corporate veil to be lifted and allow them to hold the shareholder personally liable.

Fourth, a shareholder may even be held personally liable for commitments he undertook before the corporation was constituted and received its Certificate of Incorporation. For example, he signs a lease for office space or orders necessary supplies for the start-up. The shareholder is personally liable for the obligations incurred on behalf of the company before it was constituted. To avoid this responsibility, the corporation would have to pass a motion ratifying these actions on its behalf and declare it would undertake the obligations in place of the shareholder. This, though, may not free the shareholder if the corporation fails to fulfill the obligations.

6.4.3.4 Management

The owners of the common shares in a corporation, referred as shareholders, are the persons who own the corporation.

Shareholders do not, under Federal or Quebec law, automatically acquire the power to manage the affairs of the corporation. In fact, shareholders are granted the express power to elect the Directors of the Corporation and it is the Directors who act as mandataries of, and manage, the affairs of the corporation. In order for the shareholders to acquire the power to manage the corporation, its shareholders must restrict the powers of the Directors.

Both federal and provincial laws require that the common shareholders of every corporation meet periodically. Under both federal and Québec law, the first general meetings of shareholders must be held within eighteen months after the Articles of Incorporation have been approved and subsequent general meetings of shareholders must be held at least once each 15 months. The law further requires that notices of shareholders' meetings be sent to each shareholder well in advance of the time when the meeting is to be held.

(i) The Board of Directors

In a small company with only a few shareholders, the Board of Directors may be composed of only these few persons who are also shareholders of the company. It is also possible for a Québec incorporated company, having only one shareholder, to not elect a Board of Directors at all. On the other hand, in a corporation with hundreds or even thousands of shareholders, it is not uncommon to have ten or twenty people elected to hold office on the Board of Directors.

Directors must be human beings (natural persons) of full age, apt (not under protective supervision), not bankrupt or prohibited by a court from holding such a position. It is important to note that decisions or contracts made by a director, who fails to meet these requirements, does not automatically nullify these acts.

The *CBCA and QBCA* state that directors of companies incorporated under either of these *Acts* are not required to hold shares of the corporation, and there may be any number of directors. However, if it is intended that the shares of an incorporated company be distributed to the public generally, there must be at least three directors, two of whom are neither officers nor employees of the corporation.

The federal law also provides that at least 25% percent of the directors of a corporation must be resident Canadians.

(ii) Responsibility of Directors

Section 122 of the *Canadian Business Corporations Act* states:

> Sec. 122. Duty of care of directors and officers.
>
> (1) Every director and officer of a corporation in exercising their powers and discharging their duties shall
>
> (a) act honestly and in good faith with a view to the best interests of the corporation; and
>
> (b) exercise the care, diligence and skill that a reasonably prudent person would exercise in comparable circumstances.

Section 119 of the QBCA and Art. 322 of the Civil Code impose a similar responsibility, calling upon directors to act with prudence, diligence, honesty and loyalty. These laws establish the general standards for the responsibility of directors. Failing to meet these standards, a director may be held personally liable under federal and provincial law:

a) for mixing his personal property with that of the company or benefiting personally from use of company property without permission;

b) for failure to disclose any conflict of interest which he may have;

c) for failure to disclose personal acquisition of corporation property or contracts entered into with the corporation;

d) for up to six months of unpaid wages to employees of the corporation;

e) for payment of any dividend which would render the corporation insolvent or impair the capital of the corporation;

f) for the difference, if they have issued shares for a consideration other than money, between the consideration received and the fair market value of the shares.

Except as expressly set out in these Acts, as a general rule, a director cannot be held responsible for losses sustained by the corporation. "Bad business judgment" that might place the corporation in a difficult financial situation cannot be the basis of an action for personal liability against a director, as long as the director has acted in good faith and not fraudulently or negligently.

(iii) Operation of the Corporation

In the operation of the corporation, a distinction must be drawn between policy-making and the implementation of that policy. The Board of Directors establishes what the policy of the company will be—e.g., what products to manufacture, when and where to build a new plant, whether to acquire, or merge with another company. It is then up to the officers of the corporation to carry out this policy. Thus, once the Board of Directors has made its decisions, the Chief Executive Officer (President) and other officers have the responsibility to implement this policy in the most effective way.

Officers are appointed by the Board of Directors and only natural persons can act as officers. The officers do this job of policy implementation by hiring supervisory staff (mid-management level) and employees. The instructions of the officers (e.g., Vice-President, Production) are transmitted to the supervisors or forepersons of the various departments in the plant, and these managers instruct the employees which machines to operate and what products to produce on a certain day.

Like the Board of Directors, officers are not personally liable for poor business decisions, but may be held personally liable for certain acts, such as failure to disclose any conflict of interest and fraud against the corporation.

(iv) Unanimous Shareholders' Agreement

The law also permits shareholders to take a more active role in the management of a corporation through a **Unanimous Shareholders' Agreement**. This agreement enables the shareholders to restrict the powers of the directors. This agreement may also contain many other provisions that the shareholders consider important in organizing the manner in which the corporation will be managed and to protect the rights of shareholders.

It should be noted that if shareholders take over certain management rights through a Unanimous Shareholder Agreement, they will then be held accountable to the same legal standards as the Board of Directors and could be pursued personally for failing to meet these standards.. For instance, if shareholders take over the right to issue dividends and subsequently issue dividends in violation of the law rendering the corporation insolvent, they then become personally liable to restore these amounts to the corporation.

6.4.3.5 Profits

In earlier discussion, it was pointed out that the profits earned by the corporation can be divided amongst those who hold the shares and, in this way, the shareholders obtain a return on the capital they have invested. This return is called a dividend.

It is important to note that profits earned by the company actually belong to the corporation, and the corporation is free to choose whether it will issue dividends to its shareholders. The exception to this rule is the responsibility that a company has towards preferred shareholders, who have priority over all other shareholders with respect to receiving dividends and who might also gain a right to vote should a dividend not be declared for a two year period. The decision to issue dividends is the responsibility of the Board of Directors.

6.4.3.6 Termination

The life of a company is perpetual. It continues its existence notwithstanding the death of some or even all of the shareholders. The shares are an asset in the same way as a car, jewelry or other possessions and pass on to the heirs of a deceased shareholder without an effect on the corporation. The company will exist forever, unless the shareholders decide to end its existence by surrendering its charter. Its existence may also be terminated by bankruptcy or by order of a court for violation of a provision of law.

6.4.4 Advantages and Disadvantages

Many aspects of corporations can be summed up as follows:

6.4.4.1 Advantages

- Created as a separate legal entity (a fiction of the law).
- Limitation on the liability of the owners (shareholders) for the debts of the business—no personal liability.
- Easier to attract professional managers.
- Easier to obtain outside financial support.
- Long life—does not depend on life or intention of shareholders.
- Ease of transfer of ownership (shares).
- May be incorporated under federal or provincial law.

6.4.4.2 Disadvantages

- More complex form and financial structure—usually requires lawyers and/or other professional assistance.
- Expensive to start.
- Must observe government reporting requirements.
- Lack of shareholder interest and participation in day-to-day matters.
- Double taxation.
- Difficult to keep operations and results secret.

APPENDIX "6-A"
SELECTED SECTIONS FROM
An Act Respecting the Legal Publicity of Enterprises

Chapter I
Enterprise Registrar

3. The registrar is responsible, among other things, for

(1) keeping and preserving the register described in Chapter II, receiving documents to be deposited in the register and making the register accessible to the public;

(2) registering natural persons who operate a sole proprietorship, partnerships, legal persons and groups of persons; and

(3) conferring legal existence on legal persons and recording their legal existence in the cases provided for by law, and drawing up certificates recognizing amendments to their constituting instrument.

Chapter II
Enterprise Register

12. The registrar keeps the enterprise register.

13. The register comprises all the information recorded and documents deposited in it, and includes, for each registrant and former registrant, an index of documents, a statement of information and an index of names.

Chapter III
Name

17. A registrant may not declare or use in Québec a name

(1) that is not in conformity with the Charter of the French language (chapter C-11);

(2) that includes an expression which the law reserves for another person or prohibits the registrant from using;

(3) that includes an expression that evokes an immoral, obscene or scandalous notion;

(4) that incorrectly states the registrant's juridical form or fails to state its juridical form when required by law, in view of the standards for the composition of names determined by regulation of the Government;

(5) that falsely suggests that the registrant is a non-profit group;

(6) that falsely suggests that the registrant is, or is related to, a public authority mentioned in the regulation of the Government;

(7) that falsely suggests that the registrant is related to another person, partnership or group of persons, in the cases and in view of the criteria determined by regulation of the Government;

(8) that is confusingly similar to a name used in Québec by another person, partnership or group of persons, in view of the criteria determined by regulation of the Government; or

(9) that is misleading in any other manner.

A registrant whose name is in a language other than French must declare the French version of that name used by the registrant in Québec in carrying on an activity, which includes the operation of an enterprise, or for the purpose of the possession of an immovable real right, other than a prior claim or hypothec.

The second paragraph does not apply to a natural person registered under a name comprising only his or her surname and given name.

18. For the purposes of this Act, "registrant" means any person or group of persons registered voluntarily or any person or partnership required to be registered.

20. The registrar may request that a registrant replace or change a name declared by the registrant if it is contrary to any of subparagraphs 1 to 6 of the first paragraph of section 17 or the second paragraph of that section.

If the registrant fails to comply with the request within 60 days, the registrar may, as applicable,

(1) cancel the registrant's registration, if the

name concerned is the registrant's name; or

(2) delete the name from the register, if the name concerned is another name declared by the registrant under subparagraph 2 of the first paragraph of section 33.

The registrar records in the register that the name has been refused and informs the registrant.

All information relating to a refused name appearing in a declaration is deemed unwritten.

Chapter IV
Registration, Updating of Information and Cancellation of Registration

21. The following are required to be registered:

(1) natural persons who operate a sole proprietorship, whether or not a commercial enterprise, in Québec under a name that does not include their surname and given name;

(2) general or limited partnerships constituted in Québec;

(3) partnerships not constituted in Québec if they carry on an activity in Québec, which includes the operation of an enterprise, or possess an immovable real right, other than a prior claim or hypothec, in Québec;

(4) legal persons established for a private interest and constituted in Québec;

(5) legal persons established for a private interest not constituted in Québec, or legal persons constituted in Québec and continued under the laws of a jurisdiction other than Québec, if they are domiciled in Québec, carry on an activity in Québec, which includes the operation of an enterprise, or possess an immovable real right, other than a prior claim or hypothec, in Québec;

(6) legal persons established for a private interest described in subparagraph 4 or 5 and resulting from an amalgamation other than a short-form amalgamation within the meaning of the Business Corporations Act (chapter S-31.1); and

(7) mixed enterprise companies established under the Act respecting mixed enterprise companies in the municipal sector (chapter S-25.01).

Despite subparagraph 1 of the first paragraph, natural persons who operate a tobacco retail outlet, within the meaning of the Tobacco Act (chapter T-0.01), under a name that includes their surname and given name are also required to be registered.

22. A natural person or a group of persons not required to be registered may request registration. They are registrants from the time they are registered until their registration is cancelled.

23. Despite subparagraph 1 of the first paragraph of section 21, natural persons are not required to be registered solely because they use a pseudonym in the pursuit of an artistic, literary or other cultural activity.

25. For the purposes of section 21, a person or partnership who has an address in Québec or, either directly or through a representative acting under a general mandate, has an establishment, a post office box or the use of a telephone line in Québec or performs any act for profit in Québec is presumed to be carrying on an activity or operating an enterprise in Québec.

26. A registrant who is neither domiciled nor has an establishment in Québec must designate an attorney residing in Québec, unless exempted from that rcquirement by regulation of the Minister.

31. For the purposes of this Act, "legal person constituted in Québec" means a legal person constituted under the laws of Québec and includes, except for the purposes of the second paragraph of section 36, a legal person constituted under the laws of a jurisdiction other than Québec that is continued under the laws of Québec.

32. The registration declaration, along with the fee set out in this Act, must be filed with the registrar not later than 60 days after the date on which registration becomes compulsory.

33. Unless an exemption established by regulation of the Minister applies, the registration declaration must state

(1) the registrant's name and, if the registrant was previously registered, the registrant's

Québec business number;

(2) any other name used by the registrant in Québec and by which the registrant is identified, either in carrying on an activity, which includes the operation of an enterprise, or for the purpose of the possession of an immovable real right, other than a prior claim or hypothec, if applicable;

(3) the registrant's juridical form; and

(4) the registrant's domicile.

The declaration must also state, if applicable,

(7) in order of importance, the registrant's two main activities and the code corresponding to each of them according to the classification system determined by regulation of the Minister;

(8) the addresses of the registrant's establishments in Québec, specifying which is the principal establishment, the name designating them and the two main activities carried on in the establishments and the code corresponding to each of them according to the classification system determined by regulation of the Minister;

(10) the number of employees of the registrant whose workplace is in Québec, based on the brackets determined by the Minister;

34. The registration declaration of a partnership must also contain, if applicable,

(1) the name and domicile of each partner, a statement that no other person is a member of the partnership and, in the case of a limited partnership, the name and domicile of each general partner and the names and domiciles of the three greatest contributors to the partnership among the special partners;

(2) the object pursued by the partnership;

(3) if the partnership is a limited liability partnership or is not constituted in Québec, a statement that the liability of some or all of the partners is limited; and

(4) in the case of a general partnership, the date on which it becomes or ceases to be a limited liability partnership.

35. The registration declaration of a legal person must also contain, if applicable,

(5) the names and domiciles of the three shareholders controlling the greatest number of votes, in order of importance, and identify the shareholder holding an absolute majority; and

36. The registrar must refuse to register a registrant

(1) if the registrant's name is contrary to any of subparagraphs 1 to 6 of the first paragraph of section 17 or the second paragraph of that section;

(2) if the registrant's registration declaration is incomplete or inaccurate, or is contrary to section 68 or the requirements determined by the Minister under any of sections 109, 112 or 114.

The registrar must also refuse to register a registrant who is already registered or whose registration is cancelled if the cancellation may be revoked under subdivision 3 of Division III.

The registrar informs the registrant of the reasons for the refusal.

37. The registrar registers a registrant by assigning a Québec business number to the registrant and recording in the register the date of registration and the information concerning the registrant.

39. Registrants are responsible for verifying the legality and accuracy of the declarations filed with the registrar and the documents transferred to the registrar under an agreement entered into under section 117 or 118.

45. Once a year, during the period determined by regulation of the Minister, a registrant must file an updating declaration stating that the information required by sections 33 to 35 to be contained in the register concerning the registrant is accurate or, as applicable, stating what changes should be made.

This obligation begins the year following the year in which the registrant is first registered.

The declaration of a registrant, other than a registrant described in section 46, must be filed with the annual registration fee set out in this Act.

54. The registration of a registrant is cancelled on the filing of a cancellation declaration in the cases provided for in this subdivision.

56. Not later than six months after the death of the registrant, the liquidator of the succession must file a cancellation declaration, unless the activity requiring registration is continued for the benefit of the succession.

57. If a legal person constituted in Québec is a bankrupt within the meaning of the Bankruptcy and Insolvency Act (R.S.C. 1985, c. B-3), the trustee in bankruptcy must file a cancellation declaration after being discharged by the court on completion of the administration of the legal person's estate.

68. A declaration must be signed by the registrant or the registrant's representative.

It is admissible once all fees, charges and penalties required under this Act have been paid.

Chapter VI
Publicity

98. The following information relating to a registrant may be set up against third persons from the time it is recorded in the statement of information and is proof of its content for the benefit of third persons in good faith:

(1) the registrant's name and, if the registrant was previously registered, the registrant's Québec business number;

(2) any other name used by the registrant for identification in Québec;

(3) the registrant's juridical form and the statute under which the registrant was constituted;

(4) the registrant's domicile;

(5) the domicile elected by the registrant and the name of the person mandated by the registrant to receive documents for the purposes of this Act;

(6) the names and domiciles of the directors and the positions they hold or, if all powers have been withdrawn from the board of directors by a unanimous shareholder agreement entered into in accordance with the laws of Québec or a Canadian jurisdiction other than Québec, the names and domiciles of the shareholders or third persons having assumed those powers;

(7) the date of entry into office and, if applicable, the date of cessation of office of the persons referred to in subparagraphs 6 and 10;

(8) the names and domiciles of the president, the secretary and the chief executive officer, if they are not members of the board of directors, and the positions they hold;

(9) the name and address of the registrant's attorney;

(10) the name, address and capacity of the person acting for the registrant as administrator of the property of others;

(11) the address of the registrant's establishments in Québec;

(12) the name and domicile of each partner, the fact that no other person is a member of the partnership and, in the case of a limited partnership, the name and domicile of each general partner and the names and domiciles of the three greatest contributors to the partnership among the special partners;

(13) the object pursued by the partnership;

(14) the name of the State, province or territory in which the registrant was constituted and the date of constitution;

(15) the name of the State, province or territory in which the amalgamation or division that resulted in the formation of the registrant took place, the date of the amalgamation or division and the name, domicile and Québec business number of every legal person involved in the amalgamation or division; and

(16) the date of the continuance or other transformation of the registrant.

Third persons may submit any proof to refute information contained in a document filed with the registrar or transferred under an agreement entered into under section 117 or 118.

99. Any person may consult the register.

The register may be consulted in the locations and during the hours designated by the registrar. It may also be consulted from a distance by means of technologies determined by the registrar.

101. On payment of the fee set out in this Act, the registrar may provide to any person who so requests a compilation of the information contained in statements of information.

The name and address of a natural person may not, however, be part of or the basis for such a compilation unless the compilation is requested by a person or a body referred to in any of subparagraphs 1 to 3 and 5 of the second paragraph of section 59 of the Act respecting Access to documents held by public bodies and the Protection of personal information (chapter A-2.1) or section 67 or 68 of that Act, for the purposes set out in those provisions.

105. The registrar must issue, free of charge, to any person who so requests a copy or extract of an index of documents, a statement of information or an index of names.

Chapter VIII
Inspection and Investigation

125. For the purpose of verifying compliance with this Act or a provision of an Act listed in Schedule III that confers responsibilities on the registrar, the registrar or an authorized inspector may

(1) at any reasonable hour, enter and inspect premises where activities governed by this Act are carried on;

(2) require any information relating to the carrying out of this Act or any such provision; and

(3) at any reasonable hour, demand access to anything that contains documents so that they may be inspected and copied, if there are reasonable grounds to believe that the documents contain information relating to the administration of this Act or any such provision.

Chapter IX
Remedies

133. On payment of the fee set out in this Act, an interested person other than a registrant may request that the registrar correct or delete inaccurate information from the register.

134. On payment of the fee set out in this Act, an interested person may request that the registrar order a registrant to replace or change the name the registrant uses in carrying on an activity, provided it is not the name under which the registrant was constituted, or to cease using a name, if it is contrary to this Act.

The first paragraph does not apply to a natural person who is registered voluntarily under his or her name.

APPENDIX "6-B"
SELECTED ARTICLES FROM

Civil Code of Québec

TITLE FIVE
LEGAL PERSONS

Chapter I
Juridical Personality

298. Legal persons are endowed with juridical personality. Legal persons are established in the public interest or for a private interest.

300. Both kinds of legal persons are also governed by this Code where the provisions of such Acts require to be complemented, particularly with regard to their status as legal persons, their property or their relations with other persons.

301. Legal persons have full enjoyment of civil rights.

302. Every legal person has a patrimony which may, to the extent provided by law, be divided or appropriated to a purpose. It also has the extra-patrimonial rights and obligations flowing from its nature.

303. Legal persons have capacity to exercise all their rights, and the provisions of this Code respecting the exercise of civil rights by natural persons are applicable to them, adapted as required.

They have no incapacities other than those which may result from their nature or from an express provision of law.

304. Legal persons may not exercise tutorship or curatorship to the person.

They may, however, to the extent that they are authorized by law to act as such, hold office as tutor or curator to property, liquidator of a succession, sequestrator, trustee or administrator of another legal person.

305. Every legal person has a name which is assigned to it when it is constituted, and under which it exercises its rights and performs its obligations.

It shall be assigned a name which conforms to law and which includes, where required by law, an expression that clearly indicates the juridical form assumed by the legal person.

306. A legal person may engage in an activity or identify itself under a name other than its own name. It shall give notice to the enterprise registrar by filing a declaration to that effect in accordance with the Act respecting the legal publicity of enterprises (chapter P-44.1) and, if the legal person is a syndicate of co-owners, apply for the registration of such a notice in the land register.

307. The domicile of a legal person is at the place and address of its head office.

Legal persons are distinct from their members. Their acts bind none but themselves, except as provided by law.

308. A legal person may change its name or its domicile by following the procedure established by law.

309. The functioning, the administration of the patrimony and the activities of a legal person are regulated by law, the constituting act and the by-laws; to the extent permitted by law, they may also be regulated by a unanimous agreement of the members.

In case of inconsistency between the constituting act and the by-laws, the constituting act prevails.

310. The functioning, the administration of the patrimony and the activities of a legal person are regulated by law, the constituting act and the by-laws; to the extent permitted by law, they may also be regulated by a unanimous agreement of the members.

In case of inconsistency between the constituting act and the by-laws, the constituting act prevails.

311. Legal persons act through their organs, such as the board of directors and the general meeting of the members.

312. A legal person is represented by its senior officers, who bind it to the extent of the powers vested in them by law, the constituting act or the by-laws.

313. The by-laws of a legal person set out the contractual relations existing between the legal person and its members.

314. A legal person exists in perpetuity unless otherwise provided by law or its constituting act.

315. The members of a legal person are liable toward the legal person for anything they have promised to contribute to it, unless otherwise provided by law.

316. In case of fraud with regard to the legal person, the court may, on the application of an interested person, hold the founders, directors, other senior officers or members of the legal person who have participated in the alleged act or derived personal profit therefrom liable, to the extent it indicates, for any damage suffered by the legal person.

317. In no case may a legal person set up juridical personality against a person in good faith if it is set up to dissemble fraud, abuse of right or contravention of a rule of public order.

318. The court, in deciding an action by a third person in good faith, may rule that a person or group not having status as a legal person has the same obligations as a legal person if the person or group acted as such in respect of the third person.

319. A legal person may ratify an act performed for it before it was constituted; it is then substituted for the person who acted for it.

The ratification does not effect novation; the person who acted has thenceforth the same rights and is subject to the same obligations as a mandatary in respect of the legal person.

320. A person who acts for a legal person before it is constituted is bound by the obligations so contracted, unless the contract stipulates otherwise and includes a statement to the effect that the legal person might not be constituted or might not assume the obligations subscribed in the contract.

321. A director is considered to be the mandatary of the legal person. He shall, in the performance of his duties, conform to the obligations imposed on him by law, the constituting act or the by-laws and he shall act within the limits of the powers conferred on him.

322. A director shall act with prudence and diligence.

He shall also act with honesty and loyalty in the best interest of the legal person.

323. No director may mingle the property of the legal person with his own property nor may he use for his own profit or that of a third person any property of the legal person or any information he obtains by reason of his duties, unless he is authorized to do so by the members of the legal person.

324. A director shall avoid placing himself in any situation where his personal interest would be in conflict with his obligations as a director.

A director shall declare to the legal person any interest he has in an enterprise or association that may place him in a situation of conflict of interest and of any right he may set up against it, indicating their nature and value, where applicable. The declaration of interest is recorded in the minutes of the proceedings of the board of directors or the equivalent.

325. A director may, even in carrying on his duties, acquire, directly or indirectly, rights in the property under his administration or enter into contracts with the legal person.

The director shall immediately inform the legal person of any acquisition or contract described in the first paragraph, indicating the nature and value of the rights he is acquiring, and request that the fact be recorded in the minutes of proceedings of the board of directors or the equivalent. He shall abstain, except if required, from the discussion and voting on the question. This rule does not, however, apply to matters concerning the remuneration or conditions of employment of the director.

326. Where the director of a legal person fails to give information correctly and immediately of an acquisition or a contract, the court, on the application of the legal person or a member, may, among other measures, annul the act or order the director to render account and to remit the profit or benefit realized to the legal person.

The action may be brought only within one year after knowledge is gained of the acquisition or contract.

327. Minors, persons of full age under tutorship or curatorship, bankrupts and persons prohibited by the court from holding such office are disqualified for office as directors.

However, minors and persons of full age under tutorship may be directors of associations constituted as legal persons that do not aim to make pecuniary profits and whose objects concern them.

328. The acts of a director or senior officer may not be annulled on the sole ground that he was disqualified or that his designation was irregular.

329. The court, on the application of an interested person, may prohibit a person from holding office as a director of a legal person if the person has been found guilty of an indictable offence involving fraud or dishonesty in a matter related to legal persons, or who has repeatedly violated the Acts relating to legal persons or failed to fulfil his obligations as a director.

330. No prohibition may extend beyond five years from the latest act charged.

The court may lift the prohibition under the conditions it sees fit, on the application of the person concerned by the prohibition.

335. The board of directors manages the affairs of the legal person and exercises all the powers necessary for that purpose; it may create management positions and other organs, and delegate the exercise of certain powers to the holders of those positions and to those organs.

The board of directors adopts and implements management by-laws, subject to approval by the members at the next general meeting.

The decisions of the board of directors are taken by the vote of a majority of the directors.

337. Every director is, with the other directors, liable for the decisions taken by the board of directors unless he requested that his dissent be recorded in the minutes of proceedings or the equivalent.

However, a director who was absent from a meeting of the board is presumed not to have approved the decisions taken at that meeting.

338. The directors of a legal person are designated by the members.

No person may be designated as a director without his express consent.

339. The term of office of directors is one year; at the expiry of that period, their term continues unless it is revoked.

340. The directors fill the vacancies on the board. Vacancies on the board do not prevent the directors from acting; if their number has become less than a quorum, the remaining directors may validly convene the members.

345. The general meeting is convened each year by the board of directors, or following its directives, within six months after the close of the financial period.

The first general meeting is held within six months from the constitution of the legal person.

350. Decisions of the meeting are taken by a majority of the votes given.

The vote of the members is taken by a show of hands or, upon request, by secret ballot.

355. A legal person is dissolved by the annulment of its constituting act or for any other cause provided for by the constituting act or by law.

It is also dissolved where the court confirms the fulfilment of the condition attached to the constituting act, the accomplishment of the object for which the legal person was constituted, or the impossibility of accomplishing that object, or the existence of some other legitimate cause.

356. A legal person may also be dissolved by consent of not less than two-thirds of the votes given at a general meeting convened expressly for that purpose.

The notice convening the meeting shall be sent not less than thirty days but not more than forty-five days before the meeting and not at an inopportune moment.

357. The juridical personality of the legal person continues to exist for the purposes of the liquidation.

TITLE ONE
OBLIGATIONS IN GENERAL

1518. An obligation is joint between two or more debtors where they are obligated to the creditor for the same thing but in such a way that each debtor may only be compelled to perform the obligation separately and only up to his share of the debt.

An obligation is joint between two or more creditors where each creditor may only exact the performance of his share of the claim from the common debtor.

1523. An obligation is solidary between the debtors where they are obligated to the creditor for the same thing in such a way that each of them may be compelled separately to perform the whole obligation and where performance by a single debtor releases the others towards the creditor.

1525. Solidarity between debtors is not presumed; it exists only where it is expressly stipulated by the parties or imposed by law.

Solidarity between debtors is presumed, however, where an obligation is contracted for the service or carrying on of an enterprise.

The carrying on by one or more persons of an organized economic activity, whether or not it is commercial in nature, consisting of producing, administering or alienating property, or providing a service, constitutes the carrying on of an enterprise.

Chapter X
Contracts of Partnership and of Association

2186. A contract of partnership is a contract by which the parties, in a spirit of cooperation, agree to carry on an activity, including the operation of an enterprise, to contribute thereto by combining property, knowledge or activities and to share any resulting pecuniary profits.

A contract of association is a contract by which the parties agree to pursue a common goal other than the making of pecuniary profits to be shared between the members of the association.

2187. The partnership or association is created upon the formation of the contract if no other date is indicated in the contract.

2188. Partnerships are either general partnerships, limited partnerships or undeclared partnerships.

Partnerships may also be joint-stock companies, in which case they are legal persons.

2189. A general or limited partnership is formed under a name that is common to the partners.

It shall file a registration declaration in accordance with the Act respecting the legal publicity of enterprises (chapter P-44.1); otherwise, it is deemed to be an undeclared partnership, subject to the rights of third persons in good faith.

2197. A general or limited partnership shall, in carrying on business, indicate its juridical form in its name or after its name.

Failing such indication in an act concluded by the partnership, the court, in ruling on the action of a third person in good faith, may decide that the partnership and its partners are liable, in respect of that act, in the same manner as an undeclared partnership and its partners.

Division II
General Partnerships

2198. A partner is a debtor to the partnership for everything he promises to contribute to it.

Where a person undertakes to contribute a sum of money and fails to do so, he is liable for interest from the day his contribution ought to have been made, subject to any additional damages which may be claimed from him.

2199. A contribution of property is made by transferring rights of ownership or of enjoyment and by placing the property at the disposal of the partnership.

2200. A contribution consisting in knowledge or activities is owed continuously so long as the partner who undertook to make such a contribution is a member of the partnership; the partner is liable to the partnership for any profit he realizes from the contribution.

2201. Participation in the profits of a partnership entails the obligation to share in the losses.

2202. The share of each partner in the assets, profits and losses is equal if it is not fixed in the contract.

If the contract fixes the share of each partner in only the assets, profits or losses, it is presumed to fix the share for all three cases.

2203. Any stipulation whereby a partner is

excluded from participation in the profits is without effect.

Any stipulation whereby a partner is exempt from the obligation to share in the losses may not be set up against third persons.

2204. A partner may not compete with the partnership on his own account or on behalf of a third person or take part in an activity which deprives the partnership of the property, knowledge or activity he is bound to contribute to it; any profits arising from such competition belong to the partnership, without prejudice to any remedy it may pursue.

2208. Each partner may use the property of the partnership, provided he uses it in the interest of the partnership and according to its destination, and in such a way as not to prevent the other partners from using it as they are entitled.

Each partner may also bind the partnership in the course of its activities, but the partners may oppose the transaction before it is entered into or restrict the right of a partner to bind the partnership.

2209. A partner may associate a third person with himself in his share in the partnership without the consent of the other partners, but he may not make him a member of the partnership without their consent.

2212. The partners may enter into such agreements between themselves as they consider appropriate with regard to their respective powers in the management of the affairs of the partnership.

2213. The partners may appoint one or more fellow partners or even a third person to manage the affairs of the partnership.

2215. Failing any stipulation respecting the mode of management, the partners are deemed to have conferred the power to manage the affairs of the partnership on one another.

Any act performed by a partner in respect of the common activities binds the other partners, without prejudice to their right to object, jointly or separately, to the act before it is performed.

In addition, each partner may compel the other partners to incur any expenses necessary for the preservation of the common property but one partner may not change the condition of that property without the consent of the others, regardless of how advantageous such changes may be.

2216. Every partner is entitled to participate in collective decisions, and he may not be prevented from exercising that right by the contract of partnership.

Unless otherwise stipulated in the contract, decisions are taken by the vote of a majority of the partners, regardless of the value of their interests in the partnership. However, decisions to amend the contract of partnership are taken by a unanimous vote.

2218. Notwithstanding any stipulation to the contrary, any partner may inform himself of the affairs of the partnership and consult its books and records even if he is excluded from management.

In exercising this right, the partner is bound not to impede the operations of the partnership unduly nor to prevent the other partners from exercising the same right.

2219. Each partner is a mandatary of the partnership in respect of third persons in good faith and binds the partnership for every act performed in its name in the ordinary course of its business.

No stipulation to the contrary may be set up against third persons in good faith.

2221. In respect of third persons, the partners are jointly liable for the obligations contracted by the partnership but they are solidarily liable if the obligations have been contracted for the service or operation of an enterprise of the partnership.

2222. A person who gives reason to believe that he is a partner, although he is not, may be held liable as a partner towards third persons in good faith acting in that belief.

2223. Silent partners are liable towards third persons for the same obligations as declared partners.

2224. A partnership may not make a distribution of securities to the public or issue negotiable instruments, on pain of nullity of the contracts entered into or of the securities or instruments issued and of the obligation to compensate for any injury it causes to third persons in good faith.

In such a case, the partners are solidarily liable for the obligations of the partnership.

2225. A partnership may sue and be sued in a civil action under the name it declares.

2226. A partner ceases to be a member of the partnership by the transfer or redemption of his share or upon his death, upon being placed under protective supervision or becoming bankrupt, or by the exercise of his right of withdrawal; he also ceases to be a member where such is his will, by his expulsion or by a judgment authorizing his withdrawal or ordering the seizure of his share.

2227. A partner who ceases to be a member of the partnership otherwise than by the transfer or seizure of his share may obtain the value of his share upon ceasing to be a partner, and the other partners are bound to pay him the amount of the value as soon as it is established, with interest from the day on which his membership ceased.

Failing stipulations in the contract of partnership or failing agreement among the interested persons as to the value of the share, the value is determined by an expert designated by the interested persons or, failing that, by the court. The expert or the court may, however, defer the assessment of contingent assets or liabilities.

2229. The partners may, by a majority vote, agree on the expulsion of a partner who fails to perform his obligations or hinders the carrying on of the activities of the partnership.

2230. A partnership is dissolved by the causes of dissolution provided in the contract, by the accomplishment of its object or the impossibility of accomplishing it, or by consent of all the partners. It may also be dissolved by the court for a legitimate cause.

Liquidation of the partnership is then proceeded with.

Division III
Limited Partnerships

2236. A limited partnership is a partnership consisting of one or more general partners who are the sole persons authorized to administer and bind the partnership, and of one or more special partners who are bound to furnish a contribution to the common stock of the partnership.

2237. A limited partnership may make a distribution of securities to the public to establish or increase the common stock, and issue negotiable instruments.

A third person who undertakes to make a contribution becomes a special partner of the partnership.

2238. General partners have the powers, rights and obligations of the partners of a general partnership but they are bound to render an account of their administration to the special partners.

2241. While the partnership exists, no special partner may withdraw part of his contribution in property to the common stock, in any way, unless he obtains the consent of a majority of the other partners and the property remaining after the withdrawal is sufficient to discharge the debts of the partnership.

2242. A special partner is entitled to receive his share of the profits, but if the payment of the profits reduces the common stock, every special partner who receives such a payment is bound to restore the sum necessary to cover his share of the deficit, with interest.

In the case of a partnership whose capital includes property that is consumed by its exploitation by the partnership, the special partner may receive his share of the profits only if the property remaining after the payment is sufficient to discharge the debts of the partnership.

2243. The share of a special partner in the common stock of the partnership is transferable.

In respect of third persons, the transferor remains liable for the obligations which may result from his share in the partnership while he was still a special partner.

2244. A special partner may not give other than an advisory opinion with regard to the management of the partnership.

A special partner may not negotiate any business on behalf of the partnership or act as mandatary or agent for the partnership or allow his name to be used in any act of the partnership; otherwise, he is liable in the same manner as a general partner for the obligations of the partnership resulting from such acts and, according to the importance or number of such acts, he may be liable in the same manner as a general partner for all the obligations of the partnership.

2246. Where the property of the partnership is insufficient, the general partners are solidarily liable for the debts of the partnership in respect of third persons; a special partner is liable for the debts up to the agreed amount of his contribution, notwithstanding any transfer of his share in the common stock.

Any stipulation whereby a special partner is bound to secure or assume the debts of the partnership beyond the agreed amount of his contribution is without effect.

2247. A special partner whose name appears in the firm name of the partnership is liable for the obligations of the partnership in the same manner as a general partner, unless his quality of special partner is clearly indicated.

APPENDIX "6-C"

Partnership Agreement

THIS PARTNERSHIP AGREEMENT ENTERED INTO IN THE CITY OF MONTREAL, PROVINCE OF QUEBEC ON THIS 15TH DAY OF FEBRUARY, 2013:

BETWEEN:

RICARDO PELLINI, business executive and sole proprietor of the business operated under the firm name and style of RICARDO SPORTSWEAR REG'D., located at 8755 Papineau Drive, Montreal, Québec: hereinafter referred to as

PELLINI

AND

MARIE-ALICE KENILWORTH, fashion designer and business executive, residing and domiciled at 437 Alexander Place, Brossard, Québec; hereafter referred to as

KENILWORTH

WHEREAS the parties have expressed their desire and intention to form a business partnership, they have therefore agreed as follows:

CLAUSE ONE

A business partnership is hereby formed, to be operated under the firm name and style of PELLI-KEN SPORTSWEAR MANUFACTURING REG'D., to carry on the business as contractors and manufacturers of ladies' garments and sportswear.

CLAUSE TWO

The principal office of the partnership will be located at 8755 Papineau Drive in the City of Montreal, Province of Québec, and at such other place or places as may hereafter be agreed upon by the said partners.

CLAUSE THREE

The partnership shall consist of only PELLINI and KENILWORTH and no other persons.

CLAUSE FOUR

The partnership is deemed to come into existence on and as of the First day of March 2013, and to continue until the 28th day of February 2018; it will thereafter be renewed automatically for successive periods of two years, unless a written notice to the contrary is given by one of the parties to the other not later than sixty (60) days before the current term is due to expire.

Partnership Agreement (continued)

CLAUSE FIVE

PELLINI will contribute the sum of FIFTY THOUSAND DOLLARS ($50,000.00) to the partnership; eighteen thousand dollars ($18,000.00) of this sum has already been paid towards the acquisition of machinery and fixtures which are owned by him in his name, and by this contract, he transfers all rights and titles thereto, to the partnership; in addition he has paid the rental for the premises to be occupied by the partnership for the months of March and April 2013 at the rate of One Thousand Dollars ($1,000.00) per month; and the balance of thirty thousand dollars ($30,000.00) will be paid to the partnership in cash in two instalments of fifteen thousand dollars ($15,000.00) each to be paid on the first day of March 2013 and the first June 2013 respectively.

CLAUSE SIX

KENILWORTH will contribute the sum of FIFTY THOUSAND DOLLARS ($50,000.00) to the partnership; twelve thousand dollars ($12,000.00) of this sum has already been paid towards the acquisition of patterns, designs and production rights, all of which she transfers to the partnership by this contract; the balance of thirty-eight thousand dollars ($38,000.00) will be paid in cash in four instalments as follows: ten thousand dollars to be paid on the first day of March 2013, the first date of June 2013 and the first day of September 2013 respectively; the final amount of eight thousand dollars ($8,000.00) will be paid on the first date of November 2013.

CLAUSE SEVEN

All future capital contributions to the partnership, if necessary, will be made in equal shares by both partners; all profits, debts and losses of the partnership will be divided equally between them.

CLAUSE EIGHT

And all machinery, fixtures, tools and other devices presently on the premises at the principal place of business are deemed to be the property of the partnership as and from the first day of March 2013.

CLAUSE NINE

Each partner will be entitled to draw an equal salary against the anticipated earnings of the partnership; the amount of such salary will be determined by agreement between the partners from time-to-time.

CLAUSE TEN

PELLINI will be foreman and manager of the plant, and will operate and maintain the machines until such time as the growth and expansion of the business permits other employees to be hired to carry out these functions under the supervision of PELLINI; he will be responsible for purchasing of all materials, dies, tooling, and equipment.

CLAUSE ELEVEN

KENILWORTH will be responsible for sales, for the administration of the office, and for financial management of the business of the partnership.

2

Partnership Agreement (continued)

CLAUSE TWELVE

Both partners will devote their full time and energy to the operation of the business of the partnership.

CLAUSE THIRTEEN

From and as of the first day of May 2013, the partnership will be responsible for the payment of the rent and for carrying out all of the obligations that had been undertaken by PELLINI as set out in the lease entered into between PELLINI and the landlord of the premises in which the partnership business will be located.

CLAUSE FOURTEEN

The balance of payments due under the terms of the Sales Agreement entered into by PELLINI for the machinery and other assets presently on the premises of the principal office will be paid for out of the assets of the partnership.

CLAUSE FIFTEEN

All funds of the partnership will be deposited in the bank to be chosen by the partners, and all withdrawals therefrom will be made only by cheques signed by both partners.

CLAUSE SIXTEEN

The partnership will keep proper books of accounts of all transactions of the partnership at its place of business, and such books together with vouchers, records and other relevant documents will be open at all times for inspection by either partner.

CLAUSE SEVENTEEN

Neither of the partners will, without the consent of the other partner, engage in any transaction on behalf of the partnership nor enter into it any contract requiring the expenditure of more than one thousand dollars ($1,000.00).

CLAUSE EIGHTEEN

Neither partner will, without the consent of the other partner, on behalf of the partnership, borrow or lend money, or accept any commercial paper, or execute any mortgage, bond, lease or other obligation requiring the payment of money.

CLAUSE NINETEEN

Neither partner will, without the consent of the other, assign, mortgage, or sell his or her ownership interest in the partnership or in any of the assets, capital or property of the partnership, or any part thereof, or enter into any kind of agreement as a result of which a third party will have any kind of financial interest in the partnership.

CLAUSE TWENTY

In the event the partners should agree to dissolve the business of the partnership, the ownership interest of any one the partners will be offered to the other partner before the assets of the partnership are put up for sale.

3

Partnership Agreement (continued)

CLAUSE TWENTY-ONE

In the event either of the partners becomes, as a result of accident or illness, unable to actively function as a member of the partnership business for a period exceeding three months, or in the event of the death of one of the partners, the other partner will have the right to purchase the ownership interest of the disabled or deceased partner at a price to be agreed upon following an appraisal of the value of the partnership business, such appraisal to be carried out by an independent firm of accountants.

IN WITNESS WHEREOF, THE PARTIES HAVE SET THEIR HANDS ON THE DATE AND PLACE FIRST NOTED ABOVE.

Ricardo Pellini

RICARDO PELLINI

Marie-Alice Kenilworth

MARIE-ALICE KENILWORTH

Witnessed by:

Jonathan Wizard

Jonathan Wizard

4

APPENDIX "6-D"

Sole Proprietorship Registration Form

Registraire des entreprises
Québec

RE-201 (2010-10)
Page 1

Déclaration d'immatriculation pour une personne physique exploitant une entreprise individuelle

Ce formulaire s'adresse à toute personne physique exploitant une entreprise individuelle qui désire remplir une déclaration d'immatriculation. Veuillez lire les renseignements aux pages 4 et 5 avant de remplir ce formulaire.

Réservé à l'administration
Date d'immatriculation A M J

Si vous avez déjà été immatriculé, inscrivez le NEQ qui vous avait été attribué.

Numéro d'entreprise du Québec
NEQ 2 2

Cochez les cases appropriées (le cas échéant).

☐ La personne physique est en faillite.
☐ La personne physique exploite une entreprise individuelle au Québec.

1 Identification

1.1 Nom et adresse du domicile de la personne physique

Inscrivez votre nom et votre adresse personnelle complète. Tous les établissements doivent être déclarés à la section 2.3.

☐ Madame ☐ Monsieur — Nom de famille — Prénom

Appartement — Numéro — Rue

Ville, village ou municipalité — État, province — Pays — Code postal

1.2 Domicile élu

Inscrivez l'adresse à laquelle vous désirez recevoir votre correspondance.

Nom de famille et prénom

Appartement — Numéro — Rue

Ville, village ou municipalité — État, province — Pays — Code postal

2 Informations générales

2.1 Titre des deux principales activités de la personne physique exploitant une entreprise individuelle

CAE — 1re activité — Précisez (facultatif)

CAE — 2e activité (le cas échéant) — Précisez (facultatif)

2.2 Nombre de salariés au Québec (Cochez la case appropriée.)

O ☐ Aucun	A ☐ De 1 à 5	B ☐ De 6 à 10	C ☐ De 11 à 25	D ☐ De 26 à 49
	E ☐ De 50 à 99	F ☐ De 100 à 249	G ☐ De 250 à 499	H ☐ De 500 à 749
	I ☐ De 750 à 999	J ☐ De 1 000 à 2 499	K ☐ De 2 500 à 4 999	L ☐ 5 000 et plus

Si l'espace prévu est insuffisant, joignez l'annexe 1 en indiquant votre NEQ, s'il y a lieu.

GE01 ZZ 71694849

Ministère du Revenu

Sole Proprietorship Registration Form (continued)

RE-201 (2010-10)

Page 2

2 Informations générales (suite)

2.3 Identification des établissements au Québec

- L'établissement principal doit être déclaré dans la section prévue à cette fin.
- Inscrivez le nom, l'adresse complète des établissements et les deux principales activités qui y sont exercées.

Établissement principal au Québec

Nom

Adresse — Code postal

Principales activités de cet établissement :

CAE — 1re activité — Précisez (facultatif)

CAE — 2e activité (le cas échéant) — Précisez (facultatif)

▶ **Activité à déclaration obligatoire** (Cochez la case si vous exploitez un point de vente de tabac au détail [001].) ☐

Autres établissements

Nom

Adresse — Code postal

Principales activités de cet établissement :

CAE — 1re activité — Précisez (facultatif)

CAE — 2e activité (le cas échéant) — Précisez (facultatif)

▶ **Activité à déclaration obligatoire** (Cochez la case si vous exploitez un point de vente de tabac au détail [001].) ☐

Nom

Adresse — Code postal

Principales activités de cet établissement :

CAE — 1re activité — Précisez (facultatif)

CAE — 2e activité (le cas échéant) — Précisez (facultatif)

▶ **Activité à déclaration obligatoire** (Cochez la case si vous exploitez un point de vente de tabac au détail [001].) ☐

2.4 Autres noms utilisés au Québec

Inscrivez tout autre nom utilisé dans l'exploitation de votre entreprise. Cela comprend notamment les noms d'emprunt utilisés et les noms de marchandises ou de services (marques de commerce) dont la personne physique est propriétaire ou usagère au Québec. S'il s'agit d'une marque de commerce, Précisez. Une version française est **obligatoire** pour chacun des noms déclarés dans une autre langue.

Nom

Version dans une autre langue, le cas échéant

Si l'espace prévu est insuffisant, joignez les annexes 1 et 2 en indiquant votre NEQ, s'il y a lieu.

GE02 ZZ 71694850

Numéro d'entreprise du Québec
NEQ 2 2

Sole Proprietorship Registration Form (continued)

RE-201 (2010-10)
Page 3

3 Fondé de pouvoir

Si la personne physique n'a ni domicile ni établissement au Québec ou qu'elle est dispensée par règlement de déclarer l'adresse de son domicile ou de ses établissements, inscrivez le nom et l'adresse complète d'un fondé de pouvoir résidant au Québec.

Nom de famille et prénom

Adresse

Code postal

4 Administrateur du bien d'autrui

Si vous êtes représenté par une personne chargée d'administrer l'ensemble de vos biens, inscrivez le code correspondant à la fonction de cette personne ainsi que son nom de famille, son prénom et son adresse complète. Cette personne a les droits et obligations que la Loi sur la publicité légale des entreprises confère à la personne physique exploitant l'entreprise individuelle.

Codes de fonction de l'administrateur du bien d'autrui :

CU Curateur **FI** Fiduciaire **LI** Liquidateur **LS** Liquidateur de succession **SQ** Séquestre
TU Tuteur **SY** Syndic **AU** Autre

Code | Si AU, précisez la fonction | Date de début du mandat (A M J) | Date de fin du mandat (A M J)

Nom de famille et prénom

Appartement | Numéro | Rue

Ville, village ou municipalité | État, province | Pays | Code postal

5 Signature

Je, ______________________________,
Prénom et nom de famille de la personne physique ou de la personne autorisée

domicilié au ______________________________,
Adresse

certifie que je suis la personne physique exploitant l'entreprise individuelle ou la personne autorisée par la personne physique à signer la présente déclaration, que les renseignements déclarés sont vrais et que le paiement requis accompagne la présente déclaration.

Signature de la personne autorisée | Date

Signez et retournez ce formulaire avec votre paiement.
Ne pas télécopier.

GE03 ZZ 71694851

Numéro d'entreprise du Québec
NEQ 2 2

APPENDIX "6-E"

Partnership Registration Form

Registraire des entreprises
Québec

RE-202 (2010-10)
Page 1

Déclaration d'immatriculation pour une société de personnes

Ce formulaire s'adresse à toute société de personnes qui doit remplir une déclaration d'immatriculation. Veuillez lire les renseignements aux pages 5 et 6 avant de remplir ce formulaire.

Réservé à l'administration
Date d'immatriculation A M J

Si la société de personnes a déjà été immatriculée, inscrivez le NEQ qui lui avait été attribué.

Numéro d'entreprise du Québec
NEQ 3 3

1 Identification

1.1 Nom et adresse du domicile de la société de personnes

Inscrivez le nom et l'adresse du domicile de la société de personnes. La société en nom collectif et la société en commandite constituées au Québec peuvent indiquer leur forme juridique dans leur nom ou à la suite de leur nom, ou encore en ajouter l'abréviation (SENC, SEC) à la suite de leur nom. Pour une société de personnes non constituée au Québec dont le nom est dans une autre langue que le français, déclarez la version française de ce nom s'il en existe une (sinon voir la section 4.5). Tous les établissements doivent être déclarés à la section 4.4.

Nom

Version dans une autre langue, le cas échéant

Appartement | Numéro | Rue

Ville, village ou municipalité | État, province | Pays | Code postal

1.2 Domicile élu

Inscrivez l'adresse à laquelle vous désirez recevoir votre correspondance.

Nom

Appartement | Numéro | Rue

Ville, village ou municipalité | État, province | Pays | Code postal

2 Forme juridique

Codes des formes juridiques : Inscrivez le code correspondant à la forme juridique de la société.

Société de personnes constituée au Québec ▶ **SENC** Société en nom collectif **SEC** Société en commandite **SEP** Société en participation

Société de personnes non constituée au Québec ▶ **SOC** Société de personnes

Code | Loi constitutive de la société de personnes non constituée au Québec

Société en nom collectif à responsabilité limitée (réservé aux membres d'ordres professionnels québécois) et société de personnes non constituée au Québec

Si vous êtes membre d'un ordre professionnel au sens du Code des professions, vous pouvez exercer vos activités au sein d'une société en nom collectif à responsabilité limitée si votre ordre professionnel l'autorise par règlement. Vous devez alors mentionner le fait que la responsabilité de certains ou de l'ensemble des associés est limitée et inscrire la date à laquelle la société devient ou cesse d'être à responsabilité limitée. Pour la société de personnes non constituée au Québec, vous devez seulement indiquer si la responsabilité de certains ou de l'ensemble des associés est limitée.

Cochez la case si la responsabilité de certains ou de l'ensemble des associés est limitée. ☐

Date à laquelle la société en nom collectif québécoise devient à responsabilité limitée. A M J

Date à laquelle la société en nom collectif québécoise cesse d'être à responsabilité limitée. A M J

GW01 ZZ 71874849

Ministère du Revenu

Partnership Registration Form (continued)

RE-202 (2010-10)
Page 2

3 Objet poursuivi par la société de personnes

Inscrivez brièvement l'objet poursuivi par la société.

4 Informations générales

4.1 Titre des deux principales activités de la société de personnes

CAE | 1re activité | Précisez (facultatif)

CAE | 2e activité (le cas échéant) | Précisez (facultatif)

4.2 Nombre de salariés au Québec (Cochez la case appropriée.)

- O ☐ Aucun
- A ☐ De 1 à 5
- B ☐ De 6 à 10
- C ☐ De 11 à 25
- D ☐ De 26 à 49
- E ☐ De 50 à 99
- F ☐ De 100 à 249
- G ☐ De 250 à 499
- H ☐ De 500 à 749
- I ☐ De 750 à 999
- J ☐ De 1 000 à 2 499
- K ☐ De 2 500 à 4 999
- L ☐ 5 000 et plus

4.3 Période d'existence

Pour les sociétés en nom collectif et les sociétés en commandite constituées au Québec, le fait de déclarer une date de cessation d'existence ne dispense pas de l'obligation de produire les avis de dissolution, de nomination d'un liquidateur et de clôture prévus au Code civil du Québec.

Si l'existence légale de la société de personnes est limitée dans le temps, inscrivez la date de cessation prévue. A M J

4.4 Identification des établissements au Québec

- L'établissement principal doit être déclaré dans la section prévue à cette fin.
- Pour les sociétés en commandite constituées au Québec, l'adresse du principal établissement correspond au lieu où est tenu le registre relatif aux commanditaires.
- Inscrivez le nom, l'adresse complète des établissements et les deux principales activités qui y sont exercées.

Établissement principal au Québec

Nom

Adresse | Code postal

Principales activités de cet établissement :

CAE | 1re activité | Précisez (facultatif)

CAE | 2e activité (le cas échéant) | Précisez (facultatif)

▶ **Activité à déclaration obligatoire** (Cochez la case si vous exploitez un point de vente de tabac au détail [001].) ☐

Autres établissements

Nom

Adresse | Code postal

Principales activités de cet établissement :

CAE | 1re activité | Précisez (facultatif)

CAE | 2e activité (le cas échéant) | Précisez (facultatif)

▶ **Activité à déclaration obligatoire** (Cochez la case si vous exploitez un point de vente de tabac au détail [001].) ☐

Si l'espace prévu est insuffisant, joignez l'annexe 1 en indiquant votre NEQ, s'il y a lieu.

GW02 ZZ 71874850

Numéro d'entreprise du Québec
NEQ 3 3

Partnership Registration Form (continued)

RE-202 (2010-10)
Page 3

4 Informations générales (suite)

4.5 Autres noms utilisés au Québec

Inscrivez tout autre nom utilisé dans l'exercice de vos activités, dans l'exploitation de votre entreprise ou aux fins de la possession d'un droit réel immobilier autre qu'une priorité ou une hypothèque. Cela comprend notamment les noms d'emprunt utilisés et les noms de marchandises ou de services (marques de commerce) dont la société de personnes est propriétaire ou usagère au Québec. S'il s'agit d'une marque de commerce, précisez-le. Une version française est **obligatoire** pour chacun des noms déclarés dans une autre langue.

Nom

Version dans une autre langue, le cas échéant

Si l'espace prévu est insuffisant, joignez l'annexe 2 en indiquant votre NEQ, s'il y a lieu.

5 Identification des associés

Inscrivez le code de fonction approprié, le nom et l'adresse complète de chaque associé faisant partie de la société de personnes.

- La société en nom collectif ou en participation doit déclarer les associés (AS) et indiquer qu'aucune autre personne ne fait partie de la société.
- La société en commandite doit déclarer chaque commandité (CE) ainsi que les trois commanditaires (CA) ayant fourni le plus grand apport.
- La société de personnes non constituée au Québec doit déclarer une des fonctions énumérées ci-dessous.

☐ Cochez la case pour déclarer qu'aucune autre personne ne fait partie de la société en nom collectif ou en participation.

Codes de fonction des associés :

AS Associé **CE** Commandité **CA** Commanditaire **AU** Autre (pour société de personnes non constituée au Québec)

Code | Si AU, précisez la fonction | Nom
Adresse | Code postal

Code | Si AU, précisez la fonction | Nom
Adresse | Code postal

Code | Si AU, précisez la fonction | Nom
Adresse | Code postal

Code | Si AU, précisez la fonction | Nom
Adresse | Code postal

Code | Si AU, précisez la fonction | Nom
Adresse | Code postal

Code | Si AU, précisez la fonction | Nom
Adresse | Code postal

Si l'espace prévu est insuffisant, joignez l'annexe 3 en indiquant votre NEQ, s'il y a lieu.

GW03 ZZ 71874851

Numéro d'entreprise du Québec
NEQ 3 3

Partnership Registration Form (continued)

RE-202 (2010-10)
Page 4

6 Fondé de pouvoir

Si la société de personnes n'a ni domicile ni établissement au Québec ou qu'elle est dispensée par règlement de déclarer l'adresse de son domicile ou de ses établissements, inscrivez le nom de famille, le prénom et l'adresse complète d'un fondé de pouvoir résidant au Québec.

Nom de famille et prénom

Adresse | Code postal

7 Administrateur du bien d'autrui

Si la société de personnes est représentée par une personne chargée d'administrer l'ensemble de ses biens, inscrivez le code correspondant à la fonction de cette personne ainsi que son nom de famille, son prénom et son adresse complète. Cette personne a les droits et obligations que la Loi sur la publicité légale des entreprises confère à la société de personnes.

Codes de fonction de l'administrateur du bien d'autrui :

CU Curateur **FI** Fiduciaire **LI** Liquidateur **SQ** Séquestre **SY** Syndic **AU** Autre

Code | Si AU, précisez la fonction | Date de début du mandat (A M J) | Date de fin du mandat (A M J)

Nom de famille et prénom

Appartement | Numéro | Rue

Ville, village ou municipalité | État, province | Pays | Code postal

8 Signature

Je, ____,
Prénom et nom de famille de la personne autorisée

domicilié au ____,
Adresse

certifie que je suis la personne autorisée par la société de personnes à signer la présente déclaration, que les renseignements déclarés sont vrais et que le paiement requis accompagne la présente déclaration.

______________________________ ______________________________
Signature de la personne autorisée Date

Signez et retournez ce formulaire avec votre paiement.
Ne pas télécopier.

GW04 ZZ 71874852

Numéro d'entreprise du Québec
NEQ 3 3

APPENDIX "6-F"

Federal Incorporation Forms

Industry Canada | Industrie Canada

Canada Business Corporations Act (CBCA) | Loi canadienne sur les sociétés par actions (LCSA)

Form 1

FORM 1
ARTICLES OF INCORPORATION
(SECTION 6)

FORMULAIRE 1
STATUTS CONSTITUTIFS
(ARTICLE 6)

1 – Name of the Corporation | Dénomination sociale de la société

2 – The province or territory in Canada where the registered office is situated (do not indicate the full address) | La province ou le territoire au Canada où est situé le siège social (n'indiquez pas l'adresse complète)

3 – The classes and any maximum number of shares that the corporation is authorized to issue | Catégories et tout nombre maximal d'actions que la société est autorisée à émettre

4 – Restrictions, if any, on share transfers | Restrictions sur le transfert des actions, s'il y a lieu

5 – Minimum and maximum number of directors (for a fixed number of directors, please indicate the same number in both boxes) | Nombre minimal et maximal d'administrateurs (pour un nombre fixe, veuillez indiquer le même nombre dans les deux cases)

Minimum: ☐ Maximum: ☐ | Minimal : ☐ Maximal : ☐

6 – Restrictions, if any, on the business the corporation may carry on | Limites imposées à l'activité commerciale de la société, s'il y a lieu

7 – Other provisions, if any | Autres dispositions, s'il y a lieu

8– **Incorporator's Declaration:** I hereby certify that I am authorized to sign and submit this form. | **Déclaration des fondateurs :** J'atteste que je suis autorisé à signer et à soumettre le présent formulaire.

Print Name(s) - Nom(s) en lettres moulées	Signature

Note:
Misrepresentation constitutes an offence and, on summary conviction, a person is liable to a fine not exceeding $5,000 or to imprisonment for a term not exceeding six months or both (subsection 250(1) of the CBCA).

Nota :
Faire une fausse déclaration constitue une infraction et son auteur, sur déclaration de culpabilité par procédure sommaire, est passible d'une amende maximale de 5 000 $ ou d'un emprisonnement maximal de six mois, ou de ces deux peines (paragraphe 250(1) de la LCSA).

IC 3419 (2008/08), Page 1

Canada

Federal Incorporation Forms (continued)

Industry Canada Industrie Canada
Corporations Canada Corporations Canada

Form 2

Initial Registered Office Address and First Board of Directors

(To be filed with Articles of Incorporation, Amalgamation and Continuance)
*(Sections 19 and 106 of the **Canada Business Corporations Act (CBCA)**)*

Changes to the registered office or the board of directors are to be made by filing Form 3 — Change of Registered Office Address or Form 6 — Changes Regarding Directors.

Instructions

4 At least 25 per cent of the directors of a corporation must be Canadian residents. If a corporation has four directors or less, at least one director must be a Canadian resident (subsection 105(3) of the *Canada Business Corporations Act* (CBCA)).

If the corporation is a "distributing" corporation, there must be at least three directors.

However, the board of directors of corporations operating in uranium mining, book publishing and distribution, book sale or film and video distribution must be comprised of a majority of Canadian residents (subsection 105(3.1) of the CBCA). If the space available is insufficient, please attach a schedule to the form.

5 Declaration

In the case of an incorporation, this form must be signed by the incorporator. In the case of an amalgamation or a continuance, this form must be signed by a director or an officer of the corporation (subsection 262.(2) of the CBCA).

General

The information you provide in this document is collected under the authority of the CBCA and will be stored in personal information bank number IC/PPU-049. Personal information that you provide is protected under the provisions of the *Privacy Act*. However, public disclosure pursuant to section 266 of the CBCA is permitted under the *Privacy Act*.

If you require more information, please consult our website at www.corporationscanada.ic.gc.ca or contact us at 613-941-9042 (Ottawa region), toll-free at 1-866-333-5556 or by email at corporationscanada@ic.gc.ca.

File documents online
(except for Articles of Amalgamation):
Corporations Canada Online Filing Centre:
www.corporationscanada.ic.gc.ca

Or send documents by mail:
Director General,
Corporations Canada
Jean Edmonds Tower South
9th Floor
365 Laurier Ave. West
Ottawa ON K1A 0C8

By Facsimile:
613-941-0999

1 Corporation name

2 Address of registered office (must be a street address, a P.O. Box is not acceptable)

NUMBER AND STREET NAME

CITY PROVINCE/TERRITORY POSTAL CODE

3 Mailing address (if different from the registered office)

SAME AS ABOVE ☐

ATTENTION OF

NUMBER AND STREET NAME

CITY PROVINCE/TERRITORY POSTAL CODE

4 Members of the board of directors

FIRST NAME	LAST NAME	RESIDENTIAL ADDRESS (must be a street address, a P.O. Box is not acceptable)	CANADIAN RESIDENT (Yes/No)

5 Declaration

I hereby certify that I have relevant knowledge and that I am authorized to sign and submit this form.

SIGNATURE

PRINT NAME ( ) TELEPHONE NUMBER

Note: Misrepresentation constitutes an offence and, on summary conviction, a person is liable to a fine not exceeding $5000 or to imprisonment for a term not exceeding six months or both (subsection 250(1) of the CBCA).

Canada

IC 2904 (2006/12)

APPENDIX "6-G"

Québec Incorporation Forms

Registraire des entreprises Québec

RE-200 (2010-10)
Page 1

Déclaration d'immatriculation ou déclaration initiale pour une personne morale

Ce formulaire s'adresse à toute personne morale qui doit remplir une déclaration d'immatriculation ou une déclaration initiale. Veuillez lire les renseignements aux pages 6 et 7 avant de remplir ce formulaire.

Réservé à l'administration
Date d'immatriculation A M J

Si vous avez déjà été immatriculé, inscrivez le NEQ qui vous avait été attribué.

Numéro d'entreprise du Québec
NEQ 1 1

☐ Cochez la case si la personne morale est en faillite.

Cochez la case appropriée ☐ Immatriculation ☐ Initiale

1 Identification

1.1 Nom et adresse du domicile de la personne morale

Inscrivez le nom et l'adresse complète du domicile de la personne morale. Pour une personne morale non constituée au Québec dont le nom est dans une autre langue que le français, déclarez la version française de ce nom, s'il en existe une (sinon, voir la section 4.5). Tous les établissements doivent être déclarés à la section 4.4.

Nom

Version dans une autre langue que le français, le cas échéant

Appartement | Numéro | Rue

Ville, village ou municipalité | État, province | Pays | Code postal

1.2 Domicile élu

Inscrivez l'adresse à laquelle vous désirez recevoir votre correspondance.

Nom

Appartement | Numéro | Rue

Ville, village ou municipalité | État, province | Pays | Code postal

2 Forme juridique

Inscrivez le code correspondant à la forme juridique, puis la loi constitutive, le lieu ainsi que la date de constitution de la personne morale.

Codes des formes juridiques :

CIE Compagnie **MUT** Mutuelle d'assurance **SYC** Syndicat de copropriété **COP** Coopérative **APE** Association personnifiée **AU** Autre

Code | Si AU, précisez la forme juridique | Loi constitutive

Lieu de constitution (province, État ou pays) | Date de constitution A M J

GD01 ZZ 71684849

Ministère du Revenu

Québec Incorporation Forms (continued)

RE-200 (2010-10)
Page 2

3 Dispositions particulières (s'il y a lieu)

3.1 Continuation ou transformation – Cochez la case appropriée et inscrivez l'information requise.

☐ Continuation
☐ Transformation

Loi applicable

Lieu (province, État ou pays)

Date A M J

3.2 Fusion ou scission – Cochez la case appropriée si la personne morale est issue d'une fusion ordinaire, d'une fusion simplifiée ou d'une scission et inscrivez l'information requise.

☐ Fusion ordinaire
☐ Fusion simplifiée
☐ Scission

Loi applicable

Lieu (province, État ou pays)

Date A M J

Inscrivez le nom, l'adresse du domicile et le numéro d'entreprise du Québec (NEQ), s'il y a lieu, de toutes les personnes morales faisant partie de cette fusion (les composantes) ou de cette scission.

☐ Vous avez une convention unanime des actionnaires ayant pour effet de restreindre ou de retirer les pouvoirs des administrateurs.

Nom | Numéro d'entreprise du Québec (NEQ) 1 1

Appartement | Numéro | Rue

Ville, village ou municipalité | État, province | Pays | Code postal

Nom | Numéro d'entreprise du Québec (NEQ) 1 1

Appartement | Numéro | Rue

Ville, village ou municipalité | État, province | Pays | Code postal

4 Informations générales

4.1 Titre des deux principales activités de la personne morale

CAE | 1re activité | Préciser (facultatif)

CAE | 2e activité (le cas échéant) | Préciser (facultatif)

4.2 Nombre de salariés au Québec (Cochez la case appropriée.)

O ☐ Aucun	A ☐ De 1 à 5	B ☐ De 6 à 10	C ☐ De 11 à 25	D ☐ De 26 à 49
	E ☐ De 50 à 99	F ☐ De 100 à 249	G ☐ De 250 à 499	H ☐ De 500 à 749
	I ☐ De 750 à 999	J ☐ De 1 000 à 2 499	K ☐ De 2 500 à 4 999	L ☐ 5 000 et plus

4.3 Période d'existence

Si l'existence légale de la personne morale est limitée dans le temps, inscrivez la date de cessation prévue. A M J

GD02 ZZ 71684850

Numéro d'entreprise du Québec
NEQ 1 1

Québec Incorporation Forms (continued)

RE-200 (2010-10)
Page 3

4 Informations générales (suite)

4.4 Identification des établissements au Québec

- L'établissement principal doit être déclaré dans la section prévue à cette fin.
- Inscrivez le nom, l'adresse complète des établissements et les deux principales activités qui y sont exercées.

Établissement principal au Québec

Nom

Adresse — Code postal

Principales activités de cet établissement :

CAE — 1re activité — Préciser (facultatif)

CAE — 2e activité (le cas échéant) — Préciser (facultatif)

◆ **Activité à déclaration obligatoire** (Cochez la case si vous exploitez un point de vente de tabac au détail [001].) ☐

Autres établissements

Nom

Adresse — Code postal

Principales activités de cet établissement :

CAE — 1re activité — Préciser (facultatif)

CAE — 2e activité (le cas échéant) — Préciser (facultatif)

◆ **Activité à déclaration obligatoire** (Cochez la case si vous exploitez un point de vente de tabac au détail [001].) ☐

Nom

Adresse — Code postal

Principales activités de cet établissement :

CAE — 1re activité — Préciser (facultatif)

CAE — 2e activité (le cas échéant) — Préciser (facultatif)

◆ **Activité à déclaration obligatoire** (Cochez la case si vous exploitez un point de vente de tabac au détail [001].) ☐

4.5 Autres noms utilisés au Québec

Inscrivez tout autre nom utilisé dans l'exercice de vos activités, dans l'exploitation de votre entreprise ou aux fins de la possession d'un droit réel immobilier autre qu'une priorité ou une hypothèque. Cela comprend notamment les noms d'emprunt utilisés et les noms de marchandises ou de services (marques de commerce) dont la personne morale est propriétaire ou usagère au Québec. S'il s'agit d'une marque de commerce, précisez-le. Une version française est **obligatoire** pour chacun des noms déclarés dans une autre langue.

Nom

Version dans une autre langue que le français, le cas échéant

Si l'espace prévu est insuffisant, joignez les annexes 2 et 3 en indiquant votre NEQ, s'il y a lieu.

Numéro d'entreprise du Québec
NEQ 1 1

GD03 ZZ 71684851

Québec Incorporation Forms (continued)

RE-200 (2010-10)
Page 4

5 Identification des actionnaires

Inscrivez, par ordre d'importance, le nom et l'adresse du domicile des trois actionnaires qui détiennent le plus grand nombre de voix.

Est-ce que le premier actionnaire détient plus de 50 % des voix? ☐ Oui ☐ Non

Nom du **premier** actionnaire

Adresse — Code postal

Nom du **deuxième** actionnaire

Adresse — Code postal

Nom du **troisième** actionnaire

Adresse — Code postal

6 Identification des administrateurs

Inscrivez le code de fonction approprié, les nom de famille et prénom, l'adresse du domicile et la date de début et de fin (le cas échéant) du mandat de tous les administrateurs qui sont membres du conseil d'administration. Si une personne a exercé plus d'une fonction, remplissez une section pour chacune d'entre elles.

☐ Tous les pouvoirs ont été retirés au conseil d'administration par une convention unanime des actionnaires.

Indiquez ci-dessous, les noms de famille et prénom, ainsi que l'adresse du domicile des actionnaires ou des tiers qui assument ces pouvoirs.

Codes de fonction des administrateurs : **PR** Président, **VP** Vice-président, **SE** Secrétaire, **TR** Trésorier, **ST** Secrétaire-trésorier, **AD** Administrateur, **AU** Autre

Code — Si AU, précisez la fonction — Date de début du mandat (A M J) — Date de fin du mandat (A M J)

Nom de famille et prénom

Appartement — Numéro — Rue

Ville, village ou municipalité — État, province — Pays — Code postal

Code — Si AU, précisez la fonction — Date de début du mandat (A M J) — Date de fin du mandat (A M J)

Nom de famille et prénom

Appartement — Numéro — Rue

Ville, village ou municipalité — État, province — Pays — Code postal

Si l'espace prévu est insuffisant, joignez l'annexe 4 en indiquant votre NEQ, s'il y a lieu.

GD04 ZZ 71684852

Numéro d'entreprise du Québec
NEQ 1 1

Québec Incorporation Forms (continued)

RE-200 (2010-10)
Page 5

7 Fondé de pouvoir

Si la personne morale n'a ni domicile ni établissement au Québec ou est dispensée par règlement de déclarer l'adresse de son domicile ou de ses établissements, inscrivez le nom de famille, le prénom et l'adresse complète d'un fondé de pouvoir résidant au Québec.

Nom de famille et prénom

Adresse — Code postal

8 Identification des personnes qui ne sont pas membres du conseil d'administration

Inscrivez le nom de famille, le prénom et l'adresse du domicile du président, du secrétaire et du principal dirigeant.

Nom de famille et prénom du **président**

Adresse — Code postal

Nom de famille et prénom du **secrétaire**

Adresse — Code postal

9 Administrateur du bien d'autrui

Si la personne morale est représentée par une personne chargée d'administrer l'ensemble de ses biens, inscrivez le code correspondant à la fonction de cette personne ainsi que son nom de famille, son prénom et son adresse complète. Cette personne a les droits et obligations que la Loi sur la publicité légale des entreprises confère à la personne morale.

Codes de fonction de l'administrateur du bien d'autrui :

CU Curateur **FI** Fiduciaire **LI** Liquidateur **SQ** Séquestre **SY** Syndic **AU** Autre

Code — Si AU, précisez la fonction — Date de début du mandat (A M J) — Date de fin du mandat (A M J)

Nom de famille et prénom

Appartement — Numéro — Rue

Ville, village ou municipalité — État, province — Pays — Code postal

10 Signature

Je, ______________________________ ,
Prénom et nom de famille de la personne autorisée

domicilié au ______________________________ ,
Adresse

certifie que je suis la personne autorisée par la personne morale à signer la présente déclaration, que les renseignements déclarés sont vrais et que le paiement requis, le cas échéant, accompagne la présente déclaration.

______________________________ Signature de la personne autorisée

______________________________ Date

Signez et retournez ce formulaire avec votre paiement. Ne pas télécopier.

GD05 ZZ 71684853

Numéro d'entreprise du Québec
NEQ 1 1

Québec Incorporation Forms (continued)

Registraire des entreprises
Québec

RE-301 (2010-10)
Page 1

Avis établissant l'adresse du siège et la liste des administrateurs

Ce formulaire s'adresse à toute société par actions qui désire joindre un avis établissant l'adresse du siège et la liste des administrateurs aux statuts de constitution, de continuation ou de fusion ordinaire. Veuillez lire les renseignements à la page 3 avant de remplir ce formulaire.

1 Nom
Inscrivez le nom de la société par actions et sa version dans une autre langue, s'il y a lieu.
N'inscrivez rien si vous demandez une désignation numérique au lieu d'un nom.

____

____

2 Siège
Inscrivez l'adresse complète du siège de la société par actions.

Appartement ______ Numéro ______ Rue ______

Ville, village ou municipalité ______ Province ______ Code postal ______

3 Liste des administrateurs
Inscrivez le nom de famille, le prénom et l'adresse complète de tous les administrateurs.

a) Nom de famille et prénom ______
Adresse ______ Code postal ______

b) Nom de famille et prénom ______
Adresse ______ Code postal ______

c) Nom de famille et prénom ______
Adresse ______ Code postal ______

d) Nom de famille et prénom ______
Adresse ______ Code postal ______

____
Signature de la personne autorisée

Réservé à l'administration

Signez et retournez ce formulaire avec vos statuts.
Ne pas télécopier.

Ministère du Revenu

H031 ZZ 72485149

APPENDIX "6-H"

Certificate of Incorporation

CANADA

Certificate of Incorporation

Canada Business Corporation Act

Certificat de constitution

Loi sur les sociétés commerciales canadiennes

BENSAR COMMERCE CORPORATION

Name of Corporation — Dénomination de la société

67336

Number — Numéro

I hereby certify that the above-mentioned Corporation, the Articles of Incorporation of which are attached, was incorporated under the Canada Business Corporations Act.

Je certifie par les présentes que la société mentionnée ci-haut, dont les statuts constitutifs sont joints, a été constituée en société en vertu de la Loi sur les sociétés commerciales canadiennes.

Frederick H. Sparling

Director — Directeur

July 14, 1980.

Date of Incorporation — Date de constitution

APPENDIX "6-I"
SELECTED SECTIONS FROM
The Québec Business Corporations Act

Chapter II
Constitution and Organization

3. A corporation may be constituted by one or more founders.

4. Any natural person qualified to be a director of a corporation may be the founder of a corporation.

A legal person may also be the founder of a corporation.

5. The articles of constitution must set out

(1) the name of the corporation, unless a designating number in lieu of a name has been requested from the enterprise registrar;

(2) the name and address of each founder, or the name of the founding legal person, the address of its head office and an exact reference to the Act under which it is constituted;

(3) the amount to which its share capital is limited, if applicable;

(4) the par value of its shares, if any;

(5) if there will be two or more classes of shares, the rights and restrictions attaching to the shares of each class;

(6) if a class of shares may be issued in series, the authority given to the board of directors to determine, before issue, the number of shares in, the designation of the shares of, and the rights and restrictions attaching to the shares of, each series;

(7) any restrictions on the transfer of its instruments or shares;

(8) the fixed number or the minimum and maximum number of directors; and

(9) any restrictions on its business activity.

6. The articles may set out any provision permitted by this Act to be set out in the by-laws of a corporation.

In the event of a conflict, the provisions of the articles of a corporation prevail over the provisions of the by-laws.

7. If the articles or a unanimous shareholder agreement require a greater number of votes of directors or shareholders than that required by this Act to effect any action, the provisions of the articles or of the unanimous shareholder agreement prevail.

The articles may not require a greater number of votes of shareholders to remove a director than the number required by this Act.

8. The following must be filed with the articles:

(1) a list of the directors of the corporation, containing their names and domiciles;

(2) a notice of the address of the corporation's head office;

(3) unless a designating number has been requested, a declaration stating that reasonable means have been taken to ensure that the name chosen is in compliance with the law; and

(4) any other document the Minister may require.

However, the list of directors and the notice of the address of the head office are not required to be filed if the initial declaration required under the Act respecting the legal publicity of enterprises (chapter P-44.1) is filed with the articles.

9. The articles of a corporation, signed by the founders, the documents required to be filed with them, and the fee set out in the Act respecting the legal publicity of enterprises (chapter P-44.1) must be sent to the enterprise registrar.

10. A corporation is constituted as of the date

and, if applicable, the time shown on the certificate of constitution issued by the enterprise registrar in accordance with Chapter XVIII.

The corporation is a legal person as of that time.

Division II
Organization Meeting

11. After a corporation is constituted, the board of directors holds an organization meeting at which the directors may

(1) make by-laws;

(2) adopt forms of share certificates and corporation records;

(3) authorize the issue of shares; and

(4) appoint the officers.

A founder or a director may call the organization meeting by giving not less than five days' notice to each director, stating the time and place of the meeting.

Chapter IV
Name, Head Office, Records and Documents

16. A corporation's name must not

(1) contravene the Charter of the French language (chapter C-11);

(2) include an expression which the law reserves for another person or prohibits the corporation from using;

(3) include an expression that evokes an immoral, obscene or scandalous notion;

(4) incorrectly indicate the corporation's juridical form or fail to indicate that form when required by law;

(5) falsely suggest that the corporation is a non-profit group;

(6) falsely suggest that the corporation is, or is related to, a public authority determined by government regulation;

(7) falsely suggest that the corporation is related to another person or group of persons, particularly in the cases and in view of the criteria determined by government regulation;

(8) be identical to a name reserved for or used by another person or group of persons in Québec, particularly in view of the criteria determined by government regulation;

(9) be confusingly similar to a name reserved for or used by another person or group of persons in Québec, particularly in view of the criteria determined by government regulation; or

(10) be misleading in any other manner.

17. On application and on payment of the fee set out in the Act respecting the legal publicity of enterprises (chapter P-44.1), the enterprise registrar may reserve a name for a corporation for a period of 90 days.

20. If a corporation's name does not include the term “société par actions” or “compagnie”, it must comprise the abbreviation “s.a.”, “ltée” or “inc.” at the end to indicate that the corporation is a limited-liability corporation.

22. A corporation may identify itself in a language other than French outside Québec and use that name on its negotiable instruments, invoices or purchase orders for goods or services used outside Québec or in its contracts applied outside Québec.

23. At the request of a corporation or its founders, the enterprise registrar assigns a designating number to the corporation in lieu of a name.

29. The head office of a corporation must be permanently located in Québec.

31. A corporation must prepare and maintain, at its head office, records containing

(1) the articles and the by-laws, and any unanimous shareholder agreement;

(2) minutes of meetings and resolutions of shareholders;

(3) the names and domiciles of the directors, and the dates of the beginning and end of their term of office; and

(4) a securities register.

Chapter V
Finance

43. The share capital of a corporation may be limited or unlimited. It may be constituted of shares with par value, of shares without par value or of both types of shares.

Unless otherwise provided in the articles, a corporation has an unlimited share capital and its shares are without par value.

44. The share capital of a corporation may comprise one or more classes of shares. The classes may each include one or more series of shares.

If there is more than one class of shares, the articles of the corporation must set out the rights and restrictions attaching to each class of shares.

47. The share capital of a corporation must include shares that carry

(1) the right to vote at any shareholders meeting of the corporation;

(2) the right to receive any dividend declared by the corporation; and

(3) the right to receive a share of the remaining property of the corporation on liquidation.

All such rights are not required to be attached to one class of shares.

48. Unless otherwise provided in the articles, the rights mentioned in section 47 are attached to every share.

If one of those rights is not attached to any share issued by the corporation, any restriction on that right has no effect until a share to which that right is attached is issued.

52. Unless otherwise provided in the by-laws or in a unanimous shareholder agreement and subject to section 55, shares may be issued at the times, to the persons and for the consideration the board of directors determines.

53. Shares may be issued whether or not they are fully paid.

103. Unless otherwise provided in the articles or in a unanimous shareholder agreement, the board of directors may declare and the corporation may pay a dividend either in money or property or by issuing fully paid shares or options or rights to acquire fully paid shares of the corporation.

104. A corporation may not declare and pay a dividend, except by issuing shares or options or rights to acquire shares, if there are reasonable grounds for believing that the corporation is, or would after the payment be, unable to pay its liabilities as they become due.

Chapter VI
Directors and Officers

106. The board of directors of a corporation is composed of one or more directors.

If the corporation is a reporting (public) issuer, the board of directors is composed of not fewer than three directors, at least two of whom must not be officers or employees of the corporation or an affiliate of the corporation.

108. Any natural person may be a director of a corporation, except persons disqualified for the office of director under the Civil Code or persons declared incapable by decision of a court of another jurisdiction.

109. Unless otherwise provided in the articles, a director is not required to be a shareholder.

110. The directors are elected by the shareholders, in the manner and for the term, not exceeding three years, set out in the by-laws.

112. Subject to a unanimous shareholder agreement, the board of directors exercises all the powers necessary to manage, or supervise the management of, the business and affairs of the corporation.

113. Unless otherwise provided in the articles or in a unanimous shareholder agreement, the board of directors adopts the corporation's by-laws. The by-laws are effective as of the date of the resolution of the board.

The by-laws must be submitted to the shareholders for approval at the next shareholders meeting, and the shareholders may, by ordinary resolution, ratify, reject or amend them.

116. Unless otherwise provided in the by-laws or in a unanimous shareholder agreement, the board of directors may designate the offices of the corporation, appoint directors or other persons as officers and specify their functions.

The officers are mandataries of the corporation.

119. Subject to this division, the directors are bound by the same obligations as are imposed by the Civil Code on any director of a legal person.

Consequently, in the exercise of their functions, the directors are duty-bound toward the corporation to act with prudence and diligence, honesty and loyalty and in the interest of the corporation.

In their capacity as mandataries of the corporation, the officers are bound, among other things, by the same obligations as are imposed on the directors under the second paragraph.

122. A director or officer of a corporation must disclose the nature and value of any interest he or she has in a contract or transaction to which the corporation is a party.

140. A resolution in writing, signed by all the directors entitled to vote on the resolution, has the same force as if it had been passed at a meeting of the board or, as the case may be, of a committee of the board.

154. Directors of a corporation are solidarily liable to the employees of a corporation for all debts not exceeding six months' wages payable to each such employee for services performed for the corporation while they are directors of the corporation respectively.

However, a director is not liable unless the corporation is sued for the debt within one year after it becomes due and the writ of execution is returned unsatisfied in whole or in part or unless, during that period, a liquidation order is made against the corporation or it becomes bankrupt within the meaning of that expression in the Bankruptcy and Insolvency Act (Revised Statutes of Canada, 1985, chapter B-3) and a claim for the debt is filed with the liquidator or the syndic.

155. Directors of a corporation who vote for or consent to a resolution authorizing the issue of shares for consideration payable in property or in past services are solidarily liable to the corporation for any amount by which the consideration received is less than the amount of money the corporation would have received if the shares had been issued for money on the date of the resolution.

However, a director who proves that he or she did not know and could not reasonably have known that the shares were issued for a consideration less than the amount of money the corporation should have received is not liable under the first paragraph.

156. Directors of a corporation who vote for or consent to a resolution authorizing any of the following are solidarily liable to restore to the corporation any amounts involved and not otherwise recovered by the corporation:

(4) a payment of a dividend contrary to section 104;

Chapter VII
Shareholders

163. An annual meeting of shareholders entitled to vote at such a meeting must be held not later than 18 months after the corporation is constituted and, subsequently, not later than 15 months after the last preceding annual shareholders meeting.

178. A resolution in writing signed by the sole shareholder of the corporation or by all the shareholders entitled to vote on the resolution is as valid as if it had been passed at a shareholders meeting.

179. Unless otherwise provided in the articles, each share of a corporation entitles the holder to one vote.

207. The board of directors may at any time call a special shareholders meeting.

213. All the shareholders of a corporation, whether or not their shares carry voting rights, may agree in writing among themselves or among themselves and one or more third persons to restrict the powers of the board of directors to manage, or supervise the management of, the business and affairs of the corporation, or to withdraw all such powers from the board.

214. To the extent that a unanimous

shareholder agreement restricts the powers of the board of directors to manage, or supervise the management of, the business and affairs of the corporation, or withdraws all such powers from the board, parties to the unanimous shareholder agreement who are given those powers have all the rights, powers, duties, obligations and liabilities of directors of the corporation, whether they arise under this Act or otherwise, including any defences available to the directors, and the directors are relieved of their rights, powers, duties and liabilities, including their liability for the wages of the corporation's employees, to the same extent.

216. If a unanimous shareholder agreement withdraws all powers from the board of directors and confers them on shareholders or third persons, the corporation must declare to the enterprise registrar the name and domicile of those who have assumed those powers.

The shareholders are in such a case subject to the rules of Divisions I and II, unless otherwise provided in the unanimous shareholder agreement or the by-laws.

The shareholders may choose not to establish a board of directors.

217. Decisions of a sole shareholder on whom all of the powers of the board of directors have been conferred may be made by written resolution.

Any act by such a sole shareholder on behalf of the corporation is deemed to be authorized.

Such a sole shareholder may choose not to establish a board of directors and not to appoint an auditor, and is not required to comply with the requirements of this Act relating to the by-laws, shareholders meetings and meetings of the board of directors.

224. Shareholders are not, as shareholders, liable for any act of the corporation.

However, they are debtors to the corporation for any unpaid amount on shares they hold in its share capital.

APPENDIX "6-J"
SELECTED SECTIONS FROM
The Canada Business Corporations Act

PART I
INCORPORATION

Incorporators

5. (1) One or more individuals not one of whom

(a) is less than eighteen years of age,

(b) is of unsound mind and has been so found by a court in Canada or elsewhere, or

(c) has the status of bankrupt,

may incorporate a corporation by signing articles of incorporation and complying with section 7.

Bodies corporate

(2) One or more bodies corporate may incorporate a corporation by signing articles of incorporation and complying with section 7.

Articles of incorporation

6. (1) Articles of incorporation shall follow the form that the Director fixes and shall set out, in respect of the proposed corporation,

(a) the name of the corporation;

(b) the province in Canada where the registered office is to be situated;

(c) the classes and any maximum number of shares that the corporation is authorized to issue, and

(i) if there will be two or more classes of shares, the rights, privileges, restrictions and conditions attaching to each class of shares, and

(ii) if a class of shares may be issued in series, the authority given to the directors to fix the number of shares in, and to determine the designation of, and the rights, privileges, restrictions and conditions attaching to, the shares of each series;

(d) if the issue, transfer or ownership of shares of the corporation is to be restricted, a statement to that effect and a statement as to the nature of such restrictions;

(e) the number of directors or, subject to paragraph 107(*a*), the minimum and maximum number of directors of the corporation; and

(f) any restrictions on the businesses that the corporation may carry on.

(2) The articles may set out any provisions permitted by this Act or by law to be set out in the by-laws of the corporation.
Special majorities

Delivery of articles of incorporation

7. An incorporator shall send to the Director articles of incorporation and the documents required by sections 19 and 106.

Certificate of incorporation

8. (1) Subject to subsection (2), on receipt of articles of incorporation, the Director shall issue a certificate of incorporation in accordance with section 262.

(2) The Director may refuse to issue the certificate if a notice that is required to be sent under subsection 19(2) or 106(1) indicates that the corporation, if it came into existence, would not be in compliance with this Act.

Effect of certificate

9. A corporation comes into existence on the date shown in the certificate of incorporation.

Name of corporation

10. (1) The word or expression "Limited", "Limitée", "Incorporated", "Incorporée", "Corporation" or "Société par actions de régime fédéral" or the corresponding abbreviation “Ltd.”, “Ltée”, “Inc.”, “Corp.” or “S.A.R.F.” shall be part, other than only in a figurative or descriptive sense, of the name of every corporation, but a corporation may use and be legally designated by either the full or the corresponding abbreviated form.

(3) Subject to subsection 12(1), the name of a corporation may be set out in its articles in an English form, a French form, an English form and a French form, or a combined English and French form, so long as the combined form meets the prescribed criteria. The corporation may use and may be legally designated by any such form.

Reserving name
11. (1) The Director may, on request, reserve for ninety days a name for an intended corporation or for a corporation about to change its name.

Designating number
(2) If requested to do so by the incorporators or a corporation, the Director shall assign to the corporation as its name a designating number followed by the word “Canada” and a word or expression, or the corresponding abbreviation, referred to in subsection 10(1).

Prohibited names
12. (1) A corporation shall not be incorporated or continued as a corporation under this Act with, have, carry on business under or identify itself by a name

(a) that is, as prescribed, prohibited or deceptively misdescriptive; or

(b) that is reserved for another corporation or intended corporation under section 11.

Personal liability
14. (1) Subject to this section, a person who enters into, or purports to enter into, a written contract in the name of or on behalf of a corporation before it comes into existence is personally bound by the contract and is entitled to its benefits.

(2) A corporation may, within a reasonable time after it comes into existence, by any action or conduct signifying its intention to be bound thereby, adopt a written contract made before it came into existence in its name or on its behalf…

PART III
CAPACITY AND POWERS

15. (1) A corporation has the capacity and, subject to this Act, the rights, powers and privileges of a natural person.

(2) A corporation may carry on business throughout Canada.

(3) A corporation has the capacity to carry on its business, conduct its affairs and exercise its powers in any jurisdiction outside Canada to the extent that the laws of such jurisdiction permit.

Powers of a corporation
16. (1) It is not necessary for a by-law to be passed in order to confer any particular power on the corporation or its directors.

(2) A corporation shall not carry on any business or exercise any power that it is restricted by its articles from carrying on or exercising, nor shall the corporation exercise any of its powers in a manner contrary to its articles.

PART IV
REGISTERED OFFICE AND RECORDS

32. (1) A corporation shall at all times have a registered office in the province in Canada specified in its articles.

(2) A notice of registered office in the form that the Director fixes shall be sent to the Director together with any articles that designate or change the province where the registered office of the corporation is located.

Corporate records
33. (1) A corporation shall prepare and maintain, at its registered office or at any other place in Canada designated by the directors, records containing

(a) the articles and the by-laws, and all amendments thereto, and a copy of any unanimous shareholder agreement;

(b) minutes of meetings and resolutions of shareholders;

(c) copies of all notices required by section 106 or 113; and

(d) a securities register that complies with section 50.

(2) In addition to the records described in subsection (1), a corporation shall prepare and maintain adequate accounting records and records containing minutes of meetings and resolutions of the directors and any committee thereof.

Corporate seal
23. (1) A corporation may, but need not, adopt a corporate seal, and may change a corporate seal that is adopted.

PART V
CORPORATE FINANCE

Shares
24. (1) Shares of a corporation shall be in registered form and shall be without nominal or par value.

Rights attached to shares
(3) Where a corporation has only one class of shares, the rights of the holders thereof are equal in all respects and include the rights

(a) to vote at any meeting of shareholders of the corporation;

(b) to receive any dividend declared by the corporation; and

(c) to receive the remaining property of the corporation on dissolution.

(4) The articles may provide for more than one class of shares and, if they so provide,

(a) the rights, privileges, restrictions and conditions attaching to the shares of each class shall be set out therein; and

(b) the rights set out in subsection (3) shall be attached to at least one class of shares but all such rights are not required to be attached to one class.

Issue of shares
25. (1) Subject to the articles, the by-laws and any unanimous shareholder agreement and to section 28, shares may be issued at such times and to such persons and for such consideration as the directors may determine.

(2) Shares issued by a corporation are non-assessable and the holders are not liable to the corporation or to its creditors in respect thereof.

(3) A share shall not be issued until the consideration for the share is fully paid in money or in property or past services that are not less in value than the fair equivalent of the money that the corporation would have received if the share had been issued for money.

42. A corporation shall not declare or pay a dividend if there are reasonable grounds for believing that

(a) the corporation is, or would after the payment be, unable to pay its liabilities as they become due; or

(b) the realizable value of the corporation's assets would thereby be less than the aggregate of its liabilities and stated capital of all classes.

Shareholder immunity
45. (1) The shareholders of a corporation are not, as shareholders, liable for any liability, act or default of the corporation…

PART X
DIRECTORS AND OFFICERS

Duty to manage or supervise management
102. (1) Subject to any unanimous shareholder agreement, the directors shall manage, or supervise the management of, the business and affairs of a corporation.

Number of directors
(2) A corporation shall have one or more directors but a distributing (public) corporation, any of the issued securities of which remain outstanding and are held by more than one person, shall have not fewer than three directors, at least two of whom are not officers or employees of the corporation or its affiliates.

By-laws

103. (1) Unless the articles, by-laws or a unanimous shareholder agreement otherwise provide, the directors may, by resolution, make, amend or repeal any by-laws that regulate the business or affairs of the corporation.

(2) The directors shall submit a by-law, or an amendment or a repeal of a by-law, made under subsection (1) to the shareholders at the next meeting of shareholders, and the shareholders may, by ordinary resolution, confirm, reject or amend the by-law, amendment or repeal.

Qualifications of directors

105. (1) The following persons are disqualified from being a director of a corporation:

(a) anyone who is less than eighteen years of age;

(b) anyone who is of unsound mind and has been so found by a court in Canada or elsewhere;

(c) a person who is not an individual; or

(d) a person who has the status of bankrupt.

(2) Unless the articles otherwise provide, a director of a corporation is not required to hold shares issued by the corporation.

(3) Subject to subsection (3.1), at least twenty-five per cent of the directors of a corporation must be resident Canadians. However, if a corporation has less than four directors, at least one director must be a resident Canadian.

Election of directors

106. (3) Subject to paragraph 107(*b*), shareholders of a corporation shall, by ordinary resolution at the first meeting of shareholders and at each succeeding annual meeting at which an election of directors is required, elect directors to hold office for a term expiring not later than the close of the third annual meeting of shareholders following the election.

Directors' liability

118. (1) Directors of a corporation who vote for or consent to a resolution authorizing the issue of a share under section 25 for a consideration other than money are jointly and severally, or solidarily, liable to the corporation to make good any amount by which the consideration received is less than the fair equivalent of the money that the corporation would have received if the share had been issued for money on the date of the resolution.

(2) Directors of a corporation who vote for or consent to a resolution authorizing any of the following are jointly and severally, or solidarily, liable to restore to the corporation any amounts so distributed or paid and not otherwise recovered by the corporation:

(d) a payment of a dividend contrary to section 42;

Liability of directors for wages

119. (1) Directors of a corporation are jointly and severally, or solidarily, liable to employees of the corporation for all debts not exceeding six months wages payable to each such employee for services performed for the corporation while they are such directors respectively.

(2) A director is not liable under subsection (1) unless

(a) the corporation has been sued for the debt within six months after it has become due and execution has been returned unsatisfied in whole or in part;

(b) the corporation has commenced liquidation and dissolution proceedings or has been dissolved and a claim for the debt has been proved within six months after the earlier of the date of commencement of the liquidation and dissolution proceedings and the date of dissolution; or

(c) the corporation has made an assignment or a bankruptcy order has been made against it under the Bankruptcy and Insolvency Act and a claim for the debt has been proved within six months after the date of the assignment or bankruptcy order.

(3) A director, unless sued for a debt referred to in subsection (1) while a director or within two years after ceasing to be a director, is not liable under this section.

Disclosure of interest

120. (1) A director or an officer of a corporation shall disclose to the corporation, in writing or by requesting to have it entered in the minutes of meetings of directors or of meetings of committees of directors, the nature and extent of any interest that he or she has in a material contract or material transaction, whether made or proposed, with the corporation, if the director or officer

(a) is a party to the contract or transaction;

(b) is a director or an officer, or an individual acting in a similar capacity, of a party to the contract or transaction; or

(c) has a material interest in a party to the contract or transaction.

Officers

121. Subject to the articles, the by-laws or any unanimous shareholder agreement,

(a) the directors may designate the offices of the corporation, appoint as officers persons of full capacity, specify their duties and delegate to them powers to manage the business and affairs of the corporation, except powers to do anything referred to in subsection 115(3);

Duty of care of directors and officers

122. (1) Every director and officer of a corporation in exercising their powers and discharging their duties shall

(a) act honestly and in good faith with a view to the best interests of the corporation; and

(b) exercise the care, diligence and skill that a reasonably prudent person would exercise in comparable circumstances.

(2) Every director and officer of a corporation shall comply with this Act, the regulations, articles, by-laws and any unanimous shareholder agreement.

(3) Subject to subsection 146(5), no provision in a contract, the articles, the by-laws or a resolution relieves a director or officer from the duty to act in accordance with this Act or the regulations or relieves them from liability for a breach thereof.

PART XII
SHAREHOLDERS

Place of meetings

132. (1) Meetings of shareholders of a corporation shall be held at the place within Canada provided in the by-laws or, in the absence of such provision, at the place within Canada that the directors determine.

(2) Despite subsection (1), a meeting of shareholders of a corporation may be held at a place outside Canada if the place is specified in the articles or all the shareholders entitled to vote at the meeting agree that the meeting is to be held at that place.

Calling annual meetings

133. (1) The directors of a corporation shall call an annual meeting of shareholders

(a) not later than eighteen months after the corporation comes into existence; and

(b) subsequently, not later than fifteen months after holding the last preceding annual meeting but no later than six months after the end of the corporation's preceding financial year.

Calling special meetings

(2) The directors of a corporation may at any time call a special meeting of shareholders.

Right to vote

140. (1) Unless the articles otherwise provide, each share of a corporation entitles the holder thereof to one vote at a meeting of shareholders.

Unanimous shareholder agreement

146. (1) An otherwise lawful written agreement among all the shareholders of a corporation, or among all the shareholders and one or more persons who are not shareholders, that restricts, in whole or in part, the powers of the directors to manage, or supervise the management of, the business and affairs of the corporation is valid.

(5) To the extent that a unanimous shareholder agreement restricts the powers of the directors to manage, or supervise the management of, the business and affairs of the corporation, parties to the unanimous shareholder agreement who are given that power to manage or supervise the management of the business and affairs of the corporation have all the rights, powers, duties and liabilities of a director of the corporation, whether they arise under this Act or otherwise, including any defences available to the directors, and the directors are relieved of their rights, powers, duties and liabilities, including their liabilities under section 119, to the same extent.

APPENDIX "6-K"

Share Certificate

LUSTGA4LLE6S000 TOS-80 01 05 00450 V19K NORM

Maclean Hunter

Maclean Hunter Limited Maclean Hunter Limitée

(Incorporated under the laws of the Province of Ontario)
(Constituée en vertu des lois de la province d'Ontario)

Applicable Canadian legislation necessitates certain restrictions on the right to transfer the shares represented hereby and a copy of the full text thereof is obtainable on demand and without fee from the Corporation.

Les lois canadiennes d'application exigent certaines restrictions sur le droit de transférer les actions représentées par ce certificat. Un exemplaire du texte intégral de ces restrictions est disponible sans frais sur demande à la société.

NUMBER NUMÉRO C49918

SHARES ACTIONS ***200***

C 49918

This certifies that
Les présentes attestent que

[redacted]
ST LAURENT QUE
H4L 4Y6

SPECIMEN

*200*****
200**
200
****200**
*****200*

is the registered holder of
est le détenteur immatriculé de

fully paid common shares without par value in the capital of

actions ordinaires entièrement libérées sans valeur au pair du capital-actions de

CUSIP 554749 80 4

554749 80 4

Maclean Hunter Limited — Maclean Hunter Limitée

Registration of the transfer of the shares represented by this Certificate may be made on the appropriate register of the Corporation upon surrender of this Certificate duly endorsed. There are preferences, rights, conditions, restrictions, limitations and prohibitions attaching to the shares represented by this Certificate and a copy of the full text thereof is obtainable on demand and without fee from the Corporation. This Certificate is not valid unless countersigned by the Transfer Agent and Registrar of the Corporation. In Witness Whereof, the Corporation has caused this Certificate to be signed by its duly authorized officers.

L'enregistrement d'un transfert des actions représentées par ce certificat peut être fait dans le registre pertinent de la société sur remise de ce certificat dûment endossé. Les actions représentées par ce certificat sont assujetties à des privilèges, droits, conditions, restrictions, limitations et prohibitions dont on peut obtenir sans frais le texte intégral sur demande à la société. Ce certificat n'est valable que s'il est contresigné par l'agent de transfert et le registraire de la société. En foi de quoi, la société a fait signer le présent certificat par ses dirigeants dûment autorisés.

Dated / Daté le 08 JAN 1991

Secretary
Secrétaire

Chairman of the Board
Président du conseil

COUNTERSIGNED AND REGISTERED — CONTRESIGNÉ ET ENREGISTRÉ

MONTREAL TRUST COMPANY OF CANADA
COMPAGNIE MONTRÉAL TRUST DU CANADA

TORONTO REGINA
MONTRÉAL WINNIPEG
CALGARY VANCOUVER

TRANSFER AGENT AND REGISTRAR — AGENT DE TRANSFERT ET REGISTRAIRE

BY:
PAR:

Authorized Officer — Officier autorisé

This Certificate also evidences and entitles the holder hereof to certain rights under the Corporation's Shareholder Protection Rights Plan. Please see the reverse side hereof for details.

Ce certificat confère à son porteur et atteste certains droits aux termes du régime de protection des droits des actionnaires de la société. Pour de plus amples détails, voir le verso des présentes.

These shares are transferable at the office of Montreal Trust Company of Canada in Toronto, Montreal, Calgary, Regina, Winnipeg and Vancouver.

Ces actions sont cessibles aux bureaux de Compagnie Montréal Trust du Canada à Toronto, Montréal, Calgary, Regina, Winnipeg et Vancouver.

CASE 6.1

146400 Canada Inc. v. Network Transport Ltd.

[2001] Q.J. No. 2861, Quebec Superior Court

(Excerpts of Judgment)

REASONS FOR JUDGMENT

JOEL A. SILCOFF J.:— Pursuant to an Offer to Lease (the "Offer to Lease") dated March 30, 1990 Plaintiff, 146400 Canada Inc. ("Canada Inc."), leased to an entity named in the Offer to Lease as "NETWORK TRANSPORT", a certain industrial immoveable located at 5800 Côte de Liesse Road in the Town of Mount Royal, Quebec (the "Leased Premises") for a term of five years commencing August 1, 1990 and expiring July 31, 1995 (the "Term").

Canada Inc. maintains that Defendant, Network Transport Limited, ("Network Transport Limited") was the lessee of the Leased Premises.

Network Transport Limited maintains that the Offer to Lease was signed by its president, Charles Bates, not on behalf of Network Transport Limited but rather on behalf of its wholly owned subsidiary, Network Transport (Québec) Limitée ("Network Transport (Québec)"). A formal lease was never signed and accordingly the parties acknowledge that the contractual relationship governing the Leased Premises is governed by the Offer to Lease.

Prior to the expiry of the Term, the Leased Premises were abandoned leaving a substantial amount due and owing to Canada Inc. for unpaid rent.
Network Transport (Québec) made a voluntary assignment under the An Act Respecting Bankruptcy and Insolvency [See Note 1 below] (the "Bankruptcy Act") on March 7 1994. Network Transport Limited refuses to pay the amounts claimed by Canada Inc. arguing that it was not party to the Offer to lease.

THE FACTS

By a Letter of Intent dated March 5, 1990 addressed to Claridge Properties Ltd. on the letterhead of Network Transport (Ontario) Limited and signed by Charles D. Bates, President (the "Letter of Intent"), Mr. Bates set out the terms and conditions under which the tenant would be prepared to enter into a contract of lease for the Leased Premises. The first paragraph of the Letter of Intent, states that it is submitted, ... subject to our agreement ..." (our underlining).

Accompanying the Letter of Intent is a cheque dated March 5 1990, drawn on the account of Network Transport Limited, payable to the order of Claridge Properties Ltd. in the amount of $10,000.00. The cheque, signed by Charles Bates, is drawn on the account of Network Transport Limited at the Bank of Montreal branch located in Mississauga, Ontario.

Subsequently, by letter dated March 12, 1990 addressed to Claridge Properties, again on the letterhead of Network Transport (Ontario), Mr. Bates informs the lessor:

> "Now, about our Company ... it has been in business since 1922 where it started in the City of Montreal. We worked specifically for Kraft Foods and have been with them since our inception.
> [...]
> Our group of companies includes:
> Network Transport Limited, Bert Clifford Transport Inc. and 148668 Canada Inc. operating as Therm Express.
> We are a profitable business."

By letter dated June 15, 1990 addressed to Miss Cheryl Dufour, Claridge Properties Limited, on the letterhead "Le Groupe Network Group" and signed by Gaétan Lachance, regional manager, on behalf of the "Network Group", Mr. Lachance complains of certain deficiencies in the Leased Premises and states:

> "We have now been in the Premises since May 27, and we still have at the present the following items that are still pending and work not completed..."
> (our underlining)

It is to be noted that the letter dated June 15 1990 addressed on the letterhead of "Le Groupe Network Group" includes the following companies as being part of "Le Groupe Network Group", namely: Network Transport Limited, Les Transports Network (Québec) Ltée, Network Transport (Ontario) Limited, 148668 Canada Inc. o/a Therm Express and Bert Clifford Transport.

The Offer to Lease provides, inter alia:

> "4. USE
> The Premises will be used for dispatch offices, transport, garage and storage area, parking of motor vehicles/tractor trailers and other industrial purposes."

By letter dated February 18, 1992, addressed to Mr. Michel Cohen, Samijo Management Inc. (at the time property managers for the Leased Premises), on the letterhead of "Network" and signed "Network Transport Limited"", Charles D. Bates, President, he says:

> "... We would appreciate your consideration as to the points raised and would like you to be more definite with regards to what you will do to relieve the problem of congestion in the area we have rented from you at the present time."
> (our underlining)

By letter dated October 19, 1993 addressed to Claridge Properties Ltd., on the letterhead of "Network" and signed by Charles D. Bates, President, he says:

> "You asked me, during our telephone conversation to tell you what is required to make us happy as your tenant and you further emphasised that you wanted your tenants to be satisfied. [...]

We suggest the following to rectify and satisfy us as a tenant.

1) Re-negotiate the arrangement and we move to the rear portion.
2) Abide by the offer to lease.
3) Find us a suitable building.
4) Move out the rear tenant.
5) Reduce rent by $60,000.00

There is no evidence that proposal contained in the letter of October 19, 1993 was accepted by the lessor.

Save for one occasion, payment of the base rental as well as of all other amounts payable pursuant to the Offer to Lease was made at all times by Network Transport Limited until Network Transport (Québec) made its voluntary assignment in bankruptcy.

Charles Bates is President of Network Transport Limited as well as of Network Transport (Québec). He and his family control 100 % of the outstanding shares of the capital stock of Network Transport Limited. Network Transport (Québec) is a wholly owned subsidiary of Network Transport Limited.

On March 7, 1994 Network Transport (Québec) filed a voluntary assignment under the Bankruptcy Act.

Although representatives of Canada Inc. attended the first meeting of creditors of Network Transport (Québec), Canada Inc. did not file a proof of claim as creditor of the bankrupt estate.

On May 19, 1994 Canada Inc. sent a MISE EN DEMEURE to Network Transport Limited claiming arrears of rental then owing, in the amount of $161,361.16 being the rental arrears due and owing up to May 1994.

By letter dated June 2, 1994 addressed to Messrs Phillips and Vineberg, attorneys for Canada Inc., by Mercure, Béliveau & Associés Inc. Syndics, on behalf of the bankrupt estate of Network Transport (Québec), the Trustee advised counsel for Canada Inc.:

> "L'offre de location du 30 mars 1990 à Network Transport (Québec) Limited par 146400 Canada Inc. a été annulée par le soussigné en sa qualité de responsable de l'actif de la compagnie mentionnée en titre.
> [...]
> Cette offre de location concernait strictement Network Transport (Québec) Limited et ne s'applique aucunement à toute autre compagnie reliée."

Subsequent to the abandonment of the Leased Premises, representatives of Canada Inc. made efforts to lease the Leased Premises to another tenant. Advertisements were placed in the local newspapers and brokers were advised of the availability of the Leased Premises. However, the efforts to lease were unsuccessful and the Leased Premises remained vacant.

On April 19, 2001 counsel for the parties signed a document entitled "ADMISSION OF STIPULATED FACTS" in which the following admissions are made:

1. "Subject to the Courts determination that Defendant is liable for rental arrears for the premises leased from the Plaintiff by the Defendant, Plaintiffs total claim for arrears shall amount to $238,398.25, plus GST and PST, plus interest according to the conclusions of Plaintiff's Declaration. This amount is calculated as follows:

Rental arrears for the period prior to March, 1994	$70,806.64
Rental arrears of $9,858.33 per month for the period from March, 1994 until the end of the term of the lease at July 31, 1995 (17 x $9,858.33)	$167,591.61
	$238,398.25

2. The Parties agree that Plaintiff shall amend its Declaration to claim the total amount of $238,398.25 for rental arrears, in support of which amount Plaintiffs shall not be required to produce further evidence with respect thereto;

3. In addition to contesting liability for the amount claimed by Plaintiff, Defendant reserves all its rights to plead in its defense that the amount of $238,398.25 should be reduced by an amount to be established and pleaded at trial."

ANALYSIS

Defendant Network Transport Limited argues that it was not the lessee of the Leased Premises but rather that it was its wholly owned subsidiary, Network Transport (Québec), which was the sole lessee. Network Transport Limited maintains that there is no lien de droit between Canada Inc. and itself and that it is not liable for any arrears of rental under the Offer to Lease.

In its DÉFENSE AMENDÉE, Network Transport Limited alleges that it is merely a holding corporation having no commercial operations; that its head office and all of its activities are located in the province of Ontario and that it has no activities in Quebec.

Mr. Charles Bates testified to this effect and affirmed that Network Transport Limited was merely a holding corporation, that it had no employees or activities in Quebec nor did it have any place of business or offices situate in Quebec. The annual returns filed by Network Transport Limited and the Fichier central des entreprises indicate otherwise.

Moreover, an analysis of the non-consolidated financial statements for the periods relevant to the present proceedings show total sales of Network Transport Limited alone to have been in excess of $11,000,000.00 for each of the years in question and operating losses or profits varying from a high of $209,340.00 losses for fiscal year 1992 to profits of $205,147.00 for fiscal year 1993. The corporation was more than a simple inactive holding company.

It is to be noted that the consolidated financial statements of Network Transport Limited for the periods in question were not produced as exhibits.

As previously indicated, the annual return for the period ended June 30, 1992 filed with the Inspecteur général des institutions Financières du gouvernement du Québec on behalf of Network Transport Limited and signed by Mr. Bates, indicates that the corporation had a principal office in Quebec situate in the Leased Premises, that the corporation had between 1 and 5 employees in Quebec and that the nature of the corporation's activities were not that of a holding company but rather "Code #4569: autres camionnages".

Mr. Bates acknowledged that in the preparation of the financial statement of Network Transport Limited and its subsidiaries, the auditors would take into consideration the best tax advantage for all of the companies forming part of the "Network Group" and make such inter corporate financial adjustments and charge-backs as may be in the best interest of the parent corporation and its subsidiaries.

Mr. Bates was examined on the contents of his letter dated March 12, 1990 addressed to Claridge Properties, the purpose of which, according to his testimony, was to respond to the lessor's request for financial information concerning the prospective tenant of the Leased Premises, In his letter of March 12, 1990 Mr. Bates says: "We are a profitable business.". If, as he maintains, he was referring to Network Transport (Québec), he was at best being misleading if not untruthful. The audited financial statements of Network Transport (Québec) for the fiscal period ending December 31, 1989 the period immediately prior to the March 12, 1990 letter, report a net operating loss of $174,730.00 for that period.

When asked to justify this apparent attempt to mislead, Mr. Bates' responses were less than candid and tended to cast serious doubts on the reliability and credibility of his testimony in this regard.

In a letter dated February 18, 1992 addressed by Mr. Bates, on behalf of Network Transport Limited, to the then manager of the Leased Premises, he asks that the latter:

> "... relieve the problem of congestion in the area we have rented from you ..."

When questioned on the apparent inconsistency of his testimony to the effect that the tenant was Network Transport (Québec) and the clear wording of letter of February 18, 1992 implying that Network Transport Limited was the tenant of the Leased Premises, Mr. Bates responses were not consistent with commercial logic. Mr. Bates acknowledged that several, if not all, of the companies forming the Network Group used the Leased Premises for purposes of parking and servicing their respective vehicles while in and around the Montreal area.

The Court finds that at all times prior to the execution of the Offer to Lease as well as subsequent thereto, Mr. Bates and Network Transport Limited acted in such a manner as to induce Plaintiff, Canada Inc., to believe, as reasonable business people, that they were doing business with Network Transport Limited and not with any one or more of its subsidiary companies.

Throughout the Term of the Offer to Lease, rental payments were made by cheques drawn on the account of Network Transport Limited with no indication that payment was being made on behalf of Network Transport (Québec). Despite vague and unsubstantiated allegations by Mr. Bates that the amounts paid by Network Transport Limited were adjusted or reimbursed by Network Transport (Québec) through accounting book entries, there is no proof to this effect. Indeed, the testimony of Mr. Bates was to the effect that any adjustments made with respect to inter-corporate debts among the Network Group of companies was done only to maximise the tax advantages and for no other reason.

The Court finds that Network Transport Limited is, without any legal foundation, attempting to evade its responsibility under the Offer to Lease by now claiming that the tenant of the Leased Premises was Network Transport (Québec).

Although it could be said that there is a certain ambiguity with respect to the identity of the lessee under the terms of the Offer to Lease, the Court has little doubt that the controlling force of the "Network Group of Companies", Mr. Charles Bates, induced the lessor, Canada Inc., to believe that it was dealing with Network Transport Limited as lessee of the Leased Premises.

References in the letter dated March 12, 1990 addressed by Mr. Bates to Claridge Properties, manager of the Leased Premises, from a simple reading thereof, would lead a reasonable business person to conclude that he was dealing with the parent corporation rather than one of its regional subsidiaries. It must be remembered that the purpose of the letter of March 12, 1990 was to assure Canada Inc. as to the financial wellbeing of the lessee.

Cheryl Dufour, at the time property manager of the Leased Premises, testified she believed at all times, until the events of default which gave rise to the present proceedings, that she was dealing with Network Transport Limited as lessee. In the opinion of the Court she was justified in so believing.

In view of the forgoing, the Court finds that in signing the Offer to Lease, Charles Bates acted on behalf of Network Transport Limited, and that accordingly it is responsible for the performance of the obligations assumed by the lessee therein. It is inconsistent with any logical interpretation of the documentation preceding the execution of the Offer to Lease, that the parties intended the lessee to be Network Transport (Québec).

Subsidiarily, even if one were to conclude that the Offer to Lease was signed on behalf of Network Transport (Québec) rather than Network Transport Limited, in the circumstances of the present case, the Court would be justified in piercing the corporate veil and imputing liability on the parent shareholder, Network Transport Limited.

The driving force behind the Network Transport Group of companies, Mr. Bates, had through his letters and deeds both prior to the execution of the Offer to Lease and subsequent thereto, provoked a situation which, due to his fault, induced the lessor to believe that it was dealing with the parent shareholder, Network Transport Limited, rather than its wholly owned subsidiary Network Transport (Québec). By so doing, he committed a "fraud" as contemplated by article 317 of the Civil Code of Quebec.

Article 317 C.C.Q. provides:

> "Art. 317. In no case may a legal person set up juridical personality against a person in good faith if it is set up to dissemble fraud, abuse of right or contravention of a rule of public order."

Although in law, Network Transport Limited and Network Transport (Québec) are two legal entities, quite distinct one from the other, in the circumstance of the present case, the Court retains the fact that their principal place of business in the province of Quebec, in each case, is at the same address; their activities as disclosed in the various annual reports filed on their behalf are identical; their President is, in both cases, Charles Bates; and their financial operations are inextricably bound one to the other by way of inter-company accounts and adjustments as well as by extensive cross guarantees to third party creditors of the parent and one or more of its subsidiaries.

This error as to the identity of the lessee, if indeed there was one, could have been corrected by Mr. Bates by, at the very least, having indicated on the cheques in payment of the rental due under the Offer to Lease, that payment was made on behalf of the subsidiary corporation Network Transport (Québec) and not, as would appear from the face of the cheque, on behalf of the parent Network Transport Limited. The Court can only conclude that, at the time, Mr. Bates preferred to have Canada Inc. believe it was dealing with the parent rather that its insolvent subsidiary.

Having acted in such a manner as to provoke a fundamental error with respect to the identity of the tenant and, following the execution of the Offer to Lease, making no efforts to correct this apparent error, the Court finds that the actions of Network Transport Limited constitutes a "fraud" as contemplated by article 317 C.C.Q., thereby authorising the Court to pierce the corporate veil.

See Marfoglia Construction Inc. v. 3088-1155 Quebec Inc.

In light of the foregoing, considering the letters and other documentation signed by Charles Bates on behalf of Network Transport Limited and/or its subsidiary companies and, considering the contradictory testimony given by Mr. Bates in connection with the essential elements of the contract which binds the lessor and the lessee, the Court concludes, moreover, that Mr. Bates and Network Transport Limited were in bad faith at the time of the execution of the Offer to Lease and, subsequent thereto, in the performance of their obligations pursuant to the terms thereof.

Network Transport Limited argues that in the event the Court should find it is responsible for the payment of the rent due under the Offer to Lease, the amounts payable should be reduced due to the fact that it was denied peaceable enjoyment of the Leased Premises, resulting from problems dealing with access to the parking area adjacent to the Leased Premises. Although proof has been made of an exchange of correspondence between the parties wherein Charles Bates seeks certain restitution in order to "make us happy as your tenant" there is no proof that the complaints of Mr. Bates have been substantiated and accepted by the lessor. There is a total absence of any proof of the nature as well as the amount of damages suffered by Network Transport Limited. For this reason, the Court is not disposed to reduce the amount of any condemnation for rent due and owing under the Offer to Lease.

Similarly, for the same reasons, the Court is not of the view that Network Transport Limited is justified to seek the resiliation of the Offer to Lease.

Canada Inc. seeks a condemnation against Network Transport Limited for an amount of $238,398.25, representing rental due and owing, with interest, as well as the additional indemnity contemplated by art. 1619 C.C.Q., calculated as and from May 19, 1994 date of the mise en demeure; the whole with costs as well as all applicable taxes.

In the circumstances of the present case, Network Transport Limited argues that seeing the exceptional delays in bringing the present case to a hearing on the merits, namely seven years, and seeing that the delays are, to a large extent, the responsibility of Canada Inc. the Court, exercising its discretion, should refuse the awarding of the additional indemnity.

FOR THE FOREGOING REASONS:

The Court MAINTAINS Plaintiffs action;

CONDEMNS Defendant to pay to Plaintiff the sum of $238,398.25 plus all applicable taxes, the whole with interest and, as well, the additional indemnity contemplated by article 1619 C.C.Q., calculated as and from May 19, 1994;

WITH COSTS AGAINST DEFENDANT.

LEGAL TERMS

In your reading, you came across the following terms. Be sure that you can explain each, to ensure your understanding of the material you have been reading. If you are uncertain as to the meaning of any term, review the material in the chapter for clarification. If necessary, consult a dictionary for further information or discuss the term(s) with your instructor.

enterprise
sole proprietorship
Declaration of Sole Proprietorship
personal liability
Contract of Partnership
Partnership Declaration
Limited Partnership
special partners
legal personality
Articles of Incorporation
Officers
to incorporate
dividend
transfer of shares
natural person
by-laws
Canada Business Corporations Act
Class "A" (common shares)
par value
participating
bonds/debentures

unanimous shareholder agreement
registration
liability for debts
partnership
solidary
General Partnership
general partners
corporation
business name
Certificate of Incorporation
federal objects
shares
artificial being
share certificate
registered office
directors
Québec Business Corporations Act
Class "B" (preferred) shares
cumulative
redeemable

REVIEW QUESTIONS

1. Elizabeth bought a lamp in one store, a sweater in another store, and three books in the college bookstore. Do these activities show that she is "carrying on an enterprise" within the meaning of the Civil Code?

2. Who has the authority to pass laws regulating the "personal" forms of business ownership? What is the source of this lawmaking authority?

3. What is a sole proprietorship?

   Explain the following characteristics of the sole proprietorship:

   Liability for debts
   Management
   Ownership of profits
   Legal publicity

4. Explain how a limited partnership differs from a general partnership

5. Explain how the corporate form of business ownership differs from the personal form of business ownership.

6. What is a partnership?

7. In a general commercial partnership, explain the following characteristics:

   Liability for debts
   Management
   Profit
   Legal publicity

8. What is the legal procedure for starting up a corporation?

9. It is said that with the corporate form of business ownership there is limitation of liability. To whom does this apply? Is this an advantage for all parties?

10. What are the advantages of owning shares in a corporation?

11. How can a corporation use its share structure to raise funds for the activities of the business?

12. What criteria must be met by someone who wants to incorporate a business?

13. What are the conditions for selecting a name for a business to be set up as a corporation?

14. Discuss the responsibilities of the directors of a corporation.

15. Explain the differences between Class "A" (common) shares and Class "B" (preferred) shares.

Chapter 7

EMPLOYMENT LAW

OBJECTIVES

This chapter was prepared to enable you to achieve the following objectives:

1. To understand the different bodies of law governing employment contracts.
2. To identify, analyze, and understand, the essential elements of an individual contract of employment.
4. To comprehend the rights and obligations of employees and employers.
5. To understand the purpose and interpretation of restrictive (non-competition) clauses.
6. To become familiar with the minimum standards in the *Québec Labour Standards Act*.
7. To understand the difference between an employee and a contractor.
8. To recognize what is meant by psychological harassment and what it entails.
9. To understand the different forms of termination of an employment contract.

INTRODUCTION
Section 7.1

The relationship between employee and employer has long been the subject of legal regulation. This relationship takes the form of a contract between the parties. The contract may be verbal or written, but it must conform to the rules of contracts, which will be examined in the next chapter. In addition, the employment relationship gives rise to many rights and obligations found in several of the laws of the province.

The subject of employment contracts must be considered under two broad areas of study as a means of gaining a better understanding:

1. The **individual contract**, the terms of which are negotiated and agreed to between an employee and an employer. The conditions agreed upon apply only to this particular employment relationship, and between these two parties.
2. The **collective agreement**. This is a contract between an employer and a group of employees. The group may be called a union, brotherhood, syndicat, etc. Several members of the group form a negotiating team and meet with the employer's representatives. Between them they negotiate and agree on a set of terms and conditions that will govern the employment relationship between the entire group of employees and their employer.

We shall examine only the first of the two types of employment contracts in this chapter.

THE INDIVIDUAL CONTRACT OF EMPLOYMENT
Section 7.2

7.2.1 Introduction

This contract is governed principally by the rules found in the *Civil Code of Québec*. In addition, there are important provisions in the *Québec Labour Standards Act* and in the *Québec Charter of Human Rights and Freedoms*. All three of these laws of the province must be considered in order to draw a complete picture of the individual contract of employment.

Other Québec laws that relate to employment matters include the *Act Respecting Occupational Health and Safety*, the *Act Respecting Industrial Accidents and Occupational Diseases*, the *Pay Equity Act*, and the *Employment Equity Act.*

7.2.2 The Civil Code of Québec

In the area of the individual contract, there are several characteristics to be considered with respect to the relationship between an employee and the employer. The *Civil Code* defines and outlines what constitutes an employment contract, the term, form, renewal and termination, restrictive covenants and non-competition clauses and the distinction between an employee and a contractor. The basic rules of this contract are set out in articles 2085 to 2097 of the *Civil Code*.

Selected articles from the Civil Code of Québec are reproduced in Appendix "7-A" at the end of this chapter.

7.2.2.1 The Contract

The legal contractual relationship between an employer and employee is defined by article 2085 of the *Civil Code*, which includes these essential elements:

1. it is a contract, subject to all the general rules of contract;
2. it is bilateral, i.e., it requires both parties to undertake to do something for the other:
    - the employee undertakes to do work
    - the employer undertakes to pay the employee for the work;
3. the contract requires the work to be done continuously until the termination of the contract;
4. the work must be done according to the instructions and under the direction of the employer, which requires the employee to be subordinate. This subordination is of the essence to the contract of employment. The fact that the employee's activity is under the control of the employer is reasonable, since the work is being done for the benefit of the employer;
5. the employee must personally carry out the work to be done—it cannot be delegated to someone else;
6. the contract must be for a limited time—a person cannot bind him or herself forever (unlimited duration): this would be the equivalent of slavery, and this idea is abhorrent to our society.

7.2.2.2 Term

This contract may be for a fixed term or for an indeterminate term. A contract for a **fixed term** has a clearly agreed termination date. When this date arrives, the contract is ended. No notice or other formality is required.

If the work is completed before the termination date, the employer cannot simply "lay-off" the employee. The term of the contract must be fully respected. If the employer wants to terminate the contract before the end of the term, the employer must pay the employee the full amount that would have been earned had the contract continued for the full term. Of course, the parties may agree to a settlement by which the employee receives a lesser amount and does not have to wait for the term to expire.

A contract of **indeterminate term** must not be confused with a contract of unlimited duration. As noted above, unlimited duration contracts are prohibited.

In a contract with an indeterminate term, the parties have agreed not to set a specific termination date. The contract will continue until it is terminated by one of the parties. In this case, the party wishing to terminate the contract must give notice to the other party.

If the employer wants to create a "pause" in the contract, the employee may be "laid-off" for a short period, but not more than six months. However, if either party wants to terminate the contract, the one who wants to do so must give the appropriate period of notice to the other.

7.2.2.3 Form

Aside from having to meet the requirements of a valid contract, there is no specific form required for a contract of employment. It may be verbal or written. It may be set out in a letter written by the employer to the employee or it may be a formal contract with many pages of conditions. The law leaves it entirely to the parties to determine what form they want their contract to take.

7.2.2.4 Employer / Employee Obligations and Rights

The employer's main obligations are to allow the employee to carry out the work, to pay the wage or salary agreed upon and to ensure that the work can be done safely and without danger to the employee.

The employer has the right to insist on having the work done in a particular way and on having employees follow a certain pattern of behaviour. If the employee does not conform to these rules, the employer retains the right to discipline the employee.

Disciplinary measures generally begin with a verbal and subsequently a written warning to the employee. Penalties may be applied in the form of suspension without pay for a day, a week, or more; transfer from one position to another; or demotion to a lower position. The ultimate disciplinary measure is to fire (terminate) the employee.

An employee who behaves in such a way that there is serious danger to the employer or to other employees may be dismissed on the spot without notice. Grounds for instant dismissal are: starting a fire in the plant, smoking where it is dangerous to do so, damaging the employer's equipment, stealing from the employer, fighting with other employees, falling asleep on the job, staying away from work without notifying the employer, etc. This procedure is often referred to as being "dismissed for cause".

The employee is obliged to do the work carefully, promptly and to the best of his or her ability; to be honest in dealing with the employer; and loyal, not divulge (give away) confidential information, such as trade secrets about how the employer carries on the business, unless it is a question of public security and safety (whistle blowing). After a reasonable time period has elapsed following the termination of the contract, the former employee is no longer bound to maintain information confidential. The employee, however, may never divulge information about the reputation and private life of an individual and may also be bound by a restrictive covenant or non-competition clause.

7.2.2.5 Restrictive Covenants & Non-Competition Clauses

It is not unusual for an employer to make an effort to protect his or her business by requiring employees to sign a clause restricting the employee's right to use or reveal confidential information, even after leaving the service of the employer. This restriction may state that the employee may not work for another company in the same business, and may not set up a new business in the same or even in a closely allied field to that of the employer. Clauses containing such restrictions are referred to as **non-competition clauses** or **restrictive covenants**. (The word "covenant" means an agreement.)

Such a clause would state that the employee cannot work for another firm in the same business, or start up a business, for a fixed period of time, and within a specific geographic area. Although a person may thereby be prevented from working in his or her field of experience and expertise, these clauses are considered acceptable, providing they are not unreasonable.

The reasonableness of these clauses is measured in terms of time and space. They must not cover too long a period of time and must not restrict the person from working over too wide a geographical area.

> *When Alice went to work for the railway, she signed an agreement that when she left the firm, she would not work for any other company directly or indirectly related to the railway business for a three-year period anywhere in the city of Montréal. If she violated this clause, she would have to pay the railway firm the sum of $10,000.*
>
> *After seven years, Alice was offered a job with a Montréal travel agency which specialized in selling "Vacations by Railway." This job offered her more responsibility and a much better salary. She accepted the offer and started her new job one week after leaving the railway.*
>
> *Two months later, her former employer sent her a letter of default claiming that she had violated her agreement and must either leave her new job within five days, or pay the railway $10,000.*

The question to consider is whether Alice has legally broken her agreement and is liable for the penalty. Article 2089 of the *Civil Code* refers to this type of situation.

Take note that if an employer has fired an employee without a good reason or has forced the employee to quit, article 2095 of the *Civil Code* prohibits the employer from invoking any non-competition clause previously signed by the employee.

7.2.2.6 Renewal & Termination

At the expiry of a contract with a fixed term, normally the relationship between the parties is terminated. Although the employee was originally hired for a fixed term, it may be clear from the behaviour of both parties that more work needs to be done and that neither party objects to the continuation of the employment activity.

If there is no objection from the employer and the employee continues to carry out the work for five days after the original contract expires, there is a "tacit renewal" of the contract. It is automatically renewed with the same conditions, except that it now becomes a contract with an indeterminate term. This means that to cancel the contract now requires one party to give notice to the other.

The period of notice to be given to cancel a contract with an indeterminate term is not stated in the *Civil Code*. Article 2091 simply states that the notice shall be given in "reasonable time," and this expression is not defined. It is left this way because the appropriate time period will be different for different types of work. Thus the period will vary with the type of work, its complexity, the length of time the employee has been doing this work, etc.

If the job being done is one that does not require much skill, training, education, or experience, the person doing the work will likely be able to find alternative employment quite soon. In this case, the time period would be relatively short—perhaps two weeks or one month. It will be seen, that under another Québec law, the *Labour Standards Act*, there are minimum periods of notice, based upon length of service.

If the job requires considerable education and experience, there may not be many alternative jobs available, and the employee may need many weeks or months to find an equivalent position. In this situation, the proper notice period may be two or three months or more.

For these reasons, the Civil *Code* states that in deciding how much time to give the employee, the employer should take into account the nature of the job, any special circumstances that apply to it and the period of time the employee has been doing this work.

In Article 2097 the Civil *Code* states that when a business is sold or its legal form changed, the employees who work there are not terminated as a result. Simply put, a new owner or owners take over the legal obligations of the former owner and must follow the same legal rules in order to terminate the contracts of any of the employees. Equally, if the legal form of the business is changed from a sole proprietorship to a partnership, or from a partnership to a corporation, all the employees continue to be employees of the new business structure.

When a contract of employment is terminated, the employer is required to give the employee a document called a **Certificate of Employment** stating the length of the term of employment and the kind of work done by the employee. No information about the employee's performance must appear in this certificate. If the employee wants a reference letter, it should be a separate document.

7.2.2.7 Contractors

A distinction must be made between an employee and a contractor. An employee, as discussed earlier, works under the supervision and direction of the employer. Subordination is an essential element of the employer/employee relationship. The term "contractor" refers to someone who undertakes to do a job for someone. Many firms retain the services of contractors to carry out some operations in their plant. This can range from night security duties, to cleaning the offices, laboratory testing, doing the firm's office work, or running the machines in the factory.

The relationship between a contractor and a client is quite different from the employer/employee relationship. The nature of the work to be done is identified, a price is established for the work, and the parties agree on a **contract of enterprise** or **contract for services**.

> *Maria accepted a job with Happy House Painters Inc. as a painter. She went to the houses indicated by her employer and followed the instructions given to her as to what paint to use, what brush or rollers to use, what time to start, and what time to quit. (This is an example of an employer/employee relationship.)*

A contractor does not have the same element of subordination. The contractor often decides when the job will be done, what quality of materials to use, what tools to use, and how many people will carry out the work.

> *Thomas entered into a contract with Happy House Painters Inc. to have them paint his house brown and white. He agreed with the company where the colours would go, how many coats of paint would be applied and the completion date for the job. He also agreed that the whole job would cost $2,500. (This is an example of a client/contractor relationship.)*

In this second case, Happy House Painters Inc. is a contractor, not an employee. It supplies the tools, the paint, and the people to do the work.

The difference between an employer/employee relationship and a client/contractor relationship can be summarized as follows:

1. Subordination and control—the employer has control over the work to be done, how and when it is to be carried out, whereas a client comes to an agreement with a contractor as to what work will be done, and it is the contractor who controls the job.

2. Tools and equipment—an employer owns and provides the tools used by an employee; a contractor owns his or her tools and brings them to the job.

3. Profit—an employee earns a wage or salary and no more; a contractor can increase profit by being more efficient, taking less time, using less material, etc.

4. Risk of loss—if an employee takes more time than the employer had estimated or uses more material, the employer bears the loss and must pay the employee for whatever number of hours he worked; under similar circumstances, where, for example, a contractor had estimated his cost would be $2000, and in the end the cost was actually $3000, it is the contractor, not the client, who suffers the loss.

When an employee is paid, the law requires that the employer withhold certain portions of the remuneration to pay income tax, employment insurance, pension plan contributions, etc.

When a contractor is paid, the payment is the full amount of the contract price; there are no deductions. The contractor is operating a business and is therefore responsible for making the appropriate payments on his or her behalf as well as on the behalf of any employees the contractor may have.

Selected articles from the Civil Code of Québec concerning contracts of enterprise are reproduced in Appendix "7-A" at the end of this chapter.

...as you read ask yourself...

Ideal Shipping Inc., offering courier services, contracts with ten different contractors who will each provide delivery services using their own trucks, wear the same uniforms, not compete with each other by staying within their own districts and not work for other courier services. Each will make their own profit and be their own boss. Are they contractors or employees? Why?

7.2.3 The Québec Labour Standards Act
(Loi sur les normes du travail)

This Québec law provides for several minimum conditions of work, which apply to most employees in the province. It does not apply to senior management. They must invoke the *Civil Code* and the *Québec Charter* to argue employment contract violations and discrimination.

These minimums, which concern wages, hours of work, vacations, statutory holidays, breaks, etc., are declared to be of "**public order**." This means that employer may not offer an employee any wage or other condition that is less than the minimum condition set out in the law.

> *Lucien had been out of work for several months and was desperate to find a job—any job. At one place where he applied, the owner of the business was most sympathetic, and said that he would very much like to hire Lucien but that he could not afford to pay the minimum wage required by the law.*
>
> *Lucien asked the owner how much he could afford to pay. "A dollar fifty per hour less than the minimum wage" was the answer. "But if you accept it, you will have to sign a paper stating that you know what the minimum wage is, and that you agree to accept a dollar fifty per hour less," said the owner.*
>
> *Lucien thought about it and felt that he had no choice. "I'll take it," he replied. "I have to have a job."*

Lucien and the employer have violated a very important rule in the *Québec Labour Standards Act*, so important in fact, that even after working two or three months, Lucien could file a complaint and the business owner would be required to retroactively pay him the extra $1.50 per hour. This is what is meant by "public order." No one can, by a private agreement, go below the minimum set out in the law.

The following are some of the minimum conditions set out in the *Québec Labour Standards Act*, which are declared in the law to be of "public order".

> ***Please Note that the following provisions are extracted from the Québec Labour Standards Act, and include highlights only. Section numbers of the Act are indicated in brackets.***
>
> ***Most of these provisions are subject to special exceptions in certain cases, and therefore in order to have a complete reference to the applicable legal conditions, the reader should consult the most current official edition of the Act.***

7.2.3.1 Wages

Each year, the Québec government reviews the minimum wage to determine if it should be changed. If a change is made, notices are published in all the newspapers well in advance and the change, if any, goes into effect on the date stated in the published notice (s.40).

As of 1 May 2013, the minimum wage in Québec was set at $10.15 per hour. For an employee who receives gratuities or tips, the minimum wage was set at $8.75 per hour. *(Find out if the minimum wage in effect today has changed from these figures; if so, enter the new figures here $_____ $_____).*

Wages must be paid in cash, by cheque, or by direct bank deposit (s.42). The employee must receive a pay slip showing such details as number of hours worked, hourly pay, and deductions (s.46).

Nothing may be deducted from an employee's wages unless it is required by law (such as deductions for income tax, etc.) or unless the employee has requested it in writing (such as contributions to a pension or retirement fund) (s.49).

No benefit provided by the employer may be taken into account in computing the minimum wage payable to an employee (s.41).

Wages must be paid at intervals of not more than 16 days. In the case of salaries paid to managerial personnel, these may be paid at intervals of not more than one month (s.43).

Any employee who works part-time (which means fewer hours each week than the regular employees), is entitled to receive the same hourly wage as the full-time employees who carry out the same tasks in the same place (s.41.1)

Tips received directly or indirectly by an employee, or any "gratuities" added to the customer's bill by the employer are the exclusive property of the employee. They do not belong to the employer, who has no right to tell the employee how to share them or to withhold any portion of them (s.50). The employer, however, must keep track of the tips for the purpose of calculating the portion required for the employee's personal income tax. An employer may not require an employee to pay credit card costs (s.50.1).

7.2.3.2 Hours of Work

The regular work week in Québec, for the purpose of calculating overtime is 40 hours (s.52). Overtime rates (for hours in excess of 40) are paid at time-and-one-half (s.55). If the regular rate is $10 per hour, the overtime rate is $15 per hour.

An employee may request that overtime be compensated by paid leave equivalent to the overtime worked plus 50% instead of being paid in cash. The leave must be taken during the 12 months following the overtime at a date agreed upon between the employer and the employee – otherwise the overtime must be paid (s.55).

An employee is considered to be at work (s.57) when:

- available at the place of employment and required to wait for work to be assigned
- during the break periods permitted by the employer
- travelling as required by the employer

If an employee comes to work at the required time and then is able to work only three hours or less (due to lack of materials, problems with the heating system, fire, etc.), the employee is entitled to three hours' wages at the regular rate. This is often referred to as "call-in pay." (s.58)

An employee may refuse to work more than four hours after regular daily working hours, or more than fourteen working hours per 24 hour period, whichever period is shortest (s.59.0.1).

7.2.3.3 Paid Vacations

There are two elements to the legislation relating to vacations. First, the employee is entitled to be absent while taking an annual vacation without fear of losing his or her job. Second, the employee is entitled to vacation pay while on holiday, based on the employee's gross wages during the past year.

The vacation period is determined by the length of time the employee has worked continuously for that employer. It is based on a "reference year" which runs from May 1 to April 30 each year (s.60).

If an employee has worked for less than one year for an employer, the employee is entitled to one day of vacation for every month worked during the reference year. For example, an employee who started work on February 1 would have worked three months by April 30 and therefore would be entitled to three vacation days. An employee, who started on December 1 would have worked five months by April 30 and would earn five vacation days. The maximum prescribed by law for up to one year of work is ten working days (two weeks) of vacation (s.67).

An employee who has worked one year or more, up to five years, is entitled to two weeks of vacation. An employee who has worked five years or more is entitled to three weeks of vacation. Employers may give a longer vacation period if they wish to do so, but not less! (s.68 and s.69).

An employee is entitled to know the date of the annual vacation at least four weeks in advance (s.72). The employee must take the vacation within 12 months following the end of the reference year (s.70).

An employee who receives a vacation of two weeks or less is entitled to vacation pay of four percent of the gross wages (before deductions) earned during the reference year. An employee who is entitled to three weeks' vacation receives six percent of the gross wages earned (s.74).

7.2.3.4 Paid Statutory Holidays

The government has declared the following to be holidays:

- 1 January
- Good Friday or Easter Monday (employer's choice)
- The Monday before 25 May
- The National Holiday – 24 June (or 25 June if the 24th is a Sunday)
- July 1 (or 2 July if the 1st is a Sunday)
- Labour Day (first Monday in September)
- Thanksgiving (second Monday in October)
- 25 December

For each statutory holiday, the employer must pay the employee 1/20 of the wages earned during the four complete weeks of pay before the holiday, excluding overtime (s.62)

If an employee must work on a statutory holiday, the employee is paid for the day at the usual wage plus the extra wages required under section 62, or instead of the extra wages, the employee may be granted a compensatory holiday of one day, to be taken within three weeks before or after the statutory holiday on which the employee was required to work (s.63).

If an employee is on annual leave (vacation) when a statutory holiday falls, the employee is entitled to be paid for the day or be given a compensatory day off (s.64). In many cases, when this happens, the employee obtains permission to extend the annual leave by one extra day.

To benefit from a statutory holiday, an employee must not be absent from work on the day before or on the day after the holiday (s.65).

7.2.3.5 Rest Periods

Employees are entitled to various rest periods, such as an unpaid 30-minute lunch break for every five hours of work and one day off every week (usually but not necessarily Sunday). Contrary to common belief, coffee breaks are not required by law and therefore an employer is not obliged to provide one. However, employees must be paid for the break time if the employer provides such breaks.

7.2.3.6 Other Leaves

An employee may be absent from work, and notice must be given to the employer as soon as possible (except for the first two items), for the following reasons:

- Weekly rest (s.78) – an employee is entitled to 32 consecutive hours of rest each week.
- Meal break (s.79) – an employee is entitled to a 30 minute meal break after 5 consecutive hours of work. This is not paid, unless the employee is not permitted to leave the work station.
- Sickness or accident leave (s.79.1) – after three months of service, an employee can request, in writing, up to 26 weeks of unpaid leave.
- Family Responsibilities (s.79.7) – up to 10 days per year, unpaid, may be requested by an employee to look after matters concerned with the care, health or education of a child, or the health of any other family member.
- One day paid, on the death of consort, child, parent, brother, or sister. An additional four days off, without pay, may be taken at this time (s.80).
- One day unpaid on the death of a son/daughter-in-law, brother/sister-in-law, grandparent, or grandchild (s.80.1).
- Five days off for the birth or adoption of a child. The first two of these days will be paid if the employee has been working for this employer for at least 60 days. If less than 60 days service, the employee can take 5 days off, unpaid (s.81.1)

7.2.3.7 Maternity Leave (s.81.4)

An employee may take maternity leave for not more than 18 weeks, unpaid, to begin no sooner than 16 weeks before the expected date of birth, and ending not later than 18 weeks after the week of delivery. The employer must be notified as to the start and end date of the leave. At the end of the maternity leave, the employee is entitled to return to her job and receive any increased wages or other benefits put in place while she was on leave.

7.2.3.8 Parental Leave (s.81.10)

The parents of a newborn or adopted child may have a leave of 52 consecutive weeks, but unpaid. It is possible, however, to obtain benefits through the *Québec Parental Insurance Plan*. The employer must be notified as to the start and end of this leave. An employee on maternity or parental leave who does not return to work on the expected date is considered to have resigned his or her position.

7.2.3.9 Psychological Harassment (s.81.18)

Employees are entitled to a work environment that is free from any vexatious behaviour in the form of repeated and hostile or unwanted conduct, comments, actions or gestures that affects their dignity, physical integrity or psychological integrity. A single serious act may constitute psychological harassment. Employers must take reasonable action to prevent such harassment and to put a stop to it, if it occurs. This protection is also extended to senior managers.

7.2.3.10 Notice of Termination of an Employment Contract

An employer must give written notice to terminate the employment contract of an employee who has been on staff for more than three months. The length of the notice period depends on the length of the employment period (s.82).

Length of employment	Notice period
less than 3 months	**none required**
between 3 months and 1 year	**1 week**
between 1 and 5 years	**2 weeks**
between 5 and 10 years	**4 weeks**
over 10 years	**8 weeks**

There is no notice required if the contract was for a fixed term that has expired. There is also no notice given to an employee who has committed a serious fault and is fired "for cause" (s.82.1)

Some employers prefer not to have the employee continue to work during the notice period. Instead, they pay the employee for the required period "in lieu of" (instead of) notice and the employee leaves immediately (s.83). In addition, the employee receives four percent of all gross wages earned during the current reference year as vacation pay.

The *Québec Labour Standards Act* creates a body called "**Commission des normes du travail**" (s.4). Its function is to supervise the implementation and application of the Labour Standards. It publishes information to inform employees and employers of their rights, and it receives complaints from employees and acts to help them (s.5). The Commission may carry out investigations, collect amounts due to an employee by an employer, and even sue employers on behalf of an employee, if necessary (s.39)

In order to pay the costs of operating this Commission, it is permitted to charge all employers a contribution. This is a percentage of the employers payroll, not to exceed 1% (s.29(7), and s.39.0.2). No charge is made to employees.

7.2.3.11 Dismissal not made for Good and Sufficient Cause (s. 124-128)

An employer wishing to dismiss an employee, who has been working for the employer for at least two years without interruption, must give the employee a valid reason for his dismissal. In general, the jurisprudence identifies three main reasons justifying a dismissal: an employee's incompetence, restructuring of a business and if the business is dealing with financial difficulties. Dismissals based on hiring a nephew or child instead, private matters not related or impacting the work place, jealousy against the employee and refusal by the employee to break the law in performing a task are but a few examples that may allow an employee to claim unjustified dismissal. The employee would have to file his complaint with the **Commission des relations du travail** within 45 days, or within the time frame allotted by a collective agreement, of the dismissal.

If the dismissal is found unjustified, the Commission des relations du travail may order that the employee be reinstated, order payment of lost wages to the employee and render any other decision necessary given the circumstances. Reinstatement is not possible in cases where the employment involved domestic work or care of a child, a sick person, an elderly person or somebody with a handicap.

The Québec Labour Standards Act contains some exceptions and special provisions. In order to be fully aware of all the details, it is essential to consult the Act itself. In addition, the Labour Standards Commission publishes several documents explaining the conditions that apply to employment contracts, and providing details as to the rights of employees.

Selected articles from the Québec Labour Standards Act are reproduced in Appendix "7-B" at the end of this chapter.

7.2.4 The Québec Charter of Human Rights and Freedoms

This important law was considered in Chapter 4. Sections 10 to 20 of the law can be found in that chapter. These sections deal with matters relating to employment contracts, such as the issue of discrimination in matters of employment, employment applications, and employment agencies. It is suggested that the reader review these sections at this time.

APPENDIX "7-A"
SELECTED ARTICLES FROM
The Civil Code of Québec

1458. Every person has a duty to honour his contractual undertakings.

Where he fails in this duty, he is liable for any bodily, moral or material injury he causes to the other contracting party and is liable to reparation for the injury; neither he nor the other party may in such a case avoid the rules governing contractual liability by opting for rules that would be more favourable to them.

1463. The principal is liable to reparation for injury caused by the fault of his agents and servants in the performance of their duties; nevertheless, he retains his recourses against them.

2085. A contract of employment is a contract by which a person, the employee, undertakes for a limited period to do work for remuneration, according to the instructions and under the direction or control of another person, the employer.

2086. A contract of employment is for a fixed term or an indeterminate term.

2087. The employer is bound not only to allow the performance of the work agreed upon and to pay the remuneration fixed, but also to take any measures consistent with the nature of the work to protect the health, safety and dignity of the employee.

2088. The employee is bound not only to carry on his work with prudence and diligence, but also to act faithfully and honestly and not to use any confidential information he may obtain in carrying on or in the course of his work.

These obligations continue for a reasonable time after cessation of the contract, and permanently where the information concerns the reputation and private life of another person.

2089. The parties may stipulate in writing and in express terms that, even after the termination of the contract, the employee may neither compete with his employer nor participate in any capacity whatsoever in an enterprise which would then compete with him.

Such a stipulation shall be limited, however, as to time, place and type of employment, to whatever is necessary for the protection of the legitimate interests of the employer.

The burden of proof that the stipulation is valid is on the employer.

2090. A contract of employment is tacitly renewed for an indeterminate term where the employee continues to carry on his work for five days after the expiry of the term, without objection from the employer.

2091. Either party to a contract with an indeterminate term may terminate it by giving notice of termination to the other party.

The notice of termination shall be given in reasonable time, taking into account, in particular, the nature of the employment, the special circumstances in which it is carried on and the duration of the period of work.

2092. The employee may not renounce his right to obtain compensation for any injury he suffers where insufficient notice of termination is given or where the manner of resiliation is abusive.

2093. A contract of employment terminates upon the death of the employee.

Depending on the circumstances, it may also terminate upon the death of the employer.

2094. One of the parties may, for a serious reason, unilaterally resiliate the contract of employment without prior notice.

2095. An employer may not avail himself of a stipulation of non-competition if he has resiliated the contract without a serious reason or if he has himself given the employee such a reason for resiliating the contract.

2096. Upon termination of the contract, the employer shall furnish to the employee, at his request, a certificate of employment, showing only the nature and duration of the employment and indicating the identities of the parties.

2097. A contract of employment is not terminated by alienation of the enterprise or any change in its legal structure by way of amalgamation or otherwise.

The contract is binding on the successor of the employer.

2098. A contract of enterprise or for services is a contract by which a person, the contractor or the provider of services, as the case may be, undertakes to carry out physical or intellectual work for another person, the client or to provide a service, for a price which the client binds himself to pay.

2099. The contractor or the provider of services is free to choose the means of performing the contract and no relationship of subordination exists between the contractor or the provider of services and the client in respect of such performance.

Unless a contract has been entered into specifically in view of his personal qualities or unless the very nature of the contract prevents it, the contractor or the provider of services may employ a third person to perform the contract, but its performance remains under his supervision and responsibility.

2100. The contractor and the provider of services are bound to act in the best interests of their client, with prudence and diligence. Depending on the nature of the work to be carried out or the service to be provided, they are also bound to act in accordance with usual practice and the rules of art, and, where applicable, to ensure that the work done or service provided is in conformity with the contract.

Where they are bound to produce results, they may not be relieved from liability except by proving superior force.

2109. Where the price is fixed by the contract, the client shall pay the price agreed, and may not claim a reduction of the price on the ground that the work or service required less effort or cost less than had been foreseen.

Similarly, the contractor or the provider of services may not claim an increase of the price for the opposite reason.

Unless otherwise agreed by the parties, the price fixed by the contract remains unchanged notwithstanding any modification of the original terms and conditions of performance.

APPENDIX "7-B"
SELECTED SECTIONS FROM
The Québec Labour Standards Act

DIVISION V.2
Psychological Harassment

81.18. For the purposes of this Act, "psychological harassment" means any vexatious behaviour in the form of repeated and hostile or unwanted conduct, verbal comments, actions or gestures, that affects an employee's dignity or psychological or physical integrity and that results in a harmful work environment for the employee.

A single serious incidence of such behaviour that has a lasting harmful effect on an employee may also constitute psychological harassment.

81.19. Every employee has a right to a work environment free from psychological harassment.

Employers must take reasonable action to prevent psychological harassment and, whenever they become aware of such behaviour, to put a stop to it.

81.20. The provisions of sections 81.18, 81.19, 123.7, 123.15 and 123.16, with the necessary modifications, are deemed to be an integral part of every collective agreement. An employee covered by such an agreement must exercise the recourses provided for in the agreement, insofar as any such recourse is available to employees under the agreement.

At any time before the case is taken under advisement, a joint application may be made by the parties to such an agreement to the Minister for the appointment of a person to act as a mediator.

The provisions referred to in the first paragraph are deemed to form part of the conditions of employment of every employee appointed under the Public Service Act (chapter F-3.1.1) who is not governed by a collective agreement. Such an employee must exercise the applicable recourse before the Commission de la fonction publique according to the rules of procedure established pursuant to that Act. The Commission de la fonction publique exercises for that purpose the powers provided for in sections 123.15 and 123.16 of this Act.

The third paragraph also applies to the members and officers of bodies.

DIVISION VI
Notice Of Termination Of Employment Or Layoff, And Work Certificate

82. The employer must give written notice to an employee before terminating his contract of employment or laying him off for six months or more.

The notice shall be of one week if the employee is credited with less than one year of uninterrupted service, two weeks if he is credited with one year to five years of uninterrupted service, four weeks if he is credited with five years to ten years of uninterrupted service and eight weeks if he is credited with ten years or more of uninterrupted service.

A notice of termination of employment given to an employee during the period when he is laid off is absolutely null, except in the case of employment that usually lasts for not more than six months each year due to the influence of the seasons.

This section does not deprive an employee of a right granted to him under another Act.

82.1. Section 82 does not apply to an employee

(1) who has less than three months of uninterrupted service;

(2) whose contract for a fixed term or for a specific undertaking expires;

(3) who has committed a serious fault;

(4) for whom the end of the contract of employment or the layoff is a result of superior force.

DIVISION II.1
Recourse Against Psychological Harassment

123.6. An employee who believes he has been the victim of psychological harassment may file a complaint in writing with the Commission. Such a complaint may also be filed by a non-profit organization dedicated to the defence of employees' rights on behalf of one or more employees who consent thereto in writing.

123.7. Any complaint concerning psychological harassment must be filed within 90 days of the last incidence of the offending behaviour.

123.8. On receipt of a complaint, the Commission shall make an inquiry with due dispatch.

Sections 103 to 110 shall apply to the inquiry, with the necessary modifications.

123.9. If the Commission refuses to take action following a complaint, the employee or, if applicable, the organization with the employee's written consent, may within 30 days of the Commission's decision under section 107 or 107.1, make a written request to the Commission for the referral of the complaint to the Commission des relations du travail.

123.10. The Commission may, at any time, during the inquiry and with the agreement of the parties, request the Minister to appoint a person to act as a mediator. The Commission may, at the request of the employee, assist and advise the employee during mediation.

123.11. If the employee is still bound to the employer by a contract of employment, the employee is deemed to be at work during mediation sessions.

123.12. At the end of the inquiry, if no settlement is reached between the parties and the Commission agrees to pursue the complaint, it shall refer the complaint without delay to the Commission des relations du travail.

123.13. The Commission des normes du travail may represent an employee in a proceeding under this division before the Commission des relations du travail.

123.14. The provisions of the Labour Code (chapter C-27) relating to the Commission des relations du travail, its commissioners, their decisions and the exercise of their jurisdiction, except sections 15 to 19, as well as section 100.12 of that Code apply, with the necessary modifications.

123.15. If the Commission des relations du travail considers that the employee has been the victim of psychological harassment and that the employer has failed to fulfil the obligations imposed on employers under section 81.19, it may render any decision it believes fair and reasonable, taking into account all the circumstances of the matter, including

(1) ordering the employer to reinstate the employee;

(2) ordering the employer to pay the employee an indemnity up to a maximum equivalent to wages lost;

(3) ordering the employer to take reasonable action to put a stop to the harassment;

(4) ordering the employer to pay punitive and moral damages to the employee;

(5) ordering the employer to pay the employee an indemnity for loss of employment;

(6) ordering the employer to pay for the psychological support needed by the employee for a reasonable period of time determined by the Commission;

(7) ordering the modification of the disciplinary record of the employee.

123.16. Paragraphs 2, 4 and 6 of section 123.15 do not apply to a period during which the employee is suffering from an employment injury within the meaning of the Act respecting industrial accidents and occupational diseases (chapter A-3.001) that results from psychological harassment.

Where the Commission des relations du travail considers it probable that, pursuant to section 123.15, the psychological harassment entailed an employment injury for the employee, it shall reserve its decision with regard to paragraphs 2, 4 and 6.

DIVISION III
RECOURSE AGAINST DISMISSALS NOT MADE FOR GOOD AND SUFFICIENT CAUSE

124. An employee credited with two years of uninterrupted service in the same enterprise who believes that he has not been dismissed for a good and sufficient cause may present his complaint in writing to the Commission des normes du travail or mail it to the address of the Commission des normes du travail within 45 days of his dismissal, except where a remedial procedure, other than a recourse in damages, is provided elsewhere in this Act, in another Act or in an agreement.

If the complaint is filed with the Commission des relations du travail within this period, failure to have presented it to the Commission des normes du travail cannot be set up against the complainant.

125. Upon receiving the complaint, the Commission des normes du travail may, with the agreement of the parties, appoint a person who shall endeavour to settle the complaint to the satisfaction of the interested parties. The second and third paragraphs of section 123.3 apply for the purposes of this section.

The Commission des normes du travail may require from the employer a writing containing the reasons for dismissing the employee. It must provide a copy of this writing to the employee, on demand.

126. If no settlement is reached following receipt of the complaint by the Commission des normes du travail, the Commission des normes du travail shall, without delay, refer the complaint to the Commission des relations du travail.

126.1. The Commission des normes du travail may, in a proceeding under this division, represent an employee who does not belong to a group of employees to which certification has been granted under the Labour Code (chapter C-27).

127. The provisions of the Labour Code (chapter C-27) respecting the Commission des relations du travail, its commissioners, their decisions and the exercise of their jurisdiction, and section 100.12 of the said Code apply, adapted as required, except sections 15 to 19.

128. Where the Commission des relations du travail considers that the employee has been dismissed without good and sufficient cause, the Commission may

(1) order the employer to reinstate the employee;

(2) order the employer to pay to the employee an indemnity up to a maximum equivalent to the wage he would normally have earned had he not been dismissed;

(3) render any other decision the Commission believes fair and reasonable, taking into account all the circumstances of the matter.

However, in the case of a domestic or a person whose exclusive duty is to take care of or provide care to a child or to a sick, handicapped or aged person, the Commission des relations du travail may only order the payment to the employee of an indemnity corresponding to the wage and other benefits of which he was deprived due to dismissal.

CASE 7.1

King v. BioChem Therapeutic Inc.

[2001] Q.J. No. 2166, **Quebec Superior Court**

(Excerpts of Judgment)

REASONS FOR JUDGMENT

JEANNINE M. ROUSSEAU J.:—

The Basic Facts

Dr. King and Therapeutic signed her employment contract on October 17, 1996, to begin on November 18, 1996; she was hired as Associate Director, Cancer Biology, reporting to Dr. Terry L. Bowlin, Director, Biology.

At the end of October, BioChem applied to the Canadian Government for the required work permit for Dr. King, which was issued in due course.
And she began work.

Dr. King was fired on September 8, 1997, less than one year after being hired. According to BioChem, Dr. King was fired, after having been given due warning, for insubordination and for lack of respect of colleagues and others with whom she interacted.

According to Dr. King, she was fired suddenly, having received no previous indication of being in jeopardy, her dismissal being caused by jealousy and petty complaints, some of which were false.

The evidence does not support BioChem's position, to the contrary, it supports Dr. King's position.

The trial lasted nine days; there were eleven witnesses.

The employer's case was seriously flawed: for example, there was no written warning, the evidence concerning verbal warnings was unconvincing at best, a major reproach turned out to be untrue and others were more gossip than truth.

In summary, when one examines the evidence on an overall basis, as a whole, in a continuum, it is clear that Dr. King and Therapeutic were not a good match, through no fault of Dr. King, she and Therapeutic did not merged.

What is in issue, however, is whether or not Dr. King deserved to be fired, i.e. fired for cause, and had been warned beforehand. As stated above, the answer to both questions is no.

The employer had the burden of proof to explain its reasons for terminating the employment contract of a recently recruited scientist whose scientific ability was outstanding. And it failed: the evidence does not support the employer's allegation, i.e. that Dr. King changed from the up-and-coming performer she was in March and April 1997 to an insubordinate, disrespectful non-performer in late August 1997.

Moreover, four months after her arrival, Dr. King and her team were recommended for an excellence award by Dr. Mario Thomas, Vice-President, Business Development of Therapeutic:

One month later, the April 28, 1997 memo from Dr. Bowlin, Dr. King's immediate superior, is to the same effect: Dr. King's performance to date was highly satisfactory and her probationary period to be cut short, in fact, she became a permanent employee after five and a half months, instead of six.

Prior Notice

Was Dr. King given a warning as to her performance, a warning which she would have ignored?

The Court was presented with two versions:

1. The BioChem version: Dr. King has been warned that her employment was in jeopardy.
2. The King version: no such notice was given to her; to the contrary, she had been given congratulations, early permanency, increased responsibilities; thus her termination came as a great surprise and utter shock.

The BioChem Version

It was put forth essentially by two persons: Christian Proulx and Dr. Terry Bowlin, It must be remembered Mr. Grey's testimony did not substantiate the due warning allegation, to the contrary.

Mr. Proulx, 41 years old, was the Vice-President Human Resources and Internal Communications.

He, himself, was never involved in telling Dr. King her job was in jeopardy; his information came from others, particularly Dr. Bowlin.

Thus, when Mr. Proulx states Dr. King had been warned three times, i.e. on June 30, August 6 and 13, one must examine the source of his information and go to the evidence which purports to support his statement.

Unfortunately for the employer and for Mr. Proulx' assertions, the testimony of the two persons involved in giving these alleged warnings is not convincing:

1. as to the August 6 meeting with Mr. Grey, Mr. Grey's testimony in no way substantiated the due, warning allegation, to the contrary;

2. as to the June 30 semi-annual review conducted by Dr. Bowlin and the August 13 meeting, the Court was presented with two contradictory versions, those of Dr. King and those of Dr. Bowlin.

As to the August 6 meeting, Mr. Grey confirmed that the possibility of further stock options was discussed, as Dr. King had stated.

Let us analyse BioChem's theory. If the purpose of the Grey-King meeting was to reinforce the warning purportedly given to Dr. King by Dr. Bowlin during the June 30 meeting, why were further stock options discussed, in the terms Mr. Grey said they were, i.e. he held out the prospect of "higher rewards" if matched by a significant performance? If this Grey-King meeting was to be a reinforcement of the first warning, why would President Grey even discuss the possibility of further stock options with a senior scientist who was on the second step of the staircase leading to dismissal for cause? This does not make sense; it is contradictory.

Dr. King's version makes more sense and does not contradict Mr. Grey's testimony: she was not warned of the possibility of her dismissal unless she acted differently, but she was told further options were a possibility.

The Court accepts Dr. King's version of the meeting, for various reasons:
Dr. King is a credible witness, as opposed to Dr. Bowlin, who came across as a guarded, defensive and uncomfortable witness, whose testimony was often vague and general, devoid of those details which add life and credibility to a witness' version of facts;

In summary, BioChem did not discharge its burden of proving prior notice to Dr. King.

The Employer's Evidence

Before going on to the assessment of damages, let us examine on an overall basis the employer's defence and the evidence offered.

After, nine days of trial, eleven witnesses and lengthy reflection, the Court remains perplexed as to the employer's attempt to justify Dr. King's termination.
It is not disputed that an employer is entitled to terminate the employment of an employee without cause; but in such a case, the employer must compensate the employee for the damages suffered because of such dismissal.

In this case, Dr. King's dismissal was without cause, and the various incidents put forth by BioChem were dredged up ex post facto, amplified out of context, in an attempt to cover up the real reason, whatever it may be.

The Damages Sought

Dr. King calculates the damages she incurred as follows:

. Salary: 14 months at
$125,000.00 per year $145,833.34

.	Benefits: 20%	$ 29,166.67	
.	Vacation pay: 6%	$ 8,750.00 $183,750.01	$183,750.01
.	Loss of bonus: $125,000 x 10% x 2$		$25,000.00
.	Vacation pay accrued as of May 1st, 1997: 4%		$5,833.34
.	Damages due to stress, anxiety and inconvenience		$25,000.00
.	Damages to reputation		$25,000.00
.	Relocation and placement expenses		$18,401.07
		Total:	$282,984.42

She is also claiming damages for the loss of stock options concerning 10,000 shares, 5,000 of which had been approved and 5,000 of which had been discussed with Mr. Grey.

Vacation Pay and Damages in Lieu of Notice

The vacation pay @ 4% accrued as of May 1st, 1997 does not require further explanations: $5,833 34.

As to damages pertaining to Dr. King's salary, her employment was not for a definite period of time, but for an indefinite period of time. A twelve month notice period is appropriate: $125,000,00.

The vacation pay @ 6% is to be calculated since May 1st, 1997, as Dr. King did not take any holidays during the 1997 summer, except for a day or two. It amounts to $10,000.00 ($9,999.99): 16 months x $10,416.66 x 6%.

The relocation expenses amount to $18,401.07.

The Stock Options

Exhibit P-9 is a six-page document setting out the "Directors, Officers, Employees and Consultants Stock Option Plan (Amended on June 5, 1996)".

The Plan provides that the options shall not be exercisable upon grant, but shall vest over five years, at a 20% rate per year, on the anniversary of the grant or of the date the grant became effective.

In Dr. King's case, though the grant of 5,000 stock options was agreed upon on

October 17, 1996, it still had to be approved by the board of directors, this was done around the end of the year.

When vesting time for the first 20% carne around, be it in October or December 1997, Dr. King was no longer an employee, having been fired on September 8, 1997.

This meant that, upon termination in September 1997, all non vested options became void.

> "7. Cessation of Employment, Office or Management Consulting Services
>
> > 7.1 When an Optionee ceases to be an Employee of the Company and of any of its Subsidiaries for reason, including termination, retirement or death, ceases to be a director of the Company and of any of its Subsidiaries, any Options held by the Optionee that have not yet vested shall become void upon the date of such cessation of employment unless the Board decides otherwise."
> >
> > (Exhibit P-9: BioChem Pharma Directors, Officers, Employees and Consultants Stock Option Plan (Amended on June 5, 1996.)) (Emphasis added.)

But does this mean that Dr. King is not be entitled to damages?

The answer is no: because Dr. King's cessation of employment was an unlawful termination, she is entitled to damages concerning those options that would have become vested during the 12 month notice period, i.e. the first 20% of the 5,000 options.

The exercise price could not be lower than the market price on the day immediately preceding the grant, i.e. the highest closing price on the Montreal Stock Exchange or the Toronto Stock Exchange (paragraph 5 of the Plan). During the 1996 fourth quarter, when Dr. King's options were granted, the high and low of the BioChem share were $34.50 and $26.08; during the 1997 fourth quarter, when the first 20% became vested, and thus exercisable, the high and low were $41.45 and $28.75.

Of what was Dr. King deprived? Of the possibility of buying at a lower price than the current market price and thus achieving an instantaneous increase in value.

All in all, the Court concludes that the evidence, though sparse, is sufficient to compute a minimum amount of damages, i.e. $1.51 per share

As there was a two-for-one stock split in April 1997, the 5,000 options became 10,000 and 2,000 thereof became vested in the fall of 1997.

Thus the damages pertaining to the stock options are set at $3,020.00: 2,000 options @ $1.51.

Loss of bonus

As stated in the contract of employment, the target bonus was 10% of base salary and based on department and overall corporate performance.

On the one hand, there is insufficient evidence to support the hypothesis of a quasi-automatic attribution of the bonus: the inclusion of a bonus figure in the comparisons for the Quebec tax holiday is not enough.

On the other hand, in the hypothesis of a discretionary, non-automatic award, there is no evidence to allow the Court to establish an amount: there is no evidence to compare department performance to department targets; and there is insufficient evidence to compare overall corporate performance to overall corporate targets: the BioChem annual report to shareholders provides only one pert of the corporate comparison, i.e. its performance, not the targets.

Thus, one way or the other, the claim pertaining to the loss of bonuses cannot be granted.

Stress, Anxiety and Inconvenience

The claim for damages due to stress, anxiety and inconvenience is well founded: the unjustified character of her dismissal and the manner in which it was carried out entitle Dr. King to damages, which the Court sets at $25,000.

In particular, the Court was struck by the refusal of BioChem to allow Dr. King to retrieve her personal diary-agenda from her office, thus requiring her to reconstitute, from memory and sparse notations on her home calendar (Exhibit P-12), her day-to-day activities for the 10 month period during which she carried out her duties at BioChem.

It is evident that an employer is entitled to exercise caution and to verify what documents are taken out of the premises, but retaining a personal diary-agenda without justification is a bit much: if there was, anything therein which BioChem felt it was entitled to retain, it should have explained it to the Court; if there was nothing therein of that nature, why not give it back to its author? Besides, there was a duplicate of Dr. King's agenda in the computer.

There is a flavour of pettiness arid nastiness to the whole thing.

Reputation

As to damages to reputation, Dr. King is entitled to compensation. The simple fact of having been dismissed purportedly for cause, by a major employer in a close-knit industry, carries a lingering stigma notwithstanding a judgment which vindicates the employee. The Court sets the amount of damages at $25,000.00.

Loss of Benefits

What of the 20% claimed for benefits, i.e. $29,166.67?

This is the category relating to the loss of the group insurance plan coverage: life, short and long-term disability, major medical, hospital, dental and vision care. There is no evidence to support that aspect of the claim.

There is also to be considered the Quebec tax holiday of which Dr. King benefited. As per the comparisons prepared on behalf of the employer for Dr. King before she was hired (P-10), it amounted to $27,851 per annum on a $121,000 income

In other words, Dr. King, as a Quebec resident, would normally have had to pay $55,994 in federal and Quebec income taxes, unemployment insurance and Quebec Pension Plan contributions; because of the Quebec tax holiday, amount decreased to $28,143, due to the elimination of the $27,851 Quebec income tax. Thus, Dr. King had some $27,000 or $28,000 additional disposable income: her disposable income, on a $121,000 income, was $92,857 instead of $65,006.

Without the Quebec tax holiday, such income would have had to be in the $160,000 range to provide after-tax disposable income in the $90,000 range

And if that had been the case, damages, for example vacation pay and compensation in lieu of notice, would have been calculated on income in the $160,000 range.

There is no reason to ignore this effect of the Quebec tax holiday in the assessment of damages.

The most straightforward way of compensating this item is to set the award at the same amount as the additional disposable income for the one-year notice period. Thus there shall be an award of $27,851.

In summary, Dr. King is entitled to a total amount of $240,105.41 as damages:

.	Vacation pay as of May 1st, 1997	$5,833.34
.	Damages in lieu of notice	$125,000.00
.	Vacation pay since May 1st, 1997	$10,000.00
.	Relocation expenses	$18,401,07
.	Loss of stock options	$3,020.00
.	Loss of bonus	-- nil --
.	Stress, anxiety and inconvenience	$25,000,00
.	Reputation	$25,000.00
.	Loss of benefits	$27,851.00
.	TOTAL	$240,105.41

Conclusions
The Court:
MAINTAINS the action of Ann Christie King;
DISMISSES the plea of BioChem Pharma Inc.;
CONDEMNS BioChem Pharma Inc. to pay to Ann Christie King damages in the total amount of $240,105.41, with interest at the legal rate, and the additional indemnity provided for in Article 1619 of the Civil Code of Quebec since September 15, 1997;
WITH COSTS.

CASE 7.2

Dubé v. Volcano Technologies Inc.

[2001] Q.J. No. 1208, **Quebec Superior Court**

(Excerpts of Judgment)

REASONS FOR JUDGMENT

PIERRE J. DALPHOND J.:— After 26 months of service as Production Manager at the St. Hyacinthe plant, the Plaintiff was terminated by Volcano. He now claims as indemnity an amount equivalent to 9 months of salary plus car allowance, bonuses and moral damages, the whole totalling $102,490. The Defendant considers that according to the terms of the employment agreement, Mr. Dubé is entitled to no more than 2 weeks, which it has paid to him.

THE FACTS

Mr. Dubé previously worked for ACA, where he met Mr. Jean-Yves Côté, who hired him in 1970. In 1997, Mr. Dubé was unemployed. By then, Mr. Jean-Yves Côté was the General Manager of the Volcano plant at St-Hyacinthe and in September 1997, he recruited Mr. Dubé to fill the position of Production Manager at the plant.

The employment contract provides for an annual salary of $75,000, plus a car allowance and the possibility of an annual bonus. It reads as follows:

> Monsieur, Suite aux récentes discussions que vous avez eues avec les représentants de Volcano Technologies Inc. (ci-après désignée la "Société"), il nous fait plaisir de vous offrir un emploi au sein de la Société au poste de Directeur de production. À ce titre, vous vous rapporterez à Jean-Yves Côté, Directeur général de la Société.
>
> Dans le cadre de cet emploi, vous devrez accomplir toutes les tâches, responsabilités et fonctions inhérentes à votre poste.
>
> Votre salaire annuel sera de soixante-treize mille dollars (73 000,00 $) et vous sera payable en versements égaux et réguliers à raison de mille quatre cents trois dollars et quatre-vingt-cinq cents (1 403,85 $) par semaine. Vous serez couvert par le régime d'assurance collectif de la Great West après un (1) mois de service.
>
> Vous aurez droit à un bonus annuel maximum de dix mille dollars (10 000,00 $) gagné selon des critères à discuter entre vous et Jean-Yves Côté. Vous aurez droit à une allocation de voiture de huit cent soixante dollars (860,00 $) par mois.
>
> Vous aurez droit à trois (3) semaines de vacances annuelles payées. Ces vacances pourront être prises aux époques et de la manière convenue entre vous et la Société. De plus, les vacances dues seront calculées sur la

> période de référence allant du 1er juillet au 30 juin de chaque année.
>
> Votre emploi débutera le 22 septembre 1997. Il pourra être terminé en tout temps par la Société, pour cause ou motif sérieux, avec les préavis ou indemnité équivalente prévus selon la loi sur les normes du travail.
>
> Cette offre d'emploi est conditionnelle à votre acceptation et à votre signature de la présente lettre et de l'annexe ci-après reproduite. L'ensemble de toutes ces conditions de travail constituera votre contrat de travail avec la Société.
>
> De plus, cette offre d'emploi n'est valable que pour une durée de cinq (5) jours à compter de sa réception. À l'expiration de ce délai, l'offre sera nulle et non avenue.
>
> Nous vous souhaitons que ces conditions vous soient acceptables. Si toutefois des informations supplémentaires s'avéraient nécessaires, n'hésitez pas à communiquer avec le soussigné.
>
> Nous profitons de cette occasion pour vous souhaiter la bienvenue au sein de notre équipe. Nous espérons que votre contribution sera profitable et positive à l'endroit de nous tous et que cette collaboration mutuelle se traduira par de nombreux succès et de grandes réussites.
> (...)

It is not disputed that Mr. Dubé performed his duties properly and to the complete satisfaction of Volcano. He achieved all the goals previously discussed with Mr. Côté.

However, due to the financial situation of the plant, the senior management of Volcano re-structured the operations of the company and Mr. Dubé along with 10 other employees was laid off on December 1st, 1999. He was then 53 years old. In the following days, he was paid 2 weeks' salary in lieu of notice, plus 3 weeks of vacation.

Despite numerous efforts, Mr. Dubé was unable to find new employment. In July 1999, he created his own job by becoming a consultant. Since then, he has been working 3 to 4 days a week on special assignments and seems to do well. No amount is being claimed for the period beginning in July 1999.

ARGUMENTS OF THE PARTIES

Relying on the dispositions of the Civil Code and recent case law, the Plaintiff considers to be entitled to an amount equal to 9 months of salary plus car allowance. He also claims $20,000 in bonus for his 2 years of service ($10,000/year).

Based on the reference in the employment contract to the Labour Standard Act, the Defendant argues that the Plaintiff is entitled to no more than one week per year of work. As for the bonus, it contends that the parties never agreed on how it should be determined and that the Plaintiff never asked for one while working for Volcano.

ANALYSIS AND DECISION

If there is any doubt regarding the intent of the parties with regard to the indemnity payable in case of termination, such doubt has to be resolved in favour of the Plaintiff.

The evidence shows that the issue of the indemnity payable in case of firing for or without cause or lay off was not discussed between the parties and that the paragraph including the reference to the Labour Standard Act was copied by Mr. Côté from a draft prepared in 1993 for floor employees of Mr. Côté's previous employer and not for mid manager such as Mr. Dubé.

In the Court's opinion, the reference to the Labour Standard Act in case of "terminaison pour cause ou motif sérieux" could be read as applicable only to situation related to Mr. Dubé's behaviour.

Moreover, the argument of the employer amounts to saying that when entering into the agreement, Mr. Dubé understood that he was renunciating his rights under the Civil Code to receive more than one week per year of service in case of termination. It is a well-established principle that a renunciation to a right must be clear and unambiguous. In the Court's opinion, the mere reference to the Labour Standard Act in the employment contract without further explanation or detail is not enough to constitute such a renunciation.

Therefore, there is no need to decide if the contract was one of adhesion and if the reference to the Labour Standard Act should be considered abusive (art. 1437 C.C.Q.) in light of art. 2091 C.C.Q.

As a result, the Court must determine the "délai de congé applicable" pursuant to art. 2091 C.C.Q., which in fact is based on the age of the employee, the nature of the employment, the duration of his employment, the time required to find new employment,... (Standard Broadcasting Co. c. Steward, [1994] R.J.Q. 1751 (C.A.)).

In the circumstances, the Court awards the Plaintiff an indemnity of four months i.e. eighteen weeks. Since he has already received two weeks, he is entitled to sixteen more weeks of salary.

As for the bonus, no amount is awarded because the entitlement is conditional upon the parties agreeing on the terms to determine if and when such bonus is payable. That condition was never fulfilled and it is not up to the Court to draft what the parties never elected or attempted to do; neither the Plaintiff nor the Defendant approached the other party to discuss the conditions for a yearly bonus despite the fact that the contract contemplated it. During a period of employment of over 2 years, Mr. Dubé never requested a bonus or the drafting of the terms to be applied. As for Mr. Côté, he was too busy with other problems, including the profitability of the plant, to address the issue.

Thus, this is not a case of abuse or bad faith from the employer in which the possibly of damages could be raised. The conditions had to be agreed upon and they were not even discussed after Mr. Dubé's hiring because of the poor financial conditions of the company. Since the entitlement to a bonus was conditional to terms to be agreed upon, the right to a bonus has not arisen.

As for the car allowance ($860/mo), the evidence has shown that it was provided to compensate for the costs associated with Mr. Dubé having to work in St-Hyacinthe instead of Montreal or close to his residence in Longueuil. In his testimony, the Plaintiff said that he was travelling 120 kilometres a day in order to get to and back from the plant and that the allowance was merely compensating him for the costs associated with the gas, insurance and depreciation on the car. Since he did not have to show up at the plant for work during the "délai de congé", the Court does not see why he should be compensated for expenses not incurred.

As for the claim for moral damages, it was not supported by the evidence (in fact the termination was done in a very proper way, almost friendly). In his arguments, the attorney for the Plaintiff did not really raise the issue, making it no longer a claim. It is therefore dismissed.

WHEREFORE THE COURT:

> CONDEMNS the Defendant to pay to the Plaintiff an amount equivalent to 16 weeks of salary, totalling $22,461 plus interests and indemnity as of the day of the formal demand, December 9, 1999.
> The whole with costs.

CASE 7.3

Hasanie v. Kaufel Groupe Ltd.

[2002] Q.J. No. 3551, **Quebec Superior Court**

(Excerpts of Judgment)

REASONS FOR JUDGMENT

CLAUDE LAROUCHE J.:— Plaintiff submits that he was constructively and unjustly dismissed by defendants and he is claiming from them the total sum of $674,480.70. His claim is for loss of salary and benefits, moral damages, damage to his reputation, and also for punitive damages and reimbursement of his extra-judicial legal costs.

Defendants argue that plaintiff was not constructively dismissed; that they had cause to dismiss plaintiff and that plaintiff's claim for damages is unfounded and grossly inflated.
Plaintiff is a certified management accountant since 1976. He also holds degrees in law and in commerce.

He has long experience in senior executive and professional positions. By his own admission, plaintiff was a "very senior person" in the Kaufel organisation, first as the Corporate Controller and later as the Director of Administration and Control. We could say that he was the "third person" in the corporate head office hierarchy.

He was hired by Kaufel Group Ltd. on October 1st, 1988 as a Corporate Controller. Defendant Kaufel was a public corporation specialising in the lighting industry.

As for the other defendants, they are part of one of the world's largest group of lighting and electronic components companies, and manufacturer of electrical products; they acquired the Kaufel group in November 1998.

Before Kaufel was acquired by defendants' companies, its chairman and chief executive officer was Mr. Bruce Kaufman. Mr. Roland Blais, to whom plaintiff was reporting, was the vice-president finance of Kaufel.

After the acquisition of Kaufel by defendants in November 1998, Mr. Michael B. Kenney became the president and chief executive officer. It is in that capacity that he informed the Kaufel group members that the financial operations will receive functional direction and support from Nathalie Pilon. The group was also informed that Denis Fragias, Corporate Controller, will be reporting directly to Nathalie Pilon and will assist her in the budgeting, forecasting and financial reporting functions. The organisational announcement of Kaufel group by Mr. Kenney was made known in writing as of January 28, 1999.

Plaintiff is submitting that it is clear for him that after the acquisition of Kaufel, the other defendants constructively dismissed him.

Plaintiff alleges that the constructive dismissal, which began in November 1998, was in fact confirmed by the written reorganisation announcement dated January 28, 1999, which reorganisation announcement clearly excluded him from the organised structure of Kaufel after the Thomas & Betts' acquisition.

On July 13, 1999, in a written document, defendants offered plaintiff a severance package since his employment will be terminated on a date to be agreed on.

In consideration of his period of employment cumulated up until then, and of his level of responsibility, he was offered a basic compensation indemnity corresponding to 10 months of his basic salary. It seems that plaintiff was accepting the offer in principle but he was asking for 12 months of his basic salary instead of 10 as it was offered. Finally, the offer was not accepted and the deal was to be reconsidered after plaintiff was to come back from his vacation.

Before plaintiff was back from his vacation, sometime in July 1999, defendants were made aware that plaintiff and a former employee of Kaufel, David Rycroft, had been discussing and preparing, sometime in January 1999, an offer to purchase a company named Dynergie.

It was clear then for defendants that plaintiff was involved with David Rycroft, as early as January 1999, in an offer to purchase a competing company involved in the emergency lighting business.

The written documentation obtained by defendants in July 1999, as to the activities of plaintiff with David Rycroft, appeared to defendants to indicate a serious breach of trust committed by plaintiff during his employment with Thomas & Betts.

In view of the nature of the allegations and their seriousness, defendants decided to investigate them and to provide plaintiff with the opportunity to give explanations on the said allegations and suggested that he would be accompanied by an attorney at a meeting organised in the course of said investigation.

The evidence shows that neither at that meeting nor at any relevant time after, did plaintiff provide full, truthful and satisfactory explanations to Thomas & Betts about this situation.

It is for those reasons that defendants submit therefore that they had no choice but to consider as disloyal the conduct of plaintiff showed on the occasion of both the events that took place in December 1998 and January 1999, and those pertaining to his refusal to collaborate to Thomas & Betts' investigation further to the disclosure of the correspondence as it is shown in the documentation produced as Exhibit D-1.

It is for those reasons that consequently, defendants submit that they had no choice but to rescind its decision to lay off plaintiff and to replace it by an immediate termination for cause.

A question of credibility arises concerning the initiative of plaintiff in the Dynergie affair. He testified during the trial that he was authorised in his initiative to offer the purchase of Dynergie by Roland Blais who he considered to be his immediate superior. His contentions are contradicted by the related facts of this case and by Mr. Blais himself. We have serious doubts as to his credibility.

It has been established that if the duly authorised defendants' representatives had been aware of plaintiff's initiative of January 1999, he would have been advised that his employment was terminated for cause and without severance. And this would have been decided because of breach of plaintiff's duty of loyalty during his employment.

Defendants main proposition is to the effect that every employee owes a duty of loyalty to his employer. This duty would be the very essence of the employment contract. It is important that the employee must not advance his personal interests over those of his employer. He must not place himself in a position of conflict of interest. While these obligations attached to every employee, defendants submit that persons in senior management position such as plaintiff are held to a higher standard (art. 2088 C.C.Q., Bank of Montreal v. Kuet Leong Ng, [1989] 2 R.C.S. 429, at pages 438 and 439 and Marie-France Bich, Contrat de travail et Code civil du Québec - retrospective, perspectives and expectatives, Service de la formation permanente, Barreau du Québec, Éd. Yvon Blais Inc., 1996, pages 196-198).

Defendant's fundamental position in this matter is that by taking active steps to purchase Dynergie, a competing business, while being still in his employment and while receiving his full salary and benefits, plaintiff placed himself in a position of conflict of interest and sought to advance his interests to the detriment of those of his employer.

Henceforth, Mr. Hasanie breached his duty of loyalty to his employer because he was in a very senior position; he had access to highly sensitive information which could give competitors significant competitive advantage; he commanded a substantial salary, $110,500 per annum plus benefits; he knew that his current employer Kaufel Group Ltd had been acquired by Thomas & Betts on November 4, 1998, whereupon Thomas & Betts began integrating Kaufel's operations into its own.

Plaintiff claims that Dynergie was not a competitor. The authorised representative of defendants submits that this contention is contradicted even by Mr. Hasanie's own evidence. If Dynergie were not a competitor, why was he concerned enough to seek authorisation for the transaction? Other evidence contradicts plaintiff's position as submitted by defendants:

– Exhibits D-2 to D-5 show that Dynergie and Kaufel were in the same business;
– Gary Ephraim testimony: the value of Dynergie (in bankruptcy) was in the molds and dies, on which the company could be built; he bought it with Rycroft and operated it as Luxnet in the emergency lighting business until he left in September 2000;

- Sam Rimoin testimony: "With Rycroft buying Dynergie, my job would be more difficult";
- Roland Blais testimony: "If you sale one dollar of emergency lighting, you are a competitor";
- Nathalie Pilon testimony: Dynergie was in the emergency lighting business. It was a competitor.

And finally,

- Michael Kenney testimony: Dynergie was a competitor. It quickly grew into a very substantial business.

Defendants are also submitting that taking steps to organise a competing business is grounds for dismissal for cause (Maheu Noiseux & Associés v. Roneo Vickers Canada Ltd (C.A.) [1988] R.J.Q. 1597; L.N.S Systems Inc. v. Allard, [2001] R.R.A. 813, J.E. 2001-1277 (C.S.) - in appeal, Appelant Allard has discontinued her appeal-; Sturton v. PPG Industries Canada Ltd, J.E. 84-560 (C.S.), Mr. Justice Biron at pages 17,19-21; Ducharme v. Formules municipales Ltée, J.E. 81-821 (C.S.), Mr. Justice Péloquin, at page 9).

Defendants also propose that it is immaterial that Dynergie was not a business opportunity which defendants would have pursued. Mere potential conflict of interest is sufficient to justify dismissal. In order to do so, the employer needs not to suffer actual prejudice (Felker v. Sherman Cunningham and Electro Source Inc., [2000] J.Q. no 3177, a decision of the Court of Appeal of Ontario, dated August 29, 2000, at paragraphs 14, 16 and 17; Duguay v. Maritime Welding and Rentals Ltd., [1989] N.B.J. No. 822 (Q.L.) (New-Brunswick Queen's Bench), Mr. Justice Deschênes, at page 4).

Referring to a Supreme Court decision of New-Foundland, defendants cite this proposition of Mr. Justice Goodridge, at paragraph 113 of his judgment of June 26, 1980, that "the degree of loyalty which the law imposes upon an employee is absolute. Without the informed consent of the employer, an employee may not compete or take steps to compete either directly or indirectly with his employer. If he does so there is just cause for dismissal". (King and Martin v. Harris and Hiscock, [1980], 30 N.Fld. & P.E.I.R. 118 (N. Ffld. Supreme Court).

With reference to the case of Maheu v. Vickers (at page 1599), defendants add that the employer's consent must be informed and unequivocal, preferably in writing.

Plaintiff sought to prove a "practice" at Kaufel which allowed employees to buy competing businesses. Witnesses Rimoin and Blais both deny the existence of such a practice. Defendants submit that the only evidence of such a practice that plaintiff could point out is Exhibit P-8, which was a divestiture of a non-core business contemplated by Kaufel in 1997.

Defendants indicate that plaintiff's position is not credible when he testifies that he "consulted" or "advised" Mr. Blais of his idea of pursuing the Dynergie opportunity. Blais denies ever having authorised Mr. Hasanie to do so. If plaintiff was really authorised, "why not get written confirmation", suggest defendants, as he did in 1997 with P-8 for Powerlite.

The defence is submitting that the confirmation that he was not authorised comes from Mr. Hasanie's own evidence. He had wanted to put his offer for Dynergie (Exhibit D-11) in his name or in his son's name, but he was told by "a third party" or "legal counsel" "that it was not appropriate to do so while he was still an employee of defendants". The defence suggests: "Why not reply? But I'm authorised!". Why not get a written confirmation of such purported authorisation? Because he knew if he asked Blais for authorisation, he would not get it; Blais was, in any event, in no position of authority to grant it. Plaintiff knew that if he asked the "new management", to use his own words, they too would refuse. Plaintiff knew he had no such authorisation. The fact is that he was acting covertly; despite his contention that he was authorised to pursue this opportunity from the office, he had the information package D-14 sent somewhere else (apart from sending also from his home the complete documentation of 52 pages, D-13).

Defendants argue that as an intelligent man, well educated and trained as a lawyer, plaintiff has demonstrated, at best, a clear case of wilful blindness affecting considerably his credibility. Several examples are indicated by defendants to support the proposition:

- He seems to have ignored the take-over of Kaufel by Thomas & Betts and the imposition of new authority, personified by Ms Pilon and Mr. Kenney.
- He had met with Ms Pilon, took instructions from her, even adopted the informal dress code she invited all Kaufel head office staff to adopt on November 9, 1998.
- Mr. Blais resigned as officer and director of Kaufel Group Ltd on November 5, 1998; he thereafter had a passive role only, acted as a "consultant", and had no managerial authority.
- Ms Pilon was in the premises 75% of the time, in a boardroom across the hall from plaintiff.
- Mr. Kenney was also in the premises 2-3 days a week for the first five months after the transaction, occupying Mr. Kaufman's old office on the third floor of 1800 Hymus boulevard.

In addition, defendants are submitting that in his own testimony Mr. Hasanie makes the distinction between "old management" (Kaufel) and "new management" (Thomas & Betts), thus confirming that he knew where true authority lay. Messrs Rimoin and Blais also used the same language, thus confirming that everyone knew where true authority lay.

Making reference to the case of Felker and Electro Source Inc., defendants submit that plaintiff's casual comments to Messrs Rimoin and Blais (persons not in authority) about his intention to perhaps examine the Dynergie opportunity, did not relieve him of his obligation to make full disclosure and obtain his employer's consent.

The defence submits that the burden of proving, on a balance of probabilities, that an employer has condoned disloyal conduct or has waived the right to dismiss is upon the employee who asserts such a proposition (reference is made to the judgment in the case of Duguay v. Maritime Welding & Rentals Ltd., cited above).

On the question on plaintiff's duty of loyalty, defendants are concluding that plaintiff has advanced half-truths and conjecture in support of his contention that he disclosed his involvement with Dynergie and had the requisite authorisation to proceed. Thomas & Betts asserts that Mr. Hasanie was neither open, honest nor forthright; he did not disclose all material facts; Thomas & Betts management was not fully informed of his designs. When management learned the full extent of plaintiff's involvement in late July 1999, they were entitled to dismiss him for cause.

The question now to be asked is as follows: can Thomas & Betts invoque breach of plaintiff's duty of loyalty to withdraw the severance package?

Thomas & Betts contends that it was entitled to withdraw the severance package offered to plaintiff on July 13, 1999 (Exhibit P-11), when Thomas & Betts learned in late July 1999 of plaintiff's active steps to acquire Dynergie as shown in Exhibit D-1. This because breach by the employee of his duty of loyalty goes to the very root of the employment contract (Marie-France Bich cited above at page 197).

The defence adds that the discovery of such breach, even after notification to the employee of his forthcoming dismissal on other grounds or without cause, may be relied upon to justify termination without notice (references are made to the cases of Sturton v. PPG Industries Canada Ltd cited above and Aasgard v. Harlequin Enterprises Ltd, [1993] O.J. No. 1484 (Q.L.), Ontario Court of Justice - General division, Mr. Justice Spence, at paragraphs 10, 30-35 and 37-38 and 41.

Upon learning of plaintiff's misconduct and in view of the seriousness of the matter, defendants suspended plaintiff and initiated an investigation of his conduct. Defendants submit that the employer is entitled to sufficient time to carry out an investigation of the employee's wrongful conduct (Exhibit P-12) (Duguay v. Maritime Welding and Rentals Ltd cited above and Empey v. Coastal Towing Co. Ltd, a judgment dated January 11, 1976 of the British Columbia Supreme Court, Murray G. 31 C.P.R. (2d) 157.

It is the contention of defendants that faced with plaintiff's lack of candour even when confronted with the facts, defendants had no choice but to dismiss him for cause. In support of this proposal, the defence submits some relevant references:

- During the September 1st, 1999 meeting, plaintiff made no reference to his purported disclosure of his activities (Exhibit P-17);
- During the meeting, he made no reference to any purported authorisation of his activities;
- During the meeting, he did not admit to be the author and sender of Exhibit D-1;

- Mr. Hasanie's written reply 10 days later (Exhibit P-18) is extremely evasive as to his actions of January 1999;
- In response to a precise request from T&B's counsel (Exhibit P-19), plaintiff continues to be evasive: he "does not remember" being the author and sender of Exhibit D-1 (Exhibit P-20);

It is also the submission of the defence that the employee's duty of loyalty extends to being forthright and truthful when faced with an investigation of the employee's conduct by the employer. During defendants' investigation of Mr. Hasanie's conduct, Messrs Rimoin and Blais both denied that Mr. Hasanie ever told them he was himself pursuing Dynergie. They also denied ever giving plaintiff the authorization he claims now to have received. It is the contention of defendants that both, Messrs Rimoin and Blais, confirmed these facts in their testimony at trial.

Faced with concrete evidence of plaintiff's disloyalty in January 1999 while he was a senior and highly paid employee, and his continued disloyalty demonstrated by his lack of candour during the investigation of his conduct, Thomas & Betts submit that they had no choice but to dismiss him (references were also made by defendants' attorney to Kenney testimony, Rimoin testimony in cross-examination, Exhibits D-19 and D-21, and Blais testimony).

Concerning now the constructive dismissal as alleged by plaintiff, he submits that he was constructively dismissed sometime between November 4, 1998 and January 28, 1999, dates at which his constructive dismissal was allegedly "confirmed" by the operational memo P-6. Yet, claims the defence, he complained to no one and continued collecting his salary and benefits until August 13, 1999, date of his suspension.

It is also argued by the defence that as a senior manager of Kaufel, plaintiff had witnessed many acquisitions from the buyer's side; he knew that an acquisition inevitably resulted in a reorganisation. His title has not been changed, he had not been demoted. He was even offered new responsibilities. Thomas & Betts was looking for new talent. But, as suggested by the defence, Mr. Hasanie refused to rise to the challenge. He preferred to "wait for his two-years package" (references being made to the Pilon and Hasanie's testimonies).

Referring to a judgment of this Court (Corriveau v. Sedgwick Ltd, [2000] J.Q. no 4014, J.E. 2000-2051), the defence submits that in the context of an acquisition, an employee can not anticipate his constructive dismissal. The employer must be given a reasonable time to reorganise; employees, particularly senior management, should not be jumping to any conclusions.

With reference to a judgment of the Supreme Court of Canada, defendants affirm that constructive dismissal occurs where "an employer decides unilaterally to make substantial changes to the essential terms of an employee's contract of employment, and the employee does not agree to the changes and leaves his or her job" (Farber v. Royal Trust Co., [1997] 1 S.C.R. 846, Mr. Justice Gonthier, at page 858, paragraph 24).

It is a proposition of defendants that to claim that he has been constructively dismissed, the employee must either resign or at least promptly act to protest the changes to his or her employment contract (reference is made to the case of Gilbert v. Hôpital Général de Lachine [1989] R.J.Q. 1824 (C.S.), Mr. Justice Fréchette, at pages 1827-1830).

Defendants also submit that even if plaintiff was advised of his forthcoming dismissal or considered himself constructively dismissed, he continued to be bound by his duty of loyalty to his employer (with references made to the cases of Sturton and Aasgard cited above).

We come to the conclusion that the propositions and contentions of defendants are well founded. They are based on the evidence submitted to the Court, on the law and in accordance with the different cases submitted to this Court. Unfortunately, plaintiff has not established his case of having been dismissed without cause, or having been constructively dismissed.

FOR THE ABOVE GIVEN REASONS, THIS COURT:

GRANTS defendants' plea;

DISMISSES plaintiff's action;

THE WHOLE with costs.

CASE 7.4

Copyfax Inc. v. Lambert

[2000] Q.J. No. 987, **Quebec Superior Court (Civil Division)**

(Excerpts of Judgment)

REASONS FOR JUDGMENT

IRVING J. HALPERIN J.:— The Court is seized of an application for interlocutory injunction against a former employee of Petitioner based upon a non-competition clause. The Respondent Claude Lambert (the "Employee") entered the employ of the Petitioner in February 1992 as a dispatcher. In July 1997, he assumed the function of sales representative.

The parties entered into two employment agreements during the course of their relationship. The first, dated February 24th, 1992 (P-1) was executed on the occasion of the Employee's employment as a dispatcher, while the Agreement dated July 8th, 1997, (P-2) was entered into when he became Petitioner's sales representative. The second agreement explicitly stipulates that the Employee is bound by all of the terms and conditions, and penalties stipulated in the previous agreement.

The Employment Agreement (Exhibit P-1) is almost in its entirety a series of stipulations imposing upon the Employee various conditions relating to confidentiality and non-competition upon the termination of employment. It reads as follows:

> "Montreal, Quebec, Agreement between Copyfax Inc. and Claude Lambert
>
> It is agreed that I will treat all matters pertaining to Copyfax as confidential and will not discuss Copyfax Inc. business with outside parties, as it is understood that I will be acquiring valuable information regarding customer names and lists and prices and company policies etc. etc. Also I agree not to go into the photocopy machine, supply and/or service business, whether with a Copier Supplier, on my own account or with partners, or to accept a job with any employer on the Island of Montreal or Laval or in an area of twenty-five (25) miles surrounding it, which employer would be selling photocopy machines and/or supplies in this area and which could be a competitor to Copyfax. I agree not to accept such a position for a period of fourteen months (14 mts.) from time to time I either leave or am terminated by Copyfax. Also I agree to return all merchandise, materials, manuals, lists etc. to Copyfax.
>
> And in addition to the paragraph mentioned above, It is understood that if I should accept to work for a competitor as mentioned above I shall be liable and owe Copyfax on demand $6,000 (Six Thousand Dollars) in consideration for the training that I will receive from Copyfax while being paid on the job. The training will consist of Dispatch Training

> related to Service of Copier Machines and public relations towards servicing such customers as well as continuous on the job training regarding warehouse duties etc. etc. as well as training on the job related to the specific business of copiers and its related supplies.
>
> The amount of six thousand dollars ($6,000.00) payable to Copyfax represents the costs for training prior to the termination or violation of the present contract and in no way does it serve to compensate Copyfax for any damages caused as a result of the violation of the present contract and therefore, Copyfax retains any and all of its rights and recourses to which it may be entitled to in law. And I agree to follow the rules and policies of Copyfax Inc.
>
> I agree that the above non-competing covenant is reasonable that it gives Copyfax the protection to which it is entitled and yet does not impair my ability to earn a livelihood in industries other than Photocopy machines and supplies.
>
> I agree to give Copyfax four (4) weeks notice to train my replacement should I leave Copyfax, if Copyfax so desires ..."

Exhibit P-2 dated July 8th, 1997 simply acknowledges that the previous agreement Exhibit P-1 remains in full force and effect upon the Employee assuming his new duties.

These proceedings are based upon the purported violation by the Employee of the agreements P-1 and P-2.

By judgment dated January 27th, 2000 a provisional order of injunction was issued, while on February 4th, 2000 the previously rendered order was renewed but modified by narrowing the restrictions upon the Employee in the following terms. The Employee was now required to:

> "Immediately cease doing business with any clients currently serviced by Plaintiff or on Plaintiffs current negotiation list, be it directly or indirectly with respect to the equipment etc. described in paragraph 26 of the Motion."

As to the Defendant Panasonic Canada Inc., it was ordered to "immediately cease doing business in contravention of the foregoing order with Claude Lambert or Le Groupe AMC."

The Defendant Panasonic Canada Inc. has not contested these proceedings.
Since his assumption of his new role, the Employee was Petitioner's sole sales representative and it is Petitioner's contention that "it was completely reliant after him to solicit clients, develop direct relationships with them and, ultimately increase its sales." (The Petition, paragraph 4).

In that capacity, Petitioner alleges that the Employee acquired significant knowledge of his employer's clientèle and had access to a confidential client card system and other confidential information.

The Employee on the other hand, acknowledges that he had caused to be incorporated the Respondent Le Groupe AMC Équipement de Bureau inc. in or about the month of September 1999 which has in fact been engaged in the operation of a business similar to the business carried on by the Petitioner. A serviceman has been engaged and the company Le Groupe AMC Équipement de Bureau inc. has effected four sales of equipment, two prior to his dismissal on January 21st, 2000 and two subsequent thereto.

Petitioner upon learning of the Employee's activities terminated his employment on January 21st 2000.

The evidence reveals that in July 1999 while serving as sales representative of the Petitioner, the Employee approached senior officers of the Petitioner and proposed that a new and different relationship be created whereby the Employee would leave the employ of the Petitioner and would operate as an independent dealer promoting and selling not only Petitioner's products but products of competitors as well. This proposition was turned down unequivocally by the Petitioner.

The Employee acknowledges that he has developed a business relationship with Panasonic Canada Inc. and is thereby engaged in a line of 1 business comparable to the business carried on by Plaintiff. He denies, and there is no proof to the contrary, that he effected any sales or solicited any of the entities designated as clients of the Petitioner.

There being no significant dispute on the facts, argument before the undersigned was substantially on questions of law, more specifically, the relevant criteria for the granting of an interlocutory injunction.

The 1975 Court of Appeal decision in the case of La Société de développement de la Baie James c. Robert Kenatewat continues to be the landmark decision in matters of interlocutory injunction. More particularly, the steps enumerated by Owen J. at page 183 succinctly set the standard thus:

> "At the interlocutory injunction stage these rights are apparently either (a) clear, or (b) doubtful, or (c) non-existent.
>
> (a) If it appears clear, at the interlocutory stage that the Petitioners have the rights which they invoke then the interlocutory injunction should be granted if considered necessary in accordance with the provisions of the second paragraph of Article 752 C.P.
>
> (b) However, if at this stage the existence of the rights invoked by the Petitioners appears doubtful then the Court should consider the balance of convenience and inconvenience in deciding whether an interlocutory injunction should be granted.
>
> (c) Finally if it appears, at the interlocutory stage, that the rights claimed are non-existent then the interlocutory injunction should be refused."

Nuss J. in the Court of Appeal case of Copiscope Inc. vs. TRM Copy Centers

Canada Limited, [1998] Q.J. No. 3662, at page 6 wrote:

> "if the Covenant is manifestly unreasonable then it is invalid and there is an absence of the apparent right which is an essential condition for the granting of an interlocutory injunction."

Then at page 7, he proceeds to enumerate the "well settled principles set out in the jurisprudence" which are to be applied in determining the validity of the non-competition covenant, to wit:

1) Undertakings in restraint of trade are generally against public order;
2) there may, within reasonable limits, be contractual restrictions on the freedom to conduct a specified commercial activity;
3) the validity of such restrictions is dependant on their being reasonable, particularly regarding the length of time that they are to apply and the territory where they are to be applicable;
4) furthermore, it must be shown that the restrictions are necessary for the reasonable protection of the interests of the party in whose favor they are granted;
5) if the restrictions do not meet the test of reasonability they will be struck down as being contrary to public order."

Article 2089 C.C.Q. explicitly imposes upon the employer the burden of proof as to the validity of the restrictions imposed upon an employee.

The Employee, challenges the validity of the non-competition clause on a variety of grounds inter alia, that it is unreasonable as to duration, geographic application and the modalities of its application, and in more general terms that his modest entry into a similar business offers no threat to the Petitioner. The agreements (P-1, P-2), it is further argued, are to contrats d'adhésion".

The employee also challenges the liquidated damage claim of $6,000 asserted by Plaintiff as being unreasonable particularly on the ground that the stipulated justification, namely compensation to the Petitioner of the cost incurred in training and preparing the Employee for the performance of his duties, is exaggerated and unfounded.

Finally, the Employee raises the question as to the unreasonable and excessive impact that an adverse judgment would have upon his ability to provide for his young family.

As to the territory covered by the restriction it is said to apply to "any employer on the Island of Montreal or Laval or in an area of 25 miles surrounding it..."
The use of the term "it" creates a certain ambiguity, the intention perhaps having been a reference to "them", given that two distinct areas, Montreal and Laval are mentioned. The method of calculating the restricted area appears to lack precision in that the restricted activity might be outside the 25 mile zone as regards one region but not outside the region comprising the other. No evidence on that subject was adduced.

More important is the fact that there is a restriction of 25 miles however it may be calculated.

In the Copiscope case, (supra) Nuss J. discussed the area which was subject to the restriction in that case and which was described as "a circle having a 25 mile radius." At page 8 he criticized the lack of justification of that restriction in the following terms:

> "Neither is there any reason advanced to justify this prohibition over the vast area of 5 082 square kilometers, covering any other business in which it may have an interest or in which it may wish to have an interest ..."
> (Emphasis added)

In the present case the undersigned similarly questions the reasonableness of the 25 mile prohibition.

As to the need for a 14 month restrictive period, little evidence of a persuasive nature has been adduced. Petitioner asserts that it has encountered some difficulty in finding a suitable replacement for the Employee although there was no evidence as to what measures were taken to find such an individual.

The Supreme Court case of Cameron vs. Canadian Factors Limited dealt with the question of duration and territorial ambit as regards the enforcement of a restraining covenant. At page 149, the Court held:

> "Under the Civil Code and the common law employee restraint covenants may be held invalid because of their unreasonable duration or because of their unreasonable territorial ambit, having regard in each respect to the range of businesses or activities covered by the restraining covenants. The principle raised in the present case is the application of a rule of reason to a balancing of the interests of the employer and the erstwhile employee in respect of the need of the former for protection of his business and of the latter for economic mobility, in the light of a policy that discourages limitations on personal freedom, and, specifically, on freedom of economic or employment opportunity. On this phase of the case, the five year prohibition is quite unreasonable and hence contrary to public order."

The difficulty allegedly experienced by the Petitioner in finding a replacement is somewhat surprising considering the fact that Claude Lambert the Employee, was originally engaged as a dispatcher, apparently with no particular sales knowledge or experience in that field and was later promoted to sales.

More than that however is the fact that Petitioner genuinely fears the Employee's interference with its clientèle, one would expect that a prompt replacement would be undertaken. That does not appear to have been the case, at least thusfar.

I would consider the stipulated duration of 14 months as being beyond the range of reasonableness.

The Employee alleges that the Agreement Exhibit P-1 was virtually a contrat d'adhésion in that it was prepared by the employer and required to be signed "as is" (C.C.Q. 1379). It is quite evident that there existed a major inequality of the bargaining positions of the two signatories, the one 24 years of age and only entering the job market, the other an experienced business enterprise. This is not to suggest that those facts necessarily lead to the nullity of the contract but in my respectful opinion, they bear some relevance in the process in which the Court is presently engaged.

From the point of view of the Employee, if the covenant were to be enforced given the extensive territorial ambit and duration stipulated, he would virtually be prevented from earning a livelihood and the impact upon him and is family would likely be severe.

On the other hand, the undersigned is not convinced that subject to the caveat which will be discussed below, that the Employee's continued presence in the market place during the stipulated 14 month period will cause Petitioner the prejudice it pretends.

The Court regards as important the Employee's voluntary abstention from soliciting Petitioner's clientèle. I regard that as an acknowledgement of Petitioner's entitlement to some protection in that regard.

The evidence causes the undersigned to conclude that the application of the test of balance of convenience - inconvenience generally favours the Employee for the following reasons:

(1) there is no evidence that the Petitioner's clientèle has been solicited or tampered with in any way;

(2) the prohibited area of 25 miles would have the effect of depriving the Employee of any realistic possibility of earning a livelihood given his present circumstances;

(3) that the stipulated duration of 14 months is as we have already observed, is excessive particularly since a prolonged period of exclusion would not necessarily provide the Petitioner with significantly greater security as regards its clientèle. The day of reckoning will come sooner or later when the Employee will have the opportunity of legitimately and unconditionally occupying a position in the market place.

In my respectful opinion the Petitioner has not established the apparent right which it seeks to enforce. Neither has it established that it will suffer irreparable harm or injury if the interlocutory injunction is refused, and finally the test of balance of convenience and inconvenience is to be resolved in favour of the Petitioner.

All of the foregoing will be subject to the exception that the Employee continues to respect the Ordonnance issued on February 4th by Mass J. as regards clients serviced on that date by the Petitioner or whose names appear on the "current negotiation list, be it directly or indirectly with respect to the equipment etc." described in paragraph 26 of Petitioner's Motion.

The Employee has acknowledged that he retains "certain client cards" and other material which Petitioner has described as being important to it since they contain considerable information about its clientèle. Those cards and any similar information retained by the Employee are to be returned to the Petitioner.

FOR THE FOREGOING REASONS, THE COURT:

GRANTS an interlocutory injunction to remain in effect until final judgment is rendered;

ORDERS Claude Lambert and Le Groupe AMC Équipement de Bureau inc. to immediately cease doing business with any clients currently serviced by Copifax Inc. or on its "current negotiation list" be it directly or indirectly with respect to the equipment etc. described in paragraph 28 of the Motion, for the 14 month period i.e. from January 21st, 2000 to March 21st 2001;

ORDERS Claude Lambert and Le Groupe AMC Équipement de Bureau inc. to immediately return to the Plaintiff all documents or materials, including any copies that have been made, containing any information relating to its business, including, without limiting the generality of the foregoing, all client lists, all price lists and all information pertaining to leads and follow ups, whether this information is in Lambert's possession, that of one of his family members, or that of any other employee or representative of le Groupe AMC. Équipement de Bureau inc.

Each party will pay its own costs.

CASE 7.5

A.R. Medicom Inc. v. Bergeron

[2003] Q.J. No. 18721, **Quebec Superior Court**

(Excerpts of Judgment)

The Petitioner has brought a Petition for an Interlocutory, Provisional and Permanent Injunction as well as an ordonnance de sauvegarde, has placed before the Court a request for an ordonnance de sauvegarde.

This application for a Safeguard Order is in connection with two contracts of employment containing similar but not identical non-compete clauses, signed by each of the Respondents Sylvain Bergeron and Jean Hubert.

Prior to this hearing, two provisional orders have been signed by two of my colleagues, the most recent one by Mr. Justice Bélanger which expires at midnight tonight.

The contract executed by Mr. Sylvain Bergeron on the 15th of February 1999 (P-3) is "ENTENTE DE RESPECT DE LA CONFIDENTIALITÉ, DE NON-CONCURRENCE ET DE NON-SOLLICITATION." The first paragraph reads as follows:

"1. Moyennant contrepartie valable reçue par le(la) soussigné(e) de A.R. MEDICOM INC., (ci-après MEDICOM INC.) le(la) soussigné(e) reconnaissant que ladite contrepartie est valable et suffisante pour que le(la) soussigné(e) s'engage en vertu de la présente entente, convient qu'au cours de son emploi avec MEDICOM INC., et pour une période de deux (2) années suivant la fin de cet emploi, de ne pas directement ou indirectement, travailler pour toute entreprise ayant des activités commerciales semblables ou en concurrence avec celles de Medicom inc." (Emphasis added)

The contract signed by the Respondent Hubert on the 22nd of December 1995 (P-6) is "ENTENTE DE RESPECT DE LA CONFIDENTIALITÉ ET STIPULATION DE NE PAS FAIRE". Paragraph 1. is slightly different from that which I have previously read and reads as follows:

"1. Moyennant contrepartie valable reçue par le soussigné de MEDICOM INC., (ci-après MEDICOM), le soussigné, reconnaissant que ladite contrepartie est valable et suffisante pour que le soussigné s'engage en vertu de la présente entente, convient qu'au cours de son emploi avec MEDICOM, et pour une période de trois (3) ans suivant la fin de cet emploi, de ne pas, directement ou indirectement, soit à titre de mandant, d'associé, de fondé de pouvoirs, d'actionnaire, d'employé, de consultant ou d'entrepreneur, ou par l'entremise de toute filiale ou compagnie affiliée ou autrement, travailler pour toute entreprise ayant des activités commerciales semblables ou en concurrence avec celles de MEDICOM, y être employé, y exercer [...] le tout dans les limites du territoire du Canada [...]." (Emphasis added)

To summarize the two above undertakings by each of the two Respondents, that of Mr. Bergeron is for a restriction to last two years, territorially it is worldwide, and is to prevent him from engaging in a similar commercial activity (activités commerciales semblables) or anything in competition with Medicom.

That of Mr. Hubert is for a period of three years; territorially, he is restricted to Canada, but with identical restrictions in respect of the activity, that is, any similar commercial activity or anything in competition with Medicom.

Such are the two restrictive covenants which are the basis for the application for the injunction and the request for an ordonnance de sauvegarde.

The Civil Code of Quebec, Article 2089 reads as follows [See Note 1 below]:

> "The 2089. The parties may stipulate in writing and in express terms that, even after the termination of the contract, the employee may neither compete with his employer nor participate in any capacity whatsoever in an enterprise which would then compete with him.
>
> Such a stipulation shall be limited, however, as to time, place and type of employment, to whatever is necessary for the protection of the legitimate interests of the employer.
>
> The burden of proof that the stipulation is valid is on the employer."

On a reading of the two clauses referred to above, the Court considers both to be substantially beyond what is necessary to protect the "legitimate interests of the employer".

The issue of determining whether or not the Petitioner has an appearance of right is to be placed in context such that one can determine whether the restrictive covenants themselves fall within the meaning of Art. 2089 of the Civil Code of Quebec, or whether there is other evidence, which together with the restrictive covenants give the trial judge sufficient information to determine whether there is an appearance of right.

In the case of Beau T Stop Distribution Inc. c. Mailhot, Mr. Justice Dalphond (then of the Superior Court now of the Court of Appeal) placed the issue squarely in the context of whether a restricted covenant effectively violated an apparent right to work. The restrictive covenants that are involved in this case, (P-3 and P-6), go beyond an attempt to prevent these ex-employees from competing with their employer, but as to Bergeron, it prevents him from being in a similar business anywhere in the world for a two year period, and for Hubert, for a three year period anywhere in Canada. In both cases, the issue in the restrictive covenants is not only one of non-competition or passing along confidential information, but the two clauses would actually prevent these former employees from working in their chosen field of work.

The last paragraph of Article 2089 of the Civil Code of Quebec puts the burden squarely on the shoulder of the employer to demonstrate that the stipulation is valid.

It cannot be a legitimate interest of this employer to prevent these two men from working in their field, in any capacity whatever, even if working in that field is not in competition with the business of the Petitioner.

The two clauses in question, which are the basis of the application, are, in my view, an affront to the Respondents rights to work.

There has been no demonstration to me in the documentation or in oral argument that the restrictions to which I have made reference are proportional to the essential and fundamental right of Bergeron and Hubert to earn a living.

FOR THESE REASONS, THE PETITION FOR AN ORDONNANCE DE SAUVEGARDE IS DISMISSED WITH COSTS.

ROGER E. BAKER, J.S.C.

LEGAL TERMS

In your reading, you came across the following terms. Be sure that you can explain each, to ensure your understanding of the material you have been reading. If you are uncertain as to the meaning of any term, review the material in the chapter for clarification. If necessary, consult a dictionary for further information or discuss the term(s) with your instructor.

individual contract of employment
fixed term
remuneration
call-in-pay
indeterminate term
collective agreement
prudence and diligence
employee
non-competition clause
reference year (vacations)
bilateral
subordinate
tacit renewal
restrictive covenant
statutory holidays
stipulate in writing
contractor
"diligently and in good faith"
unlimited duration
public order
confidential information

REVIEW QUESTIONS

1. Explain the meaning and importance of "subordination" in the contract of employment.

2. Discuss the differences between the contract of employment and the contract of enterprise.

3. Give an example of a contract of employment with an indeterminate term, and explain how this contract could be terminated by the employer when there is no longer any work for the employee to carry out.

4. Sunita is about to accept a job with an advertising firm. The company has asked its legal advisor to prepare a contract of employment containing a clause that will protect secret and confidential information. Prepare the clause that you believe will give the firm the protection it wants. If your clause is attacked in court as being abusive, explain why you are convinced that it is fair and valid.

5. What is "tacit renewal"? How does it relate to employment law?

6. The *Québec Labour Standards Act* establishes a number of "minimums." Select five and explain how they affect a contract of employment.

7. If an employer and employee agree in writing to conditions of employment which are below the standards in the *Act*, will this agreement be valid in law? Explain why or why not.

8. In the case described in section 7.2.2.5, explain why you would consider the non-competition clause to be valid or invalid and whether Alice should be held liable to pay the $10,000 penalty.

Chapter 8

PRINCIPLES OF CONTRACT LAW

OBJECTIVES

This chapter was prepared to enable you to achieve the following objectives:

1. To understand the nature of contracts used by businesses and individuals.
2. To explain the essential elements of a valid contract.
3. To identify the obligations that arise when parties enter into a contract.
4. To explain the basic requirements that an obligation must meet.
5. To distinguish between legal and natural obligations.
6. To analyze the legal offer and the legal acceptance which together are required for a bilateral contract to exist.
7. To understand the principles of legal capacity, especially with respect to minority, tutorship, curatorship, and protective supervision of persons of full age.
8. To understand when consent is valid and to recognize the defects of consent.

OBLIGATIONS
Section 8.1

In the discussion of forms of business ownership, we stated that the operation of a business involves the transacting of a series of acts of commerce by a merchant. If these transactions are to be respected and if the parties involved are to carry out what they agreed upon, we must be able to clearly define the conditions under which these agreements are valid and how they can be enforced. These are some of the questions we explore in this chapter. **Contracts** are what we call these business agreements that people enter into voluntarily.

Contracts create obligations. These obligations are the building blocks used to construct contracts.

For instance, the following simple example highlights the various obligations that can develop from a straight forward contract:

Billy agrees to buy Nancy's book for $10. Billy has the obligation to give Nancy the $10. Nancy has the obligation to give Billy the book.

When do these obligations come into existence? When does Billy have to pay the $10? When does Nancy have to deliver the book? What happens if Billy does not have the money to pay? What happens if Nancy's baby brother tears out many of the pages just before she is going to deliver it to Billy?

In order for an obligation to exist in law, there are three basic requirements:

1. There must be at least two parties who agree to do something for each other.
2. There must be a prestation that is the object of the obligation.
3. There must be a lawful reason for undertaking the obligation.

?...what is a prestation? It is all of these:

- a payment or performance
- the rendering of a service
- doing or not doing something

Obligations may come into existence in one of two ways. They commonly emerge from contracts, agreements that people enter into with each other. These agreements may be verbal or written. Some agreements must be in writing, according to the law, e.g., marriage contracts and hypothecs (mortgages).

They may also arise from an act carried out by someone, i.e., causing damage to a person's property or injuring someone accidentally or deliberately.

An important distinction has been drawn between "legal" and "natural" obligations. A "legal" obligation is one that is sanctioned by law and enforceable before the courts. Failure to discharge your obligation gives the person to whom you are obligated the right to demand performance and/or damages. Thus, if you agree to pay $150 per week for the rental of a truck and you do not make the payments as required, the rental company can obtain a judgment of the court against you.

A "natural" obligation is one that binds you in conscience only. Suppose for example, you owe $1,000 to a supplier of raw materials, and you do not pay the debt. If the supplier does not sue you after three years, this commercial debt is prescribed and your supplier no longer has the legal right to enforce this obligation through the courts. You still owe the $1,000, but it is now a natural rather than legal obligation. You will pay only if you feel morally bound to do so. Another example of a natural obligation is the promise to give $500 to a charitable organization every year.

CONTRACTS
Section 8.2

8.2.1 Definition

The most common source of legal obligations in business is the contract. A contract is an agreement between two or more persons which establishes legal obligations. These obligations arise out of the contract.

For example, if A sells B a car for $1,000, the obligations that arise from this transaction are:

1. A is obliged to hand the car over to B.
2. B is obliged to pay $1,000 to A.

The obligations are the consequences of the agreement or contract between two or more parties. In the above example, both A and B obligated themselves to fulfill certain acts.

A contract is a bilateral agreement since obligations operate in both directions and both parties agree to commit themselves to certain acts. Since the parties are bound by legal obligations, enforceable by the courts, a contract can be considered as creating the law between the parties with respect to the subject matter of the contract. As far as possible, the terms of the contract must be followed and applied. If the clauses of the agreement do not provide for the solution to a specific problem (e.g., where merchandise is to be delivered) then general provisions of the *Civil Code* are used to compensate the missing elements of the contract.

8.2.2 Classification of Contracts

The *Civil Code* identifies many different types of contracts, based on various criteria, and each producing different legal effects. Most often, contracts will have two or more parties negotiating their respective obligations on condition that each performs certain tasks. It is also quite common, however, that a contract may involve very little negotiation, with one party having to simply accept or reject the conditions, and in some cases one party obligating oneself to certain acts without any return from the other party. These include:

Contracts of adhesion (art. 1379) in which the conditions are drawn up by only one of the parties and the only choice available to the other party is to accept these conditions or not to enter into the contract (e.g., airline tickets and other transportation contracts).

Contracts by mutual agreement (art. 1379) in which both parties discuss and agree on all of the conditions of the contract.

Synallagmatic or bilateral contracts (art. 1380)) in which both parties have agreed to perform an obligation (e.g., "A" pays $10 to "B" and "B" gives "A" a book).

Unilateral contracts (art. 1380) in which only one party undertakes to perform an obligation (e.g., a will or a pledge to donate to charity).

Onerous contracts (art. 1381) in which each party receives something in return for undertaking an obligation to the other party (e.g., "A" receives a book and in return agrees to pay "B" $10).

Gratuitous contracts (art. 1381) in which one party undertakes an obligation that benefits the other party, but the other party does nothing for the first person (e.g., an agreement to donate money to a charity, or looking after a friend's child without being paid).

Commutative contracts (art. 1382) in which both parties know in detail how much each has to pay, and what each will receive in return (e.g., a food company buys 10,000 bushels of apples and agrees to pay $3 per bushel).

Aleatory contracts (art. 1382) in which the full extent of the obligations is uncertain at the time the contract is entered into and will only be established at a later date (e.g., a food company agrees in January to buy all of the apples the farmer will grow during the summer and pay $3 per bushel; the number of apples to be sold and the total number of dollars to be paid will be known only when the apples are harvested in August).

Contracts of instantaneous performance (art. 1383) in which there is a one-time discharge of the obligations undertaken (e.g., a bicycle is sold and delivered and the price of $175 is paid).

Contracts of successive performance (art. 1383) in which the obligation is to continue doing something on a regular basis for a specified period of time (e.g., an employment contract by which the employee goes to work every day and receives weekly pay for his or her services, or by which a contractor agrees to mow the company's front lawn once a week for a fee of $25).

Consumer contracts (art. 1384) in which a natural person (not a business) acquires, for personal use, some property or service from a business that offers such property or service to the public (such contracts are dealt with at length under the *Consumer Protection Act*).

A typical agreement may actually be a blend of several types of contracts. For instance, a one-time donation of money to a non-profit organization can be characterized as being a contract of adhesion, which is unilateral, gratuitous, commutative and of instantaneous performance.

8.2.3 Offer and Acceptance

Contracts are agreements that people enter into **voluntarily**. In order for this to occur, however, there must be a clear meeting of the minds of the people concerned (*consensus in idem*), whereby both parties clearly understand their obligations and willingly undertake to discharge them. This meeting of the minds takes place as a result of a negotiation. One party "offers" something and another party "accepts" it. If the parties agree on the same things at the same time, the contract comes into existence.

In business it is often important to identify a legitimate offer, for if an offer has clearly been made, then it requires only an acceptance to create a contract with the legal obligations that will arise from it. If, on the other hand, there is only an **invitation** to make an offer, the merchant may accept or refuse the offer.

An **offer** may be described as a clear, precise, firm proposition containing a genuine intention to enter into a binding contract. For example, is there an offer in a circular distributed door-to-door, in a newspaper ad, in a television commercial, or in a price tag of $189.95 attached to a lawn mower in a department store?

As a general rule, an offer will exist where there is specific merchandise offered for sale—e.g., the particular lawn mower with the price tag attached. Otherwise, a general newspaper ad is merely an invitation for members of the public to make an offer to the merchant. The general principle of law in Québec is that there is complete freedom of commerce and a merchant is free to deal with anyone. This principle is of course, qualified in that a merchant must have available for sale the advertised merchandise in reasonable quantities. Both federal and provincial laws govern misleading advertising and misrepresentation.

Once a specific offer is made, **acceptance** will create a contract. However the acceptance must be in the same terms as the offer. Any conditions added to the offer or any changes make it a counter-offer which itself is then subject to acceptance. An acceptance, therefore, can be described as an unqualified, unconditional assent which has been communicated to the person making the offer.

When and where does such communication take place? Art. 1387 of the *Civil Code* states that:

> *"A contract is formed when and where acceptance is received by the offeror..."*

Thus, if the two people are in the same room, talking to each other, the contract is "formed" where they are. If they are speaking on the telephone to each other, with the offeror in London and the offeree in Montréal, the contract is formed in London. If the offeree sends acceptance by fax to the offeror in Calgary, the contract is formed in Calgary.

> *The relevant articles of the Civil Code are in Appendix "8-A" at the end of this chapter.*

8.2.4 Conditions for the Formation of Contracts

Article 1385 of the *Civil Code* states that the essential elements required for the formation of a valid contract are:

1. an exchange,
2. of consents,
3. between persons,
4. having capacity to contract,
5. in any form, unless a special "form" is required,
6. a cause,
7. an object.

Each of these seven elements merits special consideration. This will enable us to evaluate a contract in order to determine whether it is valid under the terms of our *Civil Code*. Following is an explanation of each element.

8.2.4.1 Exchange – Art. 1386

The exchange of consents between the parties to a contract may be express or tacit. Consent is **express** when there is a clear indication on the part of a person, such as the statement "Yes, I am prepared to buy this printing machine for the total of $47,500."

The consent may also be **tacit** when nothing is said, but the person carries out some action to indicate acceptance, e.g., a person who walks into a barber shop, sits down in the barber's chair and, without objection, allows the barber to begin cutting his hair. Nothing has been said or written, yet it is clear the person is prepared to pay for having his hair cut. In this case there was a tacit exchange of consents.

8.2.4.2 Offer and Acceptance - Arts. 1387 to 1397

Except for specific cases for which the law provides otherwise, a contract comes into existence where and when the acceptance of the offer is received. This applies, as stated earlier, whether the parties are standing in front of each other at the time, or one party is in Québec City and the other party is in Paris, France.

If the party making an offer states that the offer will be open for a specific period of time, such as 30 days, the offer cannot be revoked (cancelled) before that time. If no time period is stated, the offer may be revoked at any time. If no acceptance is received before the time expires, the offer lapses (becomes null).

If the acceptance does not correspond to the terms of the offer, it is not really an acceptance at all. However, it may be considered as a new counter-offer. "A" offers to sell 1,000 boxes to "B" for $840. "B" says, "I'll buy them, but I'll only pay you $750." "B" has made a counter-offer, and it is now up to "A" to decide if this counter offer is acceptable or perhaps to make another counter-offer, such as offering to sell the boxes for $800.

It is important to note that silence cannot be interpreted as acceptance of an offer. If a person says nothing, the only appropriate conclusion is that the offer was refused.

A promise to enter into a contract is not the same as an acceptance. However, having promised to enter into the contract, the person cannot then change his or her mind and refuse to go through with the deal, once the promise is accepted. Such a refusal may lead to an action in damages by the person to whom the promise was made.

8.2.4.3 Consent - Qualities and Defects - Arts. 1398 to 1408

The consent to enter a contract must be given freely and willingly - "in a free and enlightened manner." There must be no undue or illegal pressure put on a person in order to obtain consent, as this will vitiate (nullify) the consent as well as the contract and all obligations contained in the contract.

The defects of consent, which render the consent invalid, are error, fraud, fear and lesion.

Error

This does not mean a simple or inexcusable error. Deciding that a recently purchased desk does not look good in the office and that its purchase was a mistake is not a legal reason to cancel the contract or refuse to pay for the desk. Another example is the purchase of art from a garage sale, which is thought to be a valuable piece, but turns out to be a fake. These are examples of a simple personal error and an inexcusable error respectively. They are not the type of errors to which the *Civil Code* refers.

When one person believes the contract is one of sale and the other honestly believes, in good faith, that it is a contract of lease, this is an error as to the nature of the contract. In this case the court may be persuaded to annul the contract.

Fraud

Fraud is closely related to error. The *Civil Code* describes this defect as an error induced by fraud. It occurs when one person tricks another into making an error or gives untrue information and, based on that information, the other person enters into a contract. A supplier tells a buyer the merchandise is made of genuine hardwood which turns out later to be imitation plastic wood, worth only half the price. A buyer in possession of the truth would not have entered into the contract at all or may have agreed to the purchase, but at a much lower price. Fraud can also occur when a seller fails to divulge relevant information.

Fear

If a person uses fear, in the form of violence or threats of violence, to extract someone's consent, such agreement is not legally valid and cannot produce any legal effects.

Fear can also be derived from the use of a position of authority over another person, such as creating a fear for one's job security. For instance, "A" threatens to fire "B" if "B" does not sell "A" a family heirloom. The contract, even if for fair market value, is not valid.

Lesion

This word comes from Roman law and the French expression meaning harm and is used in this context to refer to economic harm, such as taking financial advantage of a person who is presumed not to know better.

Lesion may be used only by persons who do not have full legal capacity, in which case it can be the basis for annulling the person's consent. If, for example, a storekeeper sells a 14-year-old a musical instrument worth $250 for $600, the law allows the contract to be annulled on the basis that the minor was not aware of the true value and was exploited (taken unfair advantage of). It may also be decided that rather than totally annulling the contract, the price should be reduced to its true level, in this case $250. Lesion may also be argued in the situation where a minor was not aware of all the financial implications of the transaction and as a consequence is unable to afford the item in question.

Lesion can apply to contracts entered into by minors and also to those entered into by persons under protective supervision.

8.2.4.4 Capacity to Contract (legal capacity)

In order for a contract to be valid, the parties must have the **legal capacity** (authority or right) to enter into contracts. A 12-year-old's physical ability to sign a contract does not mean that the 12-year-old has the legal right to enter the contract.

The law sets out specific rules as to who can and cannot legally enter into contracts.

In general, minors (persons under the age of 18) and persons under protective supervision (those who are unable, due to physical or mental illness or disability, to look after their own affairs) are declared to be legally incapable.

It is important that some provision be made to look after the legal rights of such persons.

Minors:

- if 14 years old, are considered to be of full age (over 18) for all purposes related to their employment or for operating a business.
- may validly enter into contracts to look after their ordinary and usual needs (e.g., clothing, books, food, etc.).
- may be assisted by a tutor (legal guardian) to enter certain contracts or engage in legal actions.
- can avoid responsibility for contractual undertakings for which they do not have legal capacity.
- are legally represented by their mother and father who are "of right" (automatically) tutors to the minor; if the parents cannot act as tutors, other adults may be appointed as tutors; the tutorship is supervised by a tutorship council made up of three people appointed by the members of the minor's family.
- under certain conditions a minor may be "emancipated." This means that the minor may be given legal capacity to enter contracts alone, either partially, as a result of a judicial decision, or completely, as a result of the minor's marriage.

Persons under protective supervision:

- have no legal capacity, with the result that they can no longer enter into legal contracts.
- are over the age of 18, and for reasons of physical or mental incapacity or disability, are unable to look after their own financial affairs.

8.2.4.5 Cause - Arts 1410 and 1411

A person who enters a contract has a reason for undertaking the obligations contained in the contract. It is not necessary for this reason to be expressed as part of the contract; however, if the reason is an illegal one, the contract will not be considered valid.

Thus, a person who purchases a printing machine to operate a printing business enters a valid contract. However, if the person buys the machine in order to make counterfeit money, the contract would not be enforced by a court.

8.2.4.6 Object - Arts 1412 and 1413

Every contract results in the carrying out of a juridical operation such as a sale, lease, or exchange. The only restriction the law places on the subject of a contract is the prohibition of contracts in which the object is something that is illegal or contrary to public order.

8.2.4.7 Form - Art. 1414

Most contracts do not require any particular wording or form to be used. For certain contracts, however a form specified by the law must be used to preserve the validity of the contract. This would apply to marriage contracts, hypothecs (mortgages), notarial wills, insurance policies, and collective labour agreements.

8.2.5 Nature of Nullity

Contracts entered into, which do not meet the conditions of formation discussed above, risk being declared null and to be deemed to have never existed (art. 1416). Two degrees of nullity exist; absolute nullity and relative nullity.

8.2.5.1 Absolute Nullity – Art. 1417 to 1418

A contract that contradicts or violates provisions of law deemed of public order does not meet the conditions of formation and is therefore absolutely null. In other words, a contract which puts at risk protections of the general public interest is considered absolutely null. Any interested party, be it those who have entered into the contract, a non-contracting party that can demonstrate interest, or even the court of its own motion, can invoke absolute nullity. Such nullity makes it impossible for any party to the contract to confirm it – a party cannot decide to maintain the contract regardless of the fact that it fails to meet the conditions of formation. For instance, contracting to sell body parts is contrary to public order and therefore absolute nullity can be invoked by either party or by the courts with no possibility of the contract being maintained.

8.2.5.2 Relative Nullity – Art. 1419 to 1421 and 1423

A contract that violates protections of private individual interests can be declared relatively null. Only the parties directly involved in the contract in question can invoke relative nullity. No other party may invoke this nullity, not even the court of its own motion. Unlike absolute nullity, parties who can invoke relative nullity may choose to confirm or maintain the contract regardless of the problem in the conditions of its formation. This is achieved by expressing their intent to keep the contract or by some tacit action that clearly indicates this desire. For instance, a person who donates property to another through fraud or threat can take legal action to have it declared relatively null. Because this involves the rights between these two private parties, it is also possible for the aggrieved donating party to confirm in part or in whole the contract.

8.2.5.3 Effect of Nullity – Art. 1422

A contract deemed null is considered to have never existed. The parties involved must be placed in the same state as they were before the contract was formed. Each party must return to the other party any prestation they received under the terms of the contract.

8.2.6 Interpretation of Contracts

In order to assist businesspeople and the courts to understand and interpret contracts, there are a number of articles (1425 to 1438) in the *Civil Code* that set out the principles of interpretation. Most of these are self-explanatory and will not surprise anyone, as they are rooted in fairness and good faith, key principles on which the *Civil Code* is constructed.

For example, these rules state:

- Even though words used in the contract can be interpreted in different ways, the courts should try to uncover the real intention or purpose of the parties when they originally entered the contract. (art. 1425)
- The historical nature of the relation between the parties and the circumstances must be examined when interpreting a contract. (art. 1426)
- Clauses in a contract must be interpreted in line with other clauses in the contract. (art. 1427)
- An existing clause should have an effect rather than no effect. Otherwise, why include it in the contract. (art. 1428)
- Words having multiple meaning used in a clause must be given a meaning that conforms to subject matter of the contract. (art. 1429)
- In cases of doubt over the meaning of contractual obligations, the court will favour the party that agreed to the obligations rather than the party that imposed them. Contracts are always interpreted in favour of a consumer or a party accepting the terms of a contract of adhesion. (art. 1432)
- Incidental (non-expressed) associated obligations must be recognized by the courts. (art. 1434)
- An external clause, cited in a contract, binds all parties except when it is a consumer contract or contract of adhesion in which the consumer or adhering party could not have known and was not informed of its existence. (art. 1435)
- An illegible or incomprehensible clause in a consumer or adhesion contract is null and has no effect, unless it was adequately explained. (art. 1436)
- An abusive clause, which is excessive or unreasonably detrimental to a consumer or adhering party is automatically null. (art. 1437)

- A clause that is nullified does not render the whole contract invalid if it is possible for the contract to exist without this clause. (art. 1438)

8.2.7 Performance of Contracts

Each contractual party binding itself to an obligation must fulfill his undertakings. Failure, without justification, gives the creditor under the *Civil Code* the right to:

1. Force performance through such means as an injunction or by having the obligation performed at the expense of the debtor (art. 1590, 1601, 1602);
2. Have the contract annulled by **resolution**, in which each party must restores to each other all prestations and the contract is deemed to have never existed, or cancelled by **resiliation,** in which the contract ceases to exist for the future with no restoration of prestations. But annulation or cancelation may not be possible if the default is of minor importance (art. 1590, 1604, 1606);
3. Reduce the scope of his share of related obligations (art.1590);
4. Refuse to perform his share of the obligations (art. 1591);
5. Hold on to debtor's property until he is paid for work related to the property (art.1592, 1593).

Injunctions
How do they function?

Injunction

- A creditor institutes an action seeking a court order instructing a debtor to cease doing, not do, or to perform a particular act. A permanent injunction is granted as part of the final trial judgment.

Interlocutory Injunction

- A temporary injunction may be granted for the duration of the proceedings until a trial judgment is rendered, if the plaintiff can demonstrate:
    i. Interest and seriousness of the issue;
    ii. It is necessary to avoid irreparable injury before a final judgment;
    iii. That on the balance of convenience he will suffer significantly more than the defendant.
- Possible only after an action has been instituted.

Provisional Injunction

- In case of urgency, the plaintiff can request that an injunction be issued before the defendant has received notice of an interlocutory hearing. This injunction can last no more than 10 days.

8.2.8 Default of Contracts

Prior to taking any action against the debtor, the *Civil Code* (art. 1594-1605) requires the debtor be placed in default:

1. By the contract itself, when the debtor fails to perform an obligation by a stipulated deadline;

2. By extrajudicial demand, by which the creditor sends the debtor a letter requesting performance within a certain period of time;

3. By operation of law, where the debtor fails to perform an obligation within a useful time, or failed to perform immediately in case of urgency, or where performance becomes impossible due to the debtor's fault.

If the creditor files a legal action against the debtor without placing him in default first, the debtor maintains the right to perform the obligation within a reasonable time.

8.2.9 Damages

8.2.9.1 Present Damages – Art. 1607 and 1611

Failure on the part of the debtor to fulfill his obligations may result in bodily, moral or material damages. These damages have to be directly attributed to the fault of the debtor and assessable in their present value. More specifically, in contractual matters the creditor may claim damages that were foreseen or foreseeable upon contracting.

8.2.9.2 Future Damages – Art. 1611 to 1615

It is also possible to seek future damages as long as they are certain to take place and are assessable. An example is an employee fired for unjustifiable reasons, who sues for breach of contract and requests present lost wages and future wages based on how long it will take him to find employment again. Another example is damages suffered by the owner of a trade secret. These include what was invested in the trade secret and what profit he will be deprived of in the future. Future bodily damages may also be requested on top of the evident harm suffered due to the debtor. The creditor may also make a motion to reserve the right to seek additional damages within a three year period should the present damages suffered worsen.

8.2.9.3 Punitive Damages – Art. 1621

Under certain circumstances, the failure to perform contractual obligations may even open the possibility to seek punitive damages as directed by law. Because punitive damages are meant to be used as a tool to teach the debtor a lesson and for preventative purposes, the amount awarded cannot surpass these purposes. For instance, an employer fires an employee for discriminatory reasons. This makes it possible for the creditor to seek punitive damages under the *Québec Charter of Human Rights and Freedoms*. If the creditor is awarded a too high amount that forces the employer into bankruptcy instead of paying, then the preventative nature of punitive damages would be lost. The possible loss of employment for the employees in this business would also undermine the preventative nature of punitive damages.

In calculating the amount of punitive damages, four factors must be taken into consideration: first, the gravity of the fault committed by the debtor; second, the patrimonial value of the debtor; third, the amount already awarded to the creditor for bodily, moral or material damages; and fourth, if the debtor is insured one must determine what level of damages will be covered by the insurance provider.

8.2.9.4 Penal Damages – Art. 1622 to 1623

A penal clause (penalty clause) is a contractual stipulation that is used as a means of motivating a contracting party to perform obligations. Failure to perform obligations allows the creditor to claim from the debtor the stipulated amount of damages for default. The creditor, as a general rule, may not exercise both the penal clause and require performance of the debtor's obligations.

However, it is possible for the creditor to avail himself of both the penal clause and require performance if the clause is for the purpose of punishing the debtor for time delays. For instance, the government contracts a construction company to complete a roadway within a certain time with a penal clause of $10 000 dollars a day. Should the company fail to meet the deadline, the amount paid to it will be reduced by the amount of days past the deadline.

Unlike the damages discussed in the previous sections, which require a creditor to demonstrate that the damages are directly associated to the fault of the debtor and that the creditor suffered an injury, the penal clause can be exercised without having to demonstrate that any actual damages were suffered. The simple fact of the debtor failing to meet contractual obligations that are attached to a penal clause is sufficient. In other words, the creditor need only prove the debtor violated the penal clause.

APPENDIX "8-A"
SELECTED ARTICLES *FROM*
The Civil Code of Québec

TITLE I
ENJOYMENT AND EXERCISE OF CIVIL RIGHTS

6. Every person is bound to exercise his civil rights in good faith.

7. No right may be exercised with the intent of injuring another or in an excessive and unreasonable manner which is contrary to the requirements of good faith.

TITLE I
OBLIGATIONS IN GENERAL

Chapter I
General Provisions

1371. It is of the essence of an obligation that there be persons between whom it exists, a prestation which forms its object, and, in the case of an obligation arising out of a juridical act, a cause which justifies its existence.

1372. An obligation arises from a contract or from any act or fact to which the effects of an obligation are attached by law.

1373. The object of an obligation is the prestation that the debtor is bound to render to the creditor and which consists in doing or not doing something.

The debtor is bound to render a prestation that is possible and determinate or determinable and that is neither forbidden by law nor contrary to public order.

1375. The parties shall conduct themselves in good faith both at the time the obligation is created and at the time it is performed or extinguished.

Chapter II
Contracts

Division II
Nature and Certain Classes of Contracts

1378. A contract is an agreement of wills by which one or several persons obligate themselves to one or several other persons to perform a prestation.

Contracts may be divided into contracts of adhesion and contracts by mutual agreement, synallagmatic and unilateral contracts, onerous and gratuitous contracts, commutative and aleatory contracts, and contracts of instantaneous performance or of successive performance; they may also be consumer contracts.

1379. A contract of adhesion is a contract in which the essential stipulations were imposed or drawn up by one of the parties, on his behalf or upon his instructions, and were not negotiable.

Any contract that is not a contract of adhesion is a contract by mutual agreement.

1380. A contract is synallagmatic, or bilateral, when the parties obligate themselves reciprocally, each to the other, so that the obligation of one party is correlative to the obligation of the other.

When one party obligates himself to the other without any obligation on the part of the latter, the contract is unilateral.

1381. A contract is onerous when each party obtains an advantage in return for his obligation.

When one party obligates himself to the other for the benefit of the latter without obtaining any advantage in return, the contract is gratuitous.

1382. A contract is commutative when, at the time it is formed, the extent of the obligations of the parties and of the advantages obtained by them in return is certain and determinate.

When the extent of the obligations or of the advantages is uncertain, the contract is aleatory.

1383. Where the circumstances do not preclude the performance of the obligations of the parties at one single time, the contract is a contract of instantaneous performance.

Where the circumstances absolutely require that the obligations be performed at several different times or without interruption, the contract is a contract of successive performance.

1384. A consumer contract is a contract whose field of application is delimited by legislation respecting consumer protection whereby one of the parties, being a natural person, the consumer, acquires, leases, borrows or obtains in any other manner, for personal, family or domestic purposes, property or services from the other party, who offers such property and services as part of an enterprise which he carries on.

Division III
Formation of Contracts

1385. A contract is formed by the sole exchange of consents between persons having capacity to contract, unless, in addition, the law requires a particular form to be respected as a necessary condition of its formation, or unless the parties require the contract to take the form of a solemn agreement.

It is also of the essence of a contract that it have a cause and an object.

Consent

1386. The exchange of consents is accomplished by the express or tacit manifestation of the will of a person to accept an offer to contract made to him by another person.

1387. A contract is formed when and where acceptance is received by the offeror, regardless of the method of communication used, and even though the parties have agreed to reserve agreement as to secondary terms.

Offer and Acceptance

1388. An offer to contract is a proposal which contains all the essential elements of the proposed contract and in which the offeror signifies his willingness to be bound if it is accepted.

1389. An offer to contract derives from the person who initiates the contract or the person who determines its content or even, in certain cases, the person who presents the last essential element of the proposed contract.

1390. An offer to contract may be made to a determinate or an indeterminate person, and a term for acceptance may or may not be attached to it.

Where a term is attached, the offer may not be revoked before the term expires; if none is attached, the offer may be revoked at any time before acceptance is received by the offeror.

1391. Where the offeree receives a revocation before the offer, the offer lapses, even though a term is attached to it.

1392. An offer lapses if no acceptance is received by the offeror before the expiry of the specified term or, where no term is specified, before the expiry of a reasonable time; it also lapses in respect of the offeree if he has rejected it.

The death or bankruptcy of the offeror or the offeree, whether or not a term is attached to the offer, or the institution of protective supervision in respect of either of them also causes the offer to lapse, if that event occurs before acceptance is received by the offeror.

1393. Acceptance which does not correspond substantially to the offer or which is received by the offeror after the offer has lapsed does not constitute acceptance

It may, however, constitute a new offer.

1394. Silence does not imply acceptance of an offer, subject only to the will of the parties, the law or special circumstances, such as usage or a prior business relationship.

1395. The offer of a reward made to anyone who performs a particular act is deemed to be accepted and is binding on the offeror when the act is performed, even if the person who performs the act does not know of the offer, unless, in cases which admit of it, the offer was previously revoked expressly and adequately by the offeror.

1396. An offer to contract made to a determinate person constitutes a promise to enter into the proposed contract from the moment that the offeree clearly indicates to the offeror that he intends to consider the offer and reply to it within a reasonable time or within the time stated therein.

A mere promise is not equivalent to the proposed contract; however, where the beneficiary of the promise accepts the promise or takes up his option, both he and the promisor are bound to enter into the contract, unless the beneficiary decides to enter into the contract immediately.

1397. A contract made in violation of a

promise to contract may be set up against the beneficiary of the promise, but without affecting his remedy for damages against the promisor and the person having contracted in bad faith with the promisor.

The same rule applies to a contract made in violation of a first refusal agreement.

Qualities and Defects of Consent

1398. Consent may be given only by a person who, at the time of manifesting such consent, either expressly or tacitly, is capable of binding himself.

1399. Consent may be given only in a free and enlightened manner.

It may be vitiated by error, fear or lesion.

1400. Error vitiates consent of the parties or of one of them where it relates to the nature of the contract, the object of the prestation or anything that was essential in determining that consent.

An inexcusable error does not constitute a defect of consent.

1401. Error on the part of one party induced by fraud committed by the other party or with his knowledge vitiates consent whenever, but for that error, the party would not have contracted, or would have contracted on different terms. Fraud may result from silence or concealment.

1402. Fear of serious injury to the person or property of one of the parties vitiates consent given by that party where the fear is induced by violence or threats exerted or made by or known to the other party.

Apprehended injury may also relate to another person or his property and is appraised according to the circumstances.

1403. Fear induced by the abusive exercise of a right or power or by the threat of such exercise vitiates consent.

1404. Consent to a contract the object of which is to deliver the person making it from fear of serious injury is not vitiated where the other contracting party, although aware of the state of necessity, is acting in good faith.

1405. Except in the cases expressly provided by law, lesion vitiates consent only in respect of minors and persons of full age under protective supervision.

1406. Lesion results from the exploitation of one of the parties by the other, which creates a serious disproportion between the prestations of the parties; the fact that there is a serious disproportion creates a presumption of exploitation.

In cases involving a minor or a protected person of full age, lesion may also result from an obligation that is considered to be excessive in view of the patrimonial situation of the person, the advantages he gains from the contract and the general circumstances.

1407. A person whose consent is vitiated has the right to apply for annulment of the contract; in the case of error occasioned by fraud, of fear or of lesion, he may, in addition to annulment, also claim damages or, where he prefers that the contract be maintained, apply for a reduction of his obligation equivalent to the damages he would be justified in claiming.

1408. In the case of a demand for the annulment of a contract on the ground of lesion, the court may maintain the contract where the defendant offers a reduction of his claim or an equitable pecuniary supplement.

Capacity to Contract

1409. The rules relating to the capacity to contract are laid down principally in the Book on Persons.

Cause of Contracts

1410. The cause of a contract is the reason that determines each of the parties to enter into the contract.

The cause need not be expressed.

1411. A contract whose cause is prohibited by law or contrary to public order is null.

Object of Contracts

1412. The object of a contract is the juridical operation envisaged by the parties at the time of its formation, as it emerges from all the rights and obligations created by the contract.

1413. A contract whose object is prohibited by law or contrary to public order is null.

Form of Contracts

1414. Where a particular or solemn form is required as a necessary condition of formation of a contract, it shall be observed; it shall also be observed for modifications to the contract, unless they are only accessory stipulations.

1415. A promise to enter into a contract is not subject to the form required for the contract.

Nature of Nullity

1416. Any contract which does not meet the necessary conditions of its formation may be annulled.

1417. A contract is absolutely null where the condition of formation sanctioned by its nullity is necessary for the protection of the general interest.

1418. The absolute nullity of a contract may be invoked by any person having a present and actual interest in doing so; it is invoked by the court of its own motion.

A contract that is absolutely null may not be confirmed.

1419. A contract is relatively null where the condition of formation sanctioned by its nullity is necessary for the protection of an individual interest, such as where the consent of the parties or of one of them is vitiated.

1420. The relative nullity of a contract may be invoked only by the person in whose interest it is established or by the other contracting party, provided he is acting in good faith and sustains serious injury therefrom; it may not be invoked by the court of its own motion.

A contract that is relatively null may be confirmed.

1421. Unless the nature of the nullity is clearly indicated in the law, a contract which does not meet the necessary conditions of its formation is presumed to be relatively null.

1422. A contract that is null is deemed never to have existed.

In such a case, each party is bound to restore to the other the prestations he has received.

1423. The confirmation of a contract results from the express or tacit will to renounce the invocation of its nullity.

It results only if the will to confirm is certain and evident.

1424. Where the nullity of a contract may be invoked by each of the parties or by several of them against a common opposite party to the contract, confirmation by one of them does not prevent the others from invoking nullity.

Division IV
Interpretation of Contracts

1425. The common intention of the parties rather than adherence to the literal meaning of the words shall be sought in interpreting a contract.

1426. In interpreting a contract, the nature of the contract, the circumstances in which it was formed, the interpretation which has already been given to it by the parties or which it may have received, and usage, are all taken into account.

1427. Each clause of a contract is interpreted in light of the others so that each is given the meaning derived from the contract as a whole.

1428. A clause is given a meaning that gives it some effect rather than one that gives it no effect.

1429. Words susceptible of two meanings shall be given the meaning that best conforms to the subject matter of the contract.

1430. A clause intended to eliminate doubt as to the application of the contract to a specific situation does not restrict the scope of a contract otherwise expressed in general terms.

1431. The clauses of a contract cover only what it appears that the parties intended to include, however general the terms used.

1432. In case of doubt, a contract is interpreted in favour of the person who contracted the obligation and against the person who stipulated it. In all cases, it is interpreted in favour of the adhering party or the consumer.

Division V
Effects of Contracts

1433. A contract creates obligations and, in certain cases, modifies or extinguishes them.

In some cases, it also has the effect of constituting, transferring, modifying or extinguishing real rights.

1434. A contract validly formed binds the parties who have entered into it not only as to what they have expressed in it but also as to what is incident to it according to its nature and in conformity with usage, equity or law.

1435. An external clause referred to in a contract is binding on the parties.

In a consumer contract or a contract of adhesion, however, an external clause is null if, at the time of formation of the contract, it was not expressly brought to the attention of the consumer or adhering party, unless the other party proves that the consumer or adhering party otherwise knew of it.

1436. In a consumer contract or a contract of adhesion, a clause which is illegible or incomprehensible to a reasonable person is null if the consumer or the adhering party suffers injury therefrom, unless the other party proves that an adequate explanation of the nature and scope of the clause was given to the consumer or adhering party.

1437. An abusive clause in a consumer contract or contract of adhesion is null, or the obligation arising from it may be reduced.

An abusive clause is a clause which is excessively and unreasonably detrimental to the consumer or the adhering party and is therefore not in good faith; in particular, a clause which so departs from the fundamental obligations arising from the rules normally governing the contract that it changes the nature of the contract is an abusive clause.

1438. A clause which is null does not render the contract invalid in other respects, unless it is apparent that the contract may be considered only as an indivisible whole.

The same applies to a clause without effect or deemed unwritten.

1439. A contract may not be resolved, resiliated, modified or revoked except on grounds recognized by law or by agreement of the parties.

1458. Every person has a duty to honour his contractual undertakings.

Where he fails in this duty, he is liable for any bodily, moral or material injury he causes to the other contracting party and is liable to reparation for the injury; neither he nor the other party may in such a case avoid the rules governing contractual liability by opting for rules that would be more favourable to them.

Chapter VI
Contracts

Division II
Right to Enforce Performance

1590. An obligation confers on the creditor the right to demand that the obligation be performed in full, properly and without delay.

Where the debtor fails to perform his obligation without justification on his part and he is in default, the creditor may, without prejudice to his right to the performance of the obligation in whole or in part by equivalence,

(1) force specific performance of the obligation;

(2) obtain, in the case of a contractual obligation, the resolution or resiliation of the contract or the reduction of his own correlative obligation;

(3) take any other measure provided by law to enforce his right to the performance of the obligation.

1591. Where the obligations arising from a synallagmatic contract are exigible and one of the parties fails to perform his obligation to a substantial degree or does not offer to perform it, the other party may refuse to perform his correlative obligation to a corresponding degree, unless he is bound by law, the will of the parties or usage to perform first.

1592. A party who, with the consent of the other party, has detention of property belonging to the latter has a right to retain it pending full payment of his claim against him, if the claim is exigible and is directly related to the property of which he has detention.

1593. The right of retention may be set up against anyone.

Involuntary dispossession does not extinguish a right of retention; the party exercising the right may revendicate the property, subject to the rules on prescription.

Default

1594. A debtor may be in default by the terms of the contract itself, when it contains a stipulation that the mere lapse of time for performing it will have that effect.

A debtor may also be put in default by an extrajudicial demand addressed to him by his creditor to perform the obligation, a judicial demand filed against him or the sole operation of law.

1595. The extrajudicial demand by which a creditor puts his debtor in default shall be made in writing.

If the demand does not allow the debtor sufficient time for performance, having regard to the nature of the obligation and the circumstances, the debtor may perform the obligation within a reasonable time after the demand.

1596. Where a creditor files a judicial demand against the debtor without his otherwise being in default, the debtor is entitled to perform the obligation within a reasonable time after the demand. If the obligation is performed within a reasonable time, the costs of the demand are borne by the creditor.

1597. A debtor is in default by the sole operation of law where the performance of the obligation would have been useful only within a certain time which he allowed to expire or where he failed to perform the obligation immediately despite the urgency that he do so.

A debtor is also in default by operation of law where he has violated an obligation not to do, or where specific performance of the obligation has become impossible through his fault, and also where he has made clear to the creditor his intention not to perform the obligation or where, in the case of an obligation of successive performance, he has repeatedly refused or neglected to perform it.

1598. The creditor shall prove the occurrence of one of the cases of default by operation of law notwithstanding any statement or stipulation to the contrary.

1599. An extrajudicial demand by which the creditor puts one of the solidary debtors in default has effect with respect to the other debtors.

Similarly, an extrajudicial demand made by one of the solidary creditors has effect with respect to the other creditors.

1600. Where the object of the performance is a sum of money, the debtor, although he may be granted a period of grace, is liable for injury resulting from delay in the performance of the obligation from the moment he begins to be in default.

The debtor in such a case is also liable from the same moment for any loss resulting from superior force, unless he is released thereby from his obligation.

Specific Performance

1601. A creditor may, in cases which admit of it, demand that the debtor be forced to make specific performance of the obligation.

1602. In case of default, the creditor may perform the obligation or cause it to be performed at the expense of the debtor.

A creditor wishing to avail himself of this right shall so notify the debtor in the judicial or extrajudicial demand by which he puts him in default, except in cases where the debtor is in default by operation of law or by the terms of the contract itself.

1603. The creditor may be authorized to destroy or remove, at the expense of the debtor, what has been made by the debtor in violation of an obligation not to do.

Resolution or Resiliation of Contracts and Reduction of Obligations

1604. Where the creditor does not avail himself of the right to force the specific performance of the contractual obligation of the debtor in cases which admit of it, he is entitled either to the resolution of the contract, or to its resiliation in the case of a contract of successive performance.

However and notwithstanding any stipulation to the contrary, he is not entitled to resolution or resiliation of the contract if the default of the debtor is of minor importance, unless, in the case of an obligation of successive performance, the default occurs repeatedly, but he is then entitled to a proportional reduction of his correlative obligation.

All the relevant circumstances are taken into consideration in assessing the proportional reduction of the correlative obligation. If the obligation cannot be reduced, the creditor is entitled to damages only.

1605. A contract may be resolved or resiliated without judicial proceedings where the debtor is in default by operation of law or where he has failed to perform his obligation within the time allowed in the writing putting him in default.

1606. A contract which is resolved is deemed never to have existed; each party is, in such a case, bound to restore to the other the prestations he has already received.

A contract which is resiliated ceases to exist, but only for the future.

Performance by Equivalence

1607. The creditor is entitled to damages for bodily, moral or material injury which is an immediate and direct consequence of the debtor's default.

1608. The obligation of the debtor to pay damages to the creditor is neither reduced nor altered by the fact that the creditor receives a prestation from a third person, as a result of the injury he has sustained, except so far as the third person is subrogated to the rights of the creditor.

1609. An acquittance, transaction or statement obtained from the creditor in connection with bodily or moral injury he has sustained, obtained by the debtor, an insurer or their representatives within 30 days of the act which caused the injury, is without effect if it is damaging to the creditor.

1610. The right of a creditor to damages, including punitive damages, may be assigned or transmitted.

This rule does not apply where the right of the creditor results from a breach of a personality right; in such a case, the right of the creditor to damages may not be assigned, and may be transmitted only to his heirs.

Assessment of Damages

1611. The damages due to the creditor compensate for the amount of the loss he has sustained and the profit of which he has been deprived.

Future injury which is certain and able to be assessed is taken into account in awarding damages.

1612. The loss sustained by the owner of a trade secret includes the investment expenses incurred for its acquisition, perfection and use; the profit of which he is deprived may be compensated for through payment of royalties.

1613. In contractual matters, the debtor is liable only for damages that were foreseen or foreseeable at the time the obligation was contracted, where the failure to perform the obligation does not proceed from intentional or gross fault on his part; even then, the damages include only what is an immediate and direct consequence of the nonperformance.

1614. Damages owed to the creditor for bodily injury he sustains are measured as to the future aspects of the injury according to the discount rates set by regulation of the Government, from the time such rates are set.

1615. The court, in awarding damages for bodily injury, may, for a period of not over three years, reserve the right of the creditor to apply for additional damages, if the course of his physical condition cannot be determined with sufficient precision at the time of the judgment.

1616. Damages awarded for injury are exigible in the form of capital payable in cash, unless otherwise agreed by the parties.

Where the injury sustained is bodily injury and where the creditor is a minor, however, the court may order payment, in whole or in part, in the form of an annuity or by periodic instalments, on the terms and conditions it fixes and indexed according to a fixed rate. Within three months of the date on which the minor becomes of full age, the creditor may demand immediate and discounted payment of any amount still receivable.

1617. Damages which result from delay in the performance of an obligation to pay a sum of money consist of interest at the agreed rate or, in the absence of any agreement, at the legal rate.

The creditor is entitled to the damages from the date of default without having to prove that he has sustained any injury.

A creditor may stipulate, however, that he will be entitled to additional damages, provided he justifies them.

1618. Damages other than those resulting from delay in the performance of an obligation to pay a sum of money bear interest at the rate agreed by the parties, or, in the absence of agreement, at the legal rate, from the date of default or from any other later date which the court considers appropriate, having regard to the nature of the injury and the circumstances.

1619. An indemnity may be added to the amount of damages awarded for any reason, which is fixed by applying to the amount of the damages, from either of the dates used in computing the interest on them, a percentage equal to the excess of the rate of interest fixed for claims of the State under section 28 of the Tax Administration Act (chapter A-6.002) over the rate of interest agreed by the parties or, in the absence of agreement, over the legal rate.

1620. Interest accrued on principal does not itself bear interest except where that is provided by agreement or by law or where additional interest is expressly demanded in a suit.

1621. Where the awarding of punitive damages is provided for by law, the amount of such damages may not exceed what is sufficient to fulfil their preventive purpose.

Punitive damages are assessed in the light of all the appropriate circumstances, in particular the gravity of the debtor's fault, his patrimonial situation, the extent of the reparation for which he is already liable to the creditor and, where such is the case, the fact that the payment of the damages is wholly or partly assumed by a third person.

1622. A penal clause is one by which the parties assess the anticipated damages by stipulating that the debtor will suffer a penalty if he fails to perform his obligation.

A creditor has the right to avail himself of a penal clause instead of enforcing, in cases which admit of it, the specific performance of the obligation; but in no case may he exact both the performance and the penalty, unless the penalty has been stipulated for mere delay in the performance of the obligation.

1623. A creditor who avails himself of a penal clause is entitled to the amount of the stipulated penalty without having to prove the injury he has suffered.

However, the amount of the stipulated penalty may be reduced if the creditor has benefited from partial performance of the obligation or if the clause is abusive.

CASE 8.1

Giroux v. Malik

[2000] Q.J. No. 5185, **Quebec Superior Court**

(Excerpts of Judgment)

REASONS FOR JUDGMENT

ANNE-MARIE TRAHAN J.:— What is the scope of the obligation of prudence and diligence of the purchasers of a piece of land? To what extent do they have to protect themselves from the fraud (dol) of the vendor?

I. THE ACTION

On 29 December 1999, Plaintiffs (Ms. Giroux and Mr. Fafard) buy from the Defendant (Mr. Malik) a piece of land, on Lac-de-Mai street, in Laval (the Property), from Defendant (Mr. Malik).

In January 2000, when he goes to City Hall to obtain a building permit, Mr. Fafard discovers that none will be issued: although the zoning is residential, the nature of the soil does not allow the presence of a septic tank nor does it allow the building of a dwelling.

Ms. Giroux and Mr. Fafard claim that Mr. Malik was aware of this situation since 1988 and that, by not revealing it, he has committed a fraud (dol) for which he is responsible. They are therefore claiming the refund of the sale price of $45,000 and $10,000 as damages. In his amended plea, Mr. Malik claims he told everything to his agent Mr. Yaakoubian who should have notified the Plaintiffs.

Mr. Malik testifies he advised the real estate agents and the Plaintiffs that the property was land-filled and that if they had been prudent and diligent, the Plaintiffs would have found out from the City, before signing the deed of sale, that it could not be built upon.

II. THE EVIDENCE

On 13 July 1988, Mr. Malik purchases the Property (D-1) on which he wants to build a house for his family. In order to obtain a building permit from the City, he has a rapport d'implantation prepared; he pays $1,050 for a permit and an "entrée de service" for the water supply (P-10). He also retains the services of Laboratoire de Construction 2000 inc. to do an expertise on the property in order to determine whether a septic tank can be installed. The report (P-4) dated 19 September 1988 is addressed to him and states that

> "... L'expertise réalisée sur le terrain, indique que le site se trouve dans une ancienne tourbière ou marécage. Par définition, ces dépôts sont typiques d'un mauvais drainage, ce qui a été confirmé par notre essai de percolation.

> Conséquemment, on conclut que ce terrain n'offre pas les caractéristiques de drainage requises pour l'aménagement d'une installation septique en règle avec les critères du Ministère de l'Environnement. Nous laissons aux soins de la Ville de Laval de trouver une solution alternative, si possible."

It further adds:

> "D'autre part, la nature des sols reconnus dans les sondages (remblai, terre noire et marne), nous mènent à recommander une étude par forage sur ce terrain, afin de préciser les conditions de sols plus en profondeur, car les sols reconnus à la profondeur explorée sont compressibles et ils offrent aucune portance utile pour la maison. De ce fait, on peut s'attendre que la construction des fondations sur ce terrain sera beaucoup plus dispendieuse que la moyenne ..."

In 1992 and 1995, Mr. Malik tries to sell the Property. In both cases, he notifies the real estate agent of the problem beforehand. In 1992, he receives a conditional offer from a contractor who decides not to go ahead when he realizes the nature of the problem. In 1995, the real estate agent inquires at City Hall and advises Mr. Malik that the City would allow an Eco, Flow System.

On 28 June 1999, Mr. Malik puts the Property up for sale a third time. He enters into a "contrat de courtage exclusif" (P-7) with La Capitale represented by Réjeanne Séguin and Georges Kévork Yaakoubian. The contract is in French. Subparagraphs 1. and 4. of Clause 8.2 read as follows:

> "8.2 - Le vendeur déclare de plus, à moins de stipulations contraires ci-après: (Compte tenu de l'importance que revêtent les déclarations qui suivent, le vendeur devrait s'assurer que chacun des paragraphes ci-après reflète le mieux possible la situation telle qu'il la connaît et y apporter au besoin toute modification ou addition pouvant être requises pour atteindre ce résultat.)
>
> > - n'avoir connaissance d'aucun facteur se rapportant à l'immeuble susceptible, de façon significative, d'en diminuer la valeur ou les revenus ou d'en augmenter les dépenses, sauf :
> >
> > - que la municipalité concernée fournit à l'immeuble les services d'aqueduc et d'égout - sauf l'égout.

At first, Mr. Malik states that he does not understand what P-7 says because it is in French. Nevertheless, when cross-examined as to why the words "sauf l'égout" have been written in by hand at subparagraph 4, after having answered, at first, that he did not know why, he finally recognizes that he told Mr. Yaakoubian that there was no sewer service and that the City's permission was required before installing a septic tank.

Mr. Malik's testimony as to what he told Mr. Yaakoubian is not as clear as his statement at paragraphs 20 and 21 of the Amended Plea which read as follows:

> "20. - At the time the broker's mandate was granted to Mr. Yaakoubian, the Defendant, Muhammed Hafeez Malik, informed him of the events

which occurred in 1988 with regards to the soil report and the refusal of the City of Laval to issue a construction permit and a permit to install a septic tank;

21. - Although obliged to do so, Mr. Yaakoubian failed to provide this information to the Plaintiffs;"

However, Mr. Malik says "I know the City refused to me in 1988. I did not know if it was the same in 1999" because, since 1988, he has not inquired about the situation at City Hall.

On 11 September 1999, Ms. Giroux and Mr. Fafard drive by the Property. They are considering building a new house for their family and it looks attractive to them. They call the real estate agent whose name appears on the billboard, Réjeanne Séguin, and find out the zoning is residential. Mr. Fafard checks with the City by phone and an employee, Mr. Michel Beaudoin, confirms to him that the zoning is residential.

Mr. Fafard calls upon a friend of his who is a real estate agent, Mr. Pierre Normand Paquet, to help him prepare a "Promesse d'achat" (P-2). The Plaintiffs sign it on 18 October 1999 and give the Defendant till 10:00 P.M. on 20 october 1999 to accept it.

On 20 october 1999, MM. Paquet and Yaakoubian go to Mr. Malik's residence. His son Havez is present. He accepts the offer without adding anything at clause 6 [it is similar to clause 8 of the contrat de courtage exclusif (P-7)]. The son confirms that his father asked both agents if the purchasers knew the Property had been land-filled.

Mr. Havez Malik confirms what his father stated earlier: Mr. Yaakoubian asked him if he had any documents. His father showed him the file he had with him out of which Mr. Yaakoubian took what he wanted. Mr. Malik testifies these are the only documents he gave Mr. Yaakoubian.

Ms. Giroux requests that "Dessins Drummond" prepare plans for their new house. Their fees, which amount to $1,363.06, have been paid in full (P-5).
The deed of sale was to be signed on 30 November 1999. Because November and December are busy months for Mr. Fafard who works in a garage, it is signed on 29 December 1999 (P-1).

Notary Jean-Yves Lebeau testifies he prepared the deed at Plaintiffs' request after having done a title search going back thirty years plus another deed. He says he recalls having seen the following mention:

> "Le terrain ci-dessus désigné a fait l'objet de remplissage au cours de la dernière année."

in the deed of purchase of Mr. Malik's author dated 8 December 1987 (D-2). He adds he did not draw Plaintiffs' attention to this mention since this is a situation which is found from time to time.

The signature of the Deed of Sale (P-1) on 29 December 1999 is attended by the parties and by their respective agents Mr. Paquet and Mr. Yaakoubian. While in the waiting room, Mr. Fafard asks Mr. Yaakoubian why Mr. Malik never built on the property. Mr. Yaakoubian answers Mr. Malik wanted to build a "palace" for his family but that his children were leaving one by one and that he didn't want to go ahead with his project.

Notary Lebeau proceeds as usual: he asks the parties to give some evidence of their identity, he reads the deed, he proceeds to the adjustments and to the exchange of the cheques. When reading the deed, at clause 5 of the "Déclarations du vendeur" which reads as follows :

> "Au meilleur de sa connaissance, l'immeuble ainsi que son utilisation et exploitation antérieures et actuelles respectent, et ont respecté à tout moment, en tout point, toutes les lois, les règlements, les décrets, les conventions et les politiques applicables en matière d'environnement et le vendeur n'a reçu aucun avis d'une autorité compétente, municipale, provinciale ou fédérale, à l'effet que l'immeuble n'est pas conforme aux règlements et lois en vigueur."

he asks Mr. Malik, in French, if there is any problem with the property. The answer is no. Ms. Giroux, whose English is better, wants to make sure Mr. Malik understands what is asked of him and puts the following question to him: "You're sure there is no problem with your land?". The answer is, once again, no.

Mr. Malik recalls having been asked such a question. He says he replied "look, what do you mean? This is a fill up land". He states the others laughed and joked and said "Do you hide gold or chemicals on your land?" to which he says he replied "no".

Once the Deed of Sale (P-1) is signed, Notary Lebeau hands over to the Plaintiffs a series of documents [the ones which were given by Mr. Malik to Mr. Yaakoubian on 20 October 1999 (P-10)]. When Mr. Fafard sees the "Plan d'implantation", it confirms in his mind what Mr. Yaakoubian had told him in the waiting room about Mr. Malik's intention.

The notary's fees amount to $567.22 and have been paid in full (P-5).

On 10 January 2000, Mr. Fafard goes to City Hall to obtain a building permit. He is told he must first go to the Environment Department of the City. There he meets Mr. Michel Lortie. Mr. Lortie tells him that the City requires a percolation test which takes about a week. Mr. Lortie then goes through the City's files and finds the 1988 expertise (P-4). On 13 January 2000, Mr. Lortie advises Mr. Fafard of the existence of the report and of its general contents. Mr. Fafard is taken a back: their house is sold; they have to vacate it by 27 May 2000. After having discussed the matter with Ms. Giroux, he files an access to information request with the City (P-8) in order to obtain a copy of the 1988 expertise. On 24 January 2000, the City writes Mr. Fafard reiterating that, pursuant to the 1988 expertise, the City cannot allow a septic installation to be built on the Property.

Mr. Michel Dupuis is President of Laboratoire de Construction 2000 inc. which he founded in 1987. He testifies as an expert and explains that two relatively large holes were dug on the property (about 10-12 feet long and 3 feet wide); usually, only one is dug. The technician observed what he saw, amongst others that water was found at 1,7m in hole 1 and at 2,1 m in hole 2. Mr. Dupuis explains that he does a lot of work in the Laval area. He has "soil maps" (cartes de sol) in his office which show a certain uniformity in the level of the black earth. Based on that information and on the results of the excavation, he is of the opinion that no septic system can be installed anywhere on the Property. In 1988, the Eco Flow System did not exist. Even now, it could not be installed since it requires two feet of natural soil below it "pour dissiper les eaux de rejet".

Mr. Dupuis testifies that it is not unusual that landfill is added to a property and that no specific conclusion should be drawn from such a fact.

Mr. Dupuis says that the only solution would be to connect the property to the City sewer and to build a dwelling on piles, which would greatly increase the construction costs.

Mr. Dupuis' hourly rate is $90. He was present in Court for close to four hours.
The Plaintiffs have paid, up to date, $5,597.16 in legal fees (P-5) and were given an estimate of $2,000 for the trial, for a total of $7,597.16.

Furthermore, their project of building the house of their dreams has evaporated. They had to find another house. They ended up finding one about 10 minutes from where they used to live: a small bungalow whereas they would have built a nice cottage. They also had to take steps so that their children could attend school. This was complicated by the fact that there was no more place in the neighbourhood school. Today, they are still bitter about their experience and their life savings ($45,000$) are immobilized in a worthless property.

III. ANALYSIS OF THE EVIDENCE AND FINDINGS OF THE COURT

A) THE REIMBURSEMENT OF THE SALE PRICE

The Plaintiffs have the burden of proving their case according to the preponderance of the evidence.
In the present case, the evidence is clear that Mr. Malik knew about the condition of the Property. He admitted it himself both in his amended plea and in his testimony.

The Court is also satisfied that the evidence reveals that, contrary to what he states in his amended plea, Mr. Malik did not reveal to his real estate agent the existence of the report (P-4). The two previous unsuccessful attempts to sell the property very likely deterred him from doing so. No questions were asked to Mr. Yaakoubian about this. However, Mr. Malik's testimony and the fact that reference was made only to the absence of sewer in the contrat de courtage exclusif (P-7) lead the Court to believe, in the absence of more precise evidence, that if Mr. Yaakoubian had known, he would have made mention of it in P-7. In the absence of evidence to the contrary, his good faith must be presumed.

With the few questions asked to Mr. Yaakoubian, the Court cannot assess fully his credibility on certain aspects of the evidence. For instance, how should the Court interpret the answer given by Mr. Yaakoubian to Mr. Fafard in the Notary's waiting room concerning the reason why Mr. Malik had never built on the Property. For the purposes of the present case, it is irrelevant since Article 2160 C.C.Q. provides that:

> 2160 - A mandator is liable to third persons for the acts performed by the mandatary in the performance and within the limits of his mandate unless, under the agreement or by virtue of usage, the mandatary alone is liable. The mandator is also liable for any acts which exceed the limits of the mandate, if he has ratified them."

Mr. Malik is responsible for the false answer given by Mr. Yaakoubian.

The Court cannot but note however that it finds surprising that no mention is made of the absence of sewer service at clause 6 of the Offer to purchase. This is an omission of either Mr. Malik or of Mr. Yaakoubian. In any event, Mr. Malik must bear its consequences. Mr. Malik's comment on 20 October 1999 to both real estate agents that this was a land-filled property and his statement at the Notary's on 29 December 1999 are not sufficiently clear to constitute proper notice of the problem. Both Notary Lebeau and Mr. Dupuis stated it is not unusual that soil is added to a property. Mr. Dupuis even said that no specific conclusion should be drawn from such a fact.

This is why the Court cannot accept the Defendants' suggestion that Plaintiffs' antenna should have been raised and that they should have investigated the matter more in depth. Let us remember the general principles enunciated by Articles 6 and 7 C.C.Q.:

> "6. Every person is bound to exercise his civil rights in good faith.
> 7. No right may be exercised with the intent of injuring another or in an excessive and unreasonable manner which is contrary to the requirements of good faith."

This principle is reiterated in a contractual context by Article 1375 C.C.Q.:

> "1375. The parties shall conduct themselves in good faith both at the time the obligation is created and at the time it is performed or extinguished."

Good faith is presumed. Bad faith must be proved. In the Court's opinion, the fact that Mr. Malik knew of the 1988 report (P-4) and did not reveal, directly or indirectly, its existence to the Plaintiffs is evidence of his bad faith.

What are the consequences of such behaviour which, although it may be explainable [See Note 1 below], is not excusable.

Note 1: The Court heard Mr. Malik when he said he had found himself in 1988 in the same situation as the Plaintiffs found themselves in January of this year. It is a terrible situation to be in and the Court has a lot of sympathy for Mr. Malik. However, the Court cannot make its decision based on sympathy: it must be made on the law. Let us remember what the Honourable Madam Justice Claire L'Heureux-Dubé said in the case Lapointe c. Hôpital Le Gardeur, [1992] 1 R.C.S. 351: "Guided by sympathy alone, my task here would have been much easier. As a judge, however, I must uphold the law and sympathy is a poor guide in such matters. According to law is the only guide and justice must work for both parties engaged in litigation, plaintiffs as well as defendants."

Articles 1399, 1400 and 1401 C.C.Q. read as follows:

"1399. Consent may be given only in a free and enlightened manner.

It may be vitiated by error, fear or lesion.

1400. Error vitiates consent of the parties or of one of them where it relates to the nature of the contract, the object of the prestation or anything that was essential in determining that consent.

An inexcusable error does not constitute a defect of consent.

1401. Error on the part of one party induced by fraud committed by the other party or with his knowledge vitiates consent whenever, but for that error, the party would not have contracted, or would have contracted on different terms.

Fraud may result from silence or concealment."

In the present case, the Court finds that there has been "dol" on the part of Mr. Malik which has vitiated Plaintiffs' consent.
What are the consequences of such a finding? What does the Code say?

Articles 1407 and 1705 C.C.Q. read as follows:

"1407. A person whose consent is vitiated has the right to apply for annulment of the contract; in the case of error occasioned by fraud, of fear or of lesion, he may, in addition to annulment, also claim damages or, where he prefers that the contract be maintained, apply for a reduction of his obligation equivalent to the damages he would be justified in claiming.

1705. Costs of restitution are borne by the parties, in proportion, where applicable, to the value of the prestations mutually restored.

Where one party is in bad faith, however, or where the restitution is due to his fault, the costs are borne by that party alone."

This is exactly what the Plaintiffs are requesting in their conclusions which read as follows:

"PAR CES MOTIFS, PLAISE À **LA COUR** :

CONDAMNER les défendeurs solidairement à rembourser aux demandeurs

le prix de vente, soit la somme de 45 000 $, plus les intérêts au taux légal de même que l'indemnité additionnelle prévue au Code civil du Québec depuis la demeure;

...

PRENDRE ACTE de l'offre des demandeurs de rétrocéder le terrain et de signer tous les documents nécessaires à cette rétrocession, sur paiement des sommes réclamées;

..."

This is why the Court is of the opinion that the Plaintiffs are entitled to be reimbursed of the amount of $45,000 they paid Mr. Malik.

B) THE CLAIM FOR DAMAGES

The Court finds that the Plaintiffs have suffered great stress and inconvenience because of the fact they could not build their dream house on the land they purchased from Mr. Malik. Their house was sold. They had two young children one of whom had started school; they had some difficulty registering him in school. They wanted to build a cottage; they are now living in a bungalow, 10 minutes away from where they used to live. Both of them work and they have had to cope with all the problems and difficulties arising out of this situation. Mr. Malik says he went through the same kind of experience in 1988. Therefore, he must understand what the Plaintiffs are going through.

Considering the stress, inconveniences, problems and expenses caused by Mr. Malik's dol, the Court considers the parties are entitled to the amount of $10,000 they claim as damages.

C) PROVISIONAL EXECUTION

As for the request for provisional execution, article 547 of the Code of Civil Procedure reads as follows:

"547. Notwithstanding appeal, provisional execution applies in respect of all the following matters unless, by a decision giving reasons, execution is suspended by the court: (a) possessory actions; (b) liquidation of a succession, or making an inventory; (c) urgent repairs; (d) ejectment, when there is no lease or the lease has expired or has been cancelled or annulled; (e) appointment, removal or replacement of tutors, curators or other administrators of the property of others, or revocation of the mandate given to a mandatory in anticipation of the mandator's incapacity; (f) accounting; (g) alimentary pension or allowance or custody of children; (h) judgments of sequestration; (i) (subparagraph repealed). In addition, the court may, upon application, order provisional execution in case of exceptional urgency or for any other reason deemed sufficient in particular where the fact of bringing the case to appeal is likely to cause serious or

> irreparable injury, for the whole or for part only of a judgment. In the cases provided for in this article, the court may, upon application, make provisional execution conditional upon the furnishing of security."

In the present case, the evidence reveals that the Defence is frivolous. The $45,000 paid by the Plaintiffs represent their life savings and they have nothing for it except a worthless piece of land. Furthermore, although the he recognizes that he has known about the condition of the Property since 1988, Mr. Malik does not consider he has done anything wrong. This is why the Court is of the opinion that provisional execution is warranted: the parties should not suffer the consequences of a frivolous appeal.

POUR CES MOTIFS, LE TRIBUNAL :

ACCUEILLE la présente action;

CONDAMNE les défendeurs solidairement à rembourser aux demandeurs le prix de vente, soit la somme de 45 000 $, plus les intérêts au taux légal de même que l'indemnité additionnelle prévue au Code civil du Québec depuis la mise en demeure;

CONDAMNE les défendeurs solidairement à payer aux demandeurs la somme de 10 000 $ à titre de dommages et intérêts au taux légal de même que l'indemnité additionnelle prévue au Code civil du Québec depuis la mise en demeure;

PREND ACTE de l'offre des demandeurs de rétrocéder le terrain et de signer tous les documents nécessaires à cette rétrocession, sur paiement des sommes réclamées;

ORDONNE que le présent jugement soit exécutoire nonobstant appel;
Le tout avec dépens.

* * * * *

JUGEMENT EN RECTIFICATION D'UNE ERREUR D'OMISSION (Art. 475 C.p.c.)

LA JUGE ANNE-MARIE TRAHAN:— ATTENDU qu'au paragraphe [50] du jugement rendu en la présente cause le 16 octobre 2000, il est mentionné que ledit jugement est exécutoire nonobstant appel et que cette conclusion a été omise au chapitre des conclusions;

ATTENDU qu'il s'agit là d'une erreur d'omission qui peut être corrigé aux termes de l'article 475 C.p.c.;

POUR CES MOTIFS, LE TRIBUNAL :

RECTIFIE d'office son jugement rendu le 16 octobre 2000, en y ajoutant la conclusion suivante :

"ORDONNE que le présent jugement soit exécutoire nonobstant appel."

Le tout sans frais.

CASE 8.2

Peter v. Fiasche

[2000] Q.J. No. 4880, **Quebec Superior Court**

(Excerpts of Judgment)

REASONS FOR JUDGMENT

WILLIAM FRAIBERG J.:—

INTRODUCTION

This case presents a challenging confusion of contractual cause and consent for the Court to unravel. If a purchase contravenes public order for a reason (tax evasion) known to the buyer when she makes it, can she nonetheless invoke her error induced by the vendor's fraud to justify her demand for annulment of the sale and damages? If the contract would be invalid even if she possessed perfect knowledge of all material facts, does it matter if in fact she did not? Put another way, does its ultimate irrelevance to the validity of the contract in such circumstances render any error of the buyer inexcusable?

Then, if to justify voiding the contract, the buyer invokes not her error, if inexcusable, but the offence to public order its formation represents, must she be denied restitution of the price because she knew the contract was illicit when she entered into it? Must the Court deny her all redress because she invokes her own turpitude?

THE FACTS

Plaintiff Agnes Peter ("Mrs. Gucciardo") is the wife of Francesco (a.k.a. Frank) Gucciardo ("Gucciardo") a long-time acquaintance of Defendant Biagio (a.k.a. Gino) Fiasche ("Fiasche"). Gucciardo and Fiasche are both natives of the Siculiana region of Italy, whence they immigrated to Canada with their families in the 1950's. Over many years the families maintained amiable, though not intimate, contacts as a result of the friendship between their matriarchs who visited each other from time to time.

Furthermore, Gucciardo and Fiasche associated with each other on a continuing basis as founding members of the Siculiana Association. This was an organization that perpetuated social ties among natives of that region who resided in Montreal. Fiasche once helped Gucciardo weather some political difficulties he encountered as the newly elected president of the Association. Thus it is reasonable to believe Gucciardo's claim that he trusted Fiasche and held him in high regard.

Gucciardo was also impressed by Fiasche's business success, the source of which was a restaurant kiosk ("Gino's" or "the restaurant") at the Marché de l'Ouest in Dollard-des-Ormeaux that Fiasche operated under the name "Chez Gino Smokey's (for smoked meat)". From humble beginnings, Fiasche had managed to acquire a comfortable suburban home, a condo in Florida and a Cadillac. These trappings of affluence were not lost on Gucciardo, a salaried computer programmer-analyst with a wife and four children to support. Mrs. Gucciardo did occasional clerical or interpreting work to ease the family finances. Neither she nor her husband had any business experience.

Gucciardo, and when visiting from Toronto, his brother Giacomo ("Jack") also, would often stop by Gino's for a sandwich and a chat with Fiasche. Jack expressed the thought that he might want to invest in a franchise of the restaurant in Toronto. Around Easter 1991, Fiasche informed the Gucciardo brothers he wanted to give up running the restaurant, which he would sell as a going concern, in order to expand on its success by selling franchises to others.

At the end of May 1991, Gucciardo learned his job would terminate in a month. Feeling an urgent need for a secure source of income adequate to support his family, he now began to frequent Gino's, no longer as a customer, but as its potential purchaser.

Fiasche told him the restaurant was a gold mine, capable of supporting, not one, but two families. He suggested that Gucciardo could buy one of the franchises he was offering for sale at a price of $125,000 but the real money, he said, was in the restaurant, which he wanted to sell to someone he knew.

This appealed to Gucciardo who felt he could not afford the risk of a start-up operation. He preferred to buy a going concern that was already a proven success, then run it as before, all the more so because it would be Fiasche's intended model for all the other franchises.

Though the asking price was $250,000, Gucciardo was undeterred. He succeeded in bargaining Fiasche down to $200,000, but he would have to act fast, Fiasche warned, since others were anxious to buy.

Fiasche gave Gucciardo the 1990 financial statement of the restaurant. Although it showed a loss and deficit of $6,235 on sales of $172,551, he told him this did not really mean anything because he had, in Gucciardo's words, "a special way of reporting income to the government". In fact, the restaurant was extremely profitable, generating annual sales of $300,000.

Gucciardo contends that when he asked for further details, Fiasche said he would not give away any secrets until Gucciardo showed he was a serious buyer by giving him a $100,000 deposit. When Gucciardo asked how he could do this, seeing he was about to lose his job, Fiasche suggested that he mortgage his house. Though he had finally paid off the previous hypothec only two months before after many years of debt, Gucciardo immediately applied to his bank, which approved a new loan of $100,000 by mid-June.

He borrowed another $40,000 from Jack who mortgaged his own house to come up with the money. Gucciardo planned to use $130,000 of the loans toward the purchase price, and the remaining $10,000 for professional fees and other start-up costs.

Fiasche also gave Gucciardo a draft of a franchise agreement and suggested that he have a lawyer review it. Gucciardo then phoned his boyhood friend Mark Paci ("Paci"), attorney, and after telling him he was thinking of buying the restaurant, sent him the draft agreement. Paci left on his annual vacation on June 22, 1991, leaving the document on his desk unread and without yet agreeing to represent Gucciardo.

Some time in early June 1991, the Gucciardos each spent a few hours taking orders behind the restaurant counter so they could get a feel for the business. Mrs. Gucciardo claims that while she was there a woman showed up who did not buy anything but spoke to Fiasche for some time. She went home after Fiasche told her not to stay because the visitor was a Revenue Quebec tax auditor.

That night Fiasche met the Gucciardos at their kitchen table and succeeded in persuading them to go ahead with the purchase. According to Mrs. Gucciardo, he assured them that the tax auditor had just done a routine check, which would not occur again for a few years. On a piece of paper he wrote a number of figures, including the daily sales of the restaurant. The weekly total came to $5,600, which he rounded down to $5,000.

Elsewhere on the paper, according to the Gucciardos, Fiasche's numbers showed the cost of food and salaries. Fiasche admits he told them the cost of food should be about $350 a day, or 35% of gross sales. However, he categorically denies ever stating that the restaurant sales were anything other than what the financial statement showed.

He contends that while the June 30 year-end statement was usually issued three months later, his accountant Joe Pietracupa ("Pietracupa") worked under great pressure to get out the 1991 statement on July 2 or 3 so that Gucciardo could see it before he agreed to buy the business. This statement showed an operating loss for the year of $1,482 on sales of $151,845 and an accumulated deficit of $7,717.
The Gucciardos, however, insist they did not see a 1991 statement until September, after buying the restaurant.

The above marks the fundamental point of dispute between the parties. The Gucciardos claim they would never have put down $130,000 and gone into prospective lifetime debt unless Fiasche had assured them that the sales would be as he promised at their kitchen table. They also claim that when they expressed reservations about the accuracy of Fiasche's sales figures, he promised on a piece of paper, or so he said, that if the restaurant did not prove profitable, he would buy it back for the money they paid him. According to Mrs. Gucciardo, he tore up the paper without their reading it after they sheepishly apologized for doubting his word because "he was like family".

Fiasche retorts that he made no guarantee but noted the sales figures only as a reflection of the volume Gucciardo told him the restaurant would have to generate in order to meet debt and operating costs and leave enough for a living. He insists that he never asked for a deposit of any amount and that he was surprised when Gucciardo brought him to his notary on July 5, 1991 and gave him $100,000. The notary prepared the following receipt, which Fiasche signed:

APPEARED:

GINO FIASCHE, businessman, residing at 24 Silver Pine Street, in the City of Kirkland, province of Quebec;

WHO DECLARED AS FOLLOWS:

That I have received, this day, from FRANCO GUCCIARDO, the sum of ONE HUNDRED THOUSAND DOLLARS ($100,000.00) as account for the purchase of a business known as "CHEZ GINO SMOKIES (sic)" and exploited at 11,712 De Salaberry, Marché de l'Ouest, Dollard des Ormeaux (100% of the outstanding share sic).

That the difference of ONE HUNDRED THOUSAND DOLLARS ($100,000.00) (the price being of TWO HUNDRED THOUSAND DOLLARS ($200,000.00) shall be paid when the franchise is transfer (sic) unto Franco Gucciardo within ten (10) days from these presents.

IN WITNESS WHEREOF, I have sided at Montreal, this fifth day of July nineteen hundred and ninety-one (1991).

(signed) Biagio Fiasche

Fiasche testifies that rather than apply any pressure to make a deposit and to proceed to closing thereafter, he allowed the Gucciardos to work in the restaurant on a six-week trial basis to see whether they felt it was worth his asking price. He claims he would gladly have refunded the $100,000 before closing if the Gucciardos had only asked, but they never did.

The Gucciardos began to work at the restaurant on July 5, 1991 after making the deposit. They viewed the weeks that followed as training time rather than a trial period, i.e. they felt they had already bought the restaurant. While Fiasche continued to manage the accounting during this time, Gucciardo kept all the daily sales proceeds, except for $150 to serve as the next day's opening cash.

He soon learned what he claims was the restaurant's special accounting system, although Fiasche vehemently denies such a system existed. This simply involved the preparation, after hours, of a second cash register tape for each business day that showed about half the actual sales and reallocated a large portion of otherwise taxable meal sales as non-taxable sales of sliced meat.

Gucciardo testifies that Fiasche kept a second cash register at home and that he taught him how to prepare the false tapes so as to avoid the maximum tax in the most plausible manner. According to Gucciardo, even their wives got involved in the process, meeting at Fiasche's house to prepare the false tapes when a large "backlog" of undone tapes had accumulated.

Gucciardo testifies that Fiasche bought two new cash registers for this purpose, one at the end of June 1991 and the other at the end of August. Fiasche does not deny these purchases but says he did so at the end of June only because

Gucciardo, who did not trust the existing register, insisted on the purchase of a brand new register as a condition of the sale proceeding. He adds that the second register was purchased as a backup in case the first should break down.

According to Gucciardo, Fiasche gave the false tapes and related expenses to Pietracupa at regular intervals. Pietracupa then entered them in the general ledger and used them as a basis for tax reporting, as well as the annual financial statement. Pietracupa denies this.

Fiasche testifies that during the six-week "trial" period and before, he instructed Pietracupa to allow Gucciardo unlimited access to the financial records of the company. However, Pietracupa claims he kept records only for the purpose of preparing each annual statement, returning them to Fiasche after each was prepared. He says that he did not feel it necessary to keep any copies in case of tax audit or to protect himself against professional liability and that he had never had a problem of that kind.

Moreover, Gucciardo claims he had no access to records in any case, since whenever he asked for it Pietracupa replied that he had to receive Fiasche's authorization, which never came. Gucciardo adds that once Pietracupa asked Fiasche if he would show him (Gucciardo) the black book in which he entered all the true sales. According to Gucciardo, Fiasche replied that no one would ever see his black book.

Gucciardo further relates that by the beginning of August 1991, he still had not seen the June 30, 1991 statement, so he and Jack made an appointment to see Pietracupa to review the financial records for that year with him and receive any required explanation. Jack came to Montreal for the meeting, but when the two showed up at Pietracupa's office, he was not there and could not be reached. Instead, he faxed Gucciardo a handwritten list of the monthly gross sales of the restaurant in 1991. They were considerably lower than Fiasche's kitchen table figures.

During the "trial" period the Gucciardos soon became disappointed and worried about the restaurant's low revenues. Gucciardo kept what he claims to be the true cash register tapes for July 5, 7 and 11, 1991 and only the first day matched Fiasche's kitchen table representation. He also introduced in evidence, under reserve of Fiasche's counsel's objection, the allegedly false tapes for the same days showing the reported receipts at about half the true figures.

Under reserve of the same objection, Gucciardo produced tapes for six days, June 4-9, 1991, as well as the general ledger for 1991 that Pietracupa sent him after he terminated his services as the accountant for the restaurant in 1992. These tapes show the daily receipts as being about half or less those of the three "true" tapes for July. Fiasche did not deny the veracity of the latter tapes, since his handwriting appears on them. The general ledger shows only one employee, Fiasche himself. There were at least three other people who worked in the restaurant.

The Gucciardos describe the training period as one of constant confusion, claiming that other franchisees were being trained with them in a crowded space, and that the restaurant was being used as a delivery depot for the other Smokey's restaurants. It would thus have been difficult to separate the purchases of the restaurant from the others in order to do an effective cost analysis.

They claim that while they did not do a daily calculation of sales, the "line-ups" were never the same as the first day, July 5, and the amount of money they took home decreased. Both also testified that some of the customers in the June and early July "line-ups" and in June were "fictitious", presumably consisting of Fiasche's friends recruited in order to create the desired impression of busyness. During the same six weeks, the tax auditor continued to show up but Gucciardo testifies that Fiasche told him she was just there to make sure that the cash register worked accurately.

Though they expressed their discouragement to Fiasche, he told them to be patient; that sales would pick up in August after the construction holiday in the latter half of July. When this had not happened by closing day, August 20, he told them sales would improve after Labour Day.

Paci claims that when he returned from vacation, he was surprised to learn that Gucciardo had made a deposit of $100,000. Gucciardo instructed him, to simply prepare a share purchase agreement without business warranties, saying he trusted Fiasche. According to Paci, Gucciardo seemed very optimistic. Nevertheless, Paci stated that had he accepted a mandate from him before going on vacation, he would have been very upset to learn of the deposit and would probably have withdrawn from the file. In the circumstances, however, he considered it professionally acceptable for him to document a deal Gucciardo had already made and that seemed to be the answer to his prayers for financial autonomy.

Paci quickly learned that the franchise manual referred to in the draft franchise agreement did not exist, nor did the "system" mentioned in the draft. He contends, however, that the franchise agreement was secondary to the real business objective of buying a supposedly successful restaurant as a going concern. He too saw the 1990 financial statement showing a deficit but Gucciardo told him what he had been told by Fiasche: not to worry about the deficit because not all the income was reported.

Paci went to visit the restaurant on July 15, 1991, having agreed to represent the Gucciardos four days earlier. He was not impressed by what he saw. The space was tiny, only 300 square feet, and the equipment looked as if it was "on its last legs". Although he advised Gucciardo to have an independent business appraisal made and to proceed by way of bulk sale rather than a share purchase to avoid inheriting undisclosed liabilities, Gucciardo did neither, trusting Fiasche's assurances and not wanting to incur the extra legal fees a bulk sale would entail. Meanwhile, it had been decided, at Fiasche's suggestion say the Gucciardos, to have Mrs. Gucciardo become the purchaser of record, so that Gucciardo could collect unemployment insurance for six months, using it to help finance the purchase. Mrs. Gucciardo would have transferred the shares to him later. The shares were to remain in escrow at Paci's law firm until they were fully paid. The restaurant landlord had to consent to the share purchase, since it was deemed an assignment under the lease. He did so only after Mrs. Gucciardo agreed to personally guarantee the lease.

Paci met Mrs. Gucciardo for the first time at the closing. While there was some debate at trial over what she knew or did not know, the Court is satisfied that Gucciardo informed her of the essentials of the transaction and acted as her mandatary, so that she may validly claim to be the true claimant. She particularly understood the importance of the restaurant generating sufficient sales volume, and at some level, she was also aware that the presence of a tax auditor could make for a serious problem. She never disavowed her husband's actions. The Court will therefore presume that his actions and knowledge may be imputed to her.

At closing, the Gucciardos expressed reservations about completing the purchase. Sales were low and they worried about the frequent presence of the tax auditor. Paci accepted the draft franchise agreement without change, having been persuaded that it really did not matter that much. On the other hand, he tried to protect the Gucciardos by providing that the balance of purchase price of $70,000 was to come out of positive cash flow. Fiasche's lawyer would not permit any change, however, saying that all terms had already been agreed by Gucciardo and were non-negotiable.

The Gucciardos were somewhat appeased by the inclusion of warranties in the stock purchase agreement that all tax requirements had been complied with as of July 5, 1991, the effective date of the sale, and that all liabilities of any nature had been paid as of that date. According to Paci, Fiasche also told the Gucciardos that he would never allow their family to be put on the street.

Within three weeks following the closing, however, the Gucciardos were disillusioned. Their mentor Fiasche no longer showed up every day to provide them with guidance and increased sales had not materialized, contrary to his assurances. Paci advised the Gucciardos to document their complaints. This is what they proceeded to do.

Between September 23, 1991 and February 5, 1992 they wrote 27 letters to Fiasche complaining about the quality and price of the food they had to buy from his franchise company, as well as the absence of support and guidance. They also did cost analyses in September and January showing that the cost of food exceeded 50% of sales instead of being 35% as Fiasche had promised.

The Gucciardos testify that they had to dip into their savings in order to meet all the payments to Fiasche and the bank, and they had barely enough left over for groceries. In December 1991 they met with Fiasche and asked him to buy the restaurant back from them as they say he had promised. He refused, saying he had promised only to help them if he could. He suggested that they try to sell the restaurant to another franchisee.

In December, Gucciardo began to buy salami from a nearby supermarket. He found that the retail price was less than what Fiasche had been charging wholesale. By mid-February the restaurant was buying all food directly from the

suppliers, avoiding Fiasche's mark-up. The Gucciardos complain that Fiasche wanted cash only for their purchases from February on. He retorts that they were so far behind in their payments that he did not want to extend further credit.
In February 1992 Mrs. Gucciardo sued Fiasche to have the share purchase agreement annulled based on his false representations and the failure of his franchise company to provide food of acceptable quality at reasonable prices, as well as to perform its other obligations under the franchise agreement. She claims $148,501, comprising the payments she had thus far made on account of the purchase price in the amount of $133,501 and $15,000 in damages.

In his defence, Fiasche contends that the Gucciardos had ample opportunity to verify the sales at the restaurant before and after the deposit was made and he seeks the balance of the purchase price of $66,499 by cross-demand.

In April 1992 the franchise company, 172361 Canada Inc., sued the restaurant company for the price of goods and franchise fees owed by the latter in the aggregate amount of $7,214.92. The restaurant company cross-demanded for the annulment of the franchise agreement on the basis of the franchise company's failure of performance and had the file moved to the Superior Court. Here it was eventually joined for hearing with Mrs. Gucciardo's action, which the present judgment disposes of.

POSITIONS OF THE PARTIES

Mrs. Gucciardo's position

Mrs. Gucciardo contends that the sale and franchise contracts should be resolved and Fiasche condemned to pay her damages for reasons that go both to the formation and performance of the contracts.

ISSUES

The paramount questions for the Court to decide are of fact and credibility. Did Fiasche tell the Gucciardos, as they claim and he denies, that the annual sales of the restaurant were around $300,000? Did the restaurant owe its perceived profitability to the systematic under reporting and misallocation of revenue, as they claim and he denies? If those questions are answered affirmatively, the Court must then determine whether Mrs. Gucciardo's knowledge of these factors led her to enter the agreements and the legal consequences of that knowledge. Was her error, if any, an excusable misunderstanding induced by Fiasche's fraud, or was it a deliberate wrongful choice even if she was unaware of other material facts? In the former case, the contract would be void because her consent was vitiated for a reason other than her own negligence or wilful blindness. In the second case, it would be void for want of a valid cause.

DISCUSSION

Credibility

The Court finds the Gucciardos' testimony more credible in its essentials, than that of Fiasche. The Court thinks it highly improbable that Gucciardo, with no business experience and facing unemployment, would have raised $140,000 and made a deposit of $100,000 unless Fiasche had asked for it and given assurances that the restaurant, showing a loss in two consecutive financial statements, was in fact profitable.

Considering Gucciardo's testimony, given under the protection of the Court (Art. 309 C.c.P.), that both he and Fiasche regularly prepared false tapes during the six week trial period, the payment of a purchase price not justified by the apparent sales figures, the existence of parallel tapes showing higher figures (admitted by Fiasche), the purchase of two new cash registers for the restaurant (admitted by Fiasche) and the existence of earlier tapes showing lower figures similar to those on the false tapes, the Court concludes that there was a fraudulent accounting system in place.

Gucciardo made a $100,000 deposit and agreed to buy the restaurant on the strength of Fiasche's representations that the restaurant had annual sales approaching $300,000. It is not necessary for the Court to decide whether that representation amounted to a guarantee that the sales volume would be maintained. It was at the very least a representation as to past performance.

It suffices as a reason to explain the Gucciardos' conduct and as corroboration for the Court's conclusion that by the parties' mutual consent, the entire transaction's financial viability depended on continuing a scheme of tax evasion. The Court believes that Gucciardo became Fiasche's willing apprentice in this connection after the latter enticed him with assurances that continuing to operate the restaurant in this way would be the solution for his career problems.

Formation of the Contract

Fraud

In a context where the deal was flawed at its core, all the Gucciardos' complaints of deception or misrepresentation, however well founded they believe them to be, are ultimately irrelevant.

Their fundamental complaint is that Fiasche defrauded them by grossly overstating the true weekly sales, then reneging on his promise to buy back the business if it was not profitable [See Note 1 below]. That Gucciardo had no reliable way of determining that the sales were as represented by Fiasche was an inevitable consequence of the latter not reporting almost half the gross income. It was a risk Gucciardo should have recognized, since even before making the deposit, he had seen the 1990 financial statement showing sales as $172,551, while Fiasche represented them as $300,000. He thus committed an error, though not in the sense of Art. 1400 C.c.Q.

Note 1: According to Paci who was present at closing Fiasche allayed the Gucciardos' fears of signing without a warranty of sales volume by promising to buy back the business if it was unprofitable, since he "would not allow a family with four children to be put on the street". The Gucciardos testified he also wrote a similar promise on a piece of paper when he met them in their kitchen in June. However, they never to got to see this alleged promise, since he tore up the paper after they asked to be excused for acting as if they mistrusted him.

An error of that sort - being a vitiation of consent - would have involved his being led to a perception of reality, past or present, which was untrue. Even if that were the case here, the error was inexcusable since Gucciardo's misperception of reality arose from closing his eyes to the risk he was running.

Gucciardo's "error" is better understood as one of conscious wrongful choice, since he could not avoid being aware that tax evasion was at the root of the restaurant's supposed profitability. It was disingenuous of him to testify that Fiasche told him he had a "special way of reporting income to the government", which he (Gucciardo) "did not understand" and that Fiasche would reveal to him only after he paid him $100,000. The Court believes that both Fiasche and Gucciardo lied about the deposit: Fiasche by claiming he never asked for it and Gucciardo by claiming he did not understand the illicitness of its commercial justification.

Indeed, that illicitness spawned all of the Gucciardos' difficulties that followed, as well as their belief that Fiasche betrayed them. Fiasche could not go on record by warranting that the sales were much more than officially reported; nor for the same reason could he release his black book in which the true sales supposedly were recorded. This was also why - in Fiasche's mind, reasonably - permitting the Gucciardos to be present during a trial period would allow them to assess the sales volume for themselves.

The trouble is that six weeks were not enough, especially in the distracting circumstances of their training the Gucciardos describe. It would have taken review of a whole year's true figures (presumably in the black book) to make a reasonably reliable assessment, and even then, Fiasche could not warrant their accuracy without uncovering a trail he had directed his efforts to concealing.
To compound the risk, during the trial period Gucciardo did not bother, against his lawyer's advice, to keep a record of the daily sales except for July 5, 7 and 11, 1991 nor make any cost analysis himself or through an independent accountant. He claimed at trial that it was more important for him to focus on "bonding " with his mentor Fiasche.

Had Gucciardo not seen the financial 1990 statement before paying $100,000, his conduct, however reckless, would merit the Court's sympathy. For he might then credibly have claimed he did not realize he was being taken into an illegal scheme [See Note 2 below], and that once he did, in his state of unemployment, he was trapped by circumstances he had neither the will nor the resources to resist. After all, notwithstanding Fiasche's insistence that he allowed Gucciardo a trial period, the Receipt drafted by Gucciardo's notary appears to commit him to proceed to the purchase within ten days, with no provision for return of the deposit should he for any reason be unsatisfied.

Note 2: In the Court's view this would have been an excusable error under Art. 1400 C.c.Q.

That, at any rate, was the view that Fiasche's lawyer communicated to Paci, a credible witness on the point, who in turn advised the Gucciardos they would have to go to court to get their money back should they not proceed to closing. However, if Gucciardo felt trapped, he had himself to blame in large part, for with the facts he admits to knowing, he should not have made the deposit in the first place.

In the result, the Gucciardos had nothing to guide them but their blind trust of Fiasche, the author of a fraudulent scheme. Quite apart from the illicit nature of the entire transaction, as a purely self-protective matter, they should have recognized this for the impossible situation it was and walked away. Instead, they now ask the Court to enforce a fool's bargain.

Thus, it would not have mattered that Fiasche did not provide the 1991 statement or the general ledger because both were false any way. For the same reason, the Gucciardos should not claim surprise that the tax related warranties proved to be untrue and that Revenue Quebec re-assessed the company for unpaid taxes for the three years preceding the purchase.

The tax risk would be obvious from the fact that Gucciardo knew before making the deposit at least that the restaurant company was seriously under stating its income. Even before July 5, 1991, as Mrs. Gucciardo's testimony reveals, they knew that a tax auditor was showing up at the premises. Paci alluded to the fact that both were very worried about an assessment. Gucciardo testified that he and his wife saw the presence of the tax auditor as a "dark cloud" hovering over the transaction. Heard in that context, his testimony that he believed, because Fiasche told him so, that the auditor was present simply to ensure that the cash register worked properly during a time when he was spending off-hours creating fictitious cash register tapes is hardly credible.

It is specious to claim, as Fiasche does, that the tax warranties were true on the basis that as of closing the government claimed no amount. While the formal requirements of the tax laws may have been complied with, the company was in flagrant substantive breach of them, even if no reassessment had yet issued. The Gucciardos correctly apprehended this. What else could they mean by their "dark cloud"?

Cause

Since all contracts in this case were entered into before January 1, 1994, the provisions of the Civil Code of Lower Canada govern the dispute, except to the extent that the Transitional Law causes the provisions of the Civil Code of Quebec to supersede them.

Art. 984 C.C.L.Q. provides that to be valid a contract must contain four elements:

Parties legally capable of contracting;

Their consent legally given;

Something which forms the object of the contract:

A lawful cause or consideration.

These elements are repeated, albeit in different form, in Art. 1385 C.c.Q.:

1385 A contract is formed by the sole exchange of consents between persons having capacity to contract, unless, in addition, the law requires a particular form to be respected as a necessary condition of its formation, or unless the patties require the contract to take the form of a solemn agreement.

It is also of the essence of a contract that it have a cause and an object.

Not only must the parties give their free and enlightened consent [See Note 4 below], but they must also have a valid reason to enter the contract. This reason, the motive that leads them to do so, is the cause of the contract, under both the old and new Codes. The reason may be implicit rather than express.

Note 4: Art. 1399 C.c.Q.

Civil Code of Lower Canada

Art. 989: A contract without a consideration or with an unlawful consideration has no effect; but it is not the less valid though the consideration be no expressed or be incorrectly expressed in the writing which is evidence of the contract.

Art. 990: The consideration is unlawful when it is prohibited by law, or is contrary to good morals or public order.

Civil Code of Quebec

Art. 1410: The cause of a contract is the reason that determines each of the parties to enter into the contract. (emphasis added)
The cause need not be expressed.

Art. 1411: A contract whose cause is prohibited by law or contrary to public order is null.

In the present case, Mrs. Gucciardo's obvious purpose of buying the shares of a restaurant company, the cause of her obligation, is perfectly licit. The cause of the contract, on the other hand, is Fiasche's desire to sell and hers to buy a business, apparently money-losing, for a substantial sum in the expectation that it is and will remain profitable. This is only because the parties intend that the buyer, after being schooled in the art by the seller, will continue to follow his example of systematically evading payment of most taxes affecting the business. The cause of the contract is therefore illicit.

Public Order

As viewed by the doctrine, rules of public order found in the law fall into two categories. The first is a public order of "direction" serving to protect the public

interest at large by providing political, social and economic direction. The second serves to protect individual interests through intervention in certain kinds of agreement in order to redress unequal bargaining strength between the parties.
In the present case, the cornerstone of the contract underlying its entire financial feasibility for the parties was the perpetuation of a system of falsifying documents in order to defraud the public treasury. This is an offence under the Criminal Code:

397. (1) Every one who, with intent to defraud,

(a) destroys, mutilates, alters, falsifies or makes a false entry in, or

(b) omits a material particular from, or alters a material particular in, a book, paper, writing, valuable security or document

is guilty of an indictable offence and liable to imprisonment for a term not exceeding five years.

(2) Every one who, with intent to defraud his creditors, is privy to the commission of an offence under subsection (1) is guilty of an indictable offence and liable to imprisonment for a term not exceeding five years.

The foregoing provisions are imperative rules of public order having the obvious purpose, fundamental to any civil society, of protecting citizens and the state against fraud. There is no question that under the provisions of the Civil Code of Lower Canada, which govern here, and as recognized by the Civil Code of Quebec their violation can be invoked by the Court as a ground of absolute nullity of both the share purchase contract and the franchise agreement, since both are inextricably linked.

The motives of the parties were unquestionably illicit. Fiasche desired to enrich himself by selling a fraudulent system and the Gucciardos by continuing it. Without the fraud on the treasury, there is no way either party would have entered into the contract on such terms. It was the only way the Gucciardos could service their debt of $140,000, run the business, pay Fiasche $172,000 in franchise fees and balance of price over ten years and have something left over as a decent living. There was place for payment only of enough taxes to avert the suspicion of the authorities.

Indeed, the Gucciardos' essential complaint until the Court itself raised the issue of infringement of public order was that Fiasche had not kept his promise that buying the restaurant would pay off handsomely.
Restitution

The crucial question here is whether parties to an illicit contract should have the benefit of restitution. Having harmed society by making their pact, should society rescue them when it fails? Under the Civil Code of Lower Canada the jurisprudence was unanimous in refusing restitution whenever the contract breached good morals or the criminal law. Courts took the attitude that having made their illicit bed the parties should lie in it.

In the 1985 case of Bouchard v. Bluteau, for example, our Court of Appeal denied restitution of a bribe made by a contractor to a government official who had failed to perform his half of their illicit bargain.

The more recent jurisprudence before the new Code came into force was divided over the question of whether the victim of an illicit contract gone wrong could benefit from restitution if, as in Bouchard, he was also an accomplice. Two decisions of the Cour du Québec involving pyramid sale schemes illustrate the point. In Lavoie v. Vézina it was held that the victim could not recover because she was a participant in a scheme that was criminal, regardless of her professed ignorance of the law. In Nadeau v. Doyon, on the other hand, the Court rescued the victim-participant:

It did likewise in the 1996 case of Dugal v. Villaume where the participant in the illegal pyramid contract entered in 1991, though venal, was held to be more victim than instigator.

As a result of the Court of Appeal's recent decision in Amusements St-Gervais inc. v. Legault [See Note below], it is now clear that by virtue of the second paragraph of Art. 1699 C.c.Q. the trial judge has wide discretion to grant or deny restitution as he or she sees fit in the particular circumstances of each case. The judge may deny it in the face of criminal conduct, but need not do so invariably. No special exception is made for the victim who has also participated in the act invalidated. Chief Justice Michaud held:

Note: [2000] J.Q. no 687, C.A. Québec 200-09-001361-978, AZ-50069914, J.E. 2000-550. The case dealt with whether the purchaser of prize giving snack vending machines, considered criminally illegal because of the element of chance attached to winning the prizes, could recover the price he had paid for them.

The primary objective is not to punish a transgressor but to ensure that as between the transgressors themselves, or as between them and society at large, one should not profit unduly from the annulment of the illegal bargain. As in other cases of contractual voidance, restitution has become the rule in cases of public order, its denial the exception. The judge may also opt for an intermediate form of relief by adjusting the manner or extent of restitution so as to achieve the most equitable result possible in the circumstances.

Article 1422 C.c.Q. reading,

> A contract that is null is deemed never to have existed. In such a case, each party is bound to restore to the other the prestations he has received,

Considering all the facts of this sad story, the Court sees no reason to refuse the Gucciardos restitution. Fiasche not only gulled them out of $130,000 based on the perpetuation of a criminal fraud, but he also ended up with the business that enabled him to do so, continuing to run it profitably, he claims, for another eight years. Although, based on their complicity, voiding the contract justifiably deprives the Gucciardos of entitlement to specific performance or damages, their devastating loss became Fiasche's ill-gotten gain. Therefore denying, not granting them relief would give him the undue advantage, creating the very injustice that the second paragraph of Article 1699 C.c.Q. is intended to avoid. Public order would be ill served by such an outcome.

Article 1704 C.c.Q. provides:

> Art. 1704. The fruits and revenues of the property being restored belong to the person who is bound to make restitution, and he bears the costs he has incurred to produce them. He owes no indemnity for enjoyment of the property unless that was the primary object of the prestation or unless the property was subject to rapid depreciation.
>
> If the person who is bound to make restitution is in bad faith or if the restitution is due to his fault, he is bound, after compensating of the costs, to return the fruits and revenues and indemnify the creditor for any enjoyment he has derived from the property.

In the present case Fiasche already obtained restitution of the restaurant in 1992 by taking back the premises lease he had guaranteed and buying equipment at the sale in execution of Revenue Quebec's judgment for taxes. The Gucciardos, on the other hand, have had to sue him for the return of the purchase price, which after nine years he has yet to repay. Clearly, he has been in bad faith and should therefore return any fruits and revenues derived from investing the price, but that is not possible here since no proof was made of whether and how he invested the funds. The Gucciardos remained in possession of the restaurant until June 1992 in any case, and at least until then, would have no entitlement to the fruits and revenues of the price unless they accounted for and paid their own, if any. Their possession then balances Fiasche's possession for the corresponding time.

This then leaves Fiasche's obligation to pay damages arising from his delay to refund the price. These consist of interest at the legal rate (Art. 1617 C.c.Q.) together with the additional indemnity under Article 1619 C.c.Q., should the Court award it, calculated from the date of his default. In this case that date should be July 1, 1992, 15 days after the Gucciardos' attorney advised Fiasche's that they were returning the business.

Performance

In the face of the nullity of both agreements for want of a licit cause, the Gucciardos complaint of Fiasche's failure of performance becomes moot. The Court believes that with the exception of the failure to pay the income tax assessment, the complaints are unfounded in any event.

It was unrealistic of the Gucciardos to expect that Fiasche would be able to rid them of their predicament by providing advice. The absence of a manual and of a formalized operating system were both foreseen, as were the prices, menus and quality of the food, all of which were known to the Gucciardos during the so-called trial period. It was, moreover, reasonable of Fiasche to demand cash payment for supplies. The Court must presume this reflected his legitimate desire to avoid a credit risk rather than to avoid reporting income.

The non-payment of the tax assessment, however, directly contravened Fiasche's warranty that there were no tax liabilities as of closing. His excuse that the Gucciardos did not give him a proxy to deal with Revenue Quebec is unpersuasive since his attorneys were first informed of a proposed assessment on January 24, 1992. Yet he did nothing to avoid it. The assessment for more than $19,000 was issued in March. In May 1992 Revenue Quebec threatened execution if it was not paid. This prompted the Gucciardos to abandon the business, since they lacked the funds to pay the assessment. Fiasche still did not pay it, nor give any indication he was prepared to do so, with the result that the threatened seizure and sale ensued.

The Court emphasizes, however, that even if Fiasche had done all the Gucciardos expected of him and even if all his representations as to the restaurant's profitability had been true, the entire transaction would be void because of its larcenous foundation.

Damages and Cross-Demand

It follows that the Gucciardos are not entitled to damages, pecuniary or moral, arising from a breach of the agreements, whether failure of warranty or failure of performance. Fiasche's cross-demand for the balance of the purchase price must be dismissed for the same reason.

Action on account

Given the nullity of the franchise agreement, the franchise company is not entitled to recover the arrears of royalty fees claimed in the amount of $2,140. It is, on the other hand, entitled to the recovery of $5,074.92 for goods sold and delivered, since these purchases took place individually and did not depend for their existence on the franchise agreement.

Even if one were to take the view that it is solely the franchise agreement that justified the purchases, the vendor would still be entitled to the purchase price on the basis of Article 1701 C.c.Q. The food would have to be returned by way of restitution in consequence of the nullity of the agreement. However, since it would no longer be available, having been sold or discarded, the purchaser would have to return its value instead. That value would be the highest possible, the purchase price of the foodstuffs at the time of their reception by the buyer because of the latter's bad faith deriving from its knowledge of the cause of nullity when it entered the contract.

Costs

Notwithstanding the nullity of the agreements and both parties' awareness of the cause of nullity when they entered them the Court sees no reason to depart from the usual rule that the taxable costs should be awarded to the victor. Mrs. Gucciardo's claim for restitution of the price is simply the legal consequence of the nullity of the share purchase agreement. It is fair that Fiasche pay the costs since he unjustifiably resisted restitution, even though in his own case it had already been achieved. The public interest is adequately served in the present case by denying Mrs. Gucciardo her claim in damages.

FOR ALL THE FOREGOING REASONS THE COURT:

MAINTAINS Plaintiff/Cross-Defendant Agnes Peter's action in part;

DECLARES the share purchase agreement between the parties dated July 5, 1991 null and void;

ORDERS Defendant/Cross-Plaintiff Biagio Fiasche to pay Plaintiff/Cross-Defendant Agnes Peter the sum of $133,501, with interest and the additional indemnity under Article 1619 C.c.Q. calculated from July 1, 1992 and costs;

DISMISSES Defendant/Cross-Plaintiff Biagio Fiasche's cross-demand with costs;

ORDERS the Mise-en-cause Pateras and Iezzoni to deliver to the Defendant/Cross-Plaintiff Biagio Fiasche, within 35 days of the present judgment, certificate number A-4 for 100 Class A shares of Restaurant Chez Smokey's inc. registered in the name of Agnes Peter Gucciardo issued in July 1991, or any replacement certificate in its possession since issued, without costs.

CASE 8.3

Carrefour Langelier v. Cineplex Odeon Corp.

[1999] Q.J. No. 5216, **Quebec Superior Court (Civil division)**

(Excerpts of Judgment)

REASONS FOR JUDGMENT

WILLIAM FRAIBERG J.:— While this case raises many interesting questions of civil law, the most urgent remains whether a creditor can insist upon specific performance of an obligation even though its breach causes no discernible damage. Does the remedy then offend a principle of good faith by being excessive in relation to the harm experienced or apprehended, even if it is provided for in the law and expressly anticipated in the contract?

THE FACTS

Plaintiff Carrefour Langelier ("Carrefour") is a Quebec partnership that owns and operates a shopping centre ("Shopping Centre") by that name in St. Leonard. Its principal partner is a family holding company controlled by its chief executive, Harry Glassman. Defendant Cineplex Odeon ("Cineplex") is an entertainment corporation that owns and operates cinemas and related food service concessions throughout Canada and the U.S. Defendant Cinéma Langelier inc. ("Guzzo"), the Mis-en-causes Cinéma Métropolitain 16 inc. and Cinéma Le Paradis inc., are part of a group of companies controlled by Mis-en-cause Angelo Guzzo that carry on a business in the Montreal area that is similar to Cineplex's. Since that group is commonly known as "Cinémas Guzzo", the name "Guzzo" will also be used as a convenient way of referring to it in this judgement.

After protracted negotiations, Carrefour and Cineplex signed a lease ("Lease") in April 1991 by virtue of which Carrefour constructed a multiple auditorium movie theatre ("Cinema") to order for Cineplex in the Shopping Centre. The cost of construction was approximately $3,000,000. In addition, Carrefour paid Cineplex a tenant allowance of $1,265,200. The term of the Lease was 20 years and the annual rental exceeded $500,000. Opening was scheduled for June 1991.

After the Lease was signed and before Cineplex even occupied the premises, it approached Carrefour together with representatives of Guzzo to ask its permission to assign the Lease to Guzzo based on the following representations:

1. Guzzo would operate the Cinema under Cineplex's banner and follow its criteria for operating theatres;
2. Cineplex would book all movies shown at the Cinema for Guzzo;
3. The equipment for the operation of the Cinema was to be free and clear and have a value exceeding $1,000,000;
4. Guzzo would sell the equipment to Carrefour for one dollar if it defaulted under the Lease or conditions 1 and 2 above;

5. Carrefour could refuse any further assignment or sublease if the proposed operator was not at least as financially sound as Guzzo;
6. The Cinema was to be advertised under Cineplex's name together with other Cineplex theatres in Montreal newspapers;
7. Cineplex would resume operating the Cinema if Guzzo ceased to do so because of financial difficulties.

In accordance with the above conditions, the parties signed a series of contracts ("Matrix Agreements") on June 20, 1991 consisting of:

1. An Agreement whereby Cineplex and Guzzo would continue Cineplex's banner, booking and policies in relation to the Cinema ("Operating Agreement");
2. An Assignment of Lease Agreement ("Assignment");
3. A Sale and Assignment Agreement; and
4. A Booking Agreement with a 20-year term coinciding with that of the Lease.

Carrefour consented to the Assignment in consideration of the other Matrix Agreements, especially the undertakings of Guzzo and Cineplex expressed in the Booking Agreement, which are hereafter referred to as the "Franchise Conditions". These comprised Guzzo's commitment to operate the Cinema under the Cineplex logo in accordance with Cineplex's standards, as applied throughout its organization, with Cineplex to book all films on behalf of Guzzo and to advertise the Cinema as a Cineplex theatre in the same newspaper space as it advertised its other Montreal area theatres. Cinéma Métropolitain inc. and Cinéma Le Paradis inc. were also party to the Booking Agreement in the same way as Guzzo, merging with its provisions a similar arrangement they had entered into with Cineplex in 1985. Moreover, the Mis-en-causes intervened in the Operating Agreement to guarantee Guzzo's obligations under both that agreement and the Lease. Cineplex agreed in section 13 of the Operating Agreement to take over the Cinema at Carrefour's request and operate it if Guzzo failed to cure a default within the delay provided under the Lease or the Operating Agreement.

In May 1998 Carrefour learned that Guzzo had removed the Cineplex signs on the Shopping Centre pylon, at the mall entrance leading to the Cinema and at the Cinema entrance. After its attorneys sent a notice of default to Guzzo, Carrefour also learned that the latter and Cineplex had cancelled a 1996 contract that had replaced the Booking Agreement while retaining the Franchise Conditions. Neither Guzzo nor Cineplex had sought Carrefour's permission for any of the foregoing, in spite of the Matrix Agreements. Guzzo promptly informed Carrefour that it had no intention of restoring the Cineplex signage, otherwise operating under the Cineplex name or booking movies through Cineplex.

After a delay of 30 days Carrefour exercised its right to become the owner of the Cinema equipment by having its attorneys send Guzzo a cheque for the $1 purchase price as well as an agreement of sale. It also called upon Guzzo to vacate, and for Cineplex to occupy and operate the Cinema.

By August 1998 Defendants had still refused to comply with its demands after exchanges of correspondence among counsel. Carrefour therefore brought proceedings seeking an interlocutory and a permanent injunction. It asks that Defendants be ordered to perform their obligations under the Operating Agreement, namely that Guzzo vacate the Cinema and that Cineplex occupy and operate the Cinema in accordance with the terms of the Lease ("Primary Conclusion"), or subsidiarily, that they restore the status quo ante by complying with all the Franchise Conditions ("Subsidiary Conclusion"). Carrefour also asks to be declared the owner of the Cinema equipment in either alternative.

Since each Defendant's contestation of the motion for interlocutory injunction is identical to its plea to the application for permanent injunction, Carrefour was authorized to proceed directly to trial on the latter.

PLAINTIFF'S POSITION

Plaintiff argues that it has a clear right to the relief it seeks in view of the Defendants' manifest breach, without having to prove any actual or prospective damages. Because it seeks a final, not an interlocutory injunction, it asserts that it need not concern itself about the balance of hardship between itself and the Defendants. It seeks simply the unconditional performance of the Matrix Agreements. There is no dispute that Defendants have behaved in the way Carrefour complains of. The issue is whether they should on that account be forced to behave otherwise. For that reason the Court believes it will be more helpful to analyze Plaintiffs legal arguments in the context of rebuttal to Defendants' rather than to deal with each set of arguments separately, since prima facie at any rate, Plaintiff appears to be entitled to specific performance.

DEFENDANTS' POSITION

While many issues emerge from Defendants' arguments, in general they fall into two categories. The first comprises issues that relate to the valid contracting of the obligations Plaintiff seeks to enforce. These arguments are particularly Guzzo's. It contends that its consent was vitiated by commercial duress from Cineplex and Carrefour's false representations, and that the centrepiece of the contractual matrix, the Booking Agreement, is void because it offends public order by contravening the Competition Act.

The second category of issues concerns the performance of the Operating and Booking Agreements, assuming they were validly formed in the first place. Both Defendants argue that since the essential objective of the Matrix Agreements has been attained, even if their terms have not been literally complied with, Carrefour has suffered no damage and is very unlikely ever to do so. They also claim that an injunction will not really provide the relief Carrefour seeks, exceeds the Court's powers, will likely create further litigation, make for difficult supervision and adversely affect third parties, in this case the movie-going public at large. Finally, they contend that Carrefour is acting in bad faith by insisting on a remedy unnecessarily disruptive to Defendants and completely out of proportion to any prejudice it has suffered or can anticipate.

VALIDITY OF CONTRACTS

Duress

Guzzo accuses Cineplex of forcing it to enter the Booking Agreement since not doing so meant seeing its business destroyed. This was because it feared that Cineplex, with its far greater purchasing power, would prevail on the major distributors not to supply it with first run releases. Angelo Guzzo testified that until recently challenged by his group, an unwritten rule existed that independent operators who dared to open theatres in the "backyard" of the two major exhibitors, Cineplex and Famous Players, were simply frozen out of receiving any new release exhibited by them in that territory.

In 1985 Cineplex agreed not to compete with Guzzo in the latter's established area east of Pie IX Boulevard in Montreal, where Cineplex then had only one theatre but Guzzo had two. In return, Guzzo agreed to pay Cineplex a minimum annual booking fee of $300,000. Guzzo claims, however, that the booking service was a sham from the beginning, the fee being in reality "protection" money paid to keep Cineplex at bay. Guzzo itself selected its own films from Cineplex's distributors and Cineplex did not interfere.

Angelo Guzzo related that when he saw the Cinema being built, he realized that he would be forced out of business unless Cineplex bought his theatres east of Pie IX or he bought their rights in the Cinema lease. He put the choice to Cineplex, who opted for the latter alternative, Mr. Guzzo and Cineplex then approached Harry Glassman with the proposal. Jean-Pierre Desmarais, Guzzo's lawyer for the transaction, testified that the Franchise Conditions were last minute additions insisted upon by Mr. Glassman after all the financial terms of an assignment had been agreed to. Yet the Court notes from a letter of May 15, 1991 from Mr. Desmarais to Mr. Glassman that more than a month before the closing, the Franchise Conditions were already agreed to. Mr. Glassman also testified, credibly in the view of the Court, that Cineplex's representative, Peter Mandell, assured him that although Cineplex would not run the Cinema, for all practical purposes it would be operated as if it were a Cineplex theatre and appear to the world as such.

Guzzo's defence that its consent was vitiated by duress derives from Articles 1402 and 1403 C.C.Q. The first article speaks of fear of serious injury to the person or property of a contractant induced by violence or other threats from his co-contractant. Lest there be any confusion as to what the scope of "threats" may entail, Article 1403 states that fear induced by the abusive exercise of a right or power or by the threat of such exercise vitiates consent.

The fear in this case would be that of Guzzo losing its entire business because of an inability, due to Cineplex's interference or the threat of same, to procure first run films from major suppliers as well as the threat of its opening in Guzzo's market area. In the view of the Court, a distinction has to be made between a fear of financial loss arising from competition in the normal course with a much stronger rival and a fear of such loss arising from a threat by the rival to exercise its superior power abusively. We see nothing in these facts to indicate that Guzzo, represented by able commercial counsel in entering the Matrix Agreements, had their essential clauses imposed without negotiation nor, in the absence of proof other than Guzzo's mere affirmation that it was "protection money", do we see how the $300,000 annual fee was necessarily abusive, despite the suggestion of extortion conveyed by that description. By virtue of Article 1404 C.C.Q., consent to a contract intended to deliver the person making it from fear of serious injury is not vitiated where the other contracting party, though aware of the state of necessity, is acting in good faith. Furthermore, if the $300,000 fee is lesion, Guzzo could not be relieved from it by virtue of Article 1405 C.C.Q. The assurance of a supply of profitable films and the containment of Cineplex's competition may well have been worth its money in any event. The Court is mindful that Guzzo lived with this situation for 13 years, and as late as April 1998, Vincent Guzzo was advising Cineplex that it would resist the latter's cancellation of the booking arrangements. If Guzzo was a victim, it seems to have been a willing one. The Court does not find the argument of signature under duress persuasive.

Signature under false pretences

Both Guzzo and Cineplex complain that they agreed to the Franchise Conditions because they were tricked into doing so by Harry Glassman's false representations that he had promised other tenants that there would be a Cineplex theatre in the mall. Article 1401 C.C.Q. provides that error on the part of one contractant induced by the fraud of another vitiates the first's consent when if not for the error it would not have contracted or would have done so on different terms.

Does Mr. Glassman's behaviour amount to a fraud? The Court does not think so. He would likely have told existing and prospective tenants that there would be a Cineplex theatre in the mall. The signed offer and the subsequent Lease would have been entirely consistent with that representation. He was proud and excited about the pending arrival of Cineplex, so it would be natural to tell others. That does not mean that he made contractual commitments to other tenants that Cineplex would be joining them. On the other hand, when he was informed that Cineplex wanted out and Guzzo wanted in, he was undoubtedly disappointed and worried. The Court believes his testimony that he would have been embarrassed vis-à-vis the other tenants at this turn of events and said as much to Guzzo and Cineplex.

PERFORMANCE OF THE CONTRACTS

There is nothing to enforce because the essential intent of the contracts is being satisfied

According to Defendants, the essential "prestation" of the Operating Agreement, properly interpreted, is being performed. Since 1991, Guzzo has expanded to the point where it has more screens in the Greater Montreal area than either of its much larger rivals, Cineplex or Famous Players, deals directly with the major film distributors, as they do, and shows the same kind of first run films. This proof was not contradicted. Guzzo also led proof to show its theatres are more comfortable (wider and higher seats) than most and make use of the latest audio and visual equipment. It is also a prime tenant of Ivanhoe, the real estate arm of the Caisse de Dépôt, in three major Quebec shopping centres. Apparently Ivanhoe, a far more significant real estate operator than Carrefour, has had no difficulty with cinemas in its malls being operated by Guzzo under the Guzzo name.

According to Defendants, the Quebec legislator requires scrutiny of the circumstances in which contracts are performed to determine whether their provisions are unreasonable or excessive given the essential interests the parties expressly or implicitly sought to promote or protect. In their view what may have been consciously intended, expressed as such and reasonable when a contract was entered into may no longer be so in the light of changed circumstances. These would make it unnecessary for a creditor to require the performance to protect the essential interests intended for protection by the contract.

The danger of this approach is that it invites the Court to intervene unnecessarily in the affairs of contractants whose expression of intent should normally be taken at face value. Protecting only the parties' essential interests can too easily become a means by which they evade their obligations when it no longer suits their purposes to perform them. A more appropriate standard for invoking the sanction of the Court in the interpretation and enforcement of contracts is not identification of what the parties may really need but what they really wanted when they entered the contract, as made evident by their expression then and their conduct since. Identification of the parties' needs may be a useful technique for a mediator, but not especially so for an adjudicator. The Court has seen nothing to persuade it that Carrefour's insistence on the continued performance of the Franchise Conditions is other than in conformity with the parties' original intent. Furthermore, the Court believes it would not have been beyond the foresight of the parties in 1991 that Guzzo could one day expand and become a significant movie exhibitor itself. Yet they said nothing to address that contingency. The fact that they did not should be taken as indicating they did not intend to, so that Guzzo's success since does not now become a ground to relieve it or Cineplex of the Franchise Conditions.

No prejudice suffered by Petitioner

In any case Defendants further argue, a creditor cannot enforce specific performance unless he suffers some bodily, moral or material injury (in French, "préjudice") caused by the debtor through its failure to honour its contractual undertakings. They rely on Article 1458 C.C.Q.:

> 1458. Every person has a duty to honour his contractual undertakings. Where he fails in this duty, he is liable for any bodily, moral or material injury he causes to the other contracting party and is liable to reparation for the injury; neither he nor the other party may in such a case avoid the rules governing contractual liability by opting for rules that would be more favourable to them."

According to Cineplex, civil responsibility means that every obligation, whether contractual or extra-contractual, gives rise to an obligation of reparation in case of its breach. Reparation is in fact the only available remedy, (leaving aside resiliation of the contract if the prejudice is serious enough to warrant it), but all reparation, they contend, requires some bodily, moral or material prejudice to repair. (And it may be assumed for the sake of their argument, that all prejudice must fall only into one of those three categories.)

This argument is based on a foregone conclusion that because according to some definitions, a prejudice can be "repaired" by specific performance, all specific performance necessarily requires a prejudice to repair. Yet an analysis of the first six chapters of Title One (Obligations in General) of Book Five of the Civil Code of Quebec leads instead to the conclusion that specific performance is a remedy separate from that of reparation. The latter arises only when a breach of an obligation causes some prejudice, while the former's justification is the failure to perform the obligation alone, simply because it exists, even if no prejudice results.

Thus Section 2 of Chapter 6 of the Title, entitled "Right to Enforce Performance" infers in Article 1590, styled as the "General Provision", that specific performance is normally the remedy of choice in the event of the debtor's failure to perform an obligation. The creditor has the right to demand that the obligation be performed "in full, properly and without delay". Failure to do so engenders the right to "force" specific performance, albeit by reason of Article 1601, only "in cases which admit of it". The debtor is then forced either to perform the obligation or pay the cost of its performance by the creditor or someone else at his request (Article 1602). Neither alternative depends on any pre-existing prejudice. No such qualification of the creditor's right to full, prompt and proper performance is expressed.

It is thus misleading to describe specific performance as reparation. The sole legal justification for specific performance of a contractual obligation is the will of the parties that it be performed, sanctioned by the force of the state if it is not. It is noteworthy that the Civil Code of Quebec avoids any reference to "réparation en nature" or "réparation par équivalent". It speaks more accurately of "l'exécution en nature" and "l'exécution par équivalent", neutral terms that apply to any kind of obligation.

Carrefour's burden of proof in a claim of specific performance is therefore satisfied once it establishes that there has been a breach of the Franchise Conditions. It does not have to establish any present or future prejudice, other than the loss of the performance it wishes to re-establish. Defendants' only means of escape would then be to establish that performance of the Franchise Conditions is impossible (not a case which admits of it) or would contravene public order.
A simple example may illustrate the point. If Guzzo hires a painter to paint the front of its theatre navy blue and the painter paints it black instead, it would not be a sufficient defence against Guzzo's demand that he redo the job or pay for someone else doing so, to plead that Guzzo suffers no damage from the substituted colour.

Difficulties of supervising Subsidiary Conclusion

Guzzo also argues that ordering the Subsidiary Conclusion would result in practical difficulties of applying the Booking Agreement and problems of supervision for the Court. As already stated above, however, the Court does not consider that granting the Subsidiary Conclusion necessarily implies reactivating the Booking Agreement in its entirety. It suffices that the parties comply with its provisions in their application to the Cinema. Furthermore, these provisions are not so complex, novel and difficult to comprehend or apply that the Court would likely face great difficulty in enforcing them should that ever prove necessary. The operative test is whether the terms of the injunction can be defined with precision sufficient to permit a finding of breach beyond a reasonable doubt if the Defendants are ever cited for contempt for having disobeyed it. As the late Mr. Justice Henry Steinberg so aptly said in La Compagnie de Construction Belcourt ltée v. Golden Griddle Pancake House Limited:

> "Finally, the Court must determine whether an order can be appropriately framed. In this determination, thc judgc must bcar in mind that the effect of an injunction is to transform a private obligation into a public duty. If the order is to be executory, the nature and extent of such duty must be expressed clearly so that a breach thereof be susceptible of proof beyond reasonable doubt. If the order is ambiguous and a breach cannot ever be established, the remedy itself becomes a mockery."

In recent years, Quebec courts have seen fit to grant mandatory injunctions of specific performance in more challenging circumstances than present here - resumption of operation by retail tenants of shopping centres in accordance with lengthy and complex leases being a prime example"

Other examples have included the continued provision of complex treatment by a hospital, the reinstatement of an automobile dealership by a car manufacturer and the forced re-activation of a complicated contract involving the resale of electrical power at a discount to multiple subscribers of the plaintiff after the defendant supplier had closed its operations and dispersed its personnel
Limitation of remedy to forfeiture of equipment

Guzzo argues that the sole appropriate remedy to exercise if Carrefour's complaint is well-founded is the clause of forfeiture of the equipment, a penal clause that once invoked, excludes the other conclusions sought by Carrefour. Moreover, Guzzo asserts that the penal clause should be reduced because it has already paid more than $1,000,000 for the equipment and more than $4,000,000 in rent, as well as complying with the Lease in all material respects. The Court should therefore use its discretionary power to reduce the penalty.

The Court disagrees. The clause is neither a valid penal clause nor hypothec because no sum is stipulated, as required by Articles 1622 and 2689 C.C.Q. respectively. It is also invalid as a forfeiture of the equipment by virtue of Article 1801 C.C.Q., which provides that any clause by which a creditor, with a view to securing the performance of the obligation of his debtor, reserves the right to become the irrevocable owner of the property or to dispose of it, is deemed not written.

Finally, the Court does not believe that forfeiture of the equipment was intended as a separate remedy, but rather one to be exercised with the Primary Conclusion or any other remedy that would have Guzzo evicted from the Cinema. With its ownership of the equipment already assured, Carrefour would then be in an ideal position to assure continued operation by Cineplex or some other tenant in place of Guzzo. Since the Court does not believe that Guzzo should be evicted, the question of forfeiture of equipment is, however, academic.

Carrefour's bad faith

Guzzo accuses Carrefour of bad faith for a variety of reasons. These are:

1. It obtained Defendants' agreement to use the Cineplex banner under false pretences in the first place.
2. It tacitly accepted identification of the Cinema as a Guzzo cinema by failing to complain for almost six months, though it was aware of the change.
3. It wants to trick the public, contrary to the Trade Marks Act [See Note 18 below], the Competition Act and the Quebec Consumer Protection Act.
4. Its real purpose is to harm Guzzo so as to be able to force it to pay certain charges under the Lease that have been in dispute and to be able to negotiate more favourable terms for a new Lease of an expanded Cinema area.
5. It is abusing its civil rights, in that both conclusions it seeks are excessive and unreasonable, being out of proportion to any prejudice it may suffer from the defaults complained of.

The first four grounds of Carrefour's alleged bad faith can be rapidly disposed of. Defendants have not established that they were misled by false pretences. Mr. Glassman's protests that he would be embarrassed because he had told tenants they would have Cineplex as a neighbour are not the same thing as saying he had given them contractual commitments to that effect. The use of the Cineplex trade mark by Guzzo would not harm or deceive the public, who would be able to discover that Guzzo is merely a licensee of the mark by checking the register of registered users, and the operation of the Cinema itself by one Defendant rather than another does not offend any public interest.

The argument that Carrefour tacitly accepted the situation by failing to react to the change of signs until six months had gone by is not persuasive either. Neither Defendant bothered to tell Carrefour that they had cancelled the Franchise Conditions. The only individual who would have been aware of the sign change around the time it took place was a building manager at the Shopping Centre who had no authority to consent to any change in lease conditions and whose consent was not sought in any case.

The ulterior motives attributed to Mr. Glassman are not credible. Carrefour's ongoing dispute with Guzzo over its share of real estate escalation for the Shopping Centre and its disagreement over less important matters (extra garbage disposal charges, lighting, electricity consumption, common area expenses, membership in the Merchants' Association, placement of garbage containers and opening hours) are hardly likely to have provoked such a costly reaction as the present unrelated proceedings. The parties have already been dealing with the tax escalation issue through arbitration, as called for in the Lease and they have that recourse available for the other matters as well. The same improbability attaches to Mr. Glassman's alleged use of these proceedings to force better terms from Guzzo in negotiating a major expansion of the Cinema. Imposing unrelated, protracted and expensive litigation on a prospective significant business collaborator is hardly a credible way to ensure that negotiations will continue, much less be fruitful.

This leaves Guzzo's argument that Carrefour is not in good faith because the alternative conclusions it seeks are excessive. Carrefour's good faith is presumed, the burden of proof being on Defendants to show otherwise (Article 2805 C.C.Q.).

In the view of the Court, that burden is not satisfied by simply establishing that Carrefour has not yet suffered any prejudice. As noted above, the primary purpose of specific performance is preventive, not reparative. Defendants then argue that Carrefour is presumptively acting in bad faith by claiming that it will not likely suffer any future prejudice through absence of the Cineplex name. As already stated, however, no issue of past, present or future prejudice other than the loss of the performance alone of the obligations whose performance Carrefour demands can be germane to the issue of its good faith. The relevant criteria are set forth in Article 7 C.C.Q. The right may not be exercised with the intent of injuring another, and the manner of exercise - not the fact of the exercise itself - cannot be excessive or unreasonable. If any of these elements can be proved, the creditor is presumed to be acting in bad faith, or at any rate, not in good faith.

On the facts of this case, nothing indicates that Carrefour has acted with the purpose of causing harm to either Defendant, nor that it has acted with undue haste or harshness in pursuing its remedy.

Unless the creditor acts with celerity or severity disproportionate to any prejudice that may be apprehended in the circumstances, including the loss of the performance of the obligation contracted, he is entitled to have the obligation performed in accordance with the contract. It is therefore difficult to conceive of a situation where the promisee's unvindictive, measured insistence on performance of promises made to it that are possible to perform and not contrary to public order can be the occasion for complaint by the promisor.

The promisor has a heavier burden than simply establishing that the promisee cannot prove any present or future loss. In the opinion of the Court, the test of good faith is not so rigid from the promisee's standpoint. It suffices that he can reasonably attach some value to the promise at the time he demands that it be performed. The Court believes then that the promisee's lack of good faith would be satisfied by showing that no rational person placed in the same circumstances as the promisee would likely insist on the performance at all, or when and how the promisee does so, without creating a presumption that he is acting abusively. Examples that can be imagined might be Carrefour's insistence on Guzzo's continued use of the Cineplex name after Cineplex itself had gone out of business, gone bankrupt or simply changed its name, all under circumstances where no residual value to Carrefour of any kind in the name, even if not quantifiable, could be imagined. Such a test has not been met by Defendants here.

The balance of hardship favours Guzzo and Cineplex

Defendants argue that it would create greater hardship for them if they were compelled to obey a mandatory injunction than for Carrefour if they were not, and that the Court should therefore exercise its equitable discretion to deny the remedy. That argument, at least in so far as the Primary Conclusion is concerned, finds its reflection in the Civil Code provisions that save Guzzo from losing the entire benefit of the Lease unless serious prejudice results from its default (Articles 1604, 1863 and 1875). That conclusion is not reached by comparing the relative hardship suffered by Carrefour and Guzzo dependant on whether or not the remedy is granted. The Primary Conclusion is to be denied because the breach does not justify the remedy in its own right. The question of balance of convenience is more appropriately raised in considering whether or not to grant the Subsidiary Conclusion.

Yet it is now settled jurisprudence in Quebec that a creditor seeking a final order of injunction need not prove it would suffer relatively greater prejudice than the debtor if the remedy were not granted than if it is. Unlike the interlocutory stage, the balance of convenience is then no longer relevant. The question is decided solely after a motivated recognition of the definitive rights of the parties as they flow from the law and are supported by facts derived from proof that is complete and final. No other considerations are relevant.

Indeed, as noted above, the Civil Code does not require proof of any degree of prejudice, other than the deprivation of the performance of the obligation itself. The only restraint on the granting of the remedy is that performance of the obligation be possible (not that it be free of expense or difficulty) and that it not contravene public order. Quebec courts have progressively shed their former reluctance to grant final mandatory injunctions since the remedy became available under the 1965 reform of the Code of Civil Procedure. That reluctance had stemmed from a perception that since injunction was in origin a common law remedy, then following common law principles, it was not to be granted if some other useful remedy was available to the creditor, or if the balance of convenience favoured the debtor. It is now settled law that the creditor need not exercise other recourses in preference to specific performance, even if they are available, or even if the remedy would cause relative hardship for the debtor and none for itself. The thrust of the reformed Civil Code is that specific performance is presumed to be the remedy of choice in enforcing a contract of successive performance, limited only by considerations of possibility and public order, whereas the two alternate remedies, damages and resiliation, require proof of prejudice in addition to the breach.

Conclusion

For all the foregoing reasons the Court concludes that Plaintiff Carrefour Langelier inc. is entitled to an order of permanent injunction in accordance with its Subsidiary Conclusion.

WHEREFORE THE COURT:

> ISSUES a permanent order of injunction enjoining Defendant Cinéma Langelier inc., its officers, directors, employees, representatives, agents and associates to replace the signage located at the entrance to Plaintiff's shopping centre commonly known as Carrefour Langelier, as well as above the entrance to the premises therein leased by said Defendant, as well as adjacent thereto, and on the pylon in the parking lot of the said shopping centre, with the same or equivalent signage as indicated in the photographs

comprising Exhibit P-12, so that the Cineplex Odeon name, trade mark and logo will appear to the exclusion of "Guzzo", "Guzzo Theatres" or any derivation thereof;

ORDERS Defendants Cinéma Langelier inc. and Cineplex Odeon Corporation and its successor and their officers, directors, employees, representatives, agents and associates to immediately commence all programming and display of all films of the motion picture theatre complex located at the said shopping centre in accordance with conditions and criteria established for the operation of all motion picture theatres owned and operated by the said Cineplex Odeon Corporation and its successors;

ORDERS Defendant Cineplex Odeon Corporation and its successors to immediately commence the advertisement of all motion pictures displayed at the motion picture theatre complex located at the said shopping centre under the Cineplex Odeon column, and this without distinction from the other Cineplex Odeon theatres so listed, whatsoever;

AUTHORIZES the service of such orders to be issued herein at any time, including non-juridical days, and by any lawful means;

RESERVES unto Plaintiff all of its rights and recourses against Defendant Cinéma Langelier inc., as well as the Mis-en-causes, in damages;

THE WHOLE with costs against Defendants.

CASE 8.4

Copiscope Inc. v. TRM Copy Centers (Canada) Ltd.

[1998] Q.J. No. 3662, **Quebec Court of Appeal**

(Excerpts of Judgment)

TEXT OF JUDGMENT

THE COURT:— On an appeal from a judgement of the Superior Court, district of Montreal (the Honourable Jean Normand) rendered on March 27, 1998, which, in granting an interlocutory injunction at the request of respondent, enjoined appellant from, inter alia, soliciting business operators who had contracted with respondent to terminate their contractual relationship and also enjoined appellant from placing photocopy equipment on the premises of those who had contracted with respondent for a period of one year from the termination of the contract.

Having studied the file, heard the parties and deliberated;

For the reasons given in the written opinion of Mr. Justice Joseph R. Nuss, filed herewith, with which Madam Justice Thérèse Rousseau-Houle and Mr. Justice André Denis concur:

MAINTAINS the appeal with costs;

SETS aside the judgement of the Superior Court; and

DISMISSES the motion for interlocutory injunction with costs.

REASONS FOR JUDGMENT

OPINION OF NUSS J.A.:— Appellant Copiscope Inc. (Copiscope) appeals a judgement of the Superior Court, district of Montreal (the Honourable Jean Normand) rendered on March 27, 1998, which, in granting an interlocutory injunction at the request of respondent TRM Copy Centers (Canada) Ltd. (TRM Copy), enjoined Copiscope from, inter alia, soliciting business operators who had contracted with TRM Copy or inducing them to terminate their contractual relationship. Copiscope was also enjoined from placing photocopy equipment on the premises of those who had contracted with TRM Copy for a period of one year from the termination of the contract.

Factual background

TRM Copy is in the business of offering photocopy services to the public by means of photocopy machines which are placed in stores carrying on business operations of another nature, such as dépanneurs (convenience stores) and pharmacies. In this opinion I refer to the owner of the store as the "business operator". A detailed written agreement entitled "Location Agreement" (the Contract) is entered into with each business operator. The Contract is set out in a preprinted document. It is not contested that it is a contract of adhesion within the meaning of article 1376 C.C.Q. The business operator pays TRM Copy a one-time fixed fee of $95.00 plus applicable taxes and gives the latter the right to place the TRM photocopy machine in its store. Customers of the business operator who use the photocopy services pay the fee to the business operator. The latter, in addition to providing the space for the machine, buys the photocopy paper and the ink from TRM Copy. At the end of the month, TRM Copy collects the revenue generated by the use of the photocopy machines and pays a pre-established proportion to the business operator. There is no term for the operation of the Contract, however either party can have it terminated upon giving the other party a thirty day written notice.

TRM Copy commenced operating in the Montreal area in 1992 and by 1997 had, pursuant to the Contract, installed its photocopy machines in approximately 700 hundred business locations.

The clause in the Contract in issue is headed "Noncompetition Covenant" (Covenant); it reads as follows:

> 10. Noncompetition Covenant. It is specifically acknowledged and agreed by the parties that, in connection with the provision of the Equipment and the Signs to the Business hereunder, T.R.M. has imparted and shall continue to impart to the Business throughout the term hereof certain trade secrets affecting the operation of the Equipment by the Business. It is further acknowledged and agreed by the parties that the covenants contained in this Section 10 are reasonably necessary to protect T.R.M.'s interests and that T.R.M. is reasonably entitled to such protection. The Business therefore covenants and agrees that, except as contemplated herein, it shall not at any time during the Agreement and within a period of one (1) year from the Termination Date, either directly or indirectly by way of any interest in or connection with any corporation, other entity or person, as principle, agent, shareholder, partner or in any manner whatsoever, carry on, engage in or be engaged in or connected with or be interested in or advise any person in connection with the business of making photocopy equipment available for use by the public or otherwise providing photocopy services to the public within a twenty-five (25) mile radius of the Business location. For greater certainty, during the term of this Agreement, the Business agrees that it shall not place or allow to be placed at the Business location any photocopy equipment, other than the Equipment, for use by the Business' customers. (my underlining)

Until 1996 the Contract provided that it was to be governed by and construed in accordance with the laws of the State of Oregon. Since 1996, the Contract states that it is to be governed by and construed in accordance with the laws of the Province of Quebec.

Copiscope is also in the photocopy business. Amongst its operations in the

Montreal area is one similar to the one above described conducted by T.R.M. Copy. The parties are in competition with each other.

In mid-1997, Copiscope embarked on a program to persuade (or in the words of respondent "to induce") business operators to terminate their Contracts with TRM Copy and enter into agreements with Copiscope. At times Copiscope provided the form for the thirty day termination notice to be sent to TRM Copy. In August 1997, TRM Copy sent a letter to Copiscope in which it communicated to the latter the text of the Noncompetition Covenant above set out and alleged that Copiscope was acting illegally in attempting to cause the termination of the Contracts.

Copiscope countered by alleging that the Noncompetition Covenant was illegal and that it was entitled to conduct the program upon which it was embarked. Copiscope continued to pursue its campaign of attempting to have the business operators terminate their Contracts with TRM Copy and to enter into agreements with it.

On November 18, 1997 TRM Copy instituted legal proceedings against Copiscope entitled "MOTION AND DECLARATION FOR THE ISSUANCE OF A PROVISIONAL, INTERLOCUTORY AND PERMANENT INJUNCTION". By this date Copiscope had signed approximately 21 agreements with business operators who had previously signed contracts with TRM Copy. The motion requested the following order of injunction:

> ORDER the issuance of a provisional injunction without notice, and an interlocutory and permanent injunction ordering Defendant Copiscope Inc., its officers, directors, managers, employees, representatives, agents and mandatories, and any other person having knowledge of the injunction to:
>
> a) restrain from placing or allowing to be placed at any location of a retailer contracting with Plaintiff, or so restrain for a period of one (1) year commencing from the date of termination of a retailer's Location Agreement with Plaintiff, any photocopying equipment for public use of such retailer's customers;
>
> b) restrain from soliciting or inducing by any means whatsoever any retailer contracting with Plaintiff to terminate its Location Agreement with Plaintiff or not to comply with the terms thereof, including the non-compete covenant stipulated in paragraph 10 of the standard Location Agreement, and to enter into any agreement with such retailer for the purposes of paragraph a); and
>
> c) restrain from disconnecting or tampering in any fashion with Plaintiff's photocopying equipment and signage at retail locations, either directly or indirectly, by direct act or omission, participation or inducement;

On November 20, 1997, Mass, J. dismissed the request for a provisional injunction.

The parties filed affidavits and documents and conducted cross-examinations on the affidavits. They both presented evidence on the law of the State of Oregon with respect to the validity of the Noncompetition Covenant because the Contracts executed until 1996 were to be interpreted according to the laws of that jurisdiction.

That trial judge decided that, in essence, the laws of Oregon and Quebec are to the same effect on this subject. I agree with him on this point.
By judgment dated March 27, 1998 the trial judge, in substance, granted the interlocutory injunction requested by TRM Copy.

On April 6, 1998, my colleague Mr. Justice Brossard granted leave to appeal. He also granted, in part, a motion to suspend execution of the judgment pending appeal, principally by suspending execution of the order in the paragraph which commences with the word "S'ABSTENIR" and by striking the word "indirectement" in the immediately following paragraph.

The Judgment

The trial judge came to the conclusion that TRM Copy had an apparent right. However, in his view the right was not clear and therefore he had to consider, the issues of the "balance of convenience" and whether there would be "a serious or irreparable injury" caused if the injunction were not granted. He ruled that the "balance of convenience" was in favor of TRM Copy because it was the latter's only business activity while Copiscope carried out other categories of business activities. The trial judge found that without the issue of an interlocutory injunction TRM Copy would suffer "serious or irreparable injury".

The trial judge after citing an extract from the testimony of the witness Sullo, Copiscope's Vice-President of Marketing, who confirmed that a "primary target would be a location where there would already be a copier in place".

The issue in appeal

The basic issue to be determined in this appeal is whether the Noncompetition Covenant in the Contract creates an apparent right in favor of TRM Copy which would justify the granting of an interlocutory injunction.
Analysis and discussion

Given the discretionary nature of the decision to either grant or refuse an interlocutory injunction, the Court of Appeal will not intervene unless the judge in first instance committed an error of law or did not exercise his discretion judicially.

Article 752 C.C.P. provides for the remedy of an interlocutory injunction:

> 752. In addition to an injunction, which he may demand by action, with or without other conclusions, a party may, at the commencement of or during a suit, obtain an interlocutory injunction.
>
> An interlocutory injunction may be granted when the applicant appears to be entitled to it and it is considered to be necessary in order to avoid serious or irreparable injury to him, or a factual or legal situation of such a nature as to render the final judgment ineffectual.

The Courts have elaborated a three part test to be applied in cases where an interlocutory injunction is sought. Recently, the Supreme Court of Canada referred to this test in RJR-MacDonald Inc. v. Canada (A.G.). Although that case dealt with Charter issues, the Court clearly indicated that a "three-part (...) test should be applied to applications for interlocutory injunctions (...) in both private law and Charter cases."

At the first stage, the Court must ascertain whether the applicant for the interlocutory injunction has demonstrated that its case raises a serious question to be tried. In Quebec, the "serious question" component of the test is more aptly named the stage at which it is determined whether or not the applicant has established the apparent right it is seeking to enforce. At the second stage, the applicant has to demonstrate that it will suffer irreparable harm or injury if the interlocutory injunction is refused. Finally, at the third stage, the Court considers the balance of convenience and compares the harm that will be suffered by each of the parties depending on whether or not the interlocutory injunction is granted.

In Société de développement de la Baie James et autres v. Chef Robert Kanatewat Mr. Justice Owen enunciated the three step approach in these oft cited terms:

> At the interlocutory injunction stage these rights are apparently either (a) clear, or (b) doubtful, or (c) nonexistent.
>
> (a) If it appears clear, at the interlocutory stage that the Petitioners have the rights which they invoke then the interlocutory injunction should be granted if considered necessary in accordance with the provisions of the second paragraph of Article 752 C.P. (b) However, if at this stage the existence of the rights invoked by the Petitioners appears doubtful then the Court should consider the balance of convenience and inconvenience in deciding whether an interlocutory injunction should be granted. (c) Finally if it appears, at the interlocutory stage, that the rights claimed are non-existent then the interlocutory injunction should be refused. (p. 183)

In the case before us, if the Noncompetition Covenant is valid, TRM Copy has established an apparent right which is clear. Even if TRM Copy does not establish a clear right, it must at least demonstrate that it has a right, although it may be a doubtful one, in order to fulfill the requirement of possessing an apparent right. On the other hand if the Noncompetition Covenant is not arguably valid, TRM Copy has failed to establish an apparent right and the application for interlocutory injunction should be dismissed without the necessity of addressing the issues of "balance of convenience" and "irreparable or serious injury".

Both parties submit that at the interlocutory stage we are to use the test of whether the Noncompetition Covenant is manifestly unreasonable in order to determine whether there is an apparent right. If the Covenant is manifestly unreasonable then it is invalid and there is an absence of the apparent right which is an essential condition for the granting of an interlocutory injunction.

The judge in first instance correctly identified and described the three steps to be considered, as enunciated by the jurisprudence.

However, with great respect for the trial judge, it is my opinion that the Noncompetition Covenant before us is manifestly unreasonable and therefore invalid.

The validity of the Noncompetition Covenant must be determined on the basis of well settled principles set out in the jurisprudence.

1) Undertakings in restraint of trade are generally against public order;
2) there may, within reasonable limits, be contractual restrictions on the freedom to conduct a specified commercial activity;
3) the validity of such restrictions is dependant on their being reasonable, particularly regarding the length of time that they are to apply and the territory where they are to be applicable;
4) furthermore, it must be shown that the restrictions are necessary for the reasonable protection of the interests of the party in whose favor they are granted;
5) if the restrictions do not meet the test of reasonability they will be struck down as being contrary to public order.

According to the Noncompetition Covenant in the Contract, the business operator is prevented from placing the photocopy machine of a competitor in any other store in which he may have an interest. Nor can he open a new store or go into partnership with someone else and place the photocopy machine of a competitor in the new store even if it is some twenty miles away. The restriction applies to an area which is a circle having a 25 mile radius. This covers a vast area of 5,082 square kilometres. Although the business operator is restricted from placing the machine of a competitor in another store, TRM Copy does not undertake to supply a photocopying machine in such store should it be requested to do so.

The business operator cannot buy shares in a company which operates stores and has photocopy machines of competitors on its premises. There is not even an exception made for companies whose shares are publicly traded.

If the business operator should want to go into the photocopy business either in the manufacture or distribution of machines or to work for someone in that business or connected with that business he is prevented from doing so.

All these restrictions would apply for one year after the termination of the Contract and cover an area of 5,082 square kilometres. Counsel for TRM Copy, at the hearing, submitted to the Court that according to the Covenant these restrictions would apply even if it was TRM Copy who effected the termination.

The concluding sentence of the Noncompetition Covenant standing by itself, reads:

> "For greater certainty, during the term of this Agreement, the Business agrees that it shall not place or allow to be placed at the Business location any photocopy equipment, other than the Equipment, for use by the Business' customers."

This restriction read literally would only prevent the business operator from placing the photocopy machine of a competitor on its premises during the term of the contract. Thus, if the contract is terminated, the literal meaning would suggest that the restriction would not apply thereafter because the term would be at an end. There would be no restriction for the one year period subsequent to the termination set out in the main body of the Covenant. TRM Copy does not accept this literal interpretation and argues that the restriction does apply for one year after the termination of the Contract because the one year period is mentioned earlier in the main body of the Covenant. The use of the words, in the concluding sentence, "For greater certainty..." is confusing but perhaps lends some support to this submission. However, if we are to read "one year from the Termination Date" into the concluding sentence because of this wording in the main body of the Covenant, then the concluding sentence would be inextricably bound-up in the earlier part of the Covenant and would be saturated with the unreasonable restrictions set-out which I have mentioned above. In any event there is ambiguity as to whether the one year period applies to the restriction in the concluding sentence and the ambiguity is to be interpreted against TRM Copy who is attempting to impose the restriction.

Furthermore, there is no proof of any valid reason why a business operator who decides to terminate the Contract with TRM Copy should be deprived for one year from providing the product of a competitor to its customers. Neither is there any reason advanced to justify this prohibition over the vast area of 5,082 square kilometres covering any other business in which it may have an interest or in which it may wish to have an interest. A fortiori there is absolutely no justification for TRM Copy, in the event that it is the party who terminates the Contract, to prevent the business operator from offering photocopy services of a competitor.

TRM Copy submits that it invests approximately $2,345. in the installation of each photocopy machine and assumes the risk of an unprofitable venture. Accordingly, it argues that it is entitled to the protection in the Covenant. I disagree. The restrictions set out in the Covenant are exorbitant and are grossly excessive for the reasonable protection of the interests of TRM Copy.

The beginning of the Covenant states that TRM Copy

> ... imparted and shall continue to impart to the Business throughout the term hereof certain trade secrets affecting the operation of the Equipment by the Business. It is further acknowledged and agreed by the parties that the covenants contained in this Section 10 are reasonably necessary to protect TRM's interests and that TRM is reasonably entitled to such protection. ... (my underlining)

These assertions are set out in an agreement which is a contract of adhesion. Article 1379 C.C.Q. sets out the definition of such a contract:

> Art. 1379. A contract of adhesion is a contract in which the essential stipulations were imposed or drawn up by one of the parties, on his behalf or upon his instructions, and were not negotiable.
>
> Any contract that is not a contract of adhesion is a contract by mutual agreement.

There is no evidence that the business operator has knowledge of any trade secrets. Its sole role is that of ascertaining that the machine has a supply of paper and ink and collecting the fee for its use.

There were no negotiations between the parties to the Contract; the business operator was given for signature a preprinted form prepared by TRM Copy. The assertions in the Covenant above cited do not appear to have any basis in fact. They smack of an attempt to justify manifestly unreasonable and abusive restrictions by the insertion of an illusory consideration. I attach no legal consequence to them.

I would accept the opinion of Copiscope's expert which is persuasive and based on the exact text with which we are concerned and I would conclude, at this stage, that under Oregon law, as under the law of Quebec, the Noncompetition Covenant is illegal and unenforceable.

Conclusion

In my view the Noncompetition Covenant is manifestly unreasonable and therefore invalid. It follows that respondent has not established an apparent right which is necessary for the granting of an interlocutory injunction.

For the above reasons I would maintain the appeal with costs, set aside the judgment of the Superior Court and dismiss the motion for interlocutory injunction with costs.

LEGAL TERMS

In your reading, you came across the following terms. Be sure that you can explain each, to ensure your understanding of the material you have been reading. If you are uncertain as to the meaning of any term, review the material in the chapter for clarification. If necessary, consult a dictionary for further information or discuss the term(s) with your instructor.

transaction	contract	obligation
prestation	sanction	offer
acceptance	protective supervision	lesion
capacity	cause of contract	form
object of contract	contract of adhesion	synallagmatic
onerous	tacit acceptance	emancipation
revoked	offer lapsed	vitiated
public order	bilateral agreement	presumed
consumer contract	abusive clause	null (null and void)
minor	express acceptance	

REVIEW QUESTIONS

1. How can you identify an obligation in a contract? Give three examples to illustrate your answer.

2. Explain the legal difference(s) between a written and a verbal contract.

3. Define a legal offer.

4. Define a legal acceptance. Explain where and when an acceptance is considered to be received.

5. Give an example of an invitation to make an offer.

6. How does the *Civil Code* define a contract?

7. Why is legal capacity an important element if a contract is to be considered valid? Explain the defects that may affect a person's consent.

8. Is it possible for an object in a contract to disappear? Explain.

9. If a person of full age who suffers from mental illness signs an agreement promising to sell his or her stamp collection, can the buyer force the completion of the sale? Explain your answer.

10. It two contracting parties can't agree on the meaning of a clause in their contract, what should the court look at in settling this dispute?

Chapter 9

CIVIL LIABILITY

OBJECTIVES

This chapter was prepared to enable you to achieve the following objectives:

1. To understand the difference between contractual responsibility and civil liability (responsibility).
2. To understand why civil liability is an important concept in our society.
3. To appreciate the fault concept and its role in civil liability.
4. To identify the various forms of civil liability that a person might encounter.
5. To understand the defences available to a person being sued for civil liability.
6. To identify the limits of civil liability as set by law towards balancing collective versus individual rights.

INTRODUCTION
Section 9.1

9.1.1 Description

Along with an understanding of contracts and the obligations that arise between parties to an agreement, it is essential that the reader also have a solid comprehension of **civil liability** or **civil responsibility** – these two terms are used interchangeably. The principle of civil liability holds that people must be held accountable or liable for their actions and for the consequences of their actions.

In some cases, a person may also be held responsible for injuries caused to others even though they may not personally have caused the damage. This is known as **vicarious liability**. This may take place when the damage or injury is caused by people who are under their control (children or employees) or things under their control (automobiles, machines or buildings). Therefore, under certain conditions, a party will be called upon to compensate those injured not through his direct action.

> *...before your next class...:*
> *Perform an internet search using the terms civil responsibility. What interesting cases did you discover?*

9.1.2 Contractual v. Extra-Contractual Liability

When a contract exists between people, the failure of one party to carry out the obligations that were agreed upon may result in a legal action by the other party to claim compensation for the damage the failure has caused. Article 1458 of the *Civil Code* declares that "Every person has a duty to honour his contractual undertakings."

It may happen, however, that a person causes damage to someone else, through his or her fault, even though there is no contract between them. For example, a boy throws a baseball through a window or someone accidentally knocks over a flower pot on a window ledge and it falls to the street injuring a passer-by.

In these examples, there is no "contract" between the person causing the damage and the victim. Nevertheless, since damage has been caused, and is due to the fault of another person, the one at fault is held "civilly liable" for the resulting damage. This liability will exist whether the damage was caused deliberately or unintentionally. The principle is clearly stated in article 1457 of the *Civil Code*:

> *"Every person has a duty to abide by the rules of conduct which lie upon him.....not to cause injury to another.*
>
> *"Where he is endowed with reason and fails in this duty, he is responsible for any injury he causes to another person, and is liable to reparation for the injury..."*

Whether damage results from failure to respect the obligations in a contract (contractual damage), or from the fault of someone where there is no contract (extra-contractual damage), the law clearly sets out the limitations that apply when an injured person seeks to be compensated for damages suffered. The law also strictly limits one's right to sue under both contractual and extra-contractual liability for the same damages.

The difference between these two types of actions is illustrated in the following example. John, who is renting an apartment from Mr. Bedard at 730 Querbes, was sitting one day on his balcony with his friend Sandy. Suddenly, the balcony collapsed and fell two stories down onto Ms. Manos, who happened to be walking by at that moment. All three people were seriously injured and suffered extensive physical and material damages. In this case, John would sue Mr. Bedard (the owner of the building) under article 1458 of the *Code* because of the lease, a contractual agreement, requiring the owner to provide the tenant with a safe living environment in return for a rent. For their part, Sandy and Ms. Manos would have to sue Mr. Bedard under article 1457 of the *Code* or any other related civil responsibility articles, which are discussed below, because they have no contractual relationship with him.

> *Selected articles of related to civil liability are reproduced in Appendix "9-A" at the end of this chapter.*

Personal Liability
Section 9.2

9.2.1 Conditions

In order that a person may be found personally liablc, ccrtain conditions must exist before the injured party can expect any compensation through the court system. These conditions, found in article 1457 of the *Civil Code*, require the person who caused the damage be endowed with reason, that he or she is at fault and as a result of this fault real damages were caused to another person.

9.2.1.1 Endowed With Reason

The person being sued must be endowed with reason, capable of discerning right from wrong. This means that the person has a sufficient level of intelligence and be of an age old enough to appreciate the consequences of their actions. Hence, a person whose mental faculties (due to a handicap, old age, illness or other factors) deprive them of reason, or a young child, may be free of any responsibility for their actions. In the case of a child, jurisprudence has found that a child must be at least seven years or older to be held responsible. Circumstances and characteristics of the child will determine if this rule is strictly applied. Therefore, if a person is not endowed with reason, that is, cannot tell right from wrong, they cannot be held responsible and their actions are considered to be a "*force majeur*" or **superior force** over which they have no control. In such a case, the victim may possibly seek compensation from a parent of a child or from those in charge of an older person who is not able to make this distinction.

An exception may be made under this heading for a person who causes damage while under the influence of drugs or alcohol. While these substances may result in the person being unable to distinguish right from wrong, the person may still be held liable for damage caused because the person has deliberately created this condition.

9.2.1.2 Fault

The person being sued must have committed a fault. To determine if a person is at fault, their actions, or in some cases inaction, must be compared to that of a reasonably prudent and diligent person within the context of the case at hand. Were the consequences of the person's actions foreseeable for a person who is reasonably prudent and diligent? If not, then the person is not at fault since the consequences could have not been normally foreseeable. If on the other hand the answer is positive, then the person has committed a fault that departs from acceptable standards of action in our society.

"Fault" is the violation of a duty imposed by law that requires a person to be aware of the consequences of their actions. This duty is clearly expressed in the words of Article 1457 of the *Civil Code.*

Consider the situation where Mr. Lorenzo parks outside a store to run in for a minute to get a carton of milk. He leaves his car running and unlocked and the window open. Suni, age 11, walks by, and wonders if he can move the car. The result is that he puts it in motion and the car hits the front of a store across the street. Clearly, Lorenzo should have foreseen that such event might occur that could cause damage or injury because of his thoughtlessness. He did not take the care that a reasonably prudent and diligent person would have taken. The fault in this case was failure to foresee the consequence of his action and failure to take reasonable steps to prevent such consequences, by turning off the motor and locking his car.

A person may be at fault as a result of something they did (an action), or by omitting to do something expected of them, such as not putting sand on your stairs during an ice storm.

Where more than one person have together taken part in a wrongful act that causes injury to a third party, all of said persons may be held solidarily liable for said damages (each person at fault can be held liable for 100% of the damages).

9.2.1.3 Damages

The person being sued must not only have committed a fault, but that fault must also result in actual damages suffered by the victim. A relationship between the act (fault) of the person being sued and the damages suffered by the plaintiff must exist. The damages may be **bodily** (physical injury), **moral** (psychological or mental illness or damage to a person's reputation), or **material** (medical expenses or damage to property, such as clothing, cars, houses, merchandise, or causing loss of income). The damages must be certain and in the present form, as highlighted in article 1611 of the *Civil Code,* but can also be future damages if they are certain to take place and a dollar value can be easily assessed. Future damages are also possible when a creditor, suffers bodily injury. Under article 1615 of the *Civil Code,* the creditor may petition the Court to reserve his or her right to apply for additional damages within a three year period of the initial judgment.

Damages may also be claimed by someone who indirectly suffered as a result of the actions of the person at fault. For example, a ball is thrown against a window, breaking the glass. The owner of the building can claim damages. Additionally, if someone close to the window is injured by the broken glass, the injured person may also claim compensation. Furthermore, a family member who suffered shock from having witnessed the injury, causing them to stay home from work for several days, may also be compensated for lost wages.

In addition to bodily, moral and material damages, a victim may also demonstrate the need for punitive damages. If proven the defendant's fault was intentionally and violated the victim's *Charter* protected rights, the court could be asked to award a sum of money as a punishment to teach the defendant a lesson. However, it must be noted that if the defendant was prosecuted under the criminal law for these violations and was found guilty, the victim would be foreclosed from requesting punitive damages in a civil trial. Since the intention of punitive damages is to teach the defendant a lesson, imposing punitive damages civilly after a criminal decision was rendered against the defendant would entail a double punishment for the same fault. In our legal system, a criminal prosecution's purpose is to teach the defendant a lesson also. As a result, only one punishment may generally be imposed.

9.2.1.4 The Causal Link

The fourth element required to satisfy the Court that a person is to be held liable for damages is to show that there is a causal link between the person's act or omission and the damage that was caused.

Michel was going upstairs to see his father who lived on the second floor. A step broke as he put his weight on it and he fell, injuring himself. The owner of the building knew the stairs had to be kept in good condition. The poor condition of the stairs demonstrates a fault, the damage is evident from Michel's broken arm – the only other element was whether the fault was the cause of the damages. Did the building owner comply with his duty to foresee the possibility of damage and take every precaution to avoid it? If the step had been examined a few days before the incident to ensure it was in good condition, and had been loosened that morning by some movers taking a piano up to the third floor, there might not be a causal link between the fault and the damage. The building owner cannot be expected to examine the steps several times every day to ensure their condition. Rather, a certain level of vigilance is expected, such as examinations on a reasonable and regular basis.

The link between the fault and the damage has to be proven to the satisfaction of the Court in order to succeed with a claim for compensation under Civil Liability.

9.2.2 Defences

The law offers a person being sued for civil liability some possible defences, which may exonerate them partially or totally from having to compensate another person for damages resulting from a personal act.

9.2.2.1 Victim's Actions

It is possible for the defendant to argue that the injuries sustained by the victim are directly linked to the victim's fault, the victim's acceptance of the risk or that the victim aggravated the damages suffered.

Under certain circumstances, a victim's injuries may be partially or wholly attributed to his own fault. Depending on the role the victim played in his own injuries, the person being sued may be found responsible for only a portion or none of the damages. For instance, the victim broke a leg while skating on a private ice-rink. The victim proves the injury took place because of poor ice conditions. The owner, however, demonstrates that the victim was skating in a reckless manner. As a result, the court finds the rink owner responsible for 60% percent of the victim's damages and attributes the remaining 40% percent to the victim's actions. This principle is referred to as **contributory negligence**.

The victim might also have accepted the risk when undertaking an activity or action which involves the occurrence of foreseeable and possible damages. This acceptance of risk may be possible through three different methods. The first is the signing of a contractual waiver absolving the defendant of having to compensate the victim for material damages in case of injury. Such a waiver is not enforceable however to protect the defendant from claims for bodily or moral damages. The second method of limiting liability would be displaying a notice, such as those we see in a bar or a restaurant, requiring all customers to deposit their coats in a coat-check room and stating that the owner will not be liable for any loss or damage to the coats. Posting a warning sign on your property which states "no trespassing, beware of dog" would be a third method to attempt to limit your liability if sued by a third party.

> *...as you read ask yourself...*
> *Can you think of a situation where you would be asked to sign a waiver?*
> *Does a notice prevent the owner of a stolen coat from suing the bar?*
> *If a trespasser is bitten by your dog, could he successfully sue you?*

The person being sued may also be freed of responsibility if the victim aggravates the damages due to his inaction in addressing the injury. For example, having been physically injured by the defendant, the victim refuses medical attention and as a result the injury becomes more serious. The person being sued will be held responsible only for the amount of damages suffered before the aggravation.

9.2.2.2 The Good Samaritan

Another defence may exist if someone caused damages in the process of helping others. For instance, injuring a person while helping to save them from drowning, or donating food to someone who suffers a severe allergic reaction to the food, or as a result of a person's disclosure of a trade secret for public health and safety reasons (e.g., an employee violating a contractual secrecy obligation by whistle blowing on the employer's toxic pollution of a lake). In the first two cases, the person being sued is free of any responsibility if the injury was not intentional and could not be foreseen. In the third case, the person must demonstrate the interest of the general public over that of the organization.

9.2.2.3 Superior Force

The damages caused were not within the control of the person being sued. They were unforeseeable and unstoppable acts, such as earthquakes, floods, lightening and ice storms.

9.2.2.4 Another Person made it Worse (*Novus Actus Interveniens*)

The person being sued may be found totally or partially free of liability because the fault of another weighs heavier than their own fault. Having committed a fault, another person comes along and commits an even greater fault that finally causes injury. The precedent for this defence was developed in *Baudoin v. T. W. Hand Fireworks* (1961). In this case, a few kids found some fireworks abandoned by the T.W. Hand Fireworks Company after a show. Almost all the children gave the fireworks they found to their parents who turned them over to the police. One child, however, gave the fireworks to his father who then gave them to an employee to dispose of. The employee used the fireworks in the presence of children, and one of the children was injured. The Supreme Court of Canada found the company free of any liability because the father should have disposed of the fireworks or handed them over to the police as did the other parents.

9.2.2.5 Improper Use

A defence may arise based on the fact that the object was improperly used, or used in a manner that it was not designed for. For example, if a person uses a hair dryer to remove paint from a wall and starts a fire, or uses it to defrost a window and breaks the window, or turns a lawnmower on its side and while using it to pull a rope hauling shingles up to the roof of the house, the blade breaks off and injures someone.

Indirect Liability
Section 9.3

9.3.1 Liability of Parent

A person who suffers damages due to the act or fault of a child has two possible recourses towards obtaining compensation; they may sue the child if he is at least seven years old or sue the parents. Both the child and the parents may be sued at the same time.

For the parents to be held responsible, three conditions must be fulfilled: first, the child must be a minor; second, the parent must have parental authority over the child; and third, the damages must be the result of an act or fault of the minor.

Parents may free themselves from this liability if they can demonstrate that they exercised sufficient surveillance (could not have foreseen what happened) or that they provided proper education to instil good values (taught the child the difference between right and wrong).

If a parent is held not liable for the damages caused, the Court may then hold the child liable. However, the likelihood of collecting compensation from the child may not exist if there are no assets that the child owns or will own in the near future. Note that a court judgment will give the plaintiff ten years to exercise his rights against a child.

9.3.2 Liability of a Non-Parent

A person, other than the parent (e.g. baby-sitter or teacher), may also be held liable for damages caused by a child. Similar to the responsibility of a parent, the victim has to demonstrate the existence of three conditions. The parent must have delegated authority over the child to the non-parent, the child caused the damages by an act or fault and that the child is a minor.

In their defence, a non-parent must prove adequate surveillance or education over the child during the delegated authority. Additionally, persons or organizations acting free of charge cannot be held responsible unless they personally commit a grave fault. An example of this is when a child causes damages to another while under the supervision of its grandparents.

9.3.3 Liability for Employees (Agents or Servants)

A business or organization may be held responsible for damages caused by their employees while they are carrying out their duties. For instance, a gym employee seriously injures a client during a training session; or the employee of a plumbing contractor causes a flood while installing a new water line in a manufacturing plant; or a house painter's employee drops some paint on the home-owner's sofa and ruins it.

In order to prove his right to compensation, in such an incident, the injured party needs to demonstrate that the person causing the damage was an employee, the employee was at fault, it took place during the course of their employment, and the control over the employee by the employer. By control, the law refers to the employer having some authority over the person who caused the damages. In such a case, if an employer can prove that the employee was acting for his own benefit, not within his employment functions and outside of the workplace, the employer will be free of any responsibility for damages caused to another.

9.3.4 Liability for Acts of an Animal

The owner of an animal, which has injured another party, or caused damage to property, may be held liable for such damages. The victim must demonstrate that the owner, or the person having custody (control) of the animal, failed in their surveillance of the animal.

Three points of interest must be considered. First, the animal must be domesticated. Second, both the owner and any other person given custody over the animal may be held responsible at the same time. Third, the damages caused by the animal need not be the result of direct contact. For instance, the animal can simply run into the path of a bicyclist, who avoids it, but loses control, falls and suffers injuries.

An owner or guardian of an animal can invoke superior force or the victim's fault in his defence. In the first case, the unforeseeable and unstoppable nature of the act must be proven, such as a domestic animal becoming rabid. In the second case, the victim's provocation of the animal will be considered in attributing responsibility.

9.3.5 Liability for Damage due to Ruin of an Immovable

This form of indirect civil liability was illustrated earlier in the balcony example. The owner of an immovable (building, elevator, land, etc.) may be held responsible for any damages caused by its partial or total ruin. For instance, should a building as a whole or just a part of it fall apart and subsequently injure another person, the owner is automatically presumed responsible. As in our earlier example, the balcony giving way and falling is a partial ruin. The victim would sue the building owner for failure of repairs or defect of construction.

The onus then rests on the owner, who can rebut (contradict) the allegation of fault by proving the damages were the result of the victim's fault, who may have failed to inform the owner of necessary repairs or through improper use caused the ruin resulting in his injuries. The owner may also claim superior force, such as lightning, an earthquake or flooding.

9.3.6 Liability of Manufacturer, Distributor and Seller for Safety Defects in Movables

An important business consequence of civil responsibility relates to the liability of a manufacturer, distributor and seller of movable property for damage caused by safety defects in the product. A safety defect causing liability can occur due to several reasons. First, a product may cause damages stemming from being improperly manufactured. For example, a new toaster or hair dryer whose assembly was faulty and its use causes an electrical short-circuit resulting in a fire. Second, the design of the product itself may lead to damages when being used. This could be the case with the use of specific tires on a certain model vehicle, which at high speeds catch fire or explode causing accidents. Third, a safety defect could be the result of improperly preserved or presented products. Foods going bad due to improper refrigeration or cooking and causing harm to those who consume them is a good example. Fourth, civil liability may occur when the product causes damages due to improper use as a result of a lack of information or indications of safety precautions on how the product should be handled. For instance, lawn fertilizer that fails to indicate in the instructions or label the possible danger of staining upon contact with natural stones in a patio.

The burden imposed upon the manufacturer and seller for labelling and safety instructions will depend on the very essence of the product and its complexity. The more complex the product, the greater the need for the manufacturer and seller to include detailed labels and safety instructions. The simpler the product, the less the requirement for detailed labelling and instructions. For instance, a car will require extensive warnings and instructions on how it can and should be used because of its complex nature. On the other hand, a simpler product like a hammer may have very minimal label warnings.

If an object is shown to have a safety defect, that is, it cannot be used as safely as a person should be able to expect, the liability for damage caused may rest on all of the following: the manufacturer of the object, the person who distributes it under his name, and any wholesaler or retailer of the object. These people cannot escape liability by claiming that they were unaware of the defect. If the object was sold as new (not used), they are presumed to know of the defect whether they actually knew or not.

This responsibility can be avoided if it can be proven that the victim knew of the safety defect, bought it and used the item in spite of this knowledge or could have foreseen the possibility of suffering an injury through continued use of the product. The manufacturer, distributor or seller may also free themselves of responsibility by claiming the damages were the result of a superior force, that the item was used improperly by the victim or that the defect was unforeseeable on their part and that they did not neglect to warn the purchaser of the defect the moment they became aware of its existence.

9.3.7 Responsibility for Acts of a Thing

A victim of damages caused by a thing, movable or immovable, may sue those persons who have the thing under their custody. Note that the person being sued does not have to necessarily be the owner of the thing, but simply have it under his control. For instance, a heating unit suddenly explodes and injures someone standing nearby. In his defence, the person who has custody of a thing that caused damages may argue superior force, the victim's fault or an absence of fault on his part.

LIMITING CIVIL LIABILITY Section 9.4

In an attempt to balance individual rights and the well being of the collective society, governments have on occasion limited the rights of the former by enacting legislation in support of the latter. The reasoning for such an approach vary from government to government, but general ideals such as reducing individuals' insurance costs and curtailing excessive litigation that could burden the court system are a few. Such is the case with bodily damages resulting from an automobile accident, under the *Automobile Insurance Act*, and an employment accident, under the *Workers' Compensation Act* and the *Act Respecting Industrial Accidents and Occupational Diseases*. These laws create a no-fault system in Québec, by which the government directly provides compensation to victims and removes their right to sue the person who was responsible for causing the damage.

APPENDIX "9-A"
SELECTED ARTICLES FROM
The Civil Code of Québec

Chapter III
Civil Liability

Division I
Conditions of Liability

1457. Every person has a duty to abide by the rules of conduct which lie upon him, according to the circumstances, usage or law, so as not to cause injury to another.

Where he is endowed with reason and fails in this duty, he is responsible for any injury he causes to another person by such fault and is liable to reparation for the injury, whether it be bodily, moral or material in nature.

He is also liable, in certain cases, to reparation for injury caused to another by the act or fault of another person or by the act of things in his custody.

1458. Every person has a duty to honour his contractual undertakings.

Where he fails in this duty, he is liable for any bodily, moral or material injury he causes to the other contracting party and is liable to reparation for the injury; neither he nor the other party may in such a case avoid the rules governing contractual liability by opting for rules that would be more favourable to them.

1459. A person having parental authority is liable to reparation for injury caused to another by the act or fault of the minor under his authority, unless he proves that he himself did not commit any fault with regard to the custody, supervision or education of the minor.

A person deprived of parental authority is liable in the same manner, if the act or fault of the minor is related to the education he has given to him.

1460. A person who, without having parental authority, is entrusted, by delegation or otherwise, with the custody, supervision or education of a minor is liable, in the same manner as the person having parental authority, to reparation for injury caused by the act or fault of the minor.

Where he is acting gratuitously or for reward, however, he is not liable unless it is proved that he has committed a fault.

1461. Any person who, as tutor or curator or in any other quality, has custody of a person of full age who is not endowed with reason, is not liable to reparation for injury caused by any act of the person of full age, except where he is himself guilty of a deliberate or gross fault in exercising custody.

1462. No person is liable for injury caused to another by an act or omission of a person not endowed with reason except in the cases where the conduct of the person not endowed with reason would otherwise have been considered wrongful.

1463. The principal is liable to reparation for injury caused by the fault of his agents and servants in the performance of their duties; nevertheless, he retains his recourses against them.

1464. An agent or servant of the State or of a legal person established in the public interest does not cease to act in the performance of his duties by the mere fact that he performs an act that is illegal, unauthorized or outside his competence, or by the fact that he is acting as a peace officer.

1465. A person entrusted with the custody of a thing is liable to reparation for injury resulting from the autonomous act of the thing, unless he proves that he is not at fault.

1466. The owner of an animal is liable to reparation for injury it has caused, whether the animal was under his custody or that of a third person, or had strayed or escaped.

A person making use of the animal is, together with the owner, also liable during that time.

1467. The owner of an immovable, without prejudice to his liability as custodian, is liable to reparation for injury caused by its ruin, even partial, where this has resulted from lack of repair or from a defect of construction.

1468. The manufacturer of a movable property is liable to reparation for injury caused to a third person by reason of a safety defect in the thing, even if it is incorporated with or placed in an immovable for the service or operation of the immovable.

The same rule applies to a person who distributes the thing under his name or as his own and to any supplier of the thing, whether a wholesaler or a retailer and whether or not he imported the thing.

1469. A thing has a safety defect where, having regard to all the circumstances, it does not afford the safety which a person is normally entitled to expect, particularly by reason of a defect in the design or manufacture of the thing, poor preservation or presentation of the thing, or the lack of sufficient indications as to the risks and dangers it involves or as to safety precautions.

Certain Cases of Exemption From Liability

1470. A person may free himself from his liability for injury caused to another by proving that the injury results from superior force, unless he has undertaken to make reparation for it.

A superior force is an unforeseeable and irresistible event, including external causes with the same characteristics.

1471. Where a person comes to the assistance of another person or, for an unselfish motive, disposes, free of charge, of property for the benefit of another person, he is exempt from all liability for injury that may result from it, unless the injury is due to his intentional or gross fault.

1472. A person may free himself from his liability for injury caused to another as a result of the disclosure of a trade secret by proving that considerations of general interest prevailed over keeping the secret and, particularly, that its disclosure was justified for reasons of public health or safety.

1473. The manufacturer, distributor or supplier of a movable property is not liable to reparation for injury caused by a safety defect in the property if he proves that the victim knew or could have known of the defect, or could have foreseen the injury.

Nor is he liable to reparation if he proves that, according to the state of knowledge at the time that he manufactured, distributed or supplied the property, the existence of the defect could not have been known, and that he was not neglectful of his duty to provide information when he became aware of the defect.

1474. A person may not exclude or limit his liability for material injury caused to another through an intentional or gross fault; a gross fault is a fault which shows gross recklessness, gross carelessness or gross negligence.

He may not in any way exclude or limit his liability for bodily or moral injury caused to another.

1475. A notice, whether posted or not, stipulating the exclusion or limitation of the obligation to make reparation for injury resulting from the nonperformance of a contractual obligation has effect, in respect of the creditor, only if the party who invokes the notice proves that the other party was aware of its existence at the time the contract was formed.

1476. A person may not by way of a notice exclude or limit his obligation to make reparation in respect of third persons; such a notice may, however, constitute a warning of a danger.

1477. The assumption of risk by the victim, although it may be considered imprudent having regard to the circumstances, does not entail renunciation of his remedy against the person who caused the injury.

Apportionment of Liability

1478. Where an injury has been caused by several persons, liability is shared by them in proportion to the seriousness of the fault of each.

The victim is included in the apportionment when the injury is partly the effect of his own fault.

1479. A person who is liable to reparation for an injury is not liable in respect of any aggravation of the injury that the victim could have avoided.

1480. Where several persons have jointly taken part in a wrongful act which has resulted in injury or have committed separate faults each of which may have caused the injury, and where it is impossible to determine, in either case, which of them actually caused it, they are solidarily liable for reparation thereof.

1481. Where an injury has been caused by several persons and one of them is exempted from all liability by an express provision of a special Act, the share of the liability which would have been his is assumed equally by the other persons liable for the injury.

Assessment of damages

1611. The damages due to the creditor compensate for the amount of the loss he has sustained and the profit of which he has been deprived.

Future injury which is certain and able to be assessed is taken into account in awarding damages.

1613. In contractual matters, the debtor is liable only for damages that were foreseen or foreseeable at the time the obligation was contracted, where the failure to perform the obligation does not proceed from intentional or gross fault on his part; even then, the damages include only what is an immediate and direct consequence of the nonperformance.

1614. Damages owed to the creditor for bodily injury he sustains are measured as to the future aspects of the injury according to the discount rates set by regulation of the Government, from the time such rates are set.

1615. The court, in awarding damages for bodily injury, may, for a period of not over three years, reserve the right of the creditor to apply for additional damages, if the course of his physical condition cannot be determined with sufficient precision at the time of the judgment.

CASE 9.1

Harris v. Ostromogilski

[1998] Q.J. No. 221 ,**Quebec Superior Court (Civil Division)**

(Excerpts of Judgment)

RYAN J.:— This is an amended action for $41,545.60 in damages which Plaintiff alleges he suffered at the hands of Defendant during a scuffle which took place at Defendant's residence on July 3, 1990.

Not surprisingly, each party accuses the other of having been the instigator and/or aggressor in the skirmish.

The following facts are not contested.

1) For a little over a year before the incident, Plaintiff had been leasing a taxi cab from Defendant's wife Elizabeth.

2) Every week or so, Plaintiff would go to Defendant's residence to settle his accounts with Defendant and/or the latter's wife. Notwithstanding some initial reluctance on his part, Defendant acknowledges that on every occasion, following discussions of relevant bills and Plaintiffs representations, Plaintiff would deduct the amount of repairs incurred for the vehicle during the preceding week or so and he would also occasionally negotiate and obtain credits for days when, according to Plaintiff, the latter had not used the car. Plaintiff would then pay to Defendant and/or Elizabeth Ostromogilski the difference between the amount of the rental and that of the deductions agreed upon. This payment would be made by cheque or by cash. Some 23 cheques were filed by Plaintiff to establish the fact that the amounts of the payments fluctuated considerably during the year preceding July 3, 1990.

3) On July 3, 1990, on his way to a baseball game at Olympic Stadium in Montreal, Plaintiff stopped unannounced at Defendant's residence to render his accounts for the past week or two and was duly admitted therein by Defendant and the latter's wife Elizabeth.

4) The door leading from the entrance vestibule to the interior of the premises occupied by Defendant's family opened inwards, i.e., from the street side into the short corridor (3 or 4 paces) leading to the kitchen.

5) Upon Plaintiffs arrival, he was ushered into the kitchen and joined there by Defendant whose wife and son thereupon retired to watch T.V. in an upstairs bedroom.

6) After presentation of some bills and/or a claim for idle time by Plaintiff, things turned sour and Plaintiff decided to leave the house. According to Plaintiff - uncontradicted on this point, - he had unilaterally decided to leave

and go to the baseball game, intending to return the next day to discuss matters more peaceably with Defendant's wife Elizabeth.

7) Plaintiff thereupon walked to and reached the vestibule door on his way out of the house.

From then on, the versions of the two parties are at odds. Incidentally, they were the only eye witnesses of the event heard in Court.

According to Defendant, upon reaching the hallway door, Plaintiff, presumably intending to leave the house, would have pushed Defendant while pulling the vestibule door open. This would have occurred when Defendant asked Plaintiff to immediately return the car keys and thus terminate the leasing arrangement then and there. Defendant says that he then fell "over the piano bench...I put my left hand to block my fall...I got up: Harris was still standing and we started to wrestle... we were holding hands... the kid was screaming, I was annoyed and scared...I pushed him away..." Defendant goes on: "He (Harris) was on top of me in the living room...I never pushed him down...he hit himself on the corner of the table for sure... the living room was all upside down..."

During his testimony in chief, Defendant insisted that he had not touched Plaintiff before the latter pushed him to allegedly open the vestibule door on his way out of the house. On cross-examination, however, he had to acknowledge that in testimony given on January 13, 1992 before another Court dealing with criminal proceedings instituted against him, Defendant had given a different version of this important segment of the July 3, 1990 tussle. In fact, on January 13, 1992, Defendant stated that when Plaintiff Harris refused to give him the car keys and walked to the door, he, Defendant Ostromogilski, "put my hand on his arm or shoulder..." saying "...wait a minute, don't leave I'll call police." When faced with this earlier statement, Defendant said somewhat sheepishly "...I have to accept what I said on January 13, 1992".

At trial, Defendant did not say explicitly that Harris punched him but he nevertheless insisted that he tried to "protect" himself: "...I don't recall that I tried to punch Harris...I did not push Harris...". Referred to his unequivocal statement in Court on January 13, 1992 that "...Yes, I punched him...", he merely replied that "...I don't recall...". Having observed both parties throughout the short trial, the Court cannot accept Ostromogilski's contention that his "poor English" is to blame for the above and other contradictions in his testimony before the Court.

Police officer Savage who went to the house after a telephone call made by Plaintiff as soon as the fight came to an end, testified that both Defendant's hands were swollen while Plaintiff was bleeding from the right side of the head, had red marks or bruises on his face while his glasses were broken. Defendant denies the glasses were broken and claims he put them back on Plaintiffs nose after the altercation. Likewise, he claims that Savage did not look at his hands "... to see if they were swollen...". This statement is not convincing: only Savage knows if he looked at Defendant's hands and the Court has no hesitation in accepting Savage's testimony as to what the latter saw and noticed.

According to Plaintiff, Defendant swung him around and started to beat him with his fists to the head as soon as he, Harris, reached and started to open the vestibule door: "...he shut the door... pushed me from the door...swung me around... his hands in a boxing position.. trying to punch me in the face..." Plaintiff goes on: "...I blocked a couple of blows, he hit me in the ribs, on the side of the head, face, glasses...I fell to the floor... he punched me 5 or 10 times during almost 15 minutes... he kicked me a couple of times (Plaintiff was on the floor by then) in the ribs...". Plaintiff added that while this was going on Defendant also shouted to his wife to "...get my gun, I'll kill him...". At trial, Defendant admits he may have mentioned the gun but explains that this was only to scare Harris away as Defendant was afraid for his wife and son who were crying or screaming as he was telling them to get out of the house. This particular statement was not at all credible and clearly appeared to the Court to be the result of an afterthought. It is perhaps worth noting that Defendant's version had also failed to convince the judge who found him guilty of a criminal charge of threatening to use a weapon while attacking Plaintiff on July 3, 1990, c.f. Exhibit P-9.

The additional evidence adduced by Plaintiff unquestionably corroborates or gives weight to Plaintiffs version of the altercation. For instance, the report from St Mary's Hospital - Exhibit P-12 - reveals that Defendant suffered "trauma to left hand and arm." The final diagnosis reads:

> "There has been virtually no change in the spiral fracture of the distal fifth metacarpal on the left hand. The comparison was made to the previous films on July 3rd, the fracture line persists and no callus is seen."

This annotation is certainly consistent with Savage's observation that Ostromogilski's hands were swollen and Plaintiff's version that he was struck by Defendant. It must also be borne in mind that the spiral fracture of the distal fifth metacarpal of the left hand was the only injury diagnosed on Defendant. It is also of interest to read that the doctor noted some swelling on the left hand...
The pictures of Plaintiff taken by a police photographer the day after the fight - Exhibit P-8-A - clearly show bruises and cuts eloquently descriptive of the injuries noted by Doctor Leslie Newman in the report filed as Exhibit P-1:

> "I examined Mr. Lou Harris on July 5th, 1990.
> He suffered multiple trauma on July 3rd, 1990 and had the following injuries when examined in my office.
>
> 1. laceration the left eye with three stitches
> 2. a left periorbital ecchymosis
> 3. laceration behind the right ear
> 4. laceration in the right ear with one suture
> 5. a right scalp laceration with two sutures
> 6. hematoma of the right remporal area
> 7. a fractured rib on the right chest
> 8. a 3cm. laceration on the right leg
> 9. a hematoma on the right buttock"

Nurse Joanne Lachapelle was on admission duty at Lakeshore General Hospital on July 3, 1990. She described Plaintiff's case as "semi-urgent" because of bleeding wounds to the head. She recalled that Plaintiff was "très ensanglanté..." and that she escorted him to the stitching room and laid him down as she was afraid he would lose consciousness. Suffice it to say that the injuries and condition described hereinabove are totally incompatible with Defendant's contention that they were caused by Plaintiff's mere accidental fall on or against some pieces of furniture.

On the whole, the Court concludes that Plaintiff discharged his burden of proof and established by a preponderance of evidence that he was the victim of an illegal assault by Defendant on July 3, 1990.

DAMAGES

Fortunately, Plaintiff was able to return to work some two (2) weeks after July 3. Even if Defendant claims he saw him at Mirabel airport with another car one week after the accident, this is not inconsistent with Plaintiffs claim that he may have gone to Mirabel to look for an another cab. However, Plaintiffs claim for loss of income is exaggerated as the credible proof adduced by him, i.e., his income tax returns for 1989 and 1990 (Exhibits P-6 and P-7), show an average net weekly income of about $195.00 during those two (2) years.

Plaintiffs claim of $5000.00 for "permanent psychological damages (I.P.P.) established at 5%" by Doctor Béliveau appears reasonable in the circumstances, even though Doctor Béliveau's figure of 5% was obviously arrived at somewhat arbitrarily. Plaintiffs testimony as to the symptoms recorded by Doctor Béliveau was uncontradicted and given in a straightforward manner which did not reveal unacceptable overstatements. It is reasonable and plausible to accept that plaintiff is experiencing the sequelae testified to by him. However, this is a case where the Court concludes that the nature of the discomfort included in Doctor Béliveau's 5% covers pain and suffering plus loss of enjoyment of life. Therefore, the sum of $5000.00 will cover Plaintiffs claim for those items.

In short, Plaintiff has established his claim for direct damages as follows:

Loss of income for two weeks:	$ 390.00
Perm. partial disability including pain, suffering, loss and enjoyment of life:	$ 5000.00
Broken eye glasses:	$ 336.00
Urgence Santé Ambulance:	$ 104.00
Slacks and shirt torned and bloodied:	$ 50.00
TOTAL:	$ 5880.00

Finally, Plaintiff amended paragraph 9 of his amended declaration at trial and seeks an additional $25,000.00 from Defendant as "exemplary damages...for having violated the person of plaintiff;" Plaintiff invokes arts. 1, 4 and 49 of the

Quebec Charte des Droits et Libertés de la personne, L.R.Q., c.C.-12.

Article 49 of the Charter clearly stipulates that the violation of a person's rights or "l'atteinte" must be "...illicite et intentionnelle...". The Court has already found that Defendant's attack was illicit. Was it intentional? The Court concludes that Defendant, who has a military background, is 20 years younger than Plaintiff and appears in good physical condition, willfully assaulted Plaintiff on July 3, 1990. The evidence certainly does not show that the assault was the result of a sudden and uncontrollable impulse on the part of Defendant. On the contrary, the latter acknowledges on cross-examination that he was indisposed, to say the least, towards Plaintiff who had scrapped one of Defendant's cars a few months earlier and who, he felt, was taking advantage of his "kindness". Furthermore, one must not lose sight of the fact that both parties acknowledged that Plaintiff had actually left the kitchen and was on his way out of the house before the assault. Therefore, Defendant's action in following him and assaulting Plaintiff can only have been intentional and in no palpable or proven manner due to Plaintiffs refusal to give up the car keys, something which Plaintiff had already expressed in the kitchen.

Following his conviction on two (2) criminal charges arising out of the July 3, 1990 assault, Defendant was fined a total of $2400.00 plus costs, cf. Exhibit P-9. Art. 1621 C.C.Q. stipulates clearly that the amount for punitive or example damages "may not exceed what is sufficient to fulfil their preventive purpose". The article adds that "punitive damages are assessed in the light of all the appropriate circumstances...".

According to Prof. (now J.C.A.) Baudoin, art. 1621 C.C. "vient indirectement confirmer cette règle..." established in 1987 by the Quebec Court of Appeal to the effect that an amount for punitive damages following a criminal conviction and sentence for the same set of facts may constitute "... l'imposition d'une double punition pour le même acte"

In Papadatos -vs- Sutherland, the Court of Appeal overruled the trial judge and set aside a $7000.00 award for punitive damages because the Defendant aggressor "...has already been prosecuted and punished for the same acts in the criminal court" (emphasis added). The learned attorneys did not bring this case to the Court's attention and absent any reference to contrary binding jurisprudence, this Court must of course follow and give full force to this unequivocal statement of the Court of Appeal which confirms that the preventive or deterrent purpose now mentioned in art. 1621 C.C.Q. is achieved by a criminal conviction and sentence for the same assault. I may add that in Lemieux -vs- Polyclinique St-Cyrille, the Court declined to make or see any distinction between exemplary and punitive damages.

To sum up, the Court finds Plaintiffs action is well founded to the extent of $5880.00.

As to costs, Exhibit C-1 shows that the trial date was postponed four (4) times for reasons mostly out of Defendant's control. The Court is therefore of the opinion that Defendant should not be saddled with all the costs incurred and/or pertaining to those postponements. Each party will support his own costs in connection with those adjournments.

FOR ALL THE ABOVE REASONS, THE COURT:

CONDEMNS Defendant to pay to Plaintiff the sum of $5880.00 with interest thereon calculated at the legal rate as well as the additional indemnity as provided for by law;

THE WHOLE WITH COSTS (except as noted above) against Defendant, as well as costs of $750.00 to cover Doctor Béliveau's examination and report.

CASE 9.2

Walker v. Singer

[1996] Q.J. No. 3991, **Quebec Superior Court**

(Excerpts of Judgment)

DALPHOND J.:— This is the story of a brief relationship between a man and a woman which turned sour, ending in the destruction of some of the Plaintiff's clothes followed by criminal charges against the Defendant and a complaint of sexual assault against the Plaintiff.

The Plaintiff now seeks compensation for damages to and theft of his clothes, for psychological damages, emotional stress, troubles and inconvenience, and for damages to his reputation. In addition he wants exemplary damages pursuant to sections 4 and 49 of the Québec Charter of Human Rights and Freedoms. Defendant, by way of a Cross-Demand, claims damages for troubles and inconvenience, abuse of rights and defamatory statement contained in the Declaration.

In the middle of June 1989, Walker and Singer met for the first time along the pool of a Westmount private tennis club, where Walker was hanging on daily. It seems that they took some interest in each other, as evidenced by the notes exchanged afterwards and the fact that they went together to a movie, a bar and several restaurants, in addition to frequent chats at the Club.

During that period, Walker went to pick up Singer at a large Westmount house where she was living temporarily. She introduced him to the owner, Mrs. Zito, a long time friend of her mother. Walker, who was then living in his father's small apartment where he had to sleep on a sofa, made efforts to please Zito : he drove her to Club Price, lunched with her, ... Shortly thereafter, Zito agreed to rent a room to him.

Between July 11 and 20, 1989, Singer went to Rochester for a recheck of her thyroid status (noted thyrotoxic in July 1988) at the Mayo Clinic. Her parents were there at the same time and they all stayed in the same suite at the Plaza Hotel.

During her absence, Walker moved into the room offered by Zito, bringing with him his toiletteries and part of his clothes.

When Singer returned to Montreal on July 20, Walker was waiting for her at the Dorval airport. (She claims that she never told him about her flight schedule, nor asked him to come and pick her up but admits speaking with him from Rochester; one wonders how he found out about her return schedule. Moreover she gave him at the airport a puzzle book bought for him in Rochester.) In any event, she agreed to be driven back at Zito's home, and even asked him to stop by her apartment in Cote St. Luc. During the stop, Walker took a frame containing a photograph of

Singer; according to her, he "stole" it, but admits being told about it the same day. According to Walker, on the way back she asked him to sign a document describing a phony work opportunity in his jewellery business for one of her clients, a Romanian Jewess having some expertise in that field. He refused and Singer became very upset, saying that "people do it all the time". (Singer denies this conversation; however she admits that she had then a Romanian Jewess client seeking a way to extend her stay in Canada. One wonders how Walker found out about that client.)

On Friday, July 28, 1989, Singer was told that she was pregnant and mentioned it to Walker. That very evening she went alone to a clinic and had an abortion.
On Saturday, July 29, while Walker was away, Singer walked into his room (which cannot be locked) and destroyed clothes belonging to him.

According to Walker, later on that day, Singer admitted her mischief to Walker and promised to make good for it. Singer does not recall discussing compensation. Later on that day, returning to Zito's home after a doctor's appointment, Walker saw Singer leaving with a suitcase. (She was kicked out by Zito) . Once in his room, he alleged having noticed that pieces of his wardrobe were missing. He reported the incident to the Westmount police station and took polaroid pictures of the damaged items.

At the request of the police, Walker completed on August 2, 1989, a document called "liste d'effets volés. Afterwards, an investigation was conducted by Renew Purtell of the MUC Police, who called in Singer to get her side of the story. Shortly after, criminal charges of breaking and entering and theft were filed.

At the beginning of April, Me Pepper, then the lawyer of Singer, called Purtell to inform him that Singer wanted to file a complaint of sexual assault against Walker. On April 5, she went to the police station and met with Purtell and another police officer, Lise Bergeron, who completed a document called "Événement - crime contre la personne". Singer was also asked to put down in writing the details of the alleged assault in a document called "déclaration de témoin", where she alleged to have been sexually assaulted on June 26, 1989 and beaten on July 21, 1989, all by Walker. A few days later, Purtell asked Walker to drop by the police station to answer his questions in connection with the complaint of sexual assault made by Singer. Upon the advice of his brother, Walker met with Me Julius Grey who spoke with Purtell.

On April 25, 1990, Purtell accompanied by Singer went to the Court House to meet with Me Marie Andrée Trudeau, a Crown attorney. After the meeting, the Crown recommended not to press charge against Walker and the police file was closed.

On February 19, 1991, further to an agreement between the Crown and the Defense, no evidence was put before the court in connection with the charges as laid and Singer pleaded guilty to the lesser charge of mischief, an offence punishable by summary conviction. Considering her status and the particular circumstances surrounding the affair, she was unconditionally discharged.

On March 8, 1991 Walker's attorney served a demand letter to Singer claiming $ 33,800. The writ and declaration were issued on April 2, 1991 and amended at the trial to increase the claim to $ 78,800.

SUBMISSIONS OF THE PARTIES

Walker claims damages for the replacement of his clothing. But more importantly, he alleged that as a consequence of the complaint made against him by Singer, the last 7 years of his life "have been taken away from him", forcing him to resort to medication to sleep and making it impossible for him, portrayed as a kind of rapist, to build a stable relationship with a woman.

Singer submits that the amount claimed for the clothes is grossly exaggerated, adding that what she did was a direct and consequential result of the abortion. She maintains that she was sexually assaulted by Walker, adding that no charge resulted from her complaint, thus no impact on his reputation. As for the new moral damages claimed in the amendment, she alleges that they are prescribed. With regard to punitive damages, she argues that they are not permitted, at least for the mischief, since she has already been punished in a criminal court. She concludes that Walker's procedure is abusive.

DECISION

1. Mischief and theft:

a) Singer's liability:

Singer admits that she damaged the wardrobe of Walker but stresses that she had an abortion the evening before because impregnated by Walker on June 26.

The circumstances surrounding the destruction of Walker's clothing may be relevant to the sentencing but not to the civil liability (art. 1053 C.C.L.C.). A tort (délit) was committed and Singer is responsible for the damage caused by her act.

b) Quantum of the damages:

During cross-examination, Walker acknowledged that while in California, his income was very modest. According to him, he brought from California prior to meeting Singer, summer stuff, personal toiletteries, shirts, ties and 2 or 3 costly suits. Once in Montreal, he claims to have bought shirts and suits at Brisson, an expensive men clothing store; no bill or other evidence of these purchases were filed.

According to him, his wardrobe was not only damaged (as shown by the photos) but partly stolen by Singer afterwards to erase evidence of the mischief (missing items are described in a declaration filed with the police on August 2, 1989, indicating as "valeur", the replacement costs determined after some verifications with the stores where he bought them).

According to Singer, she destroyed only two pairs of trousers, a shirt and a tie.

She also admits having taken away on the Monday, a tie, but no more, adding that Walker had very little in his room, living almost in a t-shirt, a pair of short and flip flops.

Walker declares to have paid about $ 60 to a tailor to get the necessary repairs on slightly damaged items (sewing buttons on shirts and a crest on a blue jacket, ...). As for the replacement cost of the items too damaged to be repaired or taken away, including the military crest and a tie, the Court awards only $ 700 because it considers it highly improbable that Singer would have taken away with her all the items listed on P-3, i.e. 2 suits, 2 jeans, 2 trousers and a dozen of ties while leaving behind a jacket on which she had removed the military crest and a few buttons, as well as trousers seriously damaged.

2. The complaint of sexual assault:

a) burden of proof:

In this action in civil liability arising out of the complaint, it is up to the Plaintiff to prove a fault, a prejudice and a causal connection, on the balance of probabilities.

b) the evidence:
Walker denies having had any intimate relations with Singer, adding that she had then a fiancé.

Singer affirms to the contrary, that between the moment she met Walker in mid June 1989 and June 26, 1989, she had several sexual intercourses with Walker; that she was impregnated by him during the June 26, sexual assault; and that a pregnancy resulted from this assault (to support her point, she produced a note from the doctor who performed the abortion in which he wrote "that the embryo was of age 3 1/2 to 5 weeks").

She admits that in June 1989, she went out a few times with a longtime friend who, one evening, wrote on a coaster "Why don't we marry?" and that she showed that coaster to Walker.

She remembers a visit from Sergeant detective Cupp of the RCMP in 1990, before she filed her complaint with the police, adding that she had the feeling that Walker was behind it because "of his vindictiveness and his comments to Purtell to have her disbarred".

With regard to the sexual assault, she mentioned it to her mother for the first time in April 1990 and at about the same time to Me Pepper who first called the police.

c) Court's finding:

It is hard to believe that the relationship between the parties was as limited as Walker tries to portray it. His notes reveal more love than friendship.

Assuming that it was not a case of platonic love, there is no evidence that the conception resulted from a sexual act committed on June 26 since the age of the embryo (3 1/2 to 5 weeks), assuming that the note written by the doctor of Singer and filed by her is admissible evidence and conclusive about it, covers a spectrum during which, according to Singer, she had other sexual relations with Walker.

More importantly, the behaviour of Singer that night and subsequently is not consistent with her allegation of a sexual assault by Walker on June 26.

As for the allegation that she was beaten on July 21, 1989, by Walker, it is inconsistent with the content of the notes quoted above.

It is also worth noticing that the assault and the beating were never raised in the plea to the criminal charges or in the Cross-Demand.

Adding to these facts, the silences and the evasive answers given by Singer about this event, the Court concludes that she fabricated that sexual assault story in order to get even with Walker (who was after her: criminal charges, visit to the syndic of the Bar, complaint and follow-up calls to the RCMP).

d) To make a false complaint is a tort:

As the Supreme Court of Canada has indicated in Hill c. Church of Sientology:

> "A good reputation is closely related to the innate worthiness and dignity of the individual. It is an attribute that must, just as freedom of expression, be protected by society's law."

This is particularly true in Quebec where the Québec Charter enshrines at section 4, the safeguard of one's honour, dignity and reputation as a fundamental right.

To say that a person has committed a sexual assault, when this is not true, is a serious attack to his reputation and sense of dignity. The fact that the diffamatory statement was not largely publicised, does not make it less diffamatory as pointed out in Jean-Louis Baudoin's book, La responsabilité civile

e) Damages to reputation and dignity:

Having concluded that by making a false complaint of sexual assault, Singer committed a tort, it follows that Walker is entitled to be fully compensated for the damages resulting from it.

No charge having been laid for sexual assault, Singer's allegation were never brought to the attention of the general public. However the evidence shows that Singer communicated that false accusation to the following persons: police officers, a Crown attorney, her mother and Me Pepper. The Crown attorney and Me Pepper are bound by their status not to repeat the allegation of Singer, but the mother is not.

In addition, Purtell and a representative of the police responsible for its archives, have confirmed that the complaint has been recorded in 1990 in the identification computer system used by the police; that this entry will remain until year 2000 i.e. for a period of 10 years; that in 1990, it was not the procedure to record the result of the investigation; and, that any police officer who would contact the police central information department to get information about Walker would be told that he was a suspect in a sexual assault complaint. Walker's reputation is not, according to this system, spotless.

There is also an insidious consequence of the complaint with regard to the behaviour that Walker must adopt if he becomes engaged with a woman. As he pointed out, the openness and honesty necessary for the establishment of a stable relationship with a woman required Walker to disclose the existence of the complaint. However this may cause the end of the relationship. Hopefully this problem is solved by this judgment.

Considering the very limited extent of the dissemination of the defamatory statement (law enforcement officers, Me Pepper and the mother of Singer) but also that the details of the complaint will stay in the police central system until year 2000 and not those of this judgment; considering that Singer has reiterated her defamatory remarks in the course of these proceedings; considering the insidious consequence of this attack on the image that Walker had to present to any woman with whom he may have been seriously engaged; and considering that the judgment vindicates Walker's reputation; the Court awards an amount of $ 5,000 to Walker for damages to his reputation.

e) Psychological damages, stress and inconvenience:

Walker had to replace destroyed clothes, to replace the military crest, and to make arrangements with a tailor.

There is no doubt that being asked by the police to respond to a complaint of sexual assault can be a source of stress and anxiety for any normal person.

The complaint also resulted in some troubles for Walker, such as the need to discuss the matter with his brother and seek legal advice.

Finally, the Court notes that the persistence of Walker to get Singer one way or the other, created a stressing climate for him, for which Singer is not responsible.

Considering all the factors mentioned above, the Court believes that an amount of $2,000 is appropriate.

3. Punitive damages:

Wilfully accusing someone of a serious criminal act when one knows this to be untrue, is extremely serious. Singer was told by Purtell at the time that she filed her complaint that if she was doing that to get even with Walker, she could even be charged of public mischief. Nevertheless she proceeded with her complaint, because she wanted to hurt Walker, especially Walker's reputation. In order words, Singer desired the consequences that her wrongful conduct had and more.

There was an intentional interference with the reputation, honor and dignity of Walker (art. 4 and 49 of the Québec Charter), as defined by the Supreme Court of Canada in a recent judgment, Syndicat national des employés de l'hôpital St-Ferdinand (CSN) et Fédération des affaires sociales (CSN) et Confédération des syndicats nationaux (CSN) c. Curateur public du Québec

Considering that this interference came from a member of the Bar who under oath repeated her false allegation, considering that Singer was unconditionally discharged in the criminal court for the offence of mischief and not charged of public mischief for the false complaint of sexual assault, considering that Singer has declared to have substantial income at the time of the allegation and subsequently, and considering the amounts already awarded, an additional amount of $ 3,000 appears necessary to fulfil the punitive and preventive purposes of these damages (art. 1621 C.C.Q.). For the reasons mentioned in Association des professeurs de Lignery (A.P.L.). Syndicat affilié à la C.E.Q. c. Alvetta-Comeau, this amount shall bear interest, including the additional indemnity, from the date of this judgment only.

4. Declaration to the effect that the documents filed with the police are false:

Clearly this judgment means that the content of the documents filed with the police are false. However a declaratory judgment directed to these documents would require that the MUC Police be made a party to these proceedings. Since this was not done, there is no need to discuss the existence or not of such a remedy under section 49 of the Québec Charter.

5. Cross-Demand:

Very limited evidence was brought to the Court's attention to support it. In any case, the refusal of Singer to indemnify Walker for her mischief and her subsequent false complaint against him are the causes of this action. The amounts claimed were exaggerated but Singer has not established that the action amounted to an abuse of process or that the procedures filed by the Plaintiff were diffamatory.

WHEREFORE, THE COURT:

GRANTS in part the action of Gregory Walker:
CONDEMNS Melissa Singer to pay to Gregory Walker the sum of $ 7,760 with interest plus the additional indemnity provided at article 1056 c. C.C.B.C., the whole calculated from the date when the action was instituted; and
CONDEMNS Melissa Singer to pay to Gregory Walker as punitive damages, an amount of $ 3,000 with interest plus the additional indemnity provided at article 1056 c. C.C.B.C., the whole calculated from the date of this judgment;
DISMISSES Melissa Singer's Cross-Demand;
THE WHOLE WITH COSTS (except for the expertise that should remain at the parties' expenses).

CASE 9.3

Farmakis v. Canadian Tire Corp.

[2003] O.J. No. 421, **Ontario Superior Court of Justice**

(Excerpts of Judgment)

HOILETT J.:— This is an action brought by the plaintiff for damages arising from injuries sustained by him when he fell from a ladder, which allegedly collapsed under him while he stood on the third of five steps of the ladder scraping spatter from the drywall of a residence he was building in his country of origin, Greece. The ladder, manufactured by the latter two defendants, was bought at a Canadian Tire store in Welland, Ontario, sometime in the summer of 1993. The parties have agreed on the quantum of damages, in the event that liability is found. Accordingly, the single broad issue before me is the issue of liability.

The salient points of the evidence may be briefly summarized.

Mr. Farmakis, now 54 years old, immigrated to Canada from Greece in 1973 and after a series of jobs, some in the food industry, purchased a restaurant in Welland, Ontario in 1977. He decided to build a "retirement home" in his hometown in Greece with plans to share his time between Canada and Greece. Sometime toward the end of June to early July 1993, the plaintiff, in response to a flyer or brochure, attended at the Canadian Tire store in Welland where he bought the ladder now in issue for $34.00. Mr. Farmakis found the ladder satisfactory to his needs, and made particularly appealing because it was light and easily portable. Later in the year the plaintiff moved to Greece with his family having rented out his Welland restaurant and the major portion of his Welland residence. The plaintiff's move to Greece served the twin purpose of visiting his ill mother and building his Greek residence.

The plaintiff, in anticipation of his travels to Greece, arranged for the shipment of a container full of household effects, among other things, including the ladder, made Ex. 3 in this trial. According to Mr. Farmakis, the ladder was safely packaged in rubber, plastic and cardboard, and taped. He testified that he saw the ladder packaged and was there in Greece at its unloading. He removed the ladder from its packaging, inspected it, and found it to be intact. Mr. Farmakis further testified that prior to the day, December 6, 1993, of the fateful event, he had used the ladder inside the house he was renting, next door to the one he was having built. He had never used the ladder on the construction site itself.

On the early afternoon of December 6, 1993, according to the plaintiff, he had been using the ladder for approximately one and one half-hours; in particular, he was using a scraper to scrape paint from the drywall of the house that was being built. He was standing on the third step of the 5-step ladder, and before beginning to use the ladder, he had opened up the ladder to its proper working position and verified its stability. During the approximate hour and one-half of work before the plaintiff's fall, he would move the ladder along the walls, as he had finished working at a particular site. Just before his fall, Mr. Farmakis testified, he felt like he lost his balance and he fell towards his right. He looked abortively to his right for something to hold on to in order to break his fall. He opened up his legs and tried to jump. The fall, or "jump", was some 15 or 20 feet. Mr. Farmakis' injuries and the consequential damages, not being in dispute, suffice it to say that he received emergency and early medical treatment in Greece but, for reasons which need not be canvassed, the plaintiff chose to return to Canada to be treated; that was on December 9, 1993.

Apart from testifying concerning the mechanism of his fall, the plaintiff testified that he had on many occasions inspected the ladder in the time intervening between its purchase and the time of its fall.

Although one of the principal pillars in the plaintiff's argument is that the plaintiff was not adequately warned concerning the use and risks associated with the ladder, much of the trial time was consumed with expert evidence relating to the mechanism of the fall and to compliance with industry standards of the ladder in question.

Mr. Robert John Shirer, a 1983 University of Toronto Engineering graduate, has been a professional engineer since 1985. Among other things, he has worked in the area of accident reconstruction; fire investigations and materials. Mr. Shirer was retained by the plaintiff to examine the ladder in question and to opine as to the probable cause of the alleged failure of the ladder. The ladder, which was tested at a load-bearing capacity of 800 lbs. and a performance capacity of 200 lbs., according to Mr. Shirer, should have the performance capacity of safely bearing the weight of a worker of the plaintiff's reported weight of 198 lbs., more or less. Accepting that Mr. Farmakis was standing on the third step of the ladder, facing the wall and scraping plaster from the drywall, Mr. Shirer testified that it would have been impossible for the plaintiff to generate an 800 lbs. force leading to the failure of the ladder. Mr. Shirer concluded, therefore, that there had to be a defect in the ladder that predated the purchase of the ladder by Mr. Farmakis.

Giving expert evidence on behalf of the defence were Dr. Ralph Edward Southward, a consulting engineer, Dr. Douglas Perovic, Head of the Department of Metallurgical Science and Engineering at the University, and Dr. Darrell Ogilvie-Harris, orthopaedic surgeon. Although Doctors Southward and Perovic testified at some length, their evidence in its essence is susceptible to useful distillation. Dr. Ogilvie-Harris' evidence may be even more effectively distilled. Its general purport was that the injury suffered by the plaintiff was wholly and solely consistent with a high velocity vertical impact between the right heel of the plaintiff and a hard surface.

The substance of Dr. Southward's opinion is that the ladder in issue met all industry standards and, under normal use, could not have failed in the manner suggested by the plaintiff.

Dr. Perovic, a 1986 graduate of the University of Toronto, now heads the Department of Material Science and Engineering. His qualifications to give opinion evidence in respect to the technical issues raised by this trial have been conceded; reasonably, in my opinion. Dr. Perovic's opinion, in substance, is consistent with that of Dr. Southward. Dr. Perovic takes issue with Mr. Shirer's opinion that the failure of the ladder must have resulted from damage to the ladder that pre-dated its purchase by the plaintiff.

There has been, not surprisingly, some consistency with the opinions of Mr. Shirer and Doctors Southward and Perovic. The most fundamental point of departure related to Mr. Shirer's opinion relating to pre-purchase damage to the ladder. With the greatest respect to Mr. Shirer, there is no evidence which, in my opinion, supports his views concerning pre-purchase damage to the ladder. Indeed, the evidence is all to the contrary. All the evidence, including that of Mr. Farmakis, is consistent in reporting no patent defects in the ladder, upon visual inspection. Conclusions concerning that absence of defect prior to purchase, or at any other time, were fortified by the results of testing of the ladder, chemically, structurally and microscopically.

In the face of such compelling evidence, it is difficult to elevate above the level of conjectural or speculation any suggestion of pre-purchase damage to the ladder. Equally significant is Mr. Farmakis' own version of the events proximate to his fall from the ladder. Among those circumstances is the plaintiff's evidence that he had been using the ladder for about one and one half-hours, from approximately 12:30 p.m. to 2 p.m., before his fall. Neither before nor at any time contemporaneous to the fall did the plaintiff observe the buckling of the ladder; nor did he hear any cracking sound, consistent with the sound of fracturing metal. The plaintiff, for obvious and perfectly understandable reasons, did not examine the ladder following the fall. Mr. Farmakis did not again see the ladder for approximately 1 1/2 years. His wife brought it back from Greece in the summer of 1996. Apart, therefore, from the routine use made of the ladder, it has made two cross-Atlantic trips before it was seen by any of the experts; a circumstance which renders even more speculative Mr. Shirer's evidence concerning damage prior to the plaintiff's purchase of the ladder.

Concerning the issue relating to the alleged failure of the defendants to warn the plaintiff concerning risks associated with the use of the ladder, about which more will be said later, the plaintiff testified that he removed the labels from the ladder. According to him, there were only three labels, contrary to other evidence which indicates there might have been four labels. The plaintiff was only able to produce two of the three labels he said he removed. What is clear from an examination of Ex. 3, the ladder in issue, is that there are four separate surface sites evidencing the use of adhesive, designed to keep labels affixed.

The following are areas in which it is submitted the defendant failed to warn:

1. The label on the ladder concerning the load-bearing capacity of the ladder was missing; relying, of course on the acceptance of the plaintiff's evidence that there was no such label on the ladder when originally purchased. The plaintiff claims that he would have purchased another ladder had he been aware of the 200 lb. capacity.

2. There were no personnel in the store at the time of purchase to counsel and assist the plaintiff in his choice of a ladder, or concerning the risks associated with its use.

3. There were no prominently displayed signs in the Canadian Tire store highlighting relevant features about the ladder.

The plaintiff's claim, if it is to succeed, must survive on one or the other or both of two grounds; that is, the failure of the ladder, either because of the process of its manufacture or because of a defect in the product employed in its manufacture; or, alternatively, the failure of the defendant, adequately to provide the plaintiff with a warning adequate to the nature of the product and the risks reasonably associated with its normal use. Regrettably, the plaintiff's claim fails on both grounds, for the following reasons.

I turn first to the manufacture of the ladder and the product or products employed in its manufacture. There is no evidence which, in my view, warrants the conclusion that there was any negligence on the part of the defendant in either regard. Had there been a manufacturing defect, no doubt it may have remained patent even given the passage of time. The same comments may also be validly made concerning a latent defect in the materials used; for example defects recognizable upon microscopic or other scientific examination. That, however, has not been the case.

There is no need here for theorizing, given the facts unique to this case, but even if damage had been found in the ladder, its biography from date of purchase to the date of its examination by experts was such as to leave ample opportunity for damage to the ladder caused by sources other than the defendant. I made earlier reference to the ladder's two trans-Atlantic crossings and gaps in the ladder's life concerning which there is no evidence. It may be that, given the circumstances, too much should not be made of the failure to call Mrs. Farmakis as a witness, but she was at the residence in Greece at the time of the mishap and one might, reasonably, in my view, infer that she saw the ladder in the immediate wake of the plaintiff's fall and should be able to shed some light on the condition of the ladder at that time.

I turn next to the question of the defendant's duty to warn. The law is clear that that duty is determined by the character and complexity of the product in question, as it does on the risks involved. At the low end of the range of that duty are the circumstances when there is no duty at all, given the simplicity of the product as well as the very low risks associated with its use. Or, indeed, arguably, the dangers associated with a product may be so patent and well known that the need to warn is obviated. At the other end of the spectrum are highly dangerous products the misuse of which may lead to serious bodily harm, or even death; flammable and explosive substances being examples.

Concerning the duty to warn, reference might be usefully be made to Deshane v. Deere (1993), 17 C.C.L.T. (2d) 130 (Ont. C.A.).

It is my opinion that a simple 5-step household ladder falls rather close to the bottom of the spectrum so far as the duty to warn is concerned. In the hands of an adult of average intelligence, it may well be argued that there is no duty to warn. I need not decide that issue, however, because, the evidence, viewed as a whole, supports the probable conclusion that there were four warning labels on Ex. 3, including the one as to load-bearing capacity. The comments I earlier made concerning the biography of the subject ladder are equally apposite the present circumstances. The ladder is no longer in its pristine condition; some, at least, of the warning labels having been removed from the ladder. The inability of the plaintiff to producc cven all the labels he claims to have removed cannot but serve to damage the very claim he now asserts.

The plaintiff's alternation of the ladder by the removal of label, arguably, raises the issue of "spoliation" of the evidence, a circumstance which tends further to compromise the plaintiff's claim. (ref. Spasic Estate v. Imperial Tobacco (2002), 49 O.R. (3d) 699).

The entirety of the evidence supports the conclusion that the defendant met all reasonable industry standards so far as the manufacture and labelling of the ladder was concerned, as well as in respect of the materials used.

Based on the recent decision of the Supreme Court of Canada in Fontaine v. Loewen, [1998] 156 D.L.R. (4th) 577 @ 585 the doctrine of res ipso loquitur, if not dead, is certainly in deep freeze, and should only be occasionally thawed. Be that as it may, any recourse to that doctrine must be reasoned and may not be based on conjecture. There may be no reason here to furnish an explanation for the damage to the ladder but that offered by the defence expert evidence seems most plausible, if not probable; namely, after the plaintiff lost his balance and fell, the ladder was damaged by a combination of forces, the dynamic load created by the falling body of the plaintiff being a major contributing factor.

For all the foregoing reasons, therefore, the plaintiff's action is dismissed.
Concerning the issue of costs, I shall entertain written submissions from counsel, both as to entitlement and quantum, within 30 days of the date of these reasons; after counsel have exchanged their submissions for the benefit of each other's comments.

I should add, parenthetically, that in view of the conclusions I have reached, and my reasons therefor, I do not deem it necessary to determine which of the defendants, if not both, is liable had I arrived at contrary conclusions. Had I, however, found liability based on the manufacture of the ladder or the materials used, given the nature of the relationship between Canadian Tire Corporation and its dealers, I would have had no difficulty fixing both Canadian Tire and the manufactures with liability.

Concerning the obligation relating to a warning, had I concluded that there was some breach of duty, I would have had some difficulty finding that there was some causal connection between that breach and the damages suffered by the plaintiff. There are few household items more simple in its operation than an uncomplicated step ladder.

CASE 9.4

Walford v. Jacuzzi Canada Ltd.

Ontario Court of Appeal 729

Date: 2007-10-23

FELDMAN J.A.:

[1] The appellant Correena Walford was 15 3/4 years old when she went down the slide her parents had just installed beside their 4-foot, aboveground, backyard pool, hit her chin on the bottom of the pool and broke her neck. The trial judge dismissed the appellants' claims for negligence and failure to warn against a number of defendants, including the respondent pool store that sold the mother some fittings for the slide and assured her that installing the slide with her pool would be "okay" and "no problem".The appellant Correena Walford was rendered quadriplegic by the accident. The trial judge assessed her damages at over $5 million. There is no appeal from that assessment.

[2] The sole issue of liability on the appeal is whether the pool store breached a duty of care to the appellants by telling the mother that it was "okay" and that there would be "no problem" with installing the slide on their 4-foot-deep aboveground pool, without warning her of the potential for catastrophic injury, and if so, whether that breach caused or contributed to the damage that the appellant Correena Walford suffered.

[3] In my view, the trial judge erred in finding no breach of duty by the respondent for failure to warn and no negligent misrepresentation, and for finding that Correena Walford's negligence was the sole cause of the accident. For the following reasons, I would allow the appeal.

Facts from the Reasons of the Trial Judge

[4] The Walfords had owned at least three aboveground, backyard pools, the most recent of which at the date of the accident, July 12 1996, was the Mardi Gras pool they bought second-hand and installed in 1994. It was 16 feet wide, 24 feet long, and 4 feet deep. Correena's grandfather had lived with the family until his death in April 1996 and expressed the wish that the family obtain a slide for the pool. The appellant Mrs. Marion Walford wanted to fulfill that wish using funds from her father's estate. She believed that a slide could be installed with her family's pool because the cover of the *Mardi Gras Installation Instructions*booklet that had accompanied the pool featured an illustration of a child using a slide installed at the end of the pool. However, she sought further assurances that a slide was in fact appropriate for a 4-foot-deep pool.

[5] She first contacted Pioneer Pools at their Barton Street store, where she had been a customer for two years. She bought chemicals and other pool supplies for her pool there, and a representative had attended her pool to assist with the installation of a new vinyl liner and, on another occasion, with an algae problem. Mrs. Walford relied on the expertise of the store's staff to keep her pool in proper

working order and trusted their advice. When she first called about a slide, it was to inquire whether a slide was available for a 4-foot pool. She was told that it was, but there was no floor model, the cost was over $1,000, and it had to be ordered from the manufacturer.

[6] Mrs. Walford next called the City of Hamilton building department, which told her either that they did not regulate slides or that there was no city regulation prohibiting the use of a water slide with a 4-foot pool.

[7] She subsequently saw a classified ad that Kevin Boyle had placed in *The Hamilton Spectator* offering a 10-foot pool slide manufactured by Jacuzzi for $350. She called the number and asked the man she spoke with whether the slide could be used with a 4-foot pool. He responded that he did not see a problem. She again called the City of Hamilton building department and spoke to a different official who gave her the same response as before.

[8] Before going to see the Boyles' slide, Mrs.Walford made two further inquiries for information. First she called her Pioneer Pools store and spoke to a female employee. Mrs. Walford told the employee about Mr. Boyle's advertisement and asked whether it was okay to use the slide with a 4-foot pool. The Pioneer Pools employee said that she could not see a problem. Mrs. Walford then called another pool shop, Acorn Pools, whose employee also could not foresee a problem.

[9] Eventually, Mrs. Walford went with her neighbour, Judy Dunn, to the Boyles' residence and purchased the slide for $225. The slide was quite old and had some broken parts. Mrs. Walford testified that Kevin Boyle's father, William, told her that it had been mounted on a 4-foot pool similar to hers. It turned out that the Boyles had purchased the slide 15 years earlier at a garage sale and that they had never installed it. The claim against Kevin and William Boyle for negligent misrepresentation was dismissed at trial and no appeal was taken from that part of the judgment.

[10] After purchasing the slide, Mrs. Walford loaded it into her van and drove directly to the Barton Street Pioneer Pools store. There she spoke with the store manager, Sumera Fraser, whom Mrs. Walford had dealt with before. Mrs. Walford asked Ms. Fraser to inspect the slide, which Mrs. Walford and Ms. Dunn pulled partway out of the van. Mrs. Walfordasked Ms. Fraser whether it was all right to use this slide with her 4-foot pool and she was told again that there would be no problem.

[11] The slide's installation required securing the three metal legs that support the front portion of the slide with mountings that Mrs. Walford purchased from the store. Ms. Fraser also pointed out that the tubing that supplies water to the two jets that lubricate the slide was missing, and referred Mrs. Walford to another Pioneer Pools store on Highway 53 for those parts. Mrs. Walford went to the Highway 53 Pioneer Pools store the next day. The first clerk she spoke to there directed her to an older male employee at the back of the store who was knowledgeable about the tubing.

[12] Mrs. Walford described the slide as a 10-foot-long slide manufactured by

Jacuzzi Canada, as it had been advertised. Although the slide was 10 feet in length, it was 7 feet, 6 inches high measured from the deck to the top of the handrail, 6 feet, 3 inches from the seat to the deck, and 6 feet, 6 inches from the seat to the water. The older male employee supplied Mrs. Walford with two kinds of tubing and assured her that one would fit her slide. Mrs. Walfordagain asked if it was all right to use the slide with her 4-foot-deep pool and he told her that it would be "okay." He also drew her a sketch that showed how the mountings were to be installed on the deck.

[13] Mrs. Walford testified that she felt it was important that employees of Pioneer Pools see the slide. She said that although the older male employee at the Highway 53 store did not see the slide, he appeared to be knowledgeable and she relied on his expertise. She testified that had she been told by Pioneer Pools that it was not safe to use the slide, she would not have installed it, even though she had already bought it.

[14] During all of her inquiries, Mrs. Walford did not specifically ask whether it would be *safe* to install or use the slide with a 4-foot-deep pool. However, the trial judge found that her concern was with the slide's safety. Nor was there any suggestion in the evidence that anyone's response to her inquiries would have been different had she used the word "safe" rather than "okay."

[15] That evening, the Walfords installed the slide on the deck of the pool. The next day, Correena and her next door neighbour, Shauwn Dunn, went swimming in the pool and used the slide. Mrs. Walford was very safety conscious and had firm rules for the use of the pool, including no diving, no running, and mandatory use of the ladder to get in and out. There was a "no diving" sign in a window of the house facing the pool. Either Mr. or Mrs. Walford was always present when the pool was in use. Before the children were permitted to use the slide, Mrs. Walford gathered them together and instructed them on the rules for the use of the slide. Her rules included: no pushing; no running; one person had to be down the slide before the next one started up the ladder; no one underneath the slide when one person was going down; and descending the slide only "feet first", or as Correena testified, "on their bums."

[16] Correena heeded her mother's directions and slid in a seated position the first time down, but the second time she was crouched over her knees. She slid this way because she thought it would be fun and she had done it with no restrictions on waterslides such as those at Canada's Wonderland and other large parks. Mrs. Walford watched Correena go down the slide the first time, but was distracted talking to a neighbour and did not see Correena slide the second time. When Correena entered the water head first, she went forward fast and her chin hit the bottom of the pool. She felt her body float to the top and she could not move. She had been rendered quadriplegic.

Legal Findings by the Trial Judge

[17] The original action included claims against Pioneer Pools; Kevin and William Boyle; Esther Williams Pools of Canada Inc, the manufacturer of the Mardi Gras pool; and Jacuzzi Canada Ltd., the manufacturer of the slide. The trial

judge found no liability on the part of any of the defendants, either because they were not negligent, or because their negligence did not cause the accident. The appellants appealed only against Pioneer Pools.

Causation

[24] In assessing the appellants' claim against Jacuzzi Canada, the manufacturer of the slide, the trial judge found that the slide fell far short of meeting the CPSS standard for warning labels. The slide's warning label, as well as its lettering, were smaller than the specification's requirements. The label was worn down at the edges and its lettering was grey, extremely faded, and partially missing due to weathering. The CPSS specification requires pool slide labels to be coloured, permanently attached, and tamper-proof.

[25] Neither Mrs. Walford, Correena, nor their neighbour Shauwn, who was swimming and using the slide with Correena, saw the warning label. The trial judge found that the label in its deteriorated condition was easy to miss. The warning label read:

> Enter water feet first.
> One person only on the slide at a time.
> Never stand going down the slide.

[26] The trial judge found that Jacuzzi Canada was negligent for failing to give adequate warning to users of the slide of the"extreme danger of serious injury from the improper use of the slide." He also found that pool slides can be used safely in a 4-foot pool. However, he concluded that although neither Mrs. Walford nor Correena saw the old label on the slide prior to the accident, the inadequate label was not the cause of the accident. Rather, the cause of the accident was Correena's failure to heed the warning her mother gave her to "go feet first."

Issue on the Appeal

[27] Was Pioneer Pools negligent when it failed to warn a customer, who specifically asked about the suitability of a slide for a 4-foot-deep swimming pool, that there was a serious risk of catastrophic injury due to the pool's shallow depth if a person were to descend the slide other than by sitting upright and entering the water feet first? If so, did Pioneer Pool's negligence cause or contribute to Correena's damage?

Analysis

Duty of Care

[29] In *Bow Valley Husky v. Saint John Shipbuilding*, 1997 CanLII 307 (SCC), [1997] 3 S.C.R. 1210 at 1229, the Supreme Court described the law on duty to warn as follows:

> The law may be simply stated. Manufacturers and suppliers are required to warn all those who may reasonably be affected by potentially dangerous products: *Lambert v. Lastoplex Chemicals Co.*, 1971 CanLII

> 27 (SCC), [1972] S.C.R. 569, and *Hollis v. Dow Corning Corp.*, 1995 CanLII 55 (SCC), [1995] 4 S.C.R. 634. This duty extends even to those persons who are not party to the contract of sale: *Rivtow Marine Ltd. v. Washington Iron Works*, 1973 CanLII 6 (SCC), [1974] S.C.R. 1189. The potential user must be reasonably foreseeable to the manufacturer or supplier—manufacturers and suppliers ... do not have the duty to warn the entire world about every danger that can result from improper use of their product.

[30] The duty to warn of potentially dangerous products applies only to dangers that are not obvious. In *Schulz v. Leeside Developments Ltd.* (1978), 90 D.L.R. (3d) 98, an 18-year-old boy rented a motor boat from the defendant. The teenager decided to climb over the windshield of the boat while the boat was travelling at full speed, and ride on top of the bow of the boat while holding onto a rope that was tied to a cleat on the bow. When the boat suddenly lurched, the boy fell into the water, came into contact with the propeller, and was rendered paralyzed. The British Columbia Court of Appeal found that the danger of riding on top of the bow of a speeding motor boat was an obvious one. It adopted the statement on "obvious dangers" from William L. Prosser's *Handbook of the Law of Torts*, 4thed. (St. Paul, Minn.: West Publishing, 1971) at 649:

> One limitation commonly placed upon the duty to warn, or for that matter the seller's entire liability, is that he is not liable for dangers that are known to the user, or are obvious to him, or are so commonly known that it can reasonably be assumed that the user will be familiar with them. Thus there is certainly no usual duty to warn the purchaser that a knife or an axe will cut, a match will take fire, dynamite will explode, or a hammer may mash a finger.

[32] However, where the nature and extent of the danger of using a product is not obvious and a consumer seeks reassurance from a merchant concerning the safety or propriety of a product, the answer must not be misleading. This is essentially a claim in negligent misrepresentation, augmented in the circumstances where a potentially dangerous product is involved, by the duty to warn. The five elements of a claim for negligent misrepresentation are: 1) a duty of care based on a "special relationship",2) a misleading representation, 3) negligence in making the misrepresentation, 4) reasonable reliance on the representation, 5) damage caused by the reliance. See *Queen v. Cognos,* 1993 CanLII 146 (SCC), [1993] 1 S.C.R. 87 at 110.

[33] The trial judge acknowledged that there may be a sufficiently close relationship between Mrs. Walford and Pioneer Pools to create a duty of care. I agree that there was such a relationship and that such a duty existed here. Mrs. Walford was a two-year customer of Pioneer Pools for parts and servicing and she trusted the store for help and advice regarding matters relating to her pool, including the installation of a slide. She had originally enquired about purchasing her slide from her Pioneer Pools store. It is plain on the evidence that there was a relationship of proximity between Mrs. Walfordand Pioneer Pools that created a duty of care. As the trial judge observed later in his reasons when he explained why there was no similar relationship between Mrs. Walford and the Boyles, the

men from whom she bought the slide, Mrs. Walford did not rely on them because she consulted with two pool supply businesses, "experts in the field".

[34] As McGarry J. stated in *Amin (Litigation guardian of) v. Klironomous*, [1996] O.J. No. 826 at para. 28, "it is clear that both the distributor and retailer have a duty to warn the consumer of inherent dangers with respect to the products they distribute or sell." In this case, although Pioneer Pools did not sell the slide to Mrs. Walford because they did not have one in stock and a new one would have been too expensive for her, they sold her parts for the slide she did buy, gave her instructions on how to install it, and offered her specific reassurances about installing it on her 4-foot-deep pool.

Standard of Care

[36] Having found that a duty of care existed between Pioneer Pools and Mrs. Walford, the trial judge turned to the standard of care. He was satisfied that the respondent met the standard of care when its employees told Mrs. Walford, in response to her questions, that it was "okay"or "no problem" to install a 10-foot long slide with a 4-foot-deep aboveground pool.

[38] In the context of a customer who asks a vendor of pool supplies whether it is "okay" to install a slide with a pool of a specified shallow depth, it is clear that the customer's concern is safety. There is really no other issue. The question is, once the vendor decides to answer the customer's question, does the standard of care in this context encompass a duty to warn the customer of the safety issues relevant to installing a pool slide with a 4-foot-deep pool? Or, put another way, was Pioneer Pools negligent when its employees told Mrs. Walford that it was "okay" or "no problem" to install her slide on her pool, without any qualification or warning about the dangers of using such a slide?

[39] The standard of care depends on the circumstances and the context in which the duty arises. In this case, Mrs. Walford was asking for advice and assurance that it was appropriate for her to install a slide on a 4-foot-deep aboveground pool. She asked Pioneer Pools' employees about this three times: when she bought fittings for the slide, when she obtained tubing and instructions for the slide's proper installation, and when she first called the store to inquire about buying a new slide for her pool.

[40] The respondent held itself out as having expertise regarding pools and pool accessories. Mrs. Walford trusted the respondent. No one from Pioneer Pools testified at the trial. The only evidence from Pioneer Pools was excerpts from the examination for discovery of Ms. Fraser, the manager of the Barton Street Pioneer Pools store, that were read into the record by the appellants' counsel. Ms. Fraser said she did not remember Mrs.Walford, but she had a memory of two women coming with a slide in a van and asking for tubing. She did not recall her conversation with them. She testified that she had no training regarding the propriety of using a slide with a 4-foot pool. The only information the store had on site regarding slides was a pool technician's manual and a brochure on the slide model that Pioneer Pools distributed. Nevertheless she stated that when she sold pool supplies to individuals, she would give them the benefit of her

knowledge and experience in respect of those supplies.

[41] The trial judge determined the standard of care based on the only applicable legal standard for pool safety in North America that existed at the time, the American standards promulgated in the CPSS in 1976.

[42] The trial judge also referred to the Jacuzzi Canada slide brochure and to Jacuzzi Canada owner's manual, which were attached to the report of the appellants'expert witness, for other evidence of the prevailing safety standard. The Jacuzzi Canada brochure, dated March 1, 1973, refers to its slides, including the model Mrs. Walford purchased, as "safe and serviceable." The minimum recommended water depth for that model is 4 feet. It is described as suitable for adults and children. The owners' manual, dated February 1, 1976, refers to the same 4-foot minimum water depth and recites three "safety tips", which are the same as those found on the faded label attached to the slide: *"1. Enter water feet first; 2. One person only on the slide at time; and 3. Never stand going down slide"*. The trial judge concluded that Jacuzzi Canada's printed information in 1996 would not have said anything different from the CPSS.

[56] The excerpts also show that the danger of pool slides is not something that is generally known based on "common sense." In fact, the standard recognizes that head-first belly slides are a common and popular use of a slide. Consumers will not know, however, that by entering the water head first from a pool slide, there is an unexpected and uncontrollable flipping by the body that causes the head to hit the bottom of the pool if the water is shallow. Consumers also will not know that this can and does cause paraplegia and quadriplegia, catastrophic injuries that they would not expect or anticipate from using a simple and commonly available recreational device.

[57] In other words, the danger from using a pool slide in relatively shallow water is not an obvious danger. Consumers do not know that 4 feet is the minimum depth for installing a pool slide that is usable by persons older than 13 years of age and that at such a depth, if one does not go down feet first, a significant risk of catastrophic injury arises. They do not know at what depth it becomes safe to go down head first so that the slider will not hit the bottom of the pool.

[60] Applying the correct standard of care, the respondent, Pioneer Pools, was negligent and breached its duty by failing to warn Mrs. Walford when she sought advice from its employees of the hidden danger of catastrophic injury from erecting a slide on a 4-foot-deep aboveground pool.

Causation

[61] In its recent decision in *Resurfice Corp v. Hanke* [2007] S.C.J. No. 7 at para. 7, the Supreme Court clarified that the basic test for determining causation remains the "but for" test. Mrs. Walford's uncontroverted and unchallenged evidence was that had she been warned by Pioneer Pools about the danger of using a slide with a 4-foot pool, (i.e. "but for" the failure to warn) she would not have erected the slide, even after buying it. My colleague Rouleau J.A. suggests that the trial judge implicitly rejected this evidence even though the trial judge did

not say so, and that he must have rejected it because he found the sole cause of the accident was Coreena's failure to listen to her mother when she did not go down feet first. To the contrary, the reliability of that evidence was supported by the trial judge's finding that Mrs. Walford was extremely safety conscious and cautious about her children's use of the pool, and by her many efforts to satisfy herself from knowledgeable people that it would be "okay" to install a slide with a 4-foot pool. With respect to the legal conclusion regarding causation, it appears that the trial judge's finding on causation was made without considering or applying the "but for" test.

[62] In my view, based on the evidence and applying the "but for" test: but for the failure of the respondent's employees to respond to Mrs. Walford's inquires by warning her of the risks of installing the pool slide on her 4-foot pool, she would not have erected the slide and Correena would never have been injured going down it. The breach of duty and negligence of the respondent therefore caused or contributed to Correena's injury.

Contributory Negligence

[63] Having found negligence and causation, the issue of contributory negligence arises on the appeal. The trial judge found that Correena's failure to heed her mother's admonition to only go down the slide"on her bum" was the sole cause of the accident. Because I have concluded that the negligence of the respondent caused or contributed to the accident based on the "but for" test, I must now consider whether Correena's conduct makes her to some degree legally responsible for the accident.

[64] Although Mrs. Walford gave her children many instructions and rules about using the pool, including to only slide down "on their bums" or "feet first", she did not tell them why that was important or the extent of the danger if they were to deviate from that position. Mrs.Walford did not tell them because she had not been warned herself and was consequently unaware of the nature or degree of risk she had created by installing a slide on her shallow pool. Nor could Correena have reasonably known that her behaviour was as reckless as it turned out to be, as she was accustomed to using slides installed on deeper pools that did not require her to slide down feet first to ensure safety. As the U.S. Consumer Products Safety Commission found, using a pool slide in a position other than feet first is not necessarily a dangerous practice in deep pools and head first slides are a commonly accepted means of using swimming pool slides. The risk of catastrophic injury and paralysis only arises in the context of slides installed in pools whose water depth is close to or at the CPSS' minimum depth standards. Furthermore, the cause of this risk is not immediately apparent to untutored users: it occurs principally because a slider's body flips forward uncontrollably when it enters the water, even if the slider enters the water in a straight line. Considering that Correena was unable to appreciate the nature or extent of the danger due to the absence of an authoritative warning, she clearly did not assume the risk of catastrophic injuries when she went down the slide crouched down over her knees.

[65] However, Correena does bear some responsibility for failing to heed her

mother's safety rules. Although neither Correena nor her mother could have been reasonably expected to know why sliding only feet-first was a crucial safety rule in their shallow pool—indeed, it would have been largely irrelevant if the pool had been significantly deeper—Mrs.Walford appears to have correctly intuited that sliding feet-first would have ensured her children's safety. Correena's knowing decision to ignore her mother's admonitions indicates a degree of carelessness on her part. In my view, her contribution to her loss can reasonably be fixed at 20 percent.

Result

[67] The trial judge assessed the damages in this case and there is no appeal from that assessment. I would set aside the finding of the trial judge that the respondent was not negligent and substitute a finding of negligence. I would assess the appellant Correena Walford's contributory negligence at 20 percent and award damages accordingly.

Signed: "K. Feldman J.A.", "I agree R. A. Blair J.A.".

Separate dissenting reasons delivered by P.S. Rouleau J.A., not reproduced.

CASE 9.5

Morse v. Cott Beverages West Ltd.

[2001] S.J. No. 765, **Saskatchewan Court of Queen's Bench**

(Excerpts of Judgment)

PRITCHARD J.:— On the afternoon of November 22, 1992, Tami Morse wanted a drink of pop before she left home for her basketball practice. She noticed an unopened two litre bottle of no name cola on the kitchen counter. She decided to open it but found that she was unable to turn the metal twist-off cap. She then picked up a nutcracker to get a better grip. While holding the bottle with her left hand, she used her right hand to place the nutcracker on the bottle cap. With the aid of the nutcracker, she began turning the cap counter-clockwise. As she started the turning motion, she heard a popping noise and everything instantaneously went dark. She believes that she momentarily blacked out but does remember screaming and feeling pressure on her face around the eye area.

Tami's mother was in the kitchen at the time and heard her daughter scream. Mrs. Morse immediately instructed Tami to take her contact lenses out. Mrs. Morse then put an ice pack on her daughter's eye and rushed her to the emergency department at the Pasqua Hospital in Regina. Fortunately, Tami was very quickly seen by an eye specialist who determined that her right eye had sustained a traumatic hyphema. Dr. Avram placed a drop of Atropine in the right eye, covered it with a patch and instructed Tami to have bed rest at home and to check with him for follow-up in 24 hours.

Tami followed her doctor's instructions. After her initial consultation she was terrified that she would lose sight in one eye as she could only see shadows with her right eye. She had further appointments with Dr. Avram at the Pasqua Hospital on November 23, November 26 and November 28. On November 23, Tami still could not see out of her right eye. She received further drops in the eye and continued to wear the patch. Gradually, within three to four days of the accident, she began regaining sight in her right eye and within a week her vision was, for the most part, back to normal. From November 28 to December 4 she continued to use combination antibiotic/corticosteroid drops and by December 4, she was finally able to fully resume all of her activities as her intraocular pressure was finally normal.

Following December 4, 1992, Tami continued to be monitored by Dr. Avram but less frequently as she was only seen in January and July of 1993 and again in July of 1994. During the first eight months post accident, Dr. Avram was particularly concerned that the eye injury might result in glaucoma. By July of 1993 he was satisfied that the risk of this complication was now minimal. However, in early January of 1993, Dr. Avram noted that the pupil in Tami's right eye was unusually dilated. This condition resolved itself within about a year. In January of 1993, Dr. Avram also noted the development of an anterior traumatic cataract in Tami's right eye. The cataract is small and can only be removed by surgery. At the time of trial, some nine years post injury, the cataract was not affecting Tami's eyesight. Medical intervention has therefore not been required although it may be necessary sometime in the future. Since the injury and right up to the time of trial, Tami's right eye has remained light sensitive. There is no suggestion that this condition will improve with further time.

Tami claims that the defendants are responsible in law for the injury to her eye and the resulting pain and suffering and other damages she has suffered. She has abandoned her claim in negligence and relies solely on The Consumer Products Warranties Act, R.S.S. 1978, c. 30 as am. by S.S. 1979-80, c. 17, 1980-81, c. 18 and c. 21; and 1992, c. 23 (Repealed R.S.S. 1996, c. C-30.1)(the "Act").

In particular, the plaintiff relies on the following provisions of the Act:

> 5 A person who may reasonably be expected to use, consume or be affected by a consumer product and who suffers personal injury as a result of a breach, by a retail seller or manufacturer, of a statutory warranty mentioned in paragraphs 3, 4, 5 and 6 of section 11 shall be entitled to the remedies mentioned in section 27
>
> 11 Where a consumer product is sold by a retail seller, the following warranties shall be deemed to be given by the retail seller to the consumer:
>
> > 4 that the product supplied under the contract is of acceptable quality, except that no such warranty shall be deemed to be given:
> >
> > (a) with respect to defects specifically drawn to the consumer's attention before the contract is made; or
> > (b) where the consumer examines the product before the contract is made, with respect to defects that examination ought to have revealed;
> >
> > 5 where the consumer expressly or by implication makes known to the retail seller any particular purpose for which the product is being bought, that the product supplied under the contract is reasonably fit for that purpose, whether or not that is a purpose for which such a product is commonly supplied, except that no such warranty shall be deemed to be given where the circumstances show that the consumer does not rely upon or that it is unreasonable for him to rely upon the retail seller's skill or judgment;
>
> 15 Where a consumer, a person mentioned in subsection 4(1) who derives his property or interest in a consumer product from or through a consumer, or a person mentioned in section 5 brings an action against a manufacturer for breach of one or more statutory warranties set out in paragraphs 4 and 5 of section 11, and where the consumer or person proves the poor quality, malfunctioning or breakdown of the consumer product but cannot prove the exact cause of the poor quality, malfunctioning or breakdown, and where the facts of the case are such that it is reasonable to draw an inference of a breach by the manufacturer of those statutory warranties, there shall be a

> presumption of breach of those warranties by the manufacturer but the presumption can be rebutted by proof that the poor quality, malfunctioning or breakdown of the consumer product was due to a cause not attributable to the manufacturer or that the consumer product was acceptable or fit for the purpose for which it was bought when it went out of the manufacturer's control.
>
> ...
>
> 27 A person mentioned in section 5 shall, as against the retail seller or manufacturer, be entitled to recover damages arising from personal injuries that he has suffered and that were reasonably foreseeable as liable to result from the breach.

Cott Beverages West Ltd. ("Cott") admits that it is the manufacturer of no name cola beverages sold by Westfair Foods Ltd. ("Westfair") but argues that the product in question was not defective. All parties agree that even though the Act provides for strict liability for the retail seller and manufacturer of consumer products, the burden of proving that a consumer product is not of acceptable quality or reasonably fit for its purposes still rests with the plaintiff unless the presumption under s.15 of the Act applies. It is also undisputed that even if s. 15 applies, the plaintiff must still prove, among other things, the poor quality, malfunctioning or breakdown of the product. (see Ostrowski v. United Farmers of Alberta Coop Ltd. (1987), 55 Sask. R. 282 at paras. 42-44 (Q.B.) affd 69 Sask. R. 309 (C.A.))

Clearly, there is no issue regarding the cola product itself that was bottled by Cott. The plaintiff's complaint is that she should have been able to open the twist off cap on the two litre bottle of cola by hand and that even with the assistance of the nutcracker to twist off the cap, the cap should not have exploded off the bottle as it did.

The defendants concede that the duty to supply goods of acceptable quality applies not only to the product sold but also to its container. Likewise, they concede that the statutory warranty under paragraph 5 of s. 11 applies to the consumer product's container. The only dispute is whether the injury to Tami Morse was the result of a breach of the warranties under paragraphs 4 or 5 of s. 11 of the Act.

The evidence satisfies me that the two litre bottle of no-name cola purchased by the plaintiff's mother on the early afternoon of November 22, 1992, was filled and capped on the bottling line of the defendant Cott on November 4, 1992 (the "Cola Bottle"). I am also satisfied that Westfair was the retail seller of the Cola Bottle and that on the same day that it was purchased, the plaintiff was injured in the right eye when the cap on the Cola Bottle suddenly ejected off the bottle.

The plaintiff contends that the probable cause of the sudden ejection of the cap from the bottle and the probable cause of her resulting injury was Cott's failure to employ proper quality control procedures in the bottle capping process. At the time the Cola Bottle was capped, Cott used a roll-on capping system designed by Aluminum Company of America ("Alcoa"). The Alcoa system uses an aluminum cap to seal the pop bottle. The cap is unthreaded when it is placed on the bottle. A thread roller then rolls over the cap and causes threads to be formed on the cap that match those on the bottle. At the same time, a pilfer proof roller forces the pilfer proof band at the base of the cap to be tucked under the bottle's locking ring.

The importance of a properly applied aluminum cap closure is very clearly highlighted in Alcoa's 57 page glossy, brightly coloured, spiral bound 8" by 10" brochure titled "Application of The Alcoa RO Beverage Closure" (the "Alcoa Manual"). The table of contents sets out in bold print the six topics covered in the Manual. The first topic is: The Importance Of Proper Closure Application. The three areas of discussion under this heading are shown as:

> Improperly Applied Closures Can Cause Problems Bottler's Responsibility for Quality Control Trained Personnel Are Essential to a Good Quality Control Program.

In the main body of the Aloca Manual, under the sub-heading "Improperly applied closures can cause problems", the manufacturer states that when properly applied, the Alcoa aluminum Roll-On beverage closure "is reliable, easily removable and resealable". The manufacturer then goes on to warn that when improperly applied, the closure can cause problems. In red-coloured italics, the first two of the four identified potential problems are highlighted and described as follows:

> Sometimes, ordinary pressure in a package can suddenly eject an improperly applied closure with considerable force. This can result in serious injury, often to an eye.
>
> Bottles may not be openable by hand. This may result in injury if the closure is improperly removed using a tool or some other device.

Under the sub-heading "Bottler's responsibility for quality control", the following manufacture's statement is again highlighted in red-coloured italics:

> Because of this possibility of injury, closure application quality control must be given top priority in bottling plants.

In bold black italics, the manufacturer then states:

> This brochure is not intended to offer a complete Quality Assurance program. You must design your own program in accordance with your particular operating conditions.

In ordinary black type, the manufacturer concludes this topic by stating:

> However, this brochure does include ideas and suggestions that should be included in your quality control program.

The Alcoa Manual includes suggested procedures for inspecting cap closures and other materials used in the bottling process as well as preventative maintenance and adjustment procedures for the Alcoa capping machines to ensure proper closure application. Under the heading: "The Importance of Maintaining and

Adjusting Capping Machines", the manufacturer provides the following statement in red highlighted italics:

> Warning: Any improperly adjusted or maintained capper can cause improper closure application. This can result in sudden closure ejection and serious injury, often to an eye.(p. 3.1)

In the fall of 1992, Cott was using the "RC Cola Quality Control Procedures for Testing Royal Crown Cola Co. Products, Revised March 1992" as its operating manual (the "Cott Manual"). At page 6, the Cott Manual states that the removal torque on aluminum closures should be tested hourly (each head) and that pressure testing and visual inspection should be done in accordance with the manufacturer's recommendation. The procedure for testing removal torque on aluminum closures is set out on page 15 of the Cott Manual. At the end of the seven step procedure described therein, the Cott Manual states:

> NOTE: All torque readings should fall within the allowable tolerances specified by the closure manufacturer.

A torque removal test is done by a bottler to determine how much twisting force is required to remove the cap from the bottles it is producing. As part of its quality control procedure, Cott conducts roll-on closure torque tests as well as visual inspections and cap closure proper application tests. The test results from all three tests are recorded as the readings are taken. The records maintained by Cott show that on the day that the Cola Bottle was processed, the removal torque for 16 of the 24 bottles tested was above Alcoa's specifications of "between 5 and 14 inch-pounds". Three of these 16 bottles had a torque reading of 15 which may be considered acceptable under Alcoa's specifications as they permit "an occasional reading as low as 3 inch-pounds (if the glass or plastic is still wet) or as high as 15 inch-pounds". However, notwithstanding that Cott's Manual directs that torque readings should fall within the allowable tolerances specified by Alcoa, 13 of the bottles tested on November 4, 1992, or more than half of all bottles tested, were found to be above the highest recommended torque. The records further indicate that no adjustments were made to the machinery nor were any other steps taken to ensure that production was maintained within the specified tolerances.

At page 4.4 of the Alcoa Manual under the heading "Removal torque tests", it states:

> Detailed testing procedures have not been included here because the torque test does not reliably determine proper closure application. However, the determination of high torque is important, for high torque can render the bottle unopenable by hand. This may result in injury if the closure is improperly removed using a tool or some other device.

At trial, Cott's director of technical services testified that from his own experience, removal torques in the range of 22-24 and possibly even up to 25 do not cause problems. He testified that when he was involved in production in the United States, he was able to open bottles at these torque removal levels and the product was released. Other than information contained in the Cott and Alcoa Manuals, this personal experience is the only additional evidence presented on the issue of acceptable torque removal levels.

Cott contends that the plaintiff or her mother are partially if not wholly responsible for the plaintiff's injury. It suggests that Mrs. Morse and/or the plaintiff improperly handled the Cola Bottle. Alternatively or additionally, it suggests that the plaintiff should not have used a nutcracker to open the Cola Bottle. Cott says that the more prudent thing for the plaintiff to have done was to seek assistance from her parents.

The plaintiff was sixteen years of age at the time of this incident. She was an athlete; a star basketball and baseball player. And, contrary to the position of Cott, there is absolutely nothing in the evidence to suggest that a consumer such as the plaintiff should have resorted to or required her parents' assistance to open the Cola Bottle. Indeed, there is nothing to suggest that the problem was with the plaintiff or her mother's handling of the Cola Bottle. All of the evidence points to the aluminum twist cap on the Cola Bottle being too tight for an ordinary consumer to open. In such circumstances, the plaintiff's decision to use a nutcracker was certainly foreseeable by Cott. As stated more than once by the manufacturer of the machinery used by Cott:

> ...high torque may lead the consumer to use a tool or device to aid in removing the closure. (p.1.5-Alcoa Manual, and to like effect at pp. iii and 4.4)

The Cola Bottle simply could not be opened by hand. Cott was aware or should have been aware from warnings by Alcoa that if it produced caps that were too difficult to open by hand, consumers would resort to the use of an appliance or tool. Cott was also aware or should have been aware from warnings provided by Alcoa that the use of a tool would increase the risk of injury by sudden ejection of the cap. Nevertheless, Cott produced product with closure removal torques in excess of specifications and did not warn consumers of the danger of sudden cap ejection or that if the product was not openable by hand it should be returned to the retail seller. In these circumstances, Cott can hardly complain that the plaintiff wrongly used the nutcracker to assist her in opening the Cola Bottle when that is exactly what Alcoa advised it a consumer might do when faced with a cap that was too tight to open without such assistance.

Cott also contends that through no fault of its own, it has been unable to examine the Cola Bottle or the aluminum closure cap which renders it impossible for it to counter any presumption of unmerchantability that might arise out under s. 15 of the Act.

Unfortunately, the bottle cap in question has never been available for examination by the defendants or any experts. The plaintiff's mother testified that she did not think to save the cap and that she has no recollection as to whether she ever even saw the cap. However, although the incident was not reported for some three years after the injury, Mrs. Morse did save the Cola Bottle which she gave to her daughter's solicitors when these proceedings were commenced. For discovery purposes, the solicitors made a photocopy of the label of the Cola Bottle. The photocopy was made while the label was still attached to the Cola Bottle. The Cola Bottle was also examined by a lawyer in the plaintiff's solicitors' office who testified that based on his very careful examination of the Cola Bottle, there was nothing that his non-expert eyes could detect to suggest that there might be a defect in the bottle itself. He saw no marks of any kind on the threads at the top of the bottle and based on his examination, the bottle "appeared to be in the condition that it was manufactured". Certain information stamped on the bottle could not be photocopied in the same manner as the label and the solicitor testified that he arranged for this information to be transcribed onto a post-it note that was then attached to the photocopy of the label.

A photocopy of the label and of the stamped information that was on the Cola Bottle was forwarded to the defendants' solicitors by letter dated November 7, 1996. The letter indicates that the plaintiff's solicitors were reluctant to release the Cola Bottle for inspection but they were prepared to allow it to be inspected at their offices. The defendants made no arrangements to have the Cola Bottle inspected. In May of 1997, the plaintiff's solicitors discovered that they had misplaced the Cola Bottle.

This action was commenced in 1994 and the defendants had some three years to examine the Cola Bottle but failed to do so before it was lost. Unfortunately, the aluminum cap closure was never made available to the defendants. However, none of the defendants, including Cott, has provided evidence as to how an examination of the Cola Bottle, or even more importantly, how an examination of the cap might demonstrate that the cap or the Cola Bottle were not defective; or, how such examination might establish or point to a conclusion other than that the cap was applied too tightly for an ordinary consumer to remove on her own. Given this lack of evidence, I am not satisfied that the defendants' inability to examine the Cola Bottle or the aluminum cap closure has substantially prejudiced them in this action. I am therefore not prepared to make any adverse inference based on these items not being available for inspection.

I find that on the day that the Cola Bottle was produced, Cott was not following the quality assurance recommendations of the manufacturer of the machinery being used by it. As the pressure required to remove the aluminum twist caps on over one-half of the bottles tested on that date exceeded the manufacturer's specifications, and as the plaintiff was unable to manually remove the twist top off of the Cola Bottle, I am satisfied that it is probable, indeed very likely, that the torque pressure of the Cola Bottle exceeded specifications. I therefore find that the plaintiff has established, on a balance of probabilities, the poor quality of the Cola Bottle and, on all of the evidence, I am also satisfied that it is more than reasonable to draw an inference that with respect to the Cola Bottle, Cott has breached the statutory warranties of acceptable quality and fitness.

Under the Act, the retail seller is deemed to give the consumer a warranty of acceptable quality and fitness. The retail seller is responsible for a breach of these warranties even if the breach did not originate with it. I therefore find that the statutory warranties of acceptability and fitness have been breached by the manufacturer Cott, and by the deemed manufacturer Sunfresh Limited ("Sunfresh") and by the retail seller Westfair. Sunfresh has argued that it is not a deemed manufacturer of the Cola Bottle. However, s. 2(h) of the Act states:

> 2(h) "manufacturer" means a person who carries on the business of assembling, processing or manufacturing consumer products and includes:
>
> (i) any person who attaches his brand name or causes or permits his brand name to be attached to consumer products;
> (ii) any person who describes himself or holds himself out to the public as the manufacturer of consumer products; and
> (iii) where consumer products are manufactured outside Canada and the foreign manufacturer of the products does not have a regular place of business in Canada, a person who imports or distributes such products.

The defendants have admitted that the product name "no name" is a brand name owned by Loblaws Canada and that Sunfresh holds a license from Loblaws Canada to use the name "no name". As Sunfresh has also admitted that it has permitted the brand name "no name" to be affixed to the label of the Cola Bottle, I conclude that it is a deemed manufacturer of the Cola Bottle pursuant to s. 2(h)(i) of the Act.

DAMAGES

The plaintiff experienced a significant blunt injury to her right eye. She was placed on bed rest for two days and was unable to resume full physical activities for 12 days. For at least two days she experienced the fear of her injury resulting in blindness to one eye and for another eight months she lived with the fear of developing glaucoma in her right eye. She did develop a cataract and the injured eye remains permanently photo sensitive. Although Tami suffered a serious eye injury, she was very fortunate in receiving immediate expert medical care which prevented permanent visual loss. However, as a result of the injury, she lost her starting position on her basketball team and, even when she was able to resume playing basketball, it took some additional time for her to acquire proper depth perception for the game. Before the accident, she had been rated fourth in the city for shooting. As a result of her eye injury, she did not regain a starting position on her high school team until the following year. She also gave up her back-catching position in baseball as she was afraid of the ball re-injuring her eye. As a teenager, she also experienced some difficulty from the glare of lights when driving at night and from the fluorescent lights at school. She still requires sunglasses when she is outside.

I assess general damages in the amount of $18,000.00 with pre-judgment interest thereon in accordance with The Pre-Judgment Interest Act, S.S. 1984-85-86, c. P-22.2 calculated from November, 1992 to the date of judgment. In addition, the plaintiff is entitled to $128.40 for lost income, $60.00 for the cost of replacement contact lenses, $31.95 as expenses for medical treatment, $30.00 for sunglasses and $175.00 for prescription sunglasses.

There is a small chance that the cataract in the plaintiff's right eye may require surgery more rapidly than would be anticipated from normal aging. She has requested additional special damages in the amount of $2,500.00 to cover this contingency. Although the amount requested is reasonable, the plaintiff is currently only 24 years of age and there is no evidence to suggest that cataract surgery may be required within even the next twenty years. Therefore, no separate award is allowed. In the circumstances of this case, the risk that this minor surgery may be required as the plaintiff ages has been more appropriately included as one of the considerations in the assessment of general damages.

The plaintiff also claims exemplary damages against the defendant Cott pursuant to s. 28(1) of the Act which provides:

> 28(1) In addition to any other remedy provided by this Act or any other law in force in the province, a consumer or a person mentioned in subsection (1) of section 4 or in section 5 may recover exemplary damages from any manufacturer, retail seller or warrantor who has committed a wilful and knowing violation of this Act.

In support of this claim, the plaintiff states that Cott knew or should have known:

- that it was using an aluminum roll-on closure system that required strict adherence to proper quality control procedures to reduce potential dangers from sudden cap ejection and serious personal injury to a consumer, often to an eye;

- that Cott's own test results show that during the nine production days between October 29 and November 11, 1992 almost 3 percent of the tested bottles failed the proper application test which is designed to help prevent faulty and dangerous packages from reaching the consumer; and, notwithstanding this failure rate, Cott did not re-check product that had already been bottled or recall any product;

- that the test results also show that during that same period, which includes the day the Cola Bottle was produced, Cott was producing large numbers of bottles that exceeded not only the manufacturer's recommendation for torque removal but its own testing standards, and again, it failed to make any adjustments to its equipment or recall any of the product;

- that consumers would find tight caps difficult to open with the result that they might resort to the use of a tool or other appliance for assistance;

- that in addition to not reacting to test results that were clearly outside the acceptable tolerances, Cott's quality assurance program failed to meet many of the other standards recommended by Alcoa in that: (i) Cott failed to provide Alcoa's specifications for bottles and caps to its supplier of these items; (ii) it failed to inspect new bottles and caps before putting them on the production line; (iii) it failed to change one headset on its capper daily or on any scheduled basis; (iv) it failed to conduct the recommended number of torque tests or proper application tests or visual inspections or to conduct any final inspections during production; and (v) it failed to follow Alcoa's recommended procedures when bottles failed the pressure test.

Cott acknowledges that in the fall of 1992 it was producing product with aluminum caps with removal torques in excess of those recommended by Alcoa. However, it argues that this alone does not establish that it wilfully or knowingly produced an unfit product or a product of unacceptable quality. All it means, according to Cott, is that it was producing product that it knew was outside the manufacturer's specifications. I cannot agree with this submission.

In my view, the uncontroverted inherent danger of this type of consumer packaging, coupled with the manufacturer's numerous warnings about the dangers of bottles that are difficult to open make it incumbent upon Cott to explain how it might reasonably have considered the product that it produced on November 4, 1992 to be safe and fit for the average consumer. The evidence establishes that on the day that the Cola Bottle was produced, just over 50% of the tested bottles had torque removal readings not only in excess of the highest amount specified by Alcoa, but also higher than the parameters set by Cott on its own Bottle Packaging Test Forms. Anecdotal evidence was given by Cott to the effect that because these torque test readings do not exceed 21, the Cola Bottle should have been capable of being opened by hand. Although the Cott witness was apparently able to open a similar type of product with torque readings of 22-24 or higher, the context of his evidence leads me to believe that he was opening those bottles to determine whether product with such torque readings could be released to the public. He indicated that the product was released, but in my view, this certainly does not establish that it was objectively safe or prudent to have done so.

Cott has not explained the basis for producing bottles with torque readings in excess of Alcoa's and its own testing standards. It has also not provided any objective evidence upon which one might reasonably conclude that these standards were more exacting than necessary. It has therefore failed to satisfy me that it was not wilfully jeopardizing the safety of the public by releasing inherently dangerous product that its own test results showed as having higher than recommended torque readings. In the result, I am inextricably led to the conclusion that Cott committed a wilful and knowing violation of the Act and that the plaintiff is entitled to recover exemplary damages.

In assessing the quantum of exemplary damages, the plaintiff has referred the court to the recent Ontario Court of Appeal decision in Whiten v. Pilot Insurance Co. et al (1999), 42 O.R. (3d) 641 in which the majority noted that the primary goals of punitive damages are deterrence and punishment. The plaintiff urges that any award of exemplary damages be substantial to avoid being "perceived as a mere licence fee or as a cost of doing business". Neither party has directed the court to decisions where exemplary damages have been awarded under the Act.
Although the evidence establishes that Cott is a publicly traded company with production facilities in Canada, the United States and elsewhere, there is no evidence as to the value of its assets or its profitability. I also do not know whether the same production equipment or testing procedures that were used in

1992 are applicable today. In all, I have very little evidence or other assistance on the proper measure of exemplary damages under s. 28 of the Act. After considering the evidence as a whole, I have determined that an appropriate amount for exemplary damages is double the amount of general damages or $36,000.00.

In view of the difficulty encountered by the plaintiff in obtaining disclosure of the Alcoa Manual as well as the complete text of the Cott Manual, the plaintiff has asked that she be awarded solicitor and client costs. There will be no such order, but the plaintiff shall be entitled to double column 3 taxable costs as against the defendant Cott. No other party will be entitled to costs.

LEGAL TERMS

In your reading, you came across the following terms. Be sure that you can explain each, to ensure your understanding of the material you have been reading. If you are uncertain as to the meaning of any term, review the material in the chapter for clarification. If necessary, consult a dictionary for further information or discuss the term(s) with your instructor.

responsibility	immovable	prudent and diligent
extra-contractual	damages	endowed with reason
ruin	liability	delegated authority
fault	foreseeable	solidarily
superior force	defects	contributory negligence
surveillance	movable	vicarious liability
good samaritan	no-fault	

REVIEW QUESTIONS

1. Ms. Sanders wants to sue Plowing Inc. because they damaged her property in the process of removing the snow from the driveway last winter. What article of the *Civil Code* can she use and why?

2. What are the four conditions for personal civil liability to exist?

3. Jamie (6 years old), Steven (7 years old) and Randy (7 years old) pushed around Greg (7 years old), causing him to fall, break an arm and tear his leather jacket. Can all three kids be sued? Explain.

4. Aside from Jamie, Steven and Randy, who else can be sued and why?

5. What defences can those other than Jamie, Steven and Randy plead to free themselves from civil liability from Greg's injuries?

6. What defences are available to a person sued for damages under personal civil liability?

7. ACME Inc. was moving Don's next door neighbour when one of their trucks backed-up over his child's bicycle completely destroying it. Who can Don sue for the bicycle? Explain.

8. Seeing the truck destroy the bicycle, Don approached the driver's side to complain. Not wanting to listen to Don, the employees decided to drive off and in the process rolled over Don's foot and broke his ankle. Can Don sue ACME or the driver? Explain.

9. If a consumer is injured by a defective curling iron, who would likely be held responsible?

10. If Jimmy's dog bites someone, will Jimmy be held responsible? Explain.

INDEX OF CASES

GENERAL INDEX